Rachel Donel

Rachel Donelson Jackson

The First Lady Who Never Was

BETTY BOLES ELLISON

McFarland & Company, Inc., Publishers

Jefferson, North Carolina

LIBRARY OF CONGRESS CATALOGUING-IN-PUBLICATION DATA

Names: Ellison, Betty Boles, author.
Title: Rachel Donelson Jackson : the First Lady who never was /
   Betty Boles Ellison.
Description: Jefferson, North Carolina : McFarland & Company, Inc.,
   Publishers, 2020 | Includes bibliographical references and index.
Identifiers: LCCN 2020021784 | ISBN 9781476670188
   (paperback : acid free paper) ∞
   ISBN 9781476638973 (ebook)
Subjects: LCSH: Presidents' spouses—United States—Biography. |
   Jackson, Rachel, 1767-1828. | Jackson, Andrew, 1767-1845—Marriage. |
   Generals' spouses—Tennessee—Nashville—Biography. | Plantation
   owners' spouses—Tennessee—Biography. | Plantation life—Tennessee—
   History—19th century. | Nashville (Tenn.)—Biography.
Classification: LCC E382.1.J2 E45 2020 | DDC 973.5/6092 [B]—dc23
LC record available at https://lccn.loc.gov/2020021784

BRITISH LIBRARY CATALOGUING DATA ARE AVAILABLE

ISBN (print) 978-1-4766-7018-8
ISBN (ebook) 978-1-4766-3897-3

Front cover image: a watercolor on ivory miniature of Rachel
painted by Louisa Catherine Strobel, circa 1830. It was said Jackson
wore a miniature of Rachel around his neck every day after her death
and, at night, laid it on his bedside table (Andrew Jackson's Hermitage,
Nashville, TN)

Printed in the United States of America

*McFarland & Company, Inc., Publishers
   Box 611, Jefferson, North Carolina 28640
   www.mcfarlandpub.com*

To our great-grandchildren:
Sofia Erin Franklin—Bowling Green, Kentucky,
Wyatt Alexander Richardson and
Ryann Leigh Richardson—Lebanon, Ohio

Table of Contents

Acknowledgments

As always, my family's collaboration was vital to the completion of this book. My gratitude for their assistance, patience, proofing, continued advice, great meals, flowers but, most of all, for being there. Our great-grandchildren: Sofia Erin Franklin from Bowling Green, Kentucky, and Wyatt Alexander Richardson and Ryann Leigh Richardson from Lebanon, Ohio, a wonderful light in our lives.

Donna Lou Gosney, a longtime friend from Madison, West Virginia, was always ready with advice.

Jim Strader from Louisville, Kentucky, was a valuable sounding board for my ideas about the Jacksons' complicated life.

Katie Hickey from Lexington, Kentucky, has my appreciation for being such a good friend and neighbor.

The staff of the InterLibrary Loan Department of the Lexington Public Library never blinked at my mountain of loan requests.

Joyce L. Broussard, professor of women's and southern history at California State University Northridge, provided valuable information about the divorced women of Natchez, Mississippi.

Librarians and archivists are often an author's best source. Kelley Sirko, librarian at the Metropolitan Government Archives of Nashville and Jefferson County and Kaitlyn Pettengill, archivist at the Historical Society of Pennsylvania, were most helpful. Roda Ferraro, Keeneland Association, Inc. librarian, with her staff, located rare and most valuable research material for the work.

Charlie Perdue, acquisitions editor at McFarland, had the patience of Job with my ever changing deadlines as well as a wonderful sense of humor.

There was someone else who had that kind of patience along with vast knowledge of Rachel and Andrew Jackson and their world. That was Marsha Mullin, vice-president for museum services and chief curator of The Hermitage. From the very beginning, Marsha always had an answer to my questions. Her counsel and guidance were essential in describing Rachel's world. Without Marsha, this book would not have been possible.

The advice and counsel that Dr. Humbert Nelli, my graduate school professor, gave me several years ago is still timely, still followed and still much appreciated.

Betty Boles Ellison
Lexington, Kentucky

Preface

After spending five years researching and writing a biography about a woman who yearned from a young age to be a president's wife, the tantalizing concept of doing a biography of a woman who absolutely loathed the idea of being a president's wife presented itself. It was too intriguing an idea to turn down.

There were vast differences—education, time, circumstances and politics—between the historical lives of Mary Todd Lincoln and Rachel Donelson Robards Jackson. Mary Lincoln's education was the equivalent of today's graduate degree. She was better educated than most of the members of President Abraham Lincoln's cabinet. Rachel Jackson was equally intelligent but had only a modicum of an education because her father believed only in educating his sons. Her spelling left much to be desired and she was not adept at the minuet but Rachel developed a successful business acumen operating their plantation, which created much of their wealth. Her letters, and those of her husband, have been edited for grammar but not content. Rachel learned to play musical instruments and rode horses on her father's Pittsylvania County, Virginia, plantation. She was called the most dashing horsewoman in the western country.

Rachel Jackson was almost fifty years old when Mary Todd was born into an affluent Lexington, Kentucky, family. Westward expansion began after the Revolutionary War and her father, John Donelson II, joined the procession. The expanding nation demanded adequate representation and Andrew Jackson was more than ready to lead the charge. Abraham Lincoln would later be challenged with an awesome task—preserving the Union during the Civil War. Jackson was a Democrat who remade the party in his image. Lincoln was the first president from the new Republican Party.

Many of the Lincolns' Illinois peers held the opinion that without Mary Todd, Lincoln would never have been president. He envisioned himself a United States senator but she saw him as the president and pushed him to seek that office. Rachel Jackson wanted nothing more than to live out her

1

days in the pastoral surroundings of The Hermitage with her husband, family and friends. She constantly attempted to dissuade Andrew Jackson, with little success, from seeking higher military commissions and political office. Yet, she followed him to New Orleans for the celebration of his victory there after the War of 1812, and later to Florida when he was appointed governor. Reluctantly, she was prepared to join him in the President's House in Washington.

The Lincolns were seldom separated after their marriage except for his years as a circuit lawyer in Illinois and a portion of his Congressional term in the late 1840s. After his assassination on April 15, 1865, Mary lived until July 16, 1882.

Rachel Jackson estimated that in the more than three decades of their marriage, her husband spent less than a quarter of that time in their home. She was constantly pleading with him to come home. Jackson always promised to do just that but never fulfilled the commitment.

Mary Lincoln ran her household and was a single parent half of the year when her lawyer husband was traveling the judicial circuit in Illinois, but she never ran a business. Rachel Jackson, during her husband's lengthy absences, was responsible for not only running her household but their cotton plantation, distillery, various businesses and collecting debts owed her husband.

There were also a surprising number of similarities. Each of the women came from affluent families. Rachel's father, John Donelson II, was a wealthy Virginia plantation owner and land surveyor. Mary's father was a Kentucky lawyer, businessman and politician. Both women experienced personal tragedies in their lives: Mary Lincoln in the early death of her mother and then losing two young sons, one four years old and the other eleven. Rachel Jackson, unable to have children, found herself in an abusive first marriage to an older man, Lewis Robards, in a union approved by her father. They were each strong, determined women who refused to allow their adversaries to make them victims. Once they set a course, they did not deviate from that path. Both were pilloried by the press: one during her husband's terms in office; the other during his successful presidential campaign.

While her husband was endeavoring to save the Union during the Civil War, Mary Lincoln was constantly, and incorrectly, accused of being a Confederate spy because her brother and stepbrothers fought for the Confederacy. She was also accused of being a spendthrift while refurbishing the executive mansion, which was not true. After her husband was killed, their surviving son, Robert, had her certified as an insane person. That was not true either.

Rachel Jackson's trials by the press were perpetuated by her husband's political enemies, who were convinced they could force Jackson into one of his infamous temper tantrums by persecuting his wife for living with him before Lewis Robards divorced her. Jackson kept his cool although, during the vicious 1828 presidential campaign, Rachel was called an ignorant, weak, vulgar and degraded woman unfit to associate with decent women.

Rachel Jackson, as Mary Lincoln would later do, attempted to ignore the slings and arrows delivered in newspaper articles and pamphlets.

The biggest difference between these two amazing women was that only one was a president's wife.

Introduction

Newspapers and pamphlets called her an American Jezebel, a profligate woman unfit to associate with Christian women, a convicted adulteress and a disgrace to the President's House should she live there.

She was, however, a strong, determined woman, who dealt in her own way with the social and legal restriction placed on women in the late eighteenth century. Finding herself in an abusive marriage with no remedy, she sacrificed her good name by giving her first husband a scandalous reason to divorce her.

Rachel Donelson Robards Jackson then married the love of her life, Andrew Jackson, who became the seventh President of the United States. She was a president-elect's wife, not a president's wife. She was never a first lady nor did she aspire to be. Rachel Jackson died on December 22, 1828, just weeks after her husband's successful presidential election campaign ended. Andrew Jackson was inaugurated, without his soulmate by his side, on March 4, 1829.

Why then is Rachel Jackson an important figure in American history?

She was the first presidential candidate's wife to have her morals made the focal point of an abominable presidential political campaign by her husband's opponents, the incumbent President John Quincy Adams, his Secretary of State Henry Clay and their minions. That presidential race remains, to this day, the most vile, nasty, mud-slinging, vicious campaign in American history. Not only did Jackson's political enemies call her unfit to associate with decent women, a bigamist and a convicted adulteress but his own political operatives used some of the same material to counterattack the Adams campaign. The adultery allegation was true but Jackson's enemies piled lies upon lies until Rachel was personally skewered from every direction.

Rachel was also the first presidential candidate's wife to accompany her husband on a campaign trip, their 1827 journey to New Orleans to commemorate his defeating the British in the War of 1812. Rachel Donelson grew up during the first great American land rush after the Revolutionary War. Her father and several of her brothers were land surveyors who grabbed all the

4

land they could but not always in a legal manner. Her first husband aspired to be a land baron and her second was one.

When Rachel was a teenager, her father agreed to her marriage to Lewis Robards in 1785, in Kentucky County, Virginia. Robards came from a wealthy Virginia family who immigrated to Kentucky after his father's death. Although he was the oldest son in his father's second family, William Robards passed over Lewis and named one of his brothers and his widow to administer his considerable estate. Rachel Donelson was a beautiful young woman with dark hair and eyes, a dimpled smile and a gregarious personality—she never met a stranger. Living with Robards in his widowed mother's boarding house, Rachel was thrown into the company of the single men who also lived there. If she even replied to men who spoke to her, Robards went into jealous rages. One of the Widow Robards' boarders, Peyton Short, took offense to Robards' treatment of his wife, returned to his home in Virginia to consolidate his assets with the hope of marrying her and moving to the Spanish territory in Mississippi. Robards intercepted Short's letter to his wife and went to Virginia to face him. Short gave Robards the option of a duel or $1,000. Rachel's husband was so offended by another man's attention to his wife that he took Short's money and returned to Kentucky. Robards verbally abused his wife in front of others and, some say, physically in private. Her entire family had moved back to Tennessee and she had no family support except, surprisingly enough, her mother-in-law. Elizabeth Robards took Rachel's side against her son who continued his jealous tirades. Rachel was nobody's fool and pushed back the best she could but American women in the late eighteenth century absolutely had no rights. They were simply their husbands' chattel like his lands, horses, cattle and slaves. Robards eventually contacted her mother in Tennessee and demanded that she take Rachel off his hands.

Her brother Samuel came to Kentucky in 1788 to escort her back to their mother's home near what is now Nashville. A year later, Robards arrived at the Donelsons' residence seeking a reconciliation. Apparently, he initially made an effort to settle there on his 640 acres overlooking the Cumberland River but decided, due to continued Indian raids, to live with Rachel's mother. A few months later, Robards returned to Kentucky, leaving word for Andrew Jackson, one of Mrs. Donelson's former boarders, that he could have Rachel. Robards, once back in Kentucky, felt safe enough to issue dire threats of kidnapping her. After Rachel's father's death, Robards contacted her brother-in-law Robert Hays to make sure he got his share of John Donelson's estate, which indicated he was more interested in the Donelson money and lands than in Rachel.

Exhibiting all the signs of an abused spouse, Rachel was scared of Robards and feared for her life. Mrs. Donelson agreed to let Rachel visit friends in Natchez, Mississippi. Captain Robert Stark, with whom Rachel sought transport on his flatboat, asked some of the Donelson men to provide an escort for them but they all had excuses. Jackson agreed to accompany Rachel and the other passengers for protection from Indian attacks. He returned to Nashville after the trip.

Robards asked the Virginia legislature for permission to file for divorce. His petition languished as Kentucky separated from Virginia and became a commonwealth in 1792. Word of mouth reached Nashville that Robards' filing in the Virginia General Assembly produced a divorce from Rachel. Jackson immediately headed for Natchez and they were said to have been married there but no trace of the nuptials was ever found. The Catholic Church recorded births, marriages and deaths in the Natchez District and exerted rigid control against other sects practicing their religion. A large number of Protestants lived there and some married in secret while others went outside the district to obtain a marriage license.

Rachel could have obtained a Spanish divorce from Robards while living in the Natchez District, then governed by Spain, in 1790–91. No factual evidence existed in Mississippi of the Jacksons' marriage, except by word of mouth, nor of Rachel having sought a divorce.

The Jacksons returned overland with a group of fellow travelers to Nashville and began married life. Robards petitioned the Kentucky legislature to consider his request for a divorce charging Rachel with desertion and being an adulteress. She was determined to be such in Robards' final divorce decree. Rachel and Jackson married after the Kentucky divorce decree was final. Robards, knowing his divorce was not final, had already married Hannah Winn, from Louisville, making them bigamists.

Inadvertently, the Jacksons provided the tools his political enemies used against them thirty years later; more specifically dragging Rachel's name through the mire of a nasty presidential campaign.

Her husband could have stopped it all by withdrawing from the race or declining to run in the first place. But Jackson's ego was so ravaged from manner in which the 1824 presidential campaign against Adams ended that all he envisioned was revenge. There is no doubt he loved Rachel but, from all indications, he cared more for his military career and becoming president. His continued promises to leave public life and return to Rachel and The Hermitage were empty pledges.

After the 1824 presidential election, Jackson had ninety-nine electoral votes as compared with Adams' eighty-four, William H. Crawford's forty-one and Clay's thirty-seven. Since no candidate had an Electoral College majority, the election—per the Twelfth Amendment—was decided by the House of Representatives, where Clay was speaker. After announcing he would support Adams, who received no votes in Kentucky, Clay managed the vote so that Adams received a majority in the House. Afterwards, Adams announced

Clay would be his secretary of state, an acknowledged stepping stone to the presidency the Kentuckian so badly wanted. Adams's and Clay's dirty little deal was thereafter known as the "corrupt bargain," which Jackson coined and swore to reverse in four years regardless of the scurrilous publicity that could have been a contributing factor in Rachel's death.

1

The Many Faces
of Rachel Jackson

In the nineteen decades since her death, Rachel Jackson remains almost as enigmatic now as she did in 1828. She was born in 1767, when society only recognized the worth of women as their husbands' chattel, the bearer of their children and the keeper of their homes; when fathers saw no worth in educating their daughters as compared to their sons; when mothers, busy with large families, had little time to impart more than household knowledge to their daughters, and oft times parents married off their daughters as soon as possible.

Yet, even in her own time, Rachel accomplished much that has not been recognized. Since her husband was the seventh President of the United States, Rachel was often portrayed by some historians as simply an appendage of Andrew Jackson. Others went a bit further and referred to her as a "good wife" prototype. Undoubtedly, he was the love of her life, although she was unprepared for the extended absences his military life required and the spotlight his political life produced. She weathered some very severe personal storms as a result of Jackson's choices. Had she been able to set the course for her second marriage, Rachel would have undoubtedly chosen to live her life in the domesticity of The Hermitage with her husband, the flock of nieces and nephews, wards and orphans they cared for and her large family.

A few of her letters have been preserved but many perished in the 1834 fire that destroyed potions of The Hermitage. Her words indicate a personality strong enough to survive an abusive first marriage. She chose her own method of escaping those bonds to marry the man she truly loved. Jackson's lengthy absences in their marriage forced Rachel to become proficient in managing their plantation, handling their cotton ginning and distilling businesses, overseeing planting of crops, harvesting, raising vegetables, preserving meat for winter's use and supervising the household slaves. Rachel acquired a modicum of medical knowledge that she used to care for family, friends and slaves. She furthered her interest in the domestic industries by weaving fabric for clothing. In addition, Jackson depended on her to ship him supplies for his troops whenever possible. Rachel was a strict practitioner of the religion she believed in but at times it was difficult due to her husband's political ambitions.

It was that fleeting first marriage to Lewis Robards and the manner of her escape, however, that Jackson's political enemies—John Q. Adams, Henry Clay and others—focused on which threw Rachel into the firestorm of presidential politics.

By 1824, Rachel was no longer the beauty that Jackson married. Long days outside on their plantation tanned and weathered her complexion. She undoubtedly consumed too much food during the lonely periods her husband was absent and she became quite stout. While her physique did not lessen her husband's affections, it was used in a most hurtful manner by his political enemies. The vile and venomous manner in which his opponents used Rachel's first marriage, their marriage and her physical appearance in an effort to make him lose his infamous temper failed. However, that failure probably added voters to his successful presidential campaign in 1828, not to speak of what it did to Rachel.[1]

Kathleen Kennedy and Sharon P. Ullman, in their book *Sexual Borderlands: Constructing America's Sexual Past*, called John Q. Adams' 1828 presidential campaign's treatment of Rachel "a most extra-vagrant censure." Nonetheless, the authors also saw it as an advancement of women as it challenged the stereotype of female passivity. "If a woman could be a 'modern Jezebel' (as Rachel was repeatedly called) she could also be 'a Joan of Arc' as well and exert herself as a force for righteousness," they wrote.[2]

It was doubtful if Rachel looked at her situation in that manner since she was too busy keeping them financially afloat. Rachel died on December 22, 1828, weeks before Jackson was inaugurated on March 4, 1829. A grief-stricken president-elect was sworn in, served two terms, returned to The Hermitage in 1837 and died there in 1845.

Rachel practically faded from history until Andrew Jackson, Jr., began selling of parcels of The Hermitage plantation he inherited from his parents. The younger Jackson was totally inept in financial affairs and, by 1853, had mortgaged his home. Three years later, the state of Tennessee paid him $48,000 for 500 acres including the mansion and outbuildings and allowed he and his family to live there as tenants. After his wife, Sarah Yorke Jackson, died in 1888, a group of wealthy Nashville women, including some Donelson-Jackson descendants, sprang into action, incorporated the Ladies' Hermitage Association (LHA) to save The Hermitage and purchased the mansion and twenty-five acres.[3]

The Ladies' Hermitage Association (now known as the Andrew Jackson

Foundation) was one of the earliest and most successful historic preservation organizations in the nation. In 2018, 173 years after Jackson's death, they celebrated the acquisition of The Hermitage's original 1,050 acres.[4]

The LHA worked as hard to put that acreage together as Rachel did to maintain it during her lifetime. She had no desire to leave The Hermitage to be the nation's first lady. All she wanted was to live out her last days in the peaceful surroundings of her home. In restoring The Hermitage, the LHA was also tasked with protecting the image of both Jacksons. His image, pro or con, was well established; Rachel's was woven into the background.

Sarah Jeanine Hornsby, in her Vanderbilt University thesis on how the Ladies' Hermitage Association por-

A watercolor on ivory miniature of Rachel painted by Louisa Catherine Strobel, circa 1830. It was said Jackson wore a miniature of Rachel around his neck every day after her death and, at night, laid it on his bedside table (Andrew Jackson's Hermitage, Nashville, TN).

trayed Rachel, used The Hermitage guidebooks to describe their imaging of Rachel. "The guidebooks were first published in 1905 and then edited (and updated as the books also contained inventory of artifacts at The Hermitage) by the LHA annually using the regent of that particular year as the first author," Hornsby wrote. "The earliest guidebooks dedicated the work of the LHA to Andrew Jackson and his accomplishments. The first line of the book, couched under a portrait of Jackson, read, 'In his inspiring image The Hermitage was preserved.'"[5]

From 1905 to 1917, Hornsby pointed out, guidebooks mentioned nothing about Rachel's character or her role in keeping The Hermitage running in Jackson's absences. "It was not until 1923," she continued, "that the guidebook received a major overhaul under the regency of Mrs. Walter Stokes, who later wrote a separate biography of Rachel herself under her given name, Nellie Treanor Stokes." Even then, in the fifty-page guidebook only three-quarters of a page was devoted to Rachel.[6] "Rachel's agency in Hermitage life seems, at best, to be lessened," Hornsby wrote, "and, at worst, denied in this work. Her own persona seems obliterated by the heading of the section, 'Domestic,' could apply to anything within parameter of the house and it was here that the story of Rachel was told. It is clear from this heading that the author placed Rachel in only one area of Andrew's life, his house. Indeed she seems inseparable from the home, which he was away from most of the time."[7]

The vague image of Rachel as the quiet, noble wife might have endured, Hornsby suggested, if a *Saturday Evening Post* article about Rachel by Meade Minnigerode had not appeared in 1925. "Minnigerode's Rachel Jackson," she wrote, "and the imagery it presented met with opposition from many quarters, particularly the upper classes in Tennessee. Minnigerode, unlike the LHA, [who] favored Tennessee authors before him, [S. G.] Heiskell and [A. S.] Colyar, did not rely upon [John] Overton's account of the Jacksons' marriage as the basis for his narrative. Further, instead of detailing Jackson's military exploits and describing Rachel in the background, he was interested in her own personal habits and daily routines aside from those of Jackson."[8]

It was difficult to ascertain just what infuriated the Nashvillians other than Minnigerode, who with a few exceptions, concentrated on Rachel instead of Jackson. "Shortly after the appearance in magazine form of the informal biography of Rachel Jackson, now reprinted in this volume," Minnigerode wrote, "the editors of the magazine forwarded to Mr. Minnigerode's publishers a telegram from Nashville, Tennessee, reading in part as follows. 'The people of this section are surprised and indignant at the publication … of the article by Meade Minnigerode. They were not prepared to see so unfair and inaccurate a review of such historical personages as President of the United States and his wife, and one permeated with such contemptuous and narrow prejudices as characterized the author appear in the columns of your great journal. Such a publication is an affront to the truth of history and to that justice at its bar which Tennessee holds to be due the memory of the distinguished man and woman…. A public meeting of protest will be held in the city tomorrow. E. B. Stahlman, publisher *The Nashville Banner*, Nashville Tennessee.'"[9]

More than 300 livid Nashvillians gathered at the Hermitage Hotel meeting, chaired by former Governor Benton McMillin, on May 21, 1925, to express their displeasure over Minnigerode's article. State librarian and archivist John Trotwood Moore suggested retrieving Jackson's dueling pistol, with which he killed Charles Dickerson, to settle the matter. "The old pistol which Jackson used on that memorable occasion still is preserved and I for one would glad to use it again to protect the honor of our beloved Rachel Jackson, the gracious wife of one of the greatest statesman the world has ever known," Moore espoused.[10]

"We are here to defend the honor of Andrew Jackson and his wife," Moore bragged. "In his lifetime he was not only the greatest man in Tennessee. He was the greatest man of his generation. While he lived, he needed no one to defend his honor or his wife's honor. Now that he is dead, it is our sacred duty and privilege to defend his honor. This is one of the most serious things that ever has come into the history of Tennessee and we want the world to know of our indignation."[11]

Many prominent Nashvillians—community leaders, a judge, a historian and a Congressman—wrote newspaper columns protesting Minnigerode's treatment of Jackson more so than Rachel.[12]

Minnigerode made sure the world knew of the Tennesseans' indignation as he included their meeting comments in a preface to the chapter on Rachel in his book *Some American Ladies: Seven Informal Biographies,* published the next year. It was a rather clever marketing strategy. Former Tennessee congressman and attorney John W. Gaines called Minnigerode's article, "an invasion of the grave of our beloved and the grave of his noble wife." Minnigerode was called by Gaines, "a merchant of slander, prying open the graves of the dead in order to sell slander for gold." Gaines described the writer as being vicious, venomous and insidious.[13]

Nellie Stokes said it was impossible for any person visiting The Hermitage to believe Rachel Jackson was not a woman of culture. A Miss Gentry declared, according to Minnigerode, that a man of Jackson's noble nature would have never selected as his wife a woman of the type portrayed by Mr. Minnigerode.[14]

The Nashvillians adopted a resolution, publishing in the *Tennessean,* in which Jackson was described as having few if any faults. "The portrayal of such a man as a swash-buckling roister, wine-imbibing gamester and street bully is an indefensible slander which all Tennesseans resent and which the American sense of justice strongly condemns."[15] Actually, Jackson, at one time or another, met all of those descriptions.

Rachel was practically canonized in the resolution.

The spirit of the delineation of Rachel Jackson shows that the author preferred to listen to the voice of calumny and the whispers of slander rather than take audience of the impartial of history. The attempt to hold up to ridicule and to discredit with innuendo to the woman who held sway over the heart of the foremost American of his time and illustrated Christian virtues which ennobled her demeanor in every station however exalted or exacting affronts every consideration which should control the public writer or public journal. The interesting thing about Rachel Jackson is not, perchance, that she could not spell perfectly or meet the requirements of classic English but that she could capture the heart and fire and imagination of a man like Jackson and hold his chivalrous devotion until the last day of her life.[16]

That Rachel Jackson lacked the power or repartee of a woman of the social world and that her dancing was not up to the requirements of the minuet is trivial and irrelevant. That she could live so that her distinguished husband could write her epitaph in words of noble and restrained tenderness and grief, through which truth and candor runs like a golden thread in a rich tapestry, is undying testimony of the intrinsic worth and nobleness of the woman so deeply, so tenderly loved and cherished. That one could lay violent hands upon this white flower of chivalrous love and devotion is proof of how alien is the spirit that failed to discern it.

The resolution was signed by Mrs. Walter Stokes, Regent, Ladies' Hermitage Association; Mrs. Bettie M. Donelson, President, Andrew Jackson Society; Miss Della Dortch; John W. Gaines, E. B. Stahlman, George H. Armistead, Sr., and Walter Stokes.[17]

Minnigerode acknowledged he was mistaken when he wrote it was Charles Dickinson's gun that was half-cocked in his duel with Jackson. It was Jackson's pistol which was half-cocked and the mistake was corrected. The author stated that he never received a copy of the Nashvillians' resolution and only saw it in the *Tennessean*.[18]

George P. Putnam's Sons, Minnigerode's publisher, made a most unusual defense of their author while readily admitting his mistake in the Jackson-Dickinson duel:

It is a little difficult, therefore, for Mr. Minnigerode to determine in what respect other than that no doubt manifested in his original recital of the Dickinson duel, he may have proved himself a "coward, liar, cur and rascal," and interpreter of "contemptuous and narrow prejudices," a "merchant of slander," a "cheap, common villainous prevaricator selling his rough stuff for gold" and a layer of "violent hands upon this white flower of chivalrous love and devotion." Or, as certain individuals have not hesitated to suggest, a subsidized political hack writer. In general, however, one gets the impression that Mr. Minnigerode was less surprised by the outbreak of the fundamentalist attitude towards biographical writing which greeted his article than by the astonishing lack of courtesy—amounting it would seem in some cases to libel—which adorned the transaction. In certain communities there does appear to survive a mediaeval point of view towards the fruits of not altogether unlaborious and unconscientious research about the matter scarcely requires, one could have imagined, a descent to the more unreticent levels of ungrateful abuse. At all events, always expecting the question of the pistol at half-cock, Mr. Minnigerode has at no time retracted any portion of the article under discussion."[19]

Minnigerode's mistake about Jackson's pistol certainly created a furor among the Nashvillians but here was another mistake concerning Rachel. He stated that Rachel had made only one trip to Washington, DC, but that was incorrect.[20] She was there in 1815, and again in 1824–25.[21]

Minnigerode gave an evenhanded portrayal of a frontier girl grown into a frontier woman but who had difficulties making the transition into the Pre-Victorian Era. He admitted, and there was no doubt, that Rachel and her entourage would have had struggled to adapt to the Washington social scene. "And, yet, in her own milieu in the midst of devoted friends, and on three occasions at least in the precarious glare of an unaccustomed public scrutiny, Rachel Jackson was altogether admirable," he wrote.[22]

Minnigerode used a quote by a Mrs. Seaton to describe Rachel's 1815 visit to Washington that gave "a damper to those who have used her as an argument against him. She has proven the falsity of the thousand slanders which have been industriously circulated of her awkwardness, ignorance and indecorum. I find her striking characteristics to be so unaffected simplicity of manners with great goodness of heart. So far from being denied the attention usually extended to strangers, as was predicted, she has been overpowered by the civilities of all parties."[23]

He also provided an accurate, it appeared, description of Rachel's problems with Lewis Robards and their marriage. "Rachel Robards was not the sort of girl to remain inconspicuous," he wrote. "There was nothing demure about her, nothing retiring or submissive. She liked a good time and she never failed to attract attention. Her husband, Captain Robards, was a well-educated, a handsome, passionate, tyrannical devil consumed with jealousy. According to him—although no one, not even his mother believed him—his wife was not behaving with that discretion which he had a right to expect. There were dreadful scenes and finally in 1788, a separation was agree upon and Rachel's brother, Samuel, came to take her home."[24]

The Nashvillians who objected to his magazine article should have been grateful to Minnigerode for writing that Rachel and Jackson were married in Natchez, Mississippi. He offered no proof because there was none. Somehow or other they missed that point. He was critical of Jackson, as were many others—Tennesseans among them—for having such slender knowledge of Virginia divorce laws and the decisions he made that later came back to haunt both he and Rachel.[25]

After she dealt with all the problems he created with the Charles Dickinson and John Sevier duels and the Thomas Hart Benton brawl, Minnigerode described Rachel's attitude toward her husband. "She adored him," he wrote. "She rebuked him for his sins, she strove with him for his unbelieving soul, she lamented his godless tongue and the fatal celerity of his trigger finger but she adored him."[26]

How the Nashvillians could have faulted Minnigerode's description of Rachel's first visit to New Orleans after his husband's victory over the British in the War of 1812 was unfathomable. "They helped her, of course, those fine Creole ladies," he wrote. "They told her what to do, they bought her clothes to wear, with gentle words and ministering and they set the seal of their own splendidly generous loyalty, their magnification conception of the obligation of nobility upon her goings out and comings in. They would have done this for any *Madame la Generale* punctiliously and coldly but for Rachel they did it with warm kindness because they liked her. They stood in a stately row behind her chair and watched the approaches to her dignity and guarded the portals of her negligent tongue."[27]

Hornsby wrote that the Nashvillians were offended by Minnigerode's description that Rachel suddenly got religion in the evangelical wave of preaching that swept the frontier in the early 1800s. Their complaint was that Rachel and her sisters were described as being caught up in the evangelicalism wave somehow detracted from the honesty of their faith.[28] There were those who faded after answering the call, but Rachel was not one of them. She clung to her evangelical Presbyterianism as if it were a suit of armor for the remainder of her life.

There was a different Rachel at The Hermitage, Minnigerode wrote, after she joined the church. "Salvation hung, so to speak, like the sword of Damocles above the general's unreceptive head."[29]

According to Hornsby, "Rather than meet Minnigerode's claims about Rachel's personal traits and habits, the writers of these newspaper articles worked strenuously to push Rachel's womanly role back into an unspecified trait—that of being a 'good wife.' However, exactly what being a 'good wife,' was aside from providing hospitality for her husband's guests, defied explanation. It is clear that these writers assumed that (in Rachel's case at least) a woman's function was determined only by what sort of a wife she proved to be."[30]

Apparently, Nashvillians, in opposition to Minnigerode's description of Rachel, failed to take note of the influence she held over Jackson. For example, while he was governor of Florida, Rachel complained that the citizens of Pensacola failed to observe the Sabbath. The businesses and activities she detested were closed on Sundays. "They hated her," he wrote, "just as they hated her fiery, incomprehensible general, Don Andrew Jackson, Gubernator."[31]

Hornsby asserted that local writers protested Minnigerode's treatment of Rachel because it appeared to detract from Jackson's reputation as a good man. "The editorials worked to rid the myth of damaging detail that might have detracted from the wide, sweeping claims of Jackson as a good man and as a founder of true democracy in the United States. This detail would also have assigned a specific identity to Rachel that writers were unwilling to grant. Labelling details about Rachel as 'unimportant' gives evidence to this. Not only did they object to the actual claims, for instance, that Rachel was illiterate but they considered information like this about her unnecessary."[32] Actually, Rachel was far from illiterate as her operation of The Hermitage plantation proved.

Following the Minnigerode article and book a decade later was *The Gorgeous Hussy*, a movie about Margaret O'Neal Timberlake and her marriage to John H. Eaton, Jackson's close confidant and his secretary of war, and her close relationship with the president. Joan Crawford portrayed Margaret; Robert Taylor her first husband, John Timberlake; Franchot Tone had the John Eaton role; Lionel Barrymore was the ranting and opinionated Jackson and Beulah Bondi was an ill, pipe-smoking, dried-up Rachel. The movie was based on a book of the same title written by Samuel H. Adams as a historical novel and published in 1934 by Houghton Miffin in Boston.[33] To say Adams used some poetic license in his book would be incorrect as the entire volume was poetic license.

The 103-minute MGM film cost $1,119,000 and the movie grossed $2,019,000 worldwide.[34] There was no way the studio was going to bow to the wrathful demands of Nashvillians and withdraw it from circulation.

"The image of the couple [Rachel and Jackson] in the film aroused incredible fury in Nashville," Hornsby wrote. "The LHA delivered a petition to the state legislature proposing a ban on further screenings of the film in the state of Tennessee. No action by the legislature followed but public sentiment all but burned the film in effigy. The public fury over the Minnigerode's article and book and *The Gorgeous Hussy* died down all within months of its outbreak. The memory of the harmful, slanderous images of Rachel and Andrew, however, did not. There existed the genuine fear that those who were not readily familiar with the Jacksons would take Minnigerode and *The Gorgeous Hussy* seriously."[35]

Hornsby went on to state, "The attacks on the traditional image of the domestic Rachel of the Old South prompted the LHA to provide their own truthful image of the domestic Rachel, one that gave more information than the guidebooks offered and was thus less easily misconstrued. The intent of their writing seemed to be to re-illustrate the Rachel they knew, i.e., the refined domestic Rachel appeared to be in the 1920s and 1930s in a more concrete way. However, in the following decade the LHA actually created a new image of Rachel. Their new Rachel was still gracious and hospitable but she became more managerial and directly involved in other areas of Andrew's life."[36]

Hornsby said that from 1935 to 1945 the image of Rachel made the renovation from the vague "good wife" definition into that "of a woman who had specific responsibilities in her home and community and definite opinions of the world around her and a personal stake in the political activities of her husband." These ideas, she wrote, came in opposition to Minnigerode and the film.[37]

Minnigerode, however, provided glimpses of Rachel's home life the keepers of her image apparently overlooked. He described the household's evening entertainment with nieces, nephews, wards and friends gathered to listen Rachel play the piano (or guitar) accompanied by Jackson on the flute. He described the drives Rachel and Jackson took through the Tennessee countryside in their big carriage pulled by four gray horses with footmen in blue livery and glazed hats with silver bands.[38]

In the 1930s and 1940s, Hornsby wrote, the image of Rachel emerged as a woman who had a more complex role in both public and private life. She cited books by Nellie Treanor Stokes and Mary French Caldwell illustrating that Rachel was an individual whose role demanded closer scrutiny for her own merits rather than being an appendage to the chivalrous and gentlemanly qualities of her husband. "Rachel for Stokes and Caldwell," she said, "occupied a wider space in public life and was possessed of astute intelligence and understanding. Moreover, the Rachel that they presented had other qualities such as beauty and social grace."[39]

Stokes used the words of Thomas Hart Benton, a Jackson aide during the War of 1812, to describe Rachel as a hostess during his frequent visits to The Hermitage. "She had a faculty—a rare one of retaining names and titles in a throng of visitors, addressing each one appropriately and dispensing hospitality to all with a cordially which enhances its value. No bashful youth or plain old man whose modesty sat then at the lower end of the table could escape her cordial attention any more than the titled gentlemen on her right and left. Young persons were her delight and she always had her house filled with them—clever young women and clever young men—all calling her affectionately 'Aunt Rachel.' I was young then and one of that number."[40]

Rachel's protectors in Nashville appeared to have a problem determining just what her image was or should be. "This unwillingness to confront what seemed, from some primary source material to be the real Rachel, countrified, plump and not very adept at dress and fashion," Hornsby wrote, "was manifest further in some of the portraiture that emerged in the early 1940s. When even the original portraiture of Rachel was enhances in the 1830s, the copies that circulated around Nashville and the nation reflected a desire to alter Rachel's physical appearance and demeanor."[41]

Rachel's image caught a break in 1953 when Irving Stone's novel was made into a movie, *The President's Lady*. The only problem with the title was that she was never a president's lady, only a president-elect's. Susan Hayward's portrayal of Rachel gave her beauty, fire and determination. Charlton Heston was well matched as Jackson. John Patrick's adaption of Stone's book took some poetic license and included steamy love scenes. The ninety-six-minute movie was shot in California in black and white by Twentieth Century–Fox. A decade later, the National Broadcasting Company premiered the film on their television network.[42]

The movies and television made Rachel known to millions of Americans who knew nothing about her.

From all available descriptions, Rachel was a beauty when she was young—flashing dark eyes, lustrous dark hair and a gregarious and caring personality. No portraits of that young Rachel seem to exist. It was strange that in her prime Jackson never had her portrait painted. Yet, in those years, Jackson certainly had the funds to breed, race and gamble on his Thoroughbred horses and stage and bet on cockfights.

In her University of Iowa dissertation, "America's Portraitist: Ralph E. W. Earl and the Imaging of the Jacksonian Era," Rachel E. Stephens wrote that Earl painted his first portrait of Rachel in 1817 when she was fifty years old. She is shown seated wearing a short-sleeved bodice with a satin-like skirt. Earl's apparent lack of depth perception made Rachel look even heavier.[43] The artist gave Rachel curls above her forehead and her hair was covered with a lace mantilla. Her hands were too small for her arms, a feature found in other of Earl's portraits of women. Stephens wrote that the Jackson family referred to the painting as "Rachel in her ball dress." At the time Jackson commissioned Earl to paint Rachel, Stephens wrote, he also did portraits of John Coffee and John Reid for which Jackson paid him $150.[44]

Earl arrived in Nashville in January 1817 to paint Jackson's portrait. Later that year, he married Rachel's niece, Jane Caffery. After her death and that of their infant son the next year, Earl became part of The Hermitage's entourage. After Rachel's death, he accompanied Jackson to Washington, made frequent trips back to The Hermitage, had his own room in the President's House, and then returned with Jackson when the president's second term ended. Earl died there in 1838.[45]

James C. Kelly in his *Tennessee Encyclopedia* entry on Earl reiterated Stephens' theory of Earl as a political artist with some blunt assertions. "Earl turned out numerous paintings of Jackson, some of distinction but many repetitious in nature and mediocre in quality. Politicians, especially Democrats, knew 'it did not hurt to order a portrait of General Jackson from Earl.'" Kelly elaborated on some of the artist's other talents. "He designed the invitation to Lafayette's ball in Nashville in 1825, as well as the guitar shaped driveway and concentric flower beds at The Hermitage. He also executed decorative interior painting at neighboring Tulip Grove plantation mansion."[46]

Stephens said Earl's unflattering 1817 portrait of Rachel did not fare well in the twentieth century. "In 1941, perhaps in response to the negative characterizations Mrs. Jackson was receiving, the portrait was removed from public view by the Ladies' Hermitage Association Board of Directors to 'a place where it not be seen from the hall.' In July 1948, perhaps unaware it was an Earl portrait, the board inspected the painting and called it 'a distorted and poor likeness' and determined to have it cleaned but only a month later the work was deemed not worth preserving."[47]

That particular portrait of Rachel fit the unflattering description of her in Minnigerode's book. "Her figure is rather full but loosely and carelessly dressed so that when she is seated she seems to settle into herself in a manner that is neither graceful nor elegant." Minnigerode, however, made an effort to present Nashville a contemporary's description of Rachel. "Her eyes are bright and express great kindness of heart, her face father broad and her features plain. But, withal, her face is so good-natured and motherly that you immediately feel at ease with her."[48]

Stephens wrote that Jackson was so attached to Earl's 1817 painting of Rachel he was reluctant to allow it to leave The Hermitage. "His attachment to his portraits," she wrote, "shows his devotion to his family but more importantly reveals a level of sophistication and refinement on Jackson's part in treasuring the fine arts."[49]

Andrew Jackson was painted in a uniform by The Hermitage's resident artist, Ralph E. W. Earl, who accompanied him to Washington and lived in the President's House. The portrait was painted circa 1820, after Jackson's great military victories were behind him (Andrew Jackson's Hermitage, Nashville, TN).

The devotion Jackson had for his wife's likeness, Stephens said, was also illustrated by the tours of The Hermitage given by Uncle Alfred, one of the Jacksons' last slaves, after the president's death. "During the tour, in Jackson's bedroom, he would point our Earl's portrait of Rachel over the mantel and tell how every morning Jackson would kneel before it and thank God for sparing his life so that he could look upon her face for one more day. Another account recalled, 'I found Jackson sitting at a little table with his wife's miniature, a very large one, before him propped up against some books, and between him and the picture an open book which bore the mark of long use. This was her Prayer Book. The last thing he did every night before lying down to rest, was to read in that book with that picture before his eye.'"

Earl's paintings of Rachel changed, Stephens noted, after 1824, when Jackson first ran for president. She was adorned with jewelry and stylized as an elegant companion for a future president. "Earl's numerous portraits of Mrs. Jackson served both as personal mementos for the president," she wrote, "and as a way to counter the criticism leveled against her. As an adult, she achieved significant status with her marriage to Jackson but her reputation was tarnished by the scandalous circumstances of her first marriage to Lewis Robards. When Jackson ran for the presidency the thirty-year-old disgrace was made public and she was cast as an adulterer."[50]

Rachel, in Robards' divorce decree, was legally found to be an adulterer. However, if Rachel and Jackson were married in Mississippi, as they claimed, she would have also been a bigamist.

Painting women was not Earl's forte; he did much better with men. His 1817 portrait, as well as the 1825, 1827 and 1831 portraits of Rachel, showed her in a white mantilla.[51]

Twelve other portraits of women Earl painted, or that were attributed to him, showed the subjects in either caps or bareheaded with elaborate coiffures.[52] "Traditionally, the black veils were worn by married or widowed women," an article in *Catholicism Pure & Simple* stated, "while the white veils were worn by young girls or unmarried women."[53]

The above portrait of Rachel Jackson was painted at the President's House in Washington three years after her death by Ralph E. W. Earl, copied from an earlier portrait of her. Earl accompanied Andrew Jackson to the inauguration and occupied quarters in the mansion. It is said Jackson walked into Earl's studio, saw him working on the above painting and burst into tears (Andrew Jackson's Hermitage, Nashville, TN).

Often Earl simply altered portraits he previously painted for new commissions. In 1825, Stephens wrote, John Coffee, who married Rachel's niece Mary, commissioned Earl to paint a portrait of Rachel and a pendant of Jackson. Those works were severely damaged in the fire that destroyed the Coffee home, Hickory Hill, in Florence, Alabama, during the Civil War. The repainted portrait showed Rachel in a black empire waist dress with a decorative buckle. She wore a headpiece with a sort of white shawl draped from it over her shoulders. Her jewelry appeared to be pearls. In 1827, another Earl portrait showed Rachel in the same dress but with another white collar, different headdress with a wisp of a mantilla and the topaz jewelry. She held the chain of an evening purse in her left hand. In Earl's 1831 portrait of Rachel, she was wearing the same black dress and same headdress with a longer mantilla. She wore drop earrings and an ill-fitting white lace collar. In her left hand she held a rose.[54]

The idea of Rachel as a grand dame of the Old South, Hornsby wrote, was part of the construction of a newer image bringing her into the twentieth century. "Rachel had definite influence over Jackson's public career; she remained calm and dignified even in periods of extreme stress; did not collapse under the weight of scandal and showed strength of will entirely unlike a submissive lady of the Old South."[55]

Rachel was not submissive but practically invisible in former LHA Regent Ann Harwell Wells' 1975 article in the *Tennessee Historical Quarterly* about Lafayette's 1825 visit to Nashville and The Hermitage. Aside from

In 1826, Andrew Jackson's close friend, John Coffee, who lived in Alabama, commissioned Ralph E. W. Earl to paint a portrait of Rachel Jackson and a pendant of her husband. Earl painted Rachel in the same back dress he used in the shawl collar portrait. The oil on canvas painting portrays a different headdress from the 1825 painting, a decorative buckle at the empire waist and topaz jewelry (Andrew Jackson's Hermitage, Nashville, TN).

mentioning Rachel's Washington letter about Lafayette, Wells only referenced Lafayette calling on Rachel in Nashville during the festivities. As for the elaborate dinner Rachel prepared for Lafayette at The Hermitage, Wells wrote only of Jackson, the Frenchman and his secretary's description of the Jacksons' plantation.[56]

Where Wells only mentioned Rachel twice in her article, Melissa Gismondi, in her 2017 University of Virginia dissertation, endowed Rachel with powers that posthumously influencing Andrew Jackson's Indian policies as president. "It argues," an abstract of the dissertation on the University of Virginia's website stated, "that Rachel aligned Jackson's military and political

The oil on canvas portrait of Rachel Jackson was painted by Ralph E. W. Earl circa 1825. Called the "shawl collar portrait," she has a shawl, or a shawl collar, over a black dress and under the veil falling from her mantilla. Pearls at her neck appear to be her only jewelry (Andrew Jackson's Hermitage, Nashville, TN).

career with her conservative 'avenging evangelism,' which proved a crucial tool of Jackson's empire-building. Steeped in frontier violence, Rachel saw Jackson's warfare against Indigenous peoples, the conquest of their lands and their 'removal' to reservations as part of a larger campaign to purge the U.S. of sin and create Zion on earth. This way of thinking (and feeling) justified and accelerated the violent dispossession of Indigenous peoples from southeastern North America during the War of 1812 and Jackson's presidency."[57]

According to Gismondi's dissertation abstract, a woman who had been dead for more than two years influenced the Indian Removal Act of 1830. Or, four years after her passing was responsible for Jackson ignoring the Supreme Court's 5–1 decision in *Worcester v. Georgia* which ruled that Georgia laws regarding the Cherokee Nation were unconstitutional. Rachel had been in her grave for ten years when Jackson ordered what became known as the "Trail of Tears," which removed the Cherokee people from their homes in Southeastern portion of the nation and relocated them to Oklahoma.[58]

Historic figures such as Rachel Jackson should be carefully examined within the context of the times in which they lived. Juxtaposing Rachel into the twentieth or twenty-first centuries does her a great injustice for many reasons—opinions, society, morals, expectations and the political environments changed. Scrutinize Rachel Donelson Robards Jackson within the years she lived when considering this extraordinary woman who was made the focal point of the most venomous, rancorous and vituperative presidential campaign in American history. That she even survived as long as she did was a testament to her willpower, determination and strength of character.

2

The Early Days

Rachel Donelson, a vivacious and precocious girl with a dimpled smile, great curiosity and winsome ways, grew to womanhood during the great American land rush westward after the Revolutionary War. Her father, John Donelson II, was a member of the Virginia House of Burgesses serving on committees with George Washington and Thomas Jefferson. He spent most of his time chasing Indian tribes, treatying with them, surveying frontier lands for Virginia and North Carolina and patenting choice locations for himself and his children. Rachel grew up knowing the Founding Fathers as her father's associates.[1]

Donelson, like other prominent men of his day, was afflicted with land fever and the battle for choice acreages west of the Appalachians was fierce. The Blounts—William, John Gray and Thomas—aside from their family businesses of politics, mercantile establishments, shipping, slavery and mills, accumulated at least 2.1 million acres of land in frontier America. Philadelphian Robert Morris, known as one of the financiers of the Revolutionary War, amassed approximately 2.8 million acres with his North American Land Company. The Sevier brothers, John and Valentine Jr., were not on the level of the Blount brothers and Morris when they grabbed 128,000 acres of confiscated Tory lands in North Carolina for fifty shillings per 100 acres. Donelson, closely associated with the Blounts and Seviers, was tempted to work with Morris in the accumulation of land warrants. Donelson and his family eventually accrued well over a million acres of land.[2]

Ohio Representative John C. Symmes also contributed financially to the war effort. Symmes had enough Congressional clout to ask the government for 1,000,000 acres north of the Ohio and between the two Miami rivers. He received 311,682 acres of land. Symmes' name is forever associated with the unmitigated disaster—he sold the same land twice, surveyed land that did not belong to him and reneged on requirements to set aside land for governmental and educational purposes. "Symmes never paid for nor developed the full one million acres he sought," George W. Knopper wrote in a book published by Ohio state auditor Jim Petro in 2002. "He mishandled surveys and sales to such an extent that Congress restricted his purchase to 311,682 acres, including lands reserved for special purposes."[3]

Peyton Short, unable to marry one land baron's daughter—Rachel Donelson Robards—succeeded in marrying another, Symmes' daughter Maria, whose sister Anna was the wife of President William Henry Harrison.[4]

While these men were scurrying about the country grabbing all the land they could, most of their wives were left with double responsibilities—overseeing the plantations/farms as well as running their households and raising their children.

Rachel Stockley Donelson was no different. From all indications she was born around 1730 on her great-grandfather's 3,600-acre plantation in Assawoman, Accomack County, Virginia.[5] She married John Donelson II, whose father owned ships used to import goods from England to his mercantile interests in the colonies.[6]

She raised their children, supervised the home and managed the plantation while her husband was away. Their youngest daughter, Rachel, was born in 1767. Her early years were spent exploring all the exciting places on her father's plantation in Pittsylvania County, Virginia, along the Bannister River,

Andrew Jackson commissioned a watercolor of the Stockley home in Accomack County, Virginia, in 1831. Rachel Jackson's mother, Rachel Stockley Donelson, grew up on the plantation before her marriage (Andrew Jackson's Hermitage, Nashville, TN).

with siblings, nieces and nephews. The Donelsons were a clannish group. As they married, often to their first cousins to keep wealth and power intact, they tended to settle near their parents.

Rachel was the tenth of eleven children of John Donelson II and Rachel Stockley Donelson. Alexander, the oldest son, never married. He was followed by Mary, married to Captain John Coffey. Catherine was the wife of Colonel Thomas Hutchings. Stockley Donelson, also a surveyor, landed a rich North Carolina widow, Elizabeth Glasgow Martin. Jane became the wife of Robert Hays. John III, another surveyor, married a relative, Mary Purnell. William Donelson and Charity Dickerson, like his siblings, had a large family. Samuel was married to Mary Smith. Severn and Elizabeth Rucker Donelson had twin sons. Leven, the youngest Donelson child, never married.[7]

Rachel, Samuel, Severn and Leven grew up spending their days doing assigned chores. They played nine pins, seesawed and jumped the rope on the plantation. Since their father had an iron foundry, they probably enjoying playing with hoops.[8]

The Bloomery, Donelson's iron foundry at Rocky Mount, was one of the first in Virginia and he was operating it in 1770 when Rachel was three years old. Built of granite, the southern face of the furnace measured almost 30 feet and the opening was a little over 12 feet. The furnace was cleverly placed against the side of a hill where the iron ore, charcoal and limestone flux could be dumped into the furnace from the top. Donelson's 1773 tax records indicated he had ten people working the foundry: John Holaway, Charles Holaway, Amos Spain and Thomas Bolton along with slaves Moody, Dick, Harry, Tames, Judith and Nell.[9]

Donelson's acquisition of the Bloomery was an indication of his willingness to shade the law to his advantage in land acquisitions, according to Natalie Inman's 2010 Ph.D. dissertation at Vanderbilt University. Donelson bought the property from John Wilcox in 1768 on the condition he would take over the quick-rent payments on the property. "Donelson," Inman wrote, "apparently had not yet paid Wilcox when the land was sold at auction for failure to pay the quick-rents. Although Donelson testified that he had paid the fees on behalf of Wilcox, the testimony was dismissed when it came to light that Donelson had already re-purchased the land claim from the successful bidder, James Cox. Either Donelson knew that Wilcox had not paid the quick-rents prior to the 1768 sale or Donelson purposefully defaulted on the payments to get the land at a much cheaper price. The court ruled for Cox and approved the sale to Donelson."[10]

If there was chicanery in Donelson's land acquisitions, he passed it on to his sons after he died in 1786. According to early Tennessee land grant records, File Number thirty-nine (39) lists John Donelson as having surveyed

11,520 acres of vacant land—no assignee, no grant number/date, no county, no entry number/date.[11]

Donelson's other slaves tended crops, wove cloth from cotton and wool produced on the plantation, and did household work in the one and a half story clapboard house with a long sloping roof and huge chimneys. Their furnishings, silver and other accouterments, attested to the Donelsons' wealth.[12]

The Bannister River was shallow enough in places for the Donelson children to wade and splash in the water. The river was frequented by belted kingfishers and great blue herons. Wild turkeys and bobwhite quail roamed the woodlands where Rachel learned to ride her pony. Along the banks, butterflies dithered about the Jewel weed.[13]

It was a pastoral setting for Rachel, cossetted by her family, to enjoy and fantasize about her life in the coming years, never dreaming her family would be scandalized in a notorious land fraud case in the post–Revolutionary War era or that her name would be used to demonize a candidate in a presidential campaign.

Rachel was schooled in the domestic sciences by her mother. She was a favorite of her father, but Donelson believed formal education was reserved for his sons much like a paternal uncle, Samuel Davis, a president of Princeton. He insisted his sons study surveying, politics and business. Rachel learned the domestic sciences from her mother who also taught her to sew a fine seam, read and write as well as the social graces.[14] The total extent of her education is not known. She became a prolific letter writer, expressing herself quite well if not always grammatically correct.

The son and grandson of ship owners and sailors, Donelson chose surveying over navigation for his profession. His widowed mother, Catherine Davis Donelson, who administered her husband's Maryland estate, insisted that he also study navigation, which later proved to be an asset. His sister Mary, much like Rachel, was educated by their mother but not to the extent of her brother. Mary Donelson married Hugh Henry, who later supervised Donelson's iron foundry.[15]

Prior to being elected to the House of Burgesses in 1769, Donelson was Pittsylvania County surveyor for three years. He surveyed the Virginia state line and found three settlements that actually belonged to North Carolina.[16] Donelson was absent during much of the 1771 House of Burgesses session when he was appointed to survey the Virginia state line.[17]

In the 1773 legislative session, Donelson sat on a committee with George Washington that investigated damages to tobacco lost in an Aquia warehouse fire. He served on another committee with Thomas Jefferson dealing with counterfeiting charges.[18]

Norborne Berkeley, 4th Baron de Botetourt, governor of Virginia, sent Donelson to negotiate the Treaty of Lochaber with the Cherokees. Donelson was paid £100 for his work. When Berkeley offered him the job of surveying the lands transferred from the Cherokees in the Treaty of Lochaber, Donelson jumped at the chance. Land in the new undeveloped portion of the country was the way to make his fortune. Donelson's survey made errors that took hundreds of thousands of acres from the Cherokees and added to the land set aside for settlement. In 1777, the Donelson Line was redrawn, correcting the error, resulting in a more stable relationship with the Cherokees.[19]

In May 1772, Richard D. Spence wrote that Donelson patented 1,000 acres along the Kentucky River for himself, each of his children and his sister Mary's five children, a total of 17,000 acres.[20]

During his surveying expeditions, Donelson saw more of the enormous lush, green land beyond the mountains than most of his fellow Virginians.[21] That acreage was the first of hundreds of thousands of acres of land over the mountains which he and his family accumulated bringing the Donelsons substantial wealth and political power.

Surveying was an expensive and dangerous job and surveyors usually patented choice lands for themselves. Or, they accumulated land as the price of surveying for others. William and John Donelson, however, had difficulty in collecting their land in payment for the surveying they did for William Blount and his brothers.[22]

After the Revolutionary War, another method of acquiring land was available. Virginia paid veterans for their service in varied acreage of land bounties in areas not already claimed or in Indian Territory. Depending on their ranks and if veterans served at least three years on the Continental Line, State Line, State Navy, died in service or enlisted for the entire war, they were eligible for land bounties. Veterans' heirs could sell bounty lands. Militia duty was not included.[23]

Virginia's bounty land allotments for veterans began with 100 acres for a soldier or sailor; 200 acres for a non-commissioned officer, 400 acres if they served throughout the war; 2,000 to 2,666 acres for a subaltern-cornet, subaltern-ensign (second lieutenant) or subaltern lieutenant; 2,666 to 8,000 acres for a surgeon's mate, surgeon and chaplain; 3,000 to 4,666 acres for a captain; 4,000 to 5,333 for a major; 4,500 to 6,666 acres for a lieutenant colonel; 5,000 to 8,888 acres for a colonel; 10,000-plus acres for a brigadier general, and 15,000 to 17,000 acres for a major general.[24]

In 1777 Donelson and at least one son, John III, volunteered for militia duty during the Revolutionary War to protect settlers from Indian attacks. At times, the Donelson militia was the only protection settlers had in the Ohio Valley. In the summer of 1778, Donelson and his men were assigned to march from Pittsylvania County through Franklin County across the Blue Ridge to Rocky Mount. They crossed the New River at English's Ferry and went on to Fort Patrick Henry, a stockade sitting on a bluff above the Holston River in what is now Tennessee.[25] Wherever he went, Donelson kept his eyes open for land purchases.

While her father was away on militia duty and on surveying trips, Rachel enjoyed life along the Banister River plantation. She was on her way to becoming an accomplished horsewoman. Most of Rachel's older married siblings lived nearby. She enjoyed playing with and caring for numerous nieces and nephews. Her love of music and dancing began with her learning to play the harpsichord. The first twelve years of Rachel Donelson's life were carefree, happy and uneventful for a child whose family had social, political and financial standing.[26]

That all changed in 1779.

Donelson's extended surveying trips and militia service took him away from his plantation and iron foundry, creating serious financial repercussions. He entered into a deed of trust with Hugh Innis, using his plantation and eighteen slaves as security, to deliver forty tons of iron bars in eight deliveries over a two-year period. Hugh Innis, who had two plantations on the Pigg River in Franklin County, Virginia, was a brother of Harry Innis, Kentucky's first federal district judge, who was an associate of John Brown, Lewis Robards' attorney in his successful divorce action against Rachel. "Absences on the frontier and economic and material demands of the war," Richard D. Spence wrote in the *Tennessee Historical Quarterly*, "prevented Donelson from meeting those and other obligations. By the time he returned from the Boonesborough campaign in the summer of 1778, he was on the verge of financial ruin." Donelson sold the Bloomery for £4,000 (well over half a million dollars today) to Jeremiah Early and James Calloway, who renamed it the Washington Iron Foundry. The foundry again became successful and was flourishing as late as 1836, employing more than 100 men.[27] Donelson also sold his home plantation to John Markham for £2,800.[28]

Being uprooted from the only home she had even known must have proved trying for eleven-year-old Rachel. Whether leaving her favorite haunts along the Banister River, riding trails and the rambling house were supplanted by her anticipation of adventures ahead was unknown. She would not, however, be leaving her large family.

Her father met Richard Henderson, a North Carolina lawyer and land speculator, when he was at Fort Boonesborough. Henderson had earlier purchased most of what is now Kentucky and Tennessee, called the Transylvania Colony, from the Indians, only to have the Virginia and North Carolina governments cancel the illegal transaction. The two states later each compensated Henderson with 200,000 acres, in recognition of the Transylvania Colony's so-called western improvements.[29]

Henderson had no problem in leaving his Transylvania investors in Boonesborough high and dry. The same applied to the Fort Boonesborough settlers who had to fend for themselves when Henderson abandoned them to begin a new venture in Tennessee.[30] Donelson was not unaware of Henderson's methods of operation.

Henderson was appointed a commissioner in 1779 to readjust the western and central boundaries of Virginia and North Carolina. A rather testy individual, Henderson had a disagreement with his Virginia counterpart and resigned. He made plans to settle and sell what many historians refer to as the 200,000 acres in middle Tennessee.[31] Actually, the Cumberland acreage in question was 309,760 acres. Henderson and others were also granted 200,000 acres on the Powell and Clinch Rivers.[32] Henderson carefully selected the men to lead settlers to his lands in Tennessee. He knew James Robertson from his years at the Watauga settlement in North Carolina. Henderson sent Robertson to lead a small group of men in 1779 to explore the area, called French Lick or the Big Salt Lick (now Nashville), plant corn and return to Watauga by the end of the summer. That winter, Robertson led a group of settlers, with their horses, cattle and hogs, overland to French Lick. Donelson, having sold most of his Virginia properties, moved his family to Fort Patrick Henry (now Kingsport, Tennessee) and began to build a flotilla of flatboats to transport his family, Robertson's and other settlers to new lands across the mountains.

3

The Adventure

It was just the opportunity Donelson was looking for and he jumped at the chance to lead the flotilla although it was far more dangerous then Robertson's overland route to Tennessee. Exactly when the Donelson family arrived at Fort Patrick Henry was not known. However, Donelson would have conferred with Robertson about the journey after he returned from Middle Tennessee in the late summer. Neither was it clear just how much land Henderson intended to give Robertson and Donelson for their settlement efforts.

Irene M. Griffery, in *Earliest Tennessee Land Records and Earliest Tennessee Land History,* wrote that John Donelson, Sr., was awarded three premonitions, 640 acres each, in what was later Davidson County, between the Cumberland and Stone rivers, at the Harpeth River on the south side of the Cumberland and on a branch of the Harpeth River.[1]

Donelson, from his surveying trips and negotiating with the Cherokee Indians in 1777 for the Treaty at Long Island at Cloud's Creek, was knowledgeable about the Holston River, the first part of their journey.[2] The Holston River began in Virginia and ended at its confluence with the French Broad River to form the Tennessee River.[3]

"The Holston diminished in width on the way down, varying rapidly in width and changing suddenly in depth," U.S. Army Corps of Engineers Major Dan C. Kingman later wrote. "It has a fixed regiment of bed and banks, the changes of direction are very sharp, the pools long and deep, are separated by rocky shoals." The principal obstructions, he noted, were the shoals—Tumbling Creek, Balls Battery, the Falls, Wild Waters, Harts and Freemans. Kingman's report was written in 1900, more than 120 years after the Donelson flotilla embarked on their journey down the Holston, indicating the river had changed little.[4]

Donelson began the voyage in December expecting the usual high tide during the winter. That he did so was indicative of his intense desire to make sure his family again became land wealthy even to the point of endangering their lives and those of others on the voyage.

The Tennessee River, vital to westward expansion, was only open to settlement on the upper and lower portions of the river. In between, Indian tribes controlled the Tennessee at some of its most hazardous navigational areas. The Chickasaws, from their perches on the high cliffs, could pick off settlers at will as they attempted to travel through the thirty-mile-long gorge at Walden's Ridge, near Chattanooga. If settlers made it through the gorge, they had to face the Chickamauga at Muscle Shoals with its reefs, rapids and log snags.[5]

There was only word of mouth about the difficulties maneuvering through the Muscle Shoals on the Tennessee River. For that reason, Henderson and Robertson agreed to send men to Muscle Shoals to either meet or leave a message for Donelson's party about the feasibility of traveling overland from that point to their destination.[6]

Robertson, along with 200 men, including William Donelson and his brother-in-law Hugh Henry, began their trek to the Big Salt Lick in October 1779. They loaded their wagons with provisions and herded their horses, cattle, sheep and hogs toward their destination.[7]

Donelson and other settlers continued to build boats for their water voyage. Some apparently had no resources for building the larger boats and planned to use dugouts and canoes for the trip or made arrangements for passage on the more than thirty flatboats in the flotilla.[8]

Flatboats ranged in size from 55 feet long and 16 feet wide to 100 feet long and 20 wide depending on the builder's purse and streams they planned to travel. Donelson's boat, christened *Adventure*, was probably 100 feet long and 20 feet wide. Early flatboats such as the *Adventure* were built from green wood—there was no time for the felled trees to dry out. Most flatboats were built with chine-girder construction methods where a log was split in half to create what were called gunwales. "Positioned on either side," as described by *Steamboat Times*, "they formed a ledge that held the ends of the floor planks. Wooden uprights were set into the gunwales. The heavy planks were fastened using wooden pins to the heavier timber frame. The stern and side were vertical planks of four to six feet." The sides were caulked with pitch or whatever like substance was available.[9]

A tiller control pole extended from the roof of the flatboat over the stern for navigation. It was a crude element for traversing unknown waters. Normally, the tiller was operated from or near the stern of a craft. The covered portion of the boat was situated in the middle of the craft while, at the same time, making the person steering the boat vulnerable in case of an Indian attack. The covered area, used for sleeping and eating in inclement weather, contained household goods and provisions. Openings were built into walls through which guns could be fired. Fully loaded, the flatboats drew no more than three feet of water.[10]

Rachel and her brothers Severn and Leven may have even assisted their father in building the flatboats but more than likely enjoyed playing with the log scraps left over. Rachel appeared to be an easily adaptable child who enjoyed adventure. She was embarking on the greatest journey of her young life unaware that if she was not killed by Indians she could well freeze to death or starve.

Colonel Thomas Marston Green and his family, also from Virginia, were building their flatboats on the Holston River in 1780, around the same time as Donelson. They would later play an important role in Rachel's life. Unlike the Donelsons, when the Green family reached the Mississippi River they floated their flatboats downstream to Natchez, although their original intentions were to settle in Kentucky.[11]

John Donelson had no idea how he would navigate the most treacherous part of the Tennessee River, Muscle Shoals, in what is now northern Alabama. Another unknown was the Chickamauga towns along river banks, near Chattanooga, through which he would have to pass before reaching the shoals. These, along with unpredictable weather conditions, were eminent dangers to which he was willing to expose not only his family but hundreds of other people. If he completed the journey, land wealth awaited his family. If he did not, there would have not been a Rachel Jackson toward whom her husband's enemies could aim their poison political arrows.

Not all members of John and Rachel Donelson's family traveled overland or in the flotilla. Their second oldest son, Stockley, was busy surveying lands in what are now Hawkins and Greene counties in Tennessee.[12]

When Donelson's flotilla, containing 30 to 40 crafts and 200 to 300 people, left Fort Patrick Henry on December 22, 1779, he had no idea weather conditions would produce the worst winter of the late eighteenth century. Every salt water inlet from North Carolina to Canada was completely frozen over. The ice in New York Harbor was so thick British troops marched from Manhattan to Staten Island. General George Washington's troops were immobilized at Morristown, New Jersey, under snow drifts over six feet high.[13]

Fortunately, Robertson's group reached their overland destination on December 25, three days after the Donelson flotilla left Fort Patrick Henry. They were fortunate in avoiding traveling through the terrible winter weather but that was their only asset.[14]

"Journal of a voyage, intended by God's Permission, in the good Boat Adventure, from Fort Patrick Henry on Holston River to the French Salt Springs on Cumberland River, kept by John Donelson," he began on December 22.[15]

While the weather the Donelson flotilla experienced failed to reach the disasters experienced on the East Coast, problems began on the first day of the journey. "Took our departure from the Fort and fell down the river to the mouth of Reedy Creek, where we were stopped by a fall of water and most excessive hard frost," he wrote. "After much delay and many difficulties we arrived at the mouth of Cloud's Creek on Sunday evening the 20 of February 1780, where we lay by until Sunday February 27, when we took our departure with sundry other vessels bound for the same voyage, and on the same day struck the Poor-Valley-Shoal together with Mr. Boyd and Mr. Rounsifer on which shoal we lay that afternoon and succeeding night in much distress."[16]

For nearly five weeks, the Donelson flotilla went nowhere. Historian John R. Finger attributed the delay to a drop in the water level.[17] Such a delay consumed many of the provisions they stowed on their boats. By the end of February, they were faced with the very real threat of starvation.[18]

Donelson's February 28 journal entry read, "In the morning, the water rising, we got off the shoal after landing thirty persons to lighten our boat. In attempting to land on an island received some damage and lost sundry articles and came to camp on the south shore where we joined sundry other vessels also bound down."[19]

The next couple of days the boaters only had to contend with rain.[20] The weather must have been rather confining for Rachel and her brothers—there was no place to run and play but there were plenty of chores to do. House-keeping on a flatboat was a nightmare for the Donelsons, other families and their slaves. As they used up their provisions more space was available, but personal hygiene was an unfamiliar ritual. They cooked on board only during inclement weather, or when the threat of Indian attacks prevented them from landing on the shore.

On Thursday, March 22, they reached the mouth of the French Broad River. They had been afloat for seventy-two days, had only covered around ninety miles of their 1,000-mile trip and provisions were probably rationed at this point.[21]

"Rained about half the day," Donelson wrote. "Passed the mouth of the French Broad River and about 12 o'clock, Mr. Henry's boat being driven on the point of an island by the force of the current was sunk. The crew's lives much endangered, the whole cargo much damaged, which occasioned the whole fleet to put on shore and to go their assistance but with much difficulty bailed her out and raised her, in order to take in her cargo again."[22]

The boat Donelson referenced belonged to his brother-in-law Hugh Henry, which would explain why so much time was spent on recovery efforts when other ensuing accidents were brushed aside. One can only imagine the damage to their household goods and how long, if ever, it took to dry them out.

"That same afternoon," Donelson continued, "Reuben Harrison went out a hunting and did not return that night, though many guns were fired to fetch him in." The search continued the next morning as they scoured the woods for him. "Firing many guns that day and succeeding night," he wrote, "but without success to the great grief of his parents and fellow travelers."[23]

The next day, March 4, the flotilla proceeded, leaving those on the Harrison boat and others to continue the search. Later that day, they found Reuben Harrison a considerable distance down river, where Benjamin Belew took him on his boat.[24] Donelson failed to mention if the Harrison boat and other searchers, who stayed behind, caught up with the flotilla.

He did mention that on March 5 they were joined by the Clinch River Company with whom they camped. There was a problem organizing, or re-organizing, the boats to proceed. "Got underway," Donelson wrote on March 6, "before sunrise: the morning proving very foggy, many of the fleet were bogged down; about 10 o'clock lay by for them, when collected proceeded down. Camped on the north shore, where Capt. [Thomas] Hutchings' Negro man died, being much frosted in his feet & legs."[25]

The Donelson flotilla was entering a dangerous area where they were subject to Indian attacks and the rapid current on the broad Tennessee River. "Got underway very early," he wrote on March 7, "the day proving very windy, a S.S.W. and the river being wide occasioned a high sea insomuch that some of the smaller craft were in danger. Therefore, came to the uppermost Chickamauga Town, which was then evacuated, where we lay by that afternoon and camped that night. The wife of Ephraim Peyton was here delivered of a child. Mr. Peyton has gone overland with Capt. Robertson."[26]

Donelson's luck, if it could be called that, was about to run out. Upon orders of the governors of Virginia and North Carolina, Colonel Evan Shelby gathered 500 men to annihilate the lower Chickamauga towns along the Tennessee River. The British garrison at Detroit, under the command of Colonel Henry Hamilton, was furnishing the Indians with guns, ammunition and 20,000 bushels of corn to continue the back country fighting during the Revolutionary War. Shelby was building flatboats, on which to transport his troops, in April of 1779, on the Holston River.[27]

Undoubtedly, Donelson counted on Shelby's mission being a success since it would make their voyage easier. Shelby attacked when Dragging Canoe, the Chickamauga chief, was away leading raiding parties in Georgia and South Carolina. He burned and looted the towns, confiscated their corn but the women and children escaped into the forest. Shelby's expedition, however, did not stop the return of younger Chickamauga to the lower towns where they made war on the Donelson party with a vengeance.[28]

On March 8, Donelson wrote, "Castoff at 10 o'clock & proceed down to an Indian village, which was inhabited, on the south side of the river, they invited us 'to come ashore,' called us brothers & showed signs of friendship insomuch that Mr. John Caffery [one of Donelson's sons-in-law] & my son then took on board a canoe which I had in tow & were crossing over to them, the rest of the fleet having landed on the opposite shore. After they had gone some distance, a half-breed who called himself Archy Coody with several other Indians jumped into a canoe, met them and advised them to return to the boat which they did with Coody and several canoes which left the shore & followed directly after him."[29]

Donelson said Coody and the Indians appeared to be friendly. He invited them aboard and distributed presents among them. During the gift giving, Donelson noticed a number of Indians on the other side of the stream getting into their canoes. They were armed and their faces were painted red and black.[30]

"Coody immediately made signs to his companions, ordering them to quit the boat, which they did, himself and another Indian remaining with us & telling us to move off immediately," Donelson wrote. "We had not gone far before we discovered a number of Indians armed and painted proceeding down the river, as it were, to intercept us. Coody the half-breed & his companion sailed with us for some time & and telling us that we had passed all the towns & were out of danger, left us."[31]

Coody was an Indian interpreter for the U.S. Army.[32] It was possible that during his entreaties with Indian tribes and serving in the militia, Donelson knew Coody. Otherwise, it was doubtful if he would have allowed him to remain on his flatboat.

"But we had not gone far," Donelson continued, "until we had come in sight of another Town situated likewise on the south side of the river, nearly opposite a small island. Here they again invited us to come on shore, called us brothers & observing the boats standing off for the opposite channel told us that 'their side of the river was better for boats to pass.'"[33]

A battle ensued between the travelers and the Indians. Donelson, busy shooting at their enemies, turned control of the flatboat over to Rachel. In order to steer the craft, she was exposed to the gunfire, without protection, on the roof of the flatboat.[34] Rachel was only twelve years old and, at best, had only enough strength to hold the tiller of a 100-foot-long boat on a steady course. It was possible that her father could only give her terse instructions during the gun battle. Regardless, it was an enormous responsibility to impose upon a child.

Another young woman in a similar position was not as fortunate as Rachel. While the crew of Russell Cower's flatboat was fending off the Indian attack his young daughter, Nancy, steered their craft through the narrow passage. Nancy Cower was so concentrated on keeping the boat from running aground she either did not notice that she had been shot or said nothing about her wound. Her mother eventually noticed blood on her clothing and attended to her wound, and she survived.[35]

Donelson, in his journal, made no mention of placing his youngest daughter in harm's way but wrote, "And here we must regret the unfortunate death of young M. Payne on board Capt. Blackemores boat, opposite the town where some of the enemy lay concealed."[36]

Donelson had more regrets than Payne. He was faced with the dreadful decision of separating the Stuart flatboat from the rest of the flotilla because those on board—numbering twenty-eight—had smallpox. He abandoned them to an impending Indian slaughter.[37]

"This man [Stuart] embarked with us for the western country but his family being diseased with the small-pox, it was agreed upon between him & the Company that he should keep at some distance to the rear, for fear of the infection spreading; and he was warned each night when the encampment should take place by the sound of a horn. After we had passed the Towns, the Indians, having now collected to a considerable number, observing his helpless situation, singled off from the rest of the fleet, intercepted him & killed & took prisoners the whole crew, to the great grief of the whole Company uncertain how soon we might share the same fate; their cries were distinctly heard by those boats in the rear."[38]

If she had not learned earlier, the Stuart family's tragic and painful demise taught Rachel that the primal land her father sought extracted an expensive price for settlement—a situation she would face constantly over the next few years. Rachel and her family, however, had more immediate problems dealing with their survival.

The Indians, in considerable numbers, continued to follow the flotilla down the river. Donelson said they kept pace with them until the Cumberland Mountain blocked them from sight. "We are now arriving at the place called the Whirl, or Suck, where the river is compressed within less than half its common width above by the Cumberland Mountain, which juts out on both sides." That was the hazard Archy Coody warned Donelson about, calling it a "boiling pot."[39]

What Donelson called a trivial accident in the rough waters almost ruined the expedition. John Cotton and his family were traveling in a large canoe loaded with their household goods. They boarded Robert Cartwright's flatboat for protection from the Indians and tied the canoe alongside the larger craft. Going through the boiling pot, the canoe overturned. The flotilla stopped to help Cotton save his cargo. Suddenly, Indians appeared on the opposite cliff and began shooting at them. Everybody retreated to their boats to escape the gunfire. Four people were slightly wounded before they passed the boiling pot, where the river widened. All the crafts passed through the boiling pot except Jonathan Jennings' boat.[40]

Donelson decided it was more important to continue the voyage, leaving the Jennings and their passengers to fend for themselves when their boat ran aground on a large rock. The craft was partly immersed in water and unable to move. "We were compelled to leave them," Donelson wrote, "perhaps to be slaughtered by their merciless enemies." Aboard Jennings' boat was Mrs. Ephraim Peyton, who had given birth a few days earlier.[41]

The flotilla continued on for the next two days and nights before camping ashore. Early on the morning of March 10, cries arose from boats in the rear that the Jennings family needed help. Donelson, who had left them sitting targets for the Indians, appeared surprised they appeared. "He discovered us by our fires and came up in the most wretched condition," Donelson wrote. "He states that as soon as the Indians discovered his situation they turned their whole attention to him & kept up a most galling fire on his boat." Jennings ordered his wife, son, another young man and his two slaves to throw all his good in the river while he returned the Indians' fire. Young Jennings, the passenger and a slave jumped out of the boat—that was the last anyone saw of them. Mrs. Jennings and a female slave succeeded in unloading the boat. When Mrs. Jennings pushed the boat off the rock, the craft moved so suddenly she almost lost her footing. In the furious effort to unload the boat, the Peyton infant was apparently thrown overboard. Mrs. Peyton, nonetheless, assisted the Jennings in trying to escape in their bullet-ridden boat. Donelson said that regardless of being wet and cold, Mrs. Peyton appeared to be in good health. He distributed the survivors among the other boats.[42]

Two days later, the flotilla reached Muscle Shoals, where Robertson was supposed to leave a sign for them that he had been there and whether or not it would be more practical for them to travel overland to their destination. At that point, they were only about 150 land miles from their destination.[43]

Muscle Shoals was a nightmarish collection of rock reefs, bars, boulders and projecting rocky points that permitted navigation only six months out of the year. The stream obstructions were so solid that the three New Madrid earthquakes in Western Kentucky, ranging from 7.3 to 7.5, which were felt as far away as Boston, failed to alter the shoals. Those 1811–12 earthquakes, followed by six aftershocks ranging from 5.5 to 6.3, did not move the rock formations at Muscle Shoals, Alabama.[44] A century after the Donelson flotillas passed through the shoals, the Corps of Engineers recommended removing navigational obstacles by blasting and dredging the suck and building a 14.5 mile canal around the shoals.[45]

Donelson ordered the flotilla to land when they came in sight of the shoals and look for some sign that Robertson or his men had been there. "But, to our great mortification we can find none," he wrote. "From which we conclude that it would not be prudent to make the attempt [overland] and are determined, knowing ourselves to be in imminent danger, to pursue our journey down river."[46]

The high water in the shoals made a roaring sound, which could be heard for miles. Driftwood was piled high on the land's edge. The current ran in every possible direction and the boats could be torn apart.[47]

Was Rachel scared? It was possible she sensed her father's trepidation but they really had no choice but to continue the voyage. An overland trek, from this point, meant they would have to carry their few remaining provisions. Indians continued to track them as there was a brief skirmish before they reached the shoals.[48]

"Here we did not know how soon we should be dashed to pieces and all our troubles ended at once," Donelson wrote. "Our boats frequently dragged on the bottom and appeared constantly in danger of striking. They warped as much as in a rough sea. But, by the hand of Providence we are now preserved from this danger also. I know not the length of this wonderful shoal; it had been represented to me to be 25 or 30 miles. If so, we must have descended very rapidly, as indeed we did, for we passed it in about three hours. Came to & camped on the northern shore, not far below the Shoals, for the night."[49]

Two days later, on March 14, two boats of Indians attacked the flotilla, wounding five of the passengers. When they camped and built their fires for the night, their dogs began barking. They left everything, immediately returned to their boats and found another camping place on the opposite side of the river. Since they left their food supplies and cooking utensils behind, the travelers spent a hungry night.[50]

Donelson sent his son John III and son-in-law John Caffery in a canoe back to the initial location where they found a slave, who was left behind in the rush, still sleeping by a fire. They collected the slave, utensils, food and returned to the flotilla. Five days later, they reached the Ohio River, which presented another hazard. Donelson called their situation truly disagreeable—the river was very high, the current rapid and their boats were not constructed to stem a rapid stream. "Our provisions exhausted," he wrote, "the crews almost worn down with hunger and fatigue. And know not what distance we have to go or what time it will take us to our place of destination."[51]

Some of the travelers, including Rachel's sister Mary and her husband, John Caffery, declined to continue the voyage upstream and chose to go down the Ohio to the Mississippi and on to Natchez. Another sister, Catherine, and her husband, Thomas Hutchings, headed for Illinois. "We now part," Donelson wrote regretfully, "perhaps to meet no more, for I am determined to pursue my course, happen what will."[52]

On March 21, the flotilla moved very slowly upstream toward their destination, suffering from fatigue and hunger. The Cumberland River was only fifteen miles from their entry into the Ohio but they were ten days away from reaching it.[53] "Came to the mouth of a river which I thought was the Cumberland," Donelson wrote. "Some of the company declared it could not be, it was so much smaller than expected. But I never heard of any river running between the Cumberland & Tennessee. It appeared to flow with a gentle current. We determined however to make the trial. Pushed up some distance and encamped for the night."[54]

As the river grew wider, everybody agreed it was the Cumberland. In order to move faster in the gentle current, Donelson had constructed a sail out of a bedsheet.[55] Speed was essential as their food was practically gone.

On March 26, they shot a buffalo and the next day Donelson killed a swan. Several more buffalo were harvested that week along with some herbs and greens gathered from bottom land. On March 31, the flotilla met Henderson and his men who were surveying the Virginia-North Carolina line. Henderson told them he had some corn shipped from the Falls of the Ohio (Louisville) to the Cumberland settlement. "We are now without bread and are compelled to hunt the buffalo to preserve life. Worn out with fatigue our progress at present is slow."[56]

Donelson's last entry into his journal was not enthusiastic about what they found at their destination. Thirty-three people had died since the flotilla left Fort Patrick Henry the previous December and several more were wounded. "Monday April 24, 1780. This day we arrived at our journey's end at the Big Salt Lick, where we have the pleasure of finding Capt. Robertson & his company. It is a source of satisfaction to us to be enabled to restore to him & others their families & and friends who were entrusted to our care and who, sometime hence perhaps despaired of every meeting again. Tho our prospects are dreary. We have found a few log cabins which have been built on a Cedar Bluff above the Lick by Capt. Robertson and his company."[57]

Donelson found the Big Salt Lick unsatisfactory and chose to move further up the Cumberland and settle at Clover Bottom on the Stone's River, where the family constructed three-sided buildings to live in. Often, owners used the wood from their flatboats to construct their dwellings. Whether that was what Donelson did was not known. He planted corn and cotton on the rich bottom land. Normally there would have been abundant game—buffalo, deer, elk, bear, turkey and partridge—available in the area.[58]

The extremely cold winter and heavy snows took their toll on animals that settlers normally depended on for food. The Robertson overland portion of the excursion herded cattle and hogs belonging to the settlers to the Big Salt Lick. They arrived there on Christmas Day, 1779, to find the Cumberland River already frozen over and the ground covered with deep snow. There was no place for the animals to forage and the corn they brought with them was saved for the settlers and their horses. James G. M. Ramsey, in *The Annals of Tennessee to the End of the Eighteenth Century*, speculated those animals perished from starvation.[59]

More than likely those cattle and hogs were slaughtered for meat. They settled at a salt lick, meaning salt was available for the preservation of meat. But, the Robertson party was there for three and a half months in blizzard-like conditions before the Donelson flotilla arrived and more than likely consumed most of the meat.

Rachel and her brothers, after four months confined to a flatboat, once again found themselves restricted within close borders. The horrors she witnessed during the river voyage—deaths and Indian attacks—had to affect the young girl. She was forced to grow up rather quickly. Unfortunately, her immediate future did not improve.

John Donelson must have questioned his decision to leave a relative stable lifestyle in Pittsylvania County, Virginia, regardless of financial pressures and bring his large family and slaves into the raw and unforgiving country. His son John's wife, Mary Purnell, gave birth to a son, Chesed, in the crude structure they were living in but the child died in infancy.[60] At this point, aside from his unknown agreement with Henderson, Donelson had not patented any land in Western North Carolina (Tennessee).[61] Land was the reason he uprooted his family, endured the horrendous journey on the rivers and they were still facing starvation with nothing to show for their sacrifices. There must have been terrific disappointment within the family. Donelson, having assumed the blame for listening to Richard Henderson's tale of untold riches of land, knew what he had to do.

As Indian attacks became more prolific, the Donelsons and other settlers sought protection in forts like Mansker's Station, which became terribly crowded.[62] The Donelson family alone numbered fifteen or twenty plus their thirty slaves. Early stations, or forts, were only temporary structures for protection from Indian raids and were often crudely constructed.[63]

Food was scarce and the probability of another fierce winter prompted a number of families—the Raines, Harts and Hendersons—to leave before Donelson harvested his corn crop in the fall of 1780. "Having packed his horse and given the best conveyances to the women and children and the men being furnished with such utensils and weapons as were most needed and serviceable in their hands, the party set out for Davis Station," W. Woodford Clayton wrote in the *History of Davidson County, Tennessee*.[64]

Clayton indicated the Donelson women and children were neither walking nor riding horses, meaning they were traveling by wagons or sleds. Being an iron master, it was possible that Donelson carried a wagon or some sort of sled on his flatboat or the components to build one. Exactly what route the Donelsons followed to Kentucky was unknown. Regardless, there were streams to cross. Some they probably forded; others would have required them to stop, chop down trees, bind the logs together with vines and use the rafts to cross the streams.[65]

Apparently, they had no contact with Indians and arrived at Davis

Station near Crab Orchard, Kentucky, without loss of life. Nearby Harrodsburg was a stopping point for travelers and settlers, using the Wilderness
Road, to travel from Virginia and the Carolinas to the western lands. Donelson was quite taken by Kentucky, which he once described as "that land
of promise, that terrestrial paradise and garden of Eden."[66] Davis Station,
like many of the early forts, was unable to house such large families, their
supplies and an equally large numbers of slaves.

4

A New Home

The Donelson family's tenure at Davis Station was unknown. They had the means, land and available labor to build their own housing. Pauline Burke, in her biography of Emily Donelson, wrote that John Donelson "established them temporarily on property owned by him."[1] Willard R. Jillson, in his *Old Kentucky Entries and Deeds*, listed Donelson's land holdings as 887 acres in Lincoln County (now Mercer County) on Cedar and Baldhill Creeks. The Donelson land was in the vicinity of where Rachel's future husband Lewis Robards and his family would settle a few years later. Donelson had 1,000-acres entries each on the Green River and on the southeast fork of the Licking River.[2]

Little is known about Donelson's activities immediately after the family's arrival in Kentucky other than he was corresponding with Arthur Campbell and John Sevier regarding land acquisitions in Tennessee in the early 1780s.[3]

Obviously, Donelson's first priority was the safety of his family including Rachel who was blooming into a beauty in her teenage years. She was afforded more social contacts in Kentucky than were available in Cumberland.

Their exodus from Cumberland did not shield them from Indian attacks. In the waning years of the Revolutionary War, the British, along with a few Canadians, were colluding with frontier Indians, mostly Wyandot and Shawnee, to attack settlers on the frontier. Donelson and Arthur Campbell, another surveyor, organized a meeting in Harrodsburg in the spring of 1782 out of concern Virginia was not doing enough to protect her western settlements from Indian attacks.[4]

They advocated petitioning Congress to deny Virginia ownership of the commonwealth's western lands and have the United States Congress reissue titles to those who held the lands. Major Hugh McGary, later the principal witness in Lewis Robards' divorce action against Rachel, objected violently to Donelson and Campbell's plan and broke up the meeting with his militia troops. McGary was described by those who knew him as being fractious, ill-tempered and constantly engaged in fights. Two days later, Donelson and Campbell held another meeting without an intervention by McGary and prepared petitions which were sent to Congress and the Virginia Assembly asking for separation.[5]

"The body of the people [in Kentucky] seem," General George Rogers Clark wrote Virginia Governor Benjamin Harrison on May 2, 1782, "to be alarmed for fear Virginia will give up on their interests."[6]

That was exactly what settlers feared.

Four months later, the British and Indians set up an ambush for settlers' militia at Blue Licks. "Never was the lives of so many valuable men lost more shamefully than in the late actions of the 19 August and that not a little thro the vain and seditious expressions of a major McGary," Colonel Daniel Boone wrote. Boone's son, Israel, and seventy-six other men were killed when McGary rushed into battle with only 170 men against a force of more than 500 instead of waiting for the reinforcements Colonel Benjamin Logan was bringing.[7]

The Blue Licks massacre did not personally involve Donelson's family but it did result in Virginia Governor Benjamin Harrison appointing John Donelson, along with Colonels Joseph Martin and Isaac Shelby, to form a joint commission to treat with the Cherokees and Chickasaws for peace.[8]

The intermediary between the governor and the commission was Major John Reid. When he delivered Donelson's commission the colonel was in New London, Virginia. Burke wrote that Donelson left unfinished business in Virginia when he moved his family to Fort Patrick Henry to build his flatboat.[9] Donelson, however, was involved with a new land company which planned to colonize near Muscle Shoals on the Tennessee River but first they had to determine if the site was located in what was then North Carolina or Georgia.[10]

During his travels from Virginia to the Cumberland, Donelson stopped to check on his family in Kentucky. Rachel had met a wealthy Virginian, Lewis Robards, who lived with his mother and siblings on their Cane Run plantation near Harrodsburg. The distance between the Donelson's lands on Baldhill and Cedar Creeks and that of the Robards, near Cane Run Creek, was only a few miles.[11] A handsome, older man, Robards in all probability met Rachel at the Cane Run Presbyterian Church, established in 1780 by the Reverend David Rice.[12]

Lewis Robards' career in the Revolutionary War was estimated to be twenty-eight months. The Robards brothers—Lewis, John, George and Jesse—joined the Virginia Volunteers. Lewis' half-brother William Robards, Jr., was severely wounded at Camden.[13]

Little is known about the courtship of Rachel and Robards.

Both families of a proposed union were involved before and during the courtship. The man was expected to obtain the permission of his father and the father of the intended bride.[14] Since Robards' father, William, died in Virginia in December 1783, before the family came to Kentucky, he need only obtain the permission of John Donelson.[15] On February 9, 1785, John Donelson signed the following document in the Lincoln County Clerk's office: "As there is a purpose [proposal] of marriage intended Betwn. Mr. Lewis Robards and my Daughter Rachl. Donelson Therefore if Application Should be made, you may Grant a License Accordingly. And Oblige Sir Yr. Hble. Servt, Jno. Donelson."[16] Both families looked at the wealth of the other.

Rachel brought to the marriage a gentry family with extensive land and political connections. Her father and three brothers, Stockley, John and William, had been surveying vast tracks for themselves and others. They had a close association with the Blount family—William, John Gray and Thomas—for whom John Donelson made surveys and entries for 97,000 acres of land but Donelson's portion was not known.[17]

The Donelsons eventually claimed more than 1,000,000 acres in what is now Kentucky and Tennessee, not including their Alabama lands.[18]

Did John Donelson consider that Robards, coming out of the Revolutionary War a captain, was too old for his youngest daughter? Was Donelson too busy to inquire about the war record of his youngest daughter's intended?[19] Or, to question why William Robards passed over his oldest son, Lewis, from his second family and named two other sons, George (the oldest after Lewis) and William (a son from his first marriage to Sallie Hill), along with his second wife, Elizabeth, to administer his estate.[20]

It almost appeared that Donelson was glad to have his daughter off his hands so he could devote total attention to his land business. Lewis Robards served with two half-brothers, John and William, and two brothers, George and Jesse, in the Virginia Militia during the Revolutionary War. Jesse Robards' pension deposition states his brother Lewis served six months in 1778 as a private; six months as an ensign in 1779; eight months as a lieutenant in 1780; eight months in 1781 as a captain, and was discharged during the siege of Yorktown. Jesse Robards explained that his brother's last tour of duty was eight months, from January to September 1781.[21]

Both in his depositions concerning his brother Lewis and his own service during the war, Jesse Robards stated they were under the command of Brigadier General Thomas Nelson. As commander of the Virginia Militia, Nelson, who succeeded Thomas Jefferson as governor of Virginia, was in charge of one third of the troops at the Siege of Yorktown.[22] Jesse Robards said he and his brother Lewis were honorably discharged in 1781 and that it was not common for militia to get a written discharge. Lewis's widow, Hannah, was awarded a pension of $120 a year which in 2017 had an income value of

$69,100. Jesse was awarded a pension of $56.66 a year, which had an income value of $38,900 in 2017.[23]

After his discharge, Lewis Robards returned to Goochland County.[24] Little is known of his activities in Goochland County after the war and before he immigrated to Kentucky. William Robards' will, filed a month before his death in December 1783, indicated he planned to move his entire family from Goochland across the mountains to Kentucky County.[25]

Robards owned thirty-five slaves, 10,600 acres of land, considerable livestock—cattle, sheep, hogs and was a breeder of fine horses. In addition, he had bonds, open accounts and investments. Lewis Robards, despite being passed over to administer his father's estate, fared very well. His father left 1,800 acres to be divided equally between Lewis and his brothers, George, Jesse and Joseph. Fourteen hundred acres were split between Lewis, William, John, George, Jesse, Joseph and Robert Robards. Six thousand acres were apportioned between Lewis, George, Jesse, Joseph, Robert and John Robards. In addition, Lewis received two slaves, one featherbed, furniture and thirty pounds specie. Lewis and his siblings, with the exception of James, were to inherit the estate of their maternal grandfather, Joseph Lewis. William Robards' will stated that his son James was to receive five shilling sterling as he had already received his portion of the estate.[26]

From all appearances, Rachel Donelson had made a most advantageous match.

As was the custom of the times, Rachel and Robards would have spent their courting time in her home, at church and at dancing parties.[27]

Her family undoubtedly saw advantages for her in the marriage and thought nothing of the fact she and her husband would live with his mother, which was a common practice for many newlyweds in those days. The Robards family envisioned a happy marriage for the couple. Robards was certainly aware that Rachel was a land endowed heiress and everything she inherited when her father died would belong to him.

The Widow Robards built a large stone house on their Cane Run plantation and used her original home, a log blockhouse, for boarders and travelers.[28]

Less than a month after John Donelson gave his permission for the marriage, on March 1, 1785, a marriage bond was executed by Lewis Robards. Virginia law on marriage bonds, since 1660, required the perspective groom to give bond at the courthouse of the bride's residence. The bond was pledged with two or more securities but no money was exchanged and the county clerk prepared the license for the minister conducting the ceremony. Nuptial bonding was insurance if the marriage did not take place, if either party declined to participate or if one of the parties was ineligible—underage or already married.[29]

However, the name of Robards' bride was left blank in the first paragraph of the document. Known all men by these presents that we Lewis Robards and [left blank] are held and firmly bound unto his Excellency Patrick Henry, Esquire, Governor of Virginia, in the sum of Fifty Pounds current money to the paiment [payment] whereof be made to the said Governor & his successors we bind our seals and dated this 1 day of March 1785.

The condition of the above obligation is such that whereas there is a marriage shortly intended to be solemnized between the above bound Lewis Robards and Rachel Donelson for which & license has issued if therefore there be no lawful cause to obstruct the said marriage then this obligation to be void or else to remain in full force.[30]

The document was signed by Lewis Robards and Jesse Robards in the presence of Lincoln County clerk Willis Green.[31]

The marriage presumably took place in the Donelson home or Cane Run Church. Rachel's family was there to support her and attend the wedding. Pauline W. Burke, a Donelson descendant, wrote that the family considered that Rachel had made an excellent marriage.[32]

Land business apparently kept her father away.

John Donelson, on March 10, 1785, was in North Carolina. Donelson wrote William Blount from Hillsboro, North Carolina, about the considerable number of land warrants he had accumulated, presumably for the Blounts. However, he mentioned being approached by a man named McCarthy from New Bern and a representative of Robert Morris from New York who asked Donelson to procure as much western land as possible—all the way to the banks of the Mississippi River.[33]

William Blount, apparently suspecting that Donelson might divert land to Robert Morris, wrote his brother John Gray Blount on March 28 that he advised Donelson before he left North Carolina to go to John Gray's house without delay. "You will understand," he wrote his brother, "that if you devise the making of a good bargain that you are to be a sharer in the advantages to which you may rely that Donelson will readily agree and stipulate. Donelson both in bargaining and executing is tardy, you must give him *action* or perhaps better provide that some active person shall be engaged to *execute* such a bargain as he shall make under your direction."[34]

A month later, Blount wrote his brother they had a buyer for 200,000 acres of Cumberland lands at fifty cents per acre and Donelson would make the contact. "I advise you to secure all the military land and land warrants that you can. There are a great number in the hands of William Lytle and Donelson says he will readily give a list of them if applied to do so. He offered to give Donelson a list but Donelson neglected to take it."[35]

On July 18, 1784, William Blount again wrote his brother about Donelson indicating their differences with him might have been solved. "Col. Donelson," he wrote, "will be down in September with the works in the other warrants and I believe we shall make a sweeping survey between the Clinch and Holsten as to include the mouths of both these rivers say at least 150,000-acres but Donelson himself will be a partner in it."[36]

Donelson, with the intent to move his family back to Cumberland, had surveyed some land near Nashville and entered three claims, two of 640 acres in February and March of 1784.[37] Burke wrote that those lands were in the vicinity of where The Hermitage was later built. Donelson began building a blockhouse there near a large spring while waiting for the treaty signing with the Indians to begin. In June 1785, Donelson entered a claim for another 640 acres on the south side of the Cumberland River.[38]

Donelson, while conducting his land grant/surveying business in the east, wrote his son John III on September 4, 1785, from Campbell County, Virginia, that he could move the family back to Cumberland before winter came. The letter was sent by private messenger. After assuring his son he was in good health and asking about the family, Donelson turned to land business. "I lately saw Capt. Ewing who told me that several warrants from the Military Department were sent out to your care to locate on the usual terms; I think he said to the amount of ten thousand acres. I wish among these warrants you could spare me one to secure the vacancy against my lands on the south side of the Cumberland."[39]

On April 17, 1786, young John Donelson entered grant number 115 for 640 acres in the name of his father for land on a branch of the Big Harpeth River.[40]

"I have had some conversations with Stockley Donelson [another son] concerning our business with Col. [William] Blount," Donelson continued. "He says that he has reason to trust the warrants for these lands have been issued and that we need not fear the consequence thereof. However, I shall start tomorrow morning over to Carolina in order to be satisfied in that business. I propose returning to Richmond from Carolina in order to see if it is in my power to get some goods for your family's use and return to you and my family as soon as possible. If you should find it convenient to remove to Cumberland before my return, if my family can remove at the same time, I shall have no objections. I have some debts to settle in Kentucky on my way out. I hope to be home next month. I entreat you to take particular care so as to provide that no waste be made in my corn at Cumberland. A plentiful stock of provisions is the main chance. Give every assurance to your dear mamma that I shall use every endeavor for her happiness and for every branch of the family. Your mamma's ease and happiness in every comfort of life, you and your brothers and sisters' well-being and happiness, if I could say more is the constant petition and most ardent desire of you most affectionate father, Jno. Donelson."[41]

Land business, however, prolonged Donelson's reunion with his family.

Donelson was appointed by the Georgia legislature as a commissioner (and justice of the peace) to survey land in the Big Bend area in the Tennessee River at the mouth of the Elk River in March 1785. The eight commissioners were to receive 5,000 acres each and to equally divide 50,000 acres for their work.[42]

The Mouth of the Elk, according to John Peyton, one of the commissioners, was a great resort at that time for the Indians. J. M. Lewis, who was also at Big Bend, said the Indians were dissatisfied and cross and Donelson had a talk with them. "On account of this dissatisfaction," Lewis said, "Col. John Sevier delivered them a quantity of goods and salt. After giving them the goods and salt, the Indians appeared to be more friendly."[43]

Andrew Jackson, representing the Donelson heirs, told the House of Representatives on February 9, 1818, that Donelson determined the northern boundary of Georgia "where it crossed the Tennessee and extended it east to the crossing of the Tennessee above." When Donelson and his surveying crew found the other commissioners had not arrived at the Big Bend, Jackson said, they returned to Cumberland before proceeding on to Holston to meet with them.[44]

From all indications, Donelson and John Sevier in December 1785 signed wholesale lots of land warrants for land in the Big Bend that proved worthless. When John Overall presented seventeen Big Bend land warrants, with their signatures, to the Congressional Committee on Private Land Claims in 1827, he was surprised they were useless. The state of Georgia required that a majority of the commissioners, not just two, sign the land warrants. Overall's name was not on the warrants he purchased nor were they assigned to him. The committee ruled the warrants were not valid.[45]

Just before Christmas 1785, the commissioners closed the Big Bend land office and agreed to meet there again on the first of April.[46]

Richard Spence, writing in the *Tennessee Historical Quarterly*, said that Donelson spent the winter at Long Island and did not join his family after leaving Big Bend as he was busy with land business. Andrew Jackson, in his statement to the Public Lands Committee of the Thirteenth Congress, First Session on February 9, 1818, said of Donelson, "on his return to Nashville on the duty assigned him as a commissioner and surveyor aforesaid was killed by Indians and lost all his valuables amongst which were attested copies of all the acts and resolutions of their report to the legislature of the state of Georgia, a copy of their report to the legislators and a journal of their proceedings. Those being lost aforesaid your remonstrant has been compelled to resort to the oral testimony to show that Col. Donelson in his lifetime did faithfully perform that duty assigned him and lost his life thereof." Jackson provided affidavits of John Peyton, Sr., David Henry and James M. Lewis to prove the Donelson family's claim for land due John Donelson.[47]

Not all of Donelson's papers were lost.

"From a memorandum taken by the late John Donelson in his lifetime and found amongst his papers," Jackson continued, "he intended this draft to be laid on the north side of the Tennessee River, beginning opposite the head of an island at the commencement of the Big Shoal running north 3 miles, thence up the river of complement." The committee reported out a bill for benefits of script for two dollars per acre for Donelson and the other commissioners to use to buy lands being put up for sale in Alabama. Donelson's portion of that land, as commissioner, was 11,250 acres or $22,500 in script.[48] The real worth of that $22,500 in 2017, was $664,000.[49]

5

World Turned
Upside Down

In the spring of 1786, Rachel's life began a downhill glide. Her marriage was not going well although the Widow Robards supported Rachel against her son's jealous accusations. Still a teenager, it must have been a very difficult time for Rachel, isolated, with none of her family members nearby to support and sustain her in the intricacies of her conflicts with Robards. If she saw her father when he came through Kentucky to pay some debts, such a visit would have brightened her outlook for a few days.

Would Rachel's pride have prevented her from discussing her miserable marriage with him? A woman described as the best storyteller, the best dancer, the sprightliest companion and the most dashing horsewoman in the western country would certainly have possessed an inordinate amount of pride.[1] Using that description, it was difficult to accept Rachel as being a quiet submissive woman fearful of the rages of her pathologically jealous husband. She refused to be marginalized and undoubtedly defended herself as best she could.

John Donelson was an intelligent, perceptive man accustomed to negotiating with Indian tribes. His intuition, at least, must have told him the marriage he agreed to for his youngest daughter was not going well. If Rachel did not tell him, there was common gossip about the Robards in the small Kentucky town of Harrodsburg. Donelson advanced Rachel money as he did his other children. Funds of her own would have given Rachel some measure of security, if they were not confiscated by her husband, as she owned nothing, not even the clothes on her back.

Rachel then received the news of her father's untimely death.

According to Richard D. Spence, writing in the *Tennessee Historical Quarterly*, John Donelson, as he was leaving Lincoln County, met two men, John Tully and another named Leach, who asked if they could accompany him to Cumberland where they had business. Donelson, a master woodsman, was well versed in keeping himself alive during his frequent explorations and usually traveled alone. That he acquiesced in allowing them to accompany him indicated he possibly knew them. When they reached the Barren River area on April 11, 1786, Tully and Leach wanted to stop at a spring but they said Donelson, in a rush to reach Cumberland, continued on his way. A short time later, they heard shots, mounted their horses and rode ahead. The two men said they found Donelson, still on his horse, wounded in the abdomen and one knee. The two made camp, Donelson ate some buffalo meat and died during the night. They assumed he was shot by Indians as he did not identify his assailant(s).[2]

Tully and Leach said they buried him, took his saddlebags and horse and continued on their way to Cumberland. As they forded the river, they said his saddle bags, filled with land warrants and probably money, were washed away. That was the story they told the Donelson family when they reached Cumberland. The two men guided Donelson's sons back to their father's burial place alongside the Barren River. Donelson's saddle bags were found downstream from his burial site. They contained no money; only waterlogged land documents.[3]

Did Donelson's sons take his body back to Cumberland or did they leave him there? Was his body moved at a later date? Those questions remain unanswered.

There was only circumstantial evidence to connect Tully and Leach to Donelson's death but their accounts left more questions than answers. For instance, it was unlikely that a horse would allow his rider to remain seated if a bullet came so close to the horse's body as to pierce Donelson's knee not to speak of his taking a shot in his abdomen. If there had been an Indian attack, why would they make camp at the site instead of moving on, Donelson's wounds notwithstanding? If the two men were innocent, why would Donelson not tell them who shot him? He certainly knew a gut shot was fatal.

Donelson's family, Spence wrote, was reluctant to accept Tully and Leach's account that he was killed by Indians. They maintained he was murdered by renegade white men.[4] Regardless, John Donelson was dead and his passing created numerous problems for his family, Rachel in particular.

Rachel had a gregarious persona and had always been part of her family's social interaction. Surviving Indian attacks during a 1,000-mile river voyage under the most trying conditions certainly put grit in her spine, if she needed any. Rachel, however, had two handicaps, neither of her own making. She was alone in Kentucky with no family support and, as an heiress to part of a considerable land estate, was subjected to an inequitable law which said she, as a femme covert, could own nothing.

Sir William Blackstone, the British jurist whose legal doctrines became the basis for early American laws, explained the term *femme covert*.

"By marriage, the husband and wife are one person in law; that is, the very being or legal existence of the woman is suspended during the marriage, or at least is incorporated and consolidated into that of her husband; under whose wing, protection, and cover, she performs everything; and I therefore called in our law—French a femme-covert, *foemina viro co-operta*; is said to *be covert-baron*, or under the protection and influence of her husband, her *baron* or lord; and her conditions during her marriage is called her *coverture*." Legal submission of a wife to her husband, Blackstone emphasized, was for her own protection.[5]

Rachel certainly needed protection but it was from her own husband.

After her father's death, Peyton Short, a young Virginia lawyer came to board with the Widow Robards. Short was quite taken with Rachel. A younger son, Short came to the frontier to make his fortune and was already occupied with his brother William, Thomas Jefferson's secretary while minister to France, in acquiring land.[6] Aside from being vivacious and beautiful, Rachel was an heiress, albeit a married one, to her father's wealth.

Rachel, from all indications, was only cordial toward Short's advances. Humphrey Marshall, a Kentucky state senator and historian, was a frequent visitor with friends who boarded with Mrs. Robards. Marshall said he saw nothing out of the ordinary in Rachel's demeanor with Short. Marshall described her as being unassuming, decorous and virtuous.[7]

James Overton, another Robards boarder, found great uneasiness existed between Rachel and Lewis Robards in 1787. Their dissent and shouting increased while he was there. Overton's brother John also boarded with the Widow Robards and later played a vital role in Rachel's life.[8] When Robards returned home one afternoon and found Rachel talking with Short on his mother's front porch, he verbally abused his wife and accused her not only of being unfaithful with Short but other of his mother's boarders. Short returned to Virginia to formulate plans to save Rachel from her abusive husband and acquire a beautiful and wealthy wife for himself.[9]

Short, a tall, redheaded and rather unattractive man, told his friend Henry Banks that he had great sympathy for Rachel, and wanted to marry her after her separation from Robards. He planned to convert his Virginia holdings into cash and move with her to the Spanish part of the country. Short was foolish enough to put those plans into a letter to Rachel, which her husband intercepted.[10]

Robards followed Short to Richmond, Virginia, and confronted him. Short offered him the satisfaction of a duel or a cash payment. Robards was so incensed over the man's attention to his wife that he accepted $1,000 from him.[11] The vindictive Robards, the $1,000 notwithstanding, had other plans for Short. He filed a petition to obtain permission to get a divorce from Rachel in the Virginia General Assembly naming Peyton Short as correspondent.[12]

Robards' trip from Harrodsburg to Richmond covered 404 miles as the crow flies of mountainous terrain and rivers. Based on Major Thomas Speed's records of a 1790 trip from Charlotte, North Carolina, to Danville, Kentucky, travelers averaged twelve to fifteen miles per day over that route. Robards' Richmond trip consumed more than two months of his time but he collected $1,000 from Short.[13] If Robards was so concerned about Rachel's interaction with his mother's boarders, one must speculate on what he thought she was doing during his more than two-month absence.

After he returned to Harrodsburg, Robards wrote Rachel Stockley Donelson, in Cumberland, that she should take her daughter off his hands; he no longer wanted to live with Rachel. The Widow Robards sided with Rachel against her husband as did others in the family. Rachel must have lived in a sort of purgatory with the Robards until her brother, Samuel, arrived to accompany her back to their mother's home.[14]

Ann Toplovich, in an *Ohio Valley History Journal* article, wrote that Samuel Donelson made the trip from Cumberland to Harrodsburg in late summer 1788.[15] The entire trip, 308 miles as the crow flies, would have taken at least a month, depending on the weather.[16] On their tearful parting, the Widow Robards said she loved Rachel as much as any child of her own, including her oldest son.[17]

Lewis Robards' preemption grant for 640 acres in Davidson County was dated July 10, 1788. The acreage was surveyed by Rachel's brothers John and William and the survey was dated March 13, 1786.[18] Someone had to register the grant in Davidson County in July 1788.[19] Obviously, Robards was not there. Did Robert Hays, married to Rachel's sister Jane register the grant? Hays represented Robards in other business matters. Did John and William Donelson file the grant in the summer of 1788 for Robards, who was abusing their own sister?

Rachel and Samuel probably took the same route back to Cumberland that their father followed earlier. Did they stop at the location where their father was buried? Regardless, when she arrived the Donelsons wrapped her into their family fold. "Her presence at home was a bulwark to her bereaved family," Nellie T. Stokes wrote.[20]

A year later, John Overton planned to move from the Robards' home in Kentucky to Cumberland to practice law. The Widow Robards and her son enlisted his help in affecting reconciliation between Lewis and Rachel. Lewis Robards, according to Overton, was serious about preserving his marriage.[21]

Did Robards have ulterior motives for continuing a marriage with an unhappy wife? They had been married for two years and had no children, a sign that Rachel could be barren. From all indications, Robards was also vain and egocentric. In the eighteenth century, a married woman's inability to have children reflected on her husband, absence any sign of defect in either partner.[22] Both came from large families of eleven children. Eight of Rachel's siblings produced seventy-one children—two brothers never married and one married a widow with two children.[23]

The depth of Robards' abuse of Rachel will never be known. Some sources allege that his pathological jealous rages were physical as well as verbal.[24]

There was another reason for Robards to seek reconciliation with Rachel which involved money and land. John Donelson died in April 1786, and two years later his considerable estate of real and personal property had not been settled. Donelson died intestate, without a will. Whenever his estate was settled, Robards expected to receive Rachel's inheritance as she was a femme covert.

On his arrival in Cumberland, Overton began speaking with Rachel and her mother about Robards' desire for reconciliation. Mrs. Donelson exhibited more enthusiasm for the reunion than Rachel. Eventually, Rachel agreed but only if they lived with her mother. This time she wanted the protection of her family. Robards agreed. He owned a North Carolina preemption for 1,700 acres, including the nearby 640 acres known as Hunter's Hill.[25] They planned to live with Mrs. Donelson until dangers of Indian raids abated before developing the property. Overton and Andrew Jackson were living in Mrs. Donelson's cabin.[26]

John Dowling, another of Mrs. Donelson's boarders, said Robards' actions toward Rachel were "Cruel, unmanly and unkind in the extreme." Downing said one of Robards' sisters-in-law shared his assessment. He added the breach between Robards and Rachel arose from Robards' cruel and improper conduct.[27] Did Robards abuse the Donelson slave women as he did those belonging to his family in Kentucky?

Overton's negotiated reconciliation between Rachel and Robards lasted only a few months before Robards' jealous rage found another target, Andrew Jackson.[28] Overton convinced Jackson they should move from Mrs. Donelson's to Kasper Mansker's fort. Jackson was no Peyton Short and did not turn tail and run. Instead, he questioned Robards about the injustices he was doing to his wife. Robards' temper erupted and he threatened to whip Jackson, who immediately challenged him to a duel. Robards, as usual, refused the challenge.[29] On another occasion, an acquaintance, who was standing guard watching for Indians while the Donelson women picked blackberries, told Jackson that Robards threatened him. Jackson said he would cut off Robards' ears.[30]

Robards could have easily defeated the smaller, slender man in hand-to-hand combat; pistols were another matter. Instead, he went to a magistrate and swore out a warrant for Jackson, who was arrested and given a date to appear in court. Before the two men went into the courthouse on the appointed day, Jackson asked one of the guards to borrow his hunting knife, looked at Robards, pointed the knife at him and carefully ran his fingers along the glistening blade. Robards fled the scene and his complaint was dismissed due to the plaintiff's failure to appear in court.[31]

Shortly thereafter, Robards returned to Kentucky swearing never to be seen in Cumberland again. Harriet C. Owsley, in her *Tennessee Historical Quarterly* article, *The Marriages of Rachel Donelson,* placed Robards' departure in May or June 1789. A year later, Robards made sure Rachel heard about his threat to force her to live with him in Kentucky.[32]

"She was still legally bound to Robards," H. W. Brands wrote in *Andrew Jackson: His Life and Times,* "but, the moral tie—the bond of trust and affection that makes any marriage real—had been broken by Robards' mistreatment of her which by now included infidelities Robards scarcely bothered to deny."[33]

Rachel, with her mother's backing, decided to escape Robards' reach and accompanied Colonel Robert Stark and his family downriver to Natchez in December 1789 to visit family friends, the Thomas Marston Green and Peter Bruin families, whose connection with the Donelsons reached back to Virginia and Fort Patrick Henry. If there was a Donelson connection it eventually included Jackson but the young lawyer had his own connections with the Green and Bruin families. In December, the river levels were low, making crafts vulnerable to Indian attacks. Stark asked Jackson to accompany them after being told that the Donelson men were too busy. He agreed and they arrived in Natchez in January 1790. Jackson returned to Cumberland for the April 1790 court session.[34]

Those dates indicated he tarried a month or more in Natchez area. Jackson's business and legal interests in Mississippi went back to 1788 with a trading post, cabin and racetrack on Bayou Pierre. The same year Peter Bruin settled nearby. The audacious Irish Catholic built his home atop one of four earthen mounds in Bayou Pierre, which dated back to the Native American's Coles Creek Period, AD 1000–1200.[35]

In December 1790, Robards dropped the idea of intimidating Rachel and petitioned the Virginia General Assembly for a petition to allow his divorce case against her. His attorney, John Jouett, was married to Robards' sister Sallie. Jouett represented Mercer County in the1787 and 1790 Virginia General Assemblies where he was a strong advocate for separating Kentucky County from Virginia. After separation, Jouett represented Mercer County in the Kentucky General Assembly in 1792.[36]

The Virginia General Assembly approved Robards' petition to sue for divorce. "Be it enacted by the General Assembly, that it shall and may be lawful for Lewis Roberts [Robards] to sue out of the office of the supreme court of the District of Kentucky, a writ against Rachel Roberts [Robards], which writ shall be framed by the clerk, shall express the nature of the said cause, and the defendant may appear and plead to issue, in which case, or if she does not appear within two months after such publication, it shall be set for trial by the clerk on some day in the succeeding court but may for good cause shewn to the court he continued until the succeeding term."[37]

The writ approved the discovery process—depositions taken and subpoenas issued. A jury was to be summoned to hear the case and decide if Rachel was guilty of deserting Robards and living in adultery with another man.[38]

Rumors seemed to travel faster than the cotton, tobacco, corn, furs, barrel staves and cured meats on their way downriver from Kentucky and Tennessee to Natchez.[39]

"Later research showed that a friend of Lewis Robards had planted a fake article in his own newspaper, telling that the divorce had been granted," according to the History of American Women website. Only general, not specific, attribution of that statement was provided.[40]

John Overton, returning to Cumberland from the east, stopped to visit the Widow Robards at Cane Run and she told him Lewis had written her from Virginia saying the legislature had granted him a divorce from Rachel. Nellie Stokes wrote that the Donelsons and Jackson were so delighted with the news that Jackson traveled to Mississippi as soon as possible to share the news with Rachel.[41]

Andrew Burstein, in *The Passions of Andrew Jackson*, placed Jackson's return to Natchez to tell Rachel the news of Robards' divorce action around February 1791. The couple allegedly returned to Cumberland in March 1791. The settlement of John Donelson's personal estate, in which Rachel was referred to as Rachel Jackson, began on January 28, 1791, and was closed on April 15, 1791.[42]

Robards initially failed to take advantage of the Virginia General Assembly clearing the way to hear his divorce petition. One reason could have been his portion of John Donelson's estate which at that time was unsettled. The Virginia's General Assembly approved his petition to file for divorce in December 1790. On January 9, 1791, Robards wrote Robert Hays, married to Rachel's sister Jane, concerning some business affairs he had in Cumberland. He told Hays that he expected his share of John Donelson's estate. "I shall depend on you and Mr. Overton [one of the Donelson estate's three executors] that there is no advantage taken of me in my absence at Cumberland and you will please write by the first opportunity if the estate is divided as I may know how to proceed to get my right."[43]

Seventeen days later, on January 28, the settlement of Donelson's personal estate was begun by John Overton, Robert Cartwright and Henry Bradford. His personal property included slaves, horses, cattle, hogs, furnishings, cash and funds Donelson previously advanced to his children. The value of Donelson's thirty slaves, cattle, horses and hogs was $5,026. In 2017 dollars the economic value of that figure would be $454,000, but that did not include any his land holdings.[44]

On January 21, 1789, Stockley Donelson deeded all his interest in John Donelson's estate to his mother, Rachel Donelson, for £300.[45] Whether those interests were personal or real property was not defined. Yet, on April 15, 1791, when the Donelson's personal property estate was settled, Stockley was listed as being allotted his share of slaves, horses and cattle valued at $433.[46]

There were a number of expensive and interesting items omitted from the 1791 court settlement of John Donelson's personal property in Volume I, pages 196–201, of Davidson County Wills, Inventories and Settlements when contrasted with the estate's personal property inventory submitted by the estate administrator William Donelson in 1789.[47]

William Donelson's inventory of his father's personal estate provided a picture of the family being part of the landed gentry. There were implements for clearing and cultivating land: a plow, saws, axes, augers, shovels, grubbing hoes, wedges for splitting logs—all for work done by slaves. The more elegant items—six silver spoons, most probably made from coin silver; a pair of silver sugar tongs, books, beds, furniture, a chess set, £17 and a shot glass—did not include what Rachel Stockley brought to the marriage. With the exception of the beds and furniture, none of these items were listed on the division of Donelson's personal estate in *The Papers of Andrew Jackson Volume I*. Indicative of Donelson's previous professions were surveying instruments and 230 pounds of iron.[48]

The most astounding item was a looking glass (mirror). The mirror, a fragile furnishing, most likely made the trip from Pittsylvania County, Virginia, to the Holston, survived the river voyage, the trip to Kentucky and then back to Cumberland. Donelson played chess. William Donelson's inventory listed "a few books." John Donelson obviously imbibed as there was a shot glass in the inventory. After William Donelson signed the inventory as administrator, he included a notation, "Several boxes of debt accounts."[49]

Who owed John Donelson money or who did he owe money to? Who attempted to collect those debts? If the collection was successful, what happened to the money or land, which was often used as collateral? Were the debts kept within the family?[50]

A few of those questions about Donelson's debt accounts were answered in 1805. A supplementary apportionment of $821.31 was filed in Davidson County Court. The amount was shared by Donelson's heirs. As there was no existing inventory listing Donelson's real property, this amount came from his personal property settlement.[51]

An even larger question concerned the land John Donelson owned. The only document in Davidson County Wills, Inventories and Settlements dealing with the estate of John Donelson, Sr., was the 1789 one-page inventory of his personal property, the 1791 settlement documents of that property and the 1805 supplement apportionment of his personal property.[52] No settlement was filed concerning his real property which included at least his land grants in Davidson County. He had owned 55,000-plus acres in Kentucky/Virginia. There was the 11,250 acres of Alabama land due him as a commissioner appointed by the Georgia legislature to determine the western boundaries of the state and to settle Muscle Shoals.[53]

John Donelson's land did not vanish in thin air. Land was wealth on the frontier of which all the Donelsons were well aware. Some arrangements had to be made for the legal transfer of that land if there was no court/legal inventory, division or settlement of Donelson's real holdings. Or, was it simply divided between members of Donelson's family?

Records from *American State Papers, Documents, Legislative and Executive of the Congress of the United States as Related to Public Lands*, printed in 1834, provided a partial answer. Jackson, acting as an agent on behalf of Rachel and the other John Donelson heirs, began efforts in 1815 to claim the Alabama land for the family. Rachel and her siblings were described as the "heirs and representatives of Colonel John Donelson, deceased." At no place in the government documents Jackson filed or decisions handed down was there any mention of the John Donelson estate of his real property.[54]

Jackson detailed how Donelson accepted the commission from the Georgia legislature which presented hazards to his life, at great expense and fatigue from penetrating a pathless wilderness. He neglected to mention this was what Donelson had done for half of his life and was being well paid for his efforts. Jackson, after providing affidavits from John Peyton, Sr., David Henry and James M. Lewis, was precise about the location of the land Donelson wanted. "From a memorandum taken by the said John Donelson in his lifetime and found amongst his papers, he intended his grant to be laid out on the north side of the Tennessee River beginning opposite the head of an island at the commencement of the Big Shoal running north three miles, thence east up the river of complement."[55]

"Known all men by these present," Jackson's appeal read, "that we the undersigned, the heirs and representatives of John Donelson, deceased, do nominate and appoint Gen Andrew Jackson, our true and lawful attorney, in our names and in our behalf, to apply for, ask, demand and receive for us from the State of Georgia and the General Government of the United States all the land that was due to the said John Donelson, deceased, by virtue of an act or resolution of the General Assembly of said State of Georgia and upon the receipt thereof, acquiesce and other discharges for us and in our names, or otherwise, to make sign and give hereby ratifying and confirming all and whatever shall do on the promises. In Witness thereof, we have hereunto set our hands and seals this 5th day of October 1815. Alexander Donelson, John Donelson, William Donelson, Severn Donelson, Robert Hays, Mary Caffery."[56]

"These are the nine representatives," Jackson's application continued, "of John Donelson, deceased, that is the above named set, the heirs of Samuel Donelson, deceased, and Severn Donelson, youngest son of the deceased and myself in the right of Mrs. Andrew Jackson."[57]

Marsha Mullin, The Hermitage's curator, pointed out that Jackson's reference to Severn Donelson as the youngest child of John Donelson's was in error. He was referring to Leven Donelson, not Severn, who was alive at the time he signed the document.[58]

Mary Donelson Caffery's husband, John, died in 1811, and she could legally sign the document as a femme sole unlike Rachel whose husband, acting in her stead, referred to her as only "Mrs. J." Stockley Donelson died in 1805 and had no direct heirs. His wife had remarried. Catherine Donelson Hutchings' death date in The Papers of Andrew Jackson, Volume I, was listed as 1804. Her husband, Thomas Hutchings, was also listed as dying that year.[59]

The Committee on Public Lands approved Jackson's presentation and reported out a bill in 1819, for the benefits of the Donelson heirs receiving script for two dollars per acre to buy land being offered for sale in Alabama.[60] That amounted to $22,500 for the 11,250 acres due John Donelson.[61]

Robards' concern he would lose Rachel's portion of her father's estate was accurate. By not declaring John Donelson's ownership of any land, Robards was prohibited from claiming Rachel's share. If there was no real property legally declared; there was nothing to divide. To dispute that claim, Robards would have to return to Cumberland, face Jackson, Overton and the Donelsons in a legal environment that would not have been exactly friendly to him.

Robards waited until January 24, 1792, before reviving his divorce action against Rachel because in January 1791, the process of settling John Donelson's personal property estate began. That portion of Donelson's estate was initially settled in April 1791. Rachel was listed in the settlement as Rachel Jackson and received slaves, bed, an iron pot, furnishings, a horse and two cattle. Her share was valued at $527.[62] Its real price translated into $14,200 in 2017 dollars.[63]

That was a considerable amount of money in the early 1790s and Lewis Robards did not receive a cent.

Realizing his chances of success in getting Rachel's share of her father's real property were slight, Robards chose a different path for revenge against his wife, Jackson and the Donelsons.

6

A Dangerous Choice

Lewis Robards was the recipient of the actions Rachel and Jackson handed him for his divorce proceedings and he certainly took advantage of them. The Jacksons presented themselves as a married couple in the early 1790s, and spent a few months at Jackson's cabin, trading post and racetrack on Bayou Pierre, on the northern edge of the Spanish controlled Natchez District in Mississippi. When Jackson arrived there two years earlier, Bayou Pierre was the forest primeval where the citrus scents of mango groves mixed with the seductive bloom of climbing wisteria, the honey odor of ficus and spicy evergreen cypress.[1]

An occasional white-tailed deer ventured out of the wild until startled by the gobbling of a wild turkey. Sparrows and warblers produced a constant melody of songs while scissor-tailed flycatchers darted through space. The 230,000-acre bayou was also hot with high humidity, infested with insects and filled with reptiles and amphibians along with white bass.[2]

It was in this setting that Rachel Robards and Andrew Jackson celebrated their union with friends like their neighbor Peter Bryant Bruin, who established his 1,650-acre plantation there in 1787.[3] Jackson and Bruin shared a bond from their experiences in the Revolutionary War. After he joined the Irish Rebellion of 1758, which demanded male suffrage and the end of British rule, Bruin was forced to leave the country. He built a prosperous merchant's life in Virginia but left to again fight the British. Captured in the assault on Quebec in December 1775, Bruin was a prisoner for seven months. After the war, he moved his family and several others to the Natchez District.[4]

The district's proclivity for horse racing was another attraction for Jackson and Rachel who was an accomplished horsewoman. Bruin imported fine racehorses as did other men in the district. "In Adams County and through Natchez country in those days there was a love for horse racing unmatched anywhere," Stanley Nelson wrote in a 2014 newspaper article.[5]

Aside from their affinity for horse racing, Bruin and Jackson were both merchants who saw the Bayou Pierre as being an ideal place from which to facilitate trade between Cumberland, Kentucky, and New Orleans. But first they had to sign an oath of allegiances to the Spanish crown which Jackson did on July 15, 1789. By signing the oath, duty on products coming into the district was reduced from 15 to 6 percent. In 1788, eighty-nine settlers, with five slaves, arrived in the district: fifty-seven were from Kentucky and sixteen from Cumberland.[6]

Rachel had been in the district for some time and Jackson's accounts with Natchez merchant Melling Woolley placed him there in March, April, and July 1790.[7] According to Woolley's accounts, between the billing of Jackson's March 1790 account and that of July 1790, items indicated Rachel's presence. His July account items of a tea tray, one-half yard of muslin—often used as dress trim—and two and a half yards of cloth certainly indicated a feminine presence.[8]

Rachel settled into social life in the bayou and Jackson's friends accepted them as a married couple. "For a little while," Jonathan Daniels in his book on the Natchez Trace wrote, "the young couple stayed in Jackson's log house in Bruinsberg. In a clearing on the bluff looking down on the Mississippi River and Bayou Pierre, they were at last safe together. They entertained friends who had been and were kind to Rachel."[9]

George Cochran, Jackson's Natchez business agent, confirmed in a letter on October 21, 1791, that the Jacksons presented themselves in Natchez as being married.

> While I come to the most pleasing part of this hour's employment and take the liberty of saluting Mrs. Jackson. With that satisfaction my dearest madam, I have received information of your good health, that only accustomed to look on such a friends in the nearest light of a sister can imagine. May this blessing of good health continue and may every happiness be annexed thereto. However remote, I cannot lose the remembrance of the agreeable hours I have passed in your friendly retreat at Bayou Pierre and seriously it would not be the last amongst a number of inducements I should have to receive from the hands of Mrs. Jackson so great a treasure as yr. friendship has provided that I might again enjoy the pleasure of that society I once did and still would so highly value. But, my dear madam, accustomed always to be so unlucky, & fearing that before I could accomplish what I have long so ardently withheld, the blooming prize should be snatched away by force of the more fortunate scenery of Cumberland.[10]

Obviously, Cochran considered Rachel and Jackson married to each other.

Plowing through the flowery eighteenth-century prose one was imbued with the admiration, perhaps infatuation, which permeated Cochran's feeling for Rachel. Six years later, after Rachel was charged with adultery, Cochran's feelings about his friend's wife had not changed. He wrote in a letter on April 15, 1797, "In drawing near the end of my paper, I feel a strong inclination to express myself in terms suitably expressive of my respect and esteem for Mrs. Jackson."[11]

"I have no good words to do so," Cochran continued, "I wish her all the happiness—and ardently wish I may yet in this country (for I have expectations you'll again visit it) to have her as a neighbor and friend regarded by Mrs. Cochran as she was by her quondam neighbors on Bayou Pierre. I have not yet found one of that sex that will take the name but have expectations that in the change that threatens us of laws and government it may also produce a change of situation with me—whether for better or worse depending on the circumstances, however I am determined shortly to try it."[12]

Rachel and Jackson had already left Bayou Pierre when Cochran's second letter was written. A 1792 census of Bayou Pierre listed Peter Bruin as still living there with his family but Andrew Jackson's name was not included.[13]

Different dates have been used for Rachel and Jackson's departure from Bayou Pierre. A number of writers, including Jackson's good friend John Overton, used September 1791 as the date they left Bayou Pierre. The most likely date of their departure from Natchez was the during the spring and summer of 1790 when the infamous Hugh McGary, a member of the Mercer Country Court, was absent from court sessions from February 23 to August 24, 1790. McGary, for some unknown reason, just happened to be in Natchez and was among those who made the trip to Cumberland up the Natchez Trace with the Jacksons.[14]

The Natchez Trace was noted for travelers being set upon by robbers and murderers. Four months earlier, eight travelers began their journey up the Trace. Three were murdered near the mouth of Duck River, three were never found and two survived. Rachel and Jackson made the trip without suffering any personal safety but neither ever anticipated the journey would have such devastating impact on their future lives.[15]

For their personal safety, travelers waited in Natchez for a large group to form before venturing up the Trace. More than 100 travelers accompanied Rachel and Jackson on their journey to Cumberland but one in particular, Hugh McGary, would later do them innumerable harm. McGary's brother or cousin Martin was said to be married to Betty Crawford, a Jackson cousin but the filial connection was lost on McGary who was a good friend of Lewis Robards.[16]

Like Rachel and Robards, McGary lived in Mercer County, Kentucky, where everybody knew everybody's business. Three decades later, the population of Harrodsburg, the county seat, was still only 313.[17] Robards had a store in Harrodsburg when he and Rachel lived with his mother on her Cane Run plantation.

A scandal as juicy as theirs would have been spread on several levels. Robards' nightly visits to the plantation's slave quarters created common gossip passed among those enslaved and their owners. He might have perpetuated his marital problems himself. Jackson, who had clients in Kentucky, was already an established lawyer and on his way to becoming a prominent politician. As the third partner in the trio, his adversaries later found the Robards' scandal a useful political tool. Finally, there was not too much to talk about on the still raw frontier—Indian raids, infants, crops, building cabins and arrival of newcomers—so the screaming, yelling and Rachel's fights with her husband had few peers in gossip. McGary was not one to keep his mouth shut.

From all indications, Hugh McGary did not travel much outside of Kentucky, with the known exceptions being his purchase of a slave from Mansker in Cumberland (which Jackson witnessed) and his militia activities, until he moved from Mercer County to Southern Indiana after the Robards' divorce trial. He died there in 1808.[18] The question about what was McGary, an Indian fighter and land trader, doing in Natchez at that time has never been answered.

Mary P. Hammersmith in her book, *Hugh McGary, Senior, Pioneer of Virginia, North Carolina, Kentucky and Indiana,* had no answer to that question. Hammersmith placed the Natchez trip in the summer of 1790, but gave no reason for McGary's trip to Natchez. "Worthy of noting, incidentally, is the frequency with which records crucial to this whole matter have vanished since 1827–1828," Hammersmith wrote.[19] Those were the years of Jackson's second presidential campaign.

Jonathan Daniels speculated in his book that Rachel and Jackson traveled with an entourage of servants who handled their baggage, took care of the horses, set up their tent, kindled the fires and cooked their food. The Jacksons, he wrote, would have ridden either the highly regarded Chickasaw or Kentucky horses. During the three-week trip, the party encountered streams that required rafts to cross.[20]

Beyond the Natchez District, traveling conditions on the Trace grew most uncomfortable with swamps swarming with gnats and mosquitoes. As the party progress northward, Daniels wrote, "The path became rougher, more broken and bushier." When they came to the Tennessee River, it must have reminded Rachel of the perils of the Donelson's flatboat trip. The best place travelers chose to cross, wrote Daniels, was where the river was "a quarter-of-a-mile wide and flowed with so rapid a stream that it was with difficulty a person could stand against it." Even crossing the river on a hastily constructed raft was dangerous as the craft could be rapidly swept downstream.[21]

McGary, given his bullish nature, probably made sure the Jacksons saw him every day on the Trace as a reminder that he knew Rachel was still married to Robards. There was an altercation of sorts between Jackson and McGary. Daniels referred to John Overton's later explanations that the confrontation was about Indian attacks. "Circumstances that occurred," Overton wrote three decades later, "calculated to excite in McGary as strong feeling of dislike toward General Jackson, which it is *unnecessary to detail as they relate solely* [emphasis mine] to a mediated attack by Indians."[22] The fact that Overton went to such great lengths to designate the disagreement between Jackson and McGary as a difference of opinion about Indian attacks called attention to another reason.

At that point, if the conflict between the two men was about an Indian attack, McGary actually had more experience, such as it was, than Jackson.

The clash between the two men was most likely what McGary considered the improper relationship of his friend's wife with Jackson. McGary's fiery nature probably did not keep him quiet. It may have been one of the few instances where Jackson was forced to contain his temper in order not to embarrass Rachel before the entire traveling party. What could have been a pleasant journey for Rachel turned into a stressful situation for her.

Rachel and Jackson were greeted with joyous enthusiasm by a large circle of family and friends when they reached Cumberland. Overton bragged they were beloved and esteemed by all classes.[23] Both Rachel and Jackson presented a brave and joyous public countenance. He was the attorney general of the Mero District and purchased a plantation, Popular Grove, in the Jones Bend of the Cumberland River for Rachel. His social acceptance was sealed when he was named to the board of trustees of the Davidson Academy.[24]

From all outward appearances, the future looked promising for the young couple but the Jacksons had to be aware of the cloud hanging over their relationship. That cloud turned into a storm less than two years later.

On January 24, 1792, Robards executed his petition to file for divorce against Rachel. He chose a new lawyer, John Brown, to represent him instead of his brother-in-law John Jouett, who filed the initial petition in the Virginia General Assembly. Brown studied law with some of the best legal minds in Virginia—George Wythe, Thomas Jefferson and Edmund Randolph.[25]

Brown, Kentucky's first United States senator, had his own tattered past.[26] He was said to be a member of the Spanish Conspiracy, organized by the disgraced Revolutionary War General James Wilkinson, which advocated giving land beyond the Appalachian Mountains to Spain in exchange for keeping the Mississippi River open to commerce. Wilkinson's close ties to Spain resulted in that government supposedly shipping him barrels filled with silver dollars. Whether Wilkinson shared that money with his alleged co-conspirators: Brown; Kentucky's first federal district judge Harry Innes; appellate judge Benjamin Sebastian and minister turned lawyer Caleb Wallace was not known. Later Brown, Wilkinson, Innes, Sebastian and Wallace were said to have received lifetime pensions from Spain.[27]

The Court's Writ read, "The commonwealth of Virginia to the Sheriff of Mercer County, Greetings. You are hereby again commanded to summons

Rachel Roberts [Robards] to appear before the Judges of our Supreme court for the District of Kentucky, at the Courthouse in Danville on the ninth day of their next March court to answer a charge of adultery against her by Lewis Roberts [Robards]. And have then there this Writ. Witness Christopher Greenup Clerk of our said court at the Courthouse aforesaid this 24 day of January 1792, in the year XVI of the Commonwealth."[28]

Greenup, elected governor of Kentucky in 1804, was directed to advertise Rachel's summons in the *Kentucky Gazette* on February 4, 11, 18 and 25 and in the March 5, 10, 17 and 24, 1792, issues of the Lexington newspaper.[29]

The distance between the Danville-Harrodsburg-Lexington area and Nashville as the crow flies was around 171 miles, allowing for detours. Divide the average traveling time on the trail by ten to twelve miles a day and the trip took less than three weeks. The *Kentucky Gazette* printed Rachel's summons for two months ending in March 1792.[30] It was unlikely, given the continuing westward migration after the Revolutionary War, that none of Jackson's wide range of acquaintances traveled from Danville-Harrodsburg-Lexington to Cumberland, or made the return trip, in that two-month period.[31] Consequently, it also stretched credibility that the large Donelson clan, Overton, or any of hundreds of relatives, friends, acquaintances or fellow attorneys were oblivious to Robards' finally instituting divorce action against Rachel.

The Court Writ called for Rachel to answer Robards' charges against her which included having an attorney to represent her in a hostile Kentucky setting. She certainly had access to attorneys—aside from Jackson and Overton there were lawyers in the Donelson family. Yet, they all claimed ignorance of Robards' recent legal actions.

Jackson, according to a letter from Thomas Hutchings on February 2, 1791, made trips to Kentucky during that period. Hutchings, married to Rachel's sister Catherine represented Sullivan County in the North Carolina House of Commons. He asked Jackson's assistance in collecting money Peter Turney owed him on a land warrant. When Jackson was in Kentucky, Hutchings suggested his brother Thomas Hutchings, Jr., who lived on Salt River between Harrodsburg and Danville, could assist in settling the debt.[32]

The Salt River ran through Mercer County where Rachel and Robards had lived. If Jackson made the trip, how could he have been unaware of the status of Rachel's relationship with her first husband?

Robards' divorce trial was not held in March 1792, but the following September after Kentucky statehood was finalized in June of that year. The delay not only gave Robards and his new attorney, John Brown, more time to prepare their case but also allowed more time for the Jacksons to be aware of the situation.

Jackson, Overton, the Donelsons and their friends ignored Rachel's legal summons. Whether Rachel knew about it was unknown but it stretches credibility to assume she was in ignorance of the lawsuit against her. The delay also gave Robards' attorney, John Brown, additional time to carefully select a jury.

Three divorce trial jurors, Joseph Thomas, Thomas Smith and Samuel Work could not be identified but those remaining were certainly a jury of Robards' peers with a healthy dose of influence from McGary's family. Juror John Ray was Hugh McGary's stepson. Harrison Davis, another juror, was the brother-in-law of Hugh McGary's oldest son, Robert McGary. John B. Lightfoot, the jury foreman, was a horticulturalist who came to Mercer County in 1755 from Madison County, Virginia, with his son Phillip. A member of the prominent Lightfoot family who first arrived in Virginia in 1609, John sold apple trees on the frontier and is credited with developing McAfee's Nonesuch apples.[33]

Lightfoot shared Virginia kinship with Elizabeth Woodson Lewis Robards, the plaintiff's mother. An even closer lineage existed between Lightfoot and Hannah Withers Wynn with whom Robards entered into a bigamous marriage in December 1792.[34]

James Bradsberry, if he was the same juror, was captain of a Mississippi company of mounted spies in the War of 1812.[35]

Juror Gabriel Slaughter was a native of Culpeper County, Virginia. Only two counties—Orange and Louisa—separated Robards' home county of Goochland from Culpepper. Slaughter, who was Kentucky governor from 1816 to 1820, arrived in Mercer County shortly before the divorce trial began.[36]

John Miles, a native of Augusta County, Virginia, was known to be in Mercer County, Kentucky, in 1792 and was selected as a juror.[37] Another juror, John Meaux, was from Botetourt County, Virginia. Meaux moved to Mercer County in 1784 and accumulated considerable wealth with sixty slaves, 2,500 acres of land and a stable of twenty-five horses. Meaux was a noteworthy figure because at his death, with the exception of giving ten cows and ten ewes each to his two grandsons, he emancipated his slaves and directed his property and real estate be divided between them.[38]

When Jackson was running for president in 1827, Meaux claimed little memory of sitting on the divorce jury. "I recollect being on the jury when Robards obtained his divorce, but have ... [missing words] the most distant recollection of what evidence was offered on the trial."[39]

Little is known about juror Benjamin Lawless, from Halifax County, Virginia, other than he witnessed a deposition in the estate of Richard Swan in Washington County, Kentucky, and was practically penniless by 1822.[40]

More is known about the plaintiff's two witnesses, John Cowan, a member of the original James Harrod company who settled and built Fort Harrod in 1774–75, and Hugh McGary, who observed the Jacksons' behavior during the Natchez Trace trip. The relationships between Robards, Cowan and

McGary raised questions about the validity of their testimony. Cowan and McGary were appointed in 1788 as justices of the peace in Lincoln County (before Mercer was formed and after Virginia divided Kentucky County into Lincoln, Jefferson and Fayette counties). Robards, in an effort to collect debts owed his mercantile establishment, would have had interactions with both in that capacity. Cowan and McGary had served as sheriffs of Lincoln County and would have served any legal papers Robards filed. McGary was appointed lieutenant colonel in the militia with Robards serving under him as a captain.[41]

The same court McGary was once a member of found him guilty on May 10, 1783, of betting on a mare at Humble's Race Path, near Harrodsburg. "Said Hugh McGary, gentleman, be deemed an infamous gambler and that he shall not be eligible to any office of trust or honor within this state [Virginia]—pursuant to an act of Assembly entitled, an Act to suppress excessive gambling."[42]

Even then, many in Mercer County wanted nothing to do with McGary and for good reason. This was almost two years after the Revolutionary War Battle of Blue Licks, August 19, 1781, in which Colonel Daniel Boone excoriated McGary for his shameful and seditious actions that resulted in the loss of seventy-seven frontiersmen including his son Israel. Colonels John Todd and Stephen Trigg, two prominent Kentucky leaders, were also killed. McGary shouted a challenge to the undermanned militia, if they were not cowards, to follow him in attacking the Wyandot instead of waiting for General Benjamin Logan and his reinforcement of 500 militiamen.[43]

Attempting to shift blame from himself, McGary said Todd and Trigg gave the order to advance. It was a handy ploy since the dead men were unable to defend themselves. Colonel Boone said differently as did Colonel Arthur Campbell, who agreed with John Donelson at Harrodsburg in 1782 on separation from Virginia but they were opposed by McGary. "Never was the lives of so many valuable [men] lost more shamefully than in the late actions of the 19 August," Colonel Boone wrote, "and that not a little thro the vain and seditious expressions of a Major McGary."[44]

McGary, nonetheless, continued to attach himself to the militia, riding with General Benjamin Logan in the summer of 1786 in a raid on a Shawnee village in Ohio. The Shawnee Chief Moluntha, who was married to the late Chief Cornstalk's sister the Grenadier Squaw was captured in what is now Logan County, Ohio. General Logan specifically warned McGary not to molest the prisoners. Ignoring him, McGary advanced and asked Moluntha if he was at the Battle of Blue Licks. Moluntha indicated that he was. McGary grabbed an axe and slashed open the chief's head before running away. McGary's separation from the militia occurred shortly thereafter.[45]

An incident at McGary's Station in Mercer County that same year indicated he was as savage and uncivilized as the worst Indian. One of his stepsons was killed in an attack on McGary's Station. The next day, McGary found an Indian wearing his stepson's shirt. He not only killed the Indian but returned home with his body, hacked it apart and fed the flesh to his dogs.[46]

Robards's principal witness, McGary, had known Jackson since 1789 when Kasper Mansker bought a slave from McGary at Cumberland. Jackson and Charles Hamman were witnesses to the £100 sale.[47] The two men were not strangers when they travelled the Natchez Trace together.

From all indications, McGary took great satisfaction in testifying that, while on their journey up the Natchez Trace, Rachel and Jackson slept under the same blanket.[48] Ann Toplovich, in an article in the *Ohio Valley Historical Journal,* gave credit to McGary, describing him as a Kentucky war hero, for the seemingly effortless divorce.[49]

"Robards could not have obtained a divorce with lesser proof," Hammersmith wrote. "If McGary was summons to testify, and the extant records do show that he was, then he was under oath to tell the truth."[50]

Had Rachel answered the summons and appeared in the Danville court along with Jackson, Overton and the entire Cumberland bar to defend her, the divorce trial verdict would have been no different.

"Jackson's friends later were at much pains to prove that McGary had only seen the Jacksons on the trip up the Trace after they believed they were legally married," Daniels wrote.[51] To subscribe to Daniels' theory would have made the Jacksons bigamists.

On September 27, 1793, Lightfoot read the jury's verdict. "Specified upon their [jurors] do say that the defendant Rachel Robards hath deserted the plaintiff Lewis Robards and hath and does still live in adultery with another man. It is therefore considered by the court that the marriage between Plaintiff and Defendant be dissolved."[52]

The court directed Lewis Robards to pay Hugh McGary four shillings and two pence for his two-days of testimony in the divorce trial.[53]

Lewis Robards and Rachel, having committed bigamy and adultery respectively, were finally divorced. Hannah Withers Winn was also a bigamist for having married Robards in Jefferson County in December 1792.[54] The Robards remarried on November 9, 1793, according to the *Register of the Kentucky State Historical Society* and raised their ten children in Bullitt County, Kentucky. However, in her 1839 application for Robards' Revolutionary War pension, Hannah Robards gave their marriage date as December 29, 1792. Hannah signed the pension application form with an "X."[55] Robards died there in April 1815.[56]

Rachel and Andrew Jackson were married on January 17, 1794, after much urging by John Overton over Jackson's opposition.[57] Jackson felt they were already married. "He swore, damn it, he would not consider a second marriage since Rachel was his wife before God and in the 'understanding of every person in the country,'" Daniels wrote. "Overton's counsel prevailed."[58] The ritual was conducted by Rachel's brother-in-law Robert Hays, who was a justice of the peace in Davidson County.[59]

Jackson, an attorney, has been faulted by historians for not knowing the difference between Robards' petition asking legislative permission to file for a divorce and his actual filing for a divorce in Virginia courts. Author Harriet Owsley pointed out that that Jackson had never practiced law in Virginia, only in North Carolina and what later became Tennessee.[60] Andrew Jackson had no reason to be familiar with Virginia divorce laws. Absolute divorce was not then legal in Colonial North Carolina. When North Carolina became a state in 1789, only separations, with maintenance or alimony, were granted by the General Court and on very few occasions.[61]

Generations of biographers spent untold years attempting to figure out if, when and where the Jacksons were married in Mississippi. Rachel and Andrew Jackson said they were married there without mentioning any specific place or date.

Biographers and Jackson's political opponents never found any evidence of the Jacksons' marriage in Mississippi. The district of Natchez, Mississippi, at that time was under Spanish control and the Catholic Church maintained records of marriages, births and deaths. The Jacksons were not Catholic and could not be married in a Catholic church.

Jonathan Daniels speculated the Jacksons might have been married by one of the Irish Catholic priests who were there to convert the increasing number of American settlers.[62]

Other speculation of the Jacksons' Mississippi nuptials ranged from their being married in the drawing room of Thomas Maston Green's plantation home to a double log cabin in Bayou Pierre to her having applied for and received a Spanish divorce to not being married at all.

The Donelsons were related to or had known most of the prosperous families from Virginia to Georgia. There were close enough personal relations between the two families for Rachel to spend several months with Thomas M. Green, Jr., and his family at their Springfield plantation and a lesser amount of time with his brother Abner Green and his family at their Second Creek plantation.

Jackson had his own connection to the Greens which began around 1788 with his excursion into the Natchez District of Spanish controlled Mississippi. The following year, Colonel Thomas Maston Green gave Jackson his power of attorney.[63] Jackson also had political and business dealings with one of Colonel Green's sons-in-law, Cato West.[64]

The Green families maintained for decades that the Jacksons were married in their drawing room at Springfield. Thomas Maston Green's great-great-great-great-granddaughter Laura Lake Ihrie was certain of that fact. "Jackson and Mrs. Robards were married in the great, big downstairs room at Springfield," she recalled in 1937. "I have been told that many times, not only by my mother but by other members of the family."[65]

The plantation house told a different story, according to Dawn Maddox, architectural historian at the Mississippi Department of Archives and History, who conducted the survey for the structure's nomination for the National Register of Historic Places. Maddox found that the house was built not by the elder Green, but by his son Thomas Maston Green, Jr. "Its decorative woodcarving is one factor which suggests that Springfield was built at a later date than 1791, the year that Andrew Jackson-Rachel Robards marriage allegedly took place there." Maddox wrote. "It seems unlikely that the Adamesque mode of interior architecture would have penetrated the Old Southwest a decade prior to its ascendancy in such centers of the au courant as Boston, Salem and Charleston. On the other hand, it is possible that the woodwork is of a later period than the house itself."[66]

Jefferson County resident E. R. Jones, in a 1910 article in the *Publication of the Mississippi Historical Society*, disputed the Jacksons being married there. Jones said he was born in 1804 and grew up at Belle Grove across from the Natchez Trace home of Rachel Robards. "Mrs. Robards, so the old people of the time while I was growing up around Greenville, told me she owned her own farm near Greenville and had on it a double log house with an open hall and here they say she was married to General Jackson." Jones further cited his friendship with Allen Colier, a former slaved owned by Thomas Marston Green. He quoted Colier as saying the Green great house (Springfield) had not been built when the Jacksons married. "I remember it," Jones quoted Colier as saying, "Miss Robards didn't have to go over there to be married when she had a good house of her own right by what we call the Jackson Spring." Jones was critical of historians William H. McCardle and Robert Lowry for their account of the Robards-Jackson wedding taking place at Springfield.[67]

McCardle and Lowry wrote about Rachel's visits with the Green families and gave an account of the Jacksons' wedding. "The next year, 1791, Andrew Jackson returned to Natchez and during the summer of that year, he and Mrs. Rachel Robards were married at the residence of Thomas Marston Green in Jefferson County." They added the ceremony was conducted by Thomas Marston Green, Sr., a justice of the peace of Bourbon County, Georgia.[68]

Green had been instrumental in the establishment of Bourbon County, Georgia, in the movement to extend that state's westward boundary to the Mississippi River over the objections of Spain. He was a justice of the peace for that county. However, Bourbon County, Georgia, was viable for only three years, 1785 to 1788. The formation of Bourbon County, Georgia, and its repeal was the basis for the Yazoo Land Fraud. Consequently, if Thomas Green married the Jacksons in 1791, he did so without legal authority.[69]

The two historians, quoting from *The Memories of Fifty Years* by W. H. Sparks, maintained Rachel Robards had applied for a divorce from the Spanish tribunals. "At the time of her [Rachel] coming to the home of Thomas M. Green, the civil authority was a disputed one, most of the people acknowledged the Spanish authorities' acts. A suit was instituted for a divorce and a decree was granted by a Spanish tribunal. There was probably little ceremony or strictness of legal proceedings in the matter, as all government and law was equivocal and of but little force just at that time in the country."[70]

Dunbar Rowland in *Mississippi: Comprising Sketches of County, Towns, Institutions and Persons,* maintained that Rachel was granted a divorce from Robards in Spanish controlled Natchez District but offered no proof.[71]

In his 1933 biography of Andrew Jackson, Marquis James was skeptical of Spanish divorces in Natchez. "This seems impossible for two reasons: the extreme difficulty of obtaining divorces under Spanish law and that, if true, there would have been no need two years later for a second ceremony."[72]

Recent research by historians questioned James' theory that Spanish divorces were extremely difficult to arrange in Natchez.

"Women in the Natchez district understood their moral and legal rights and customarily approached the bench determined to protect themselves and their families," Joyce L. Broussard wrote in the second volume of *Mississippi Women: Their Histories, Their Lives.* "Of fifty-five Mississippi divorce cases filed between 1789 and 1817, twenty-three of them were initiated by women; forty-two were granted. By the time of statehood, 1817, several dozen Mississippi women had sued successfully for divorce and most of them had filed petitions in the Natchez District, home to the lion's share of the state's white population."[73]

"Unfortunately," Broussard continued, "the outcome of the entire record of divorce petitions is unknown due to the scattered sources and the unorganized array of records. The majority of petitions have been located either in county records or state archives but the final decrees in numerous cases have been lost."[74]

Therefore, if Rachel applied for and received a Spanish divorce those documents were among the lost records Broussard mentioned.

Rachel Donelson Robards certainly had the political contacts in Natchez to obtain a Spanish divorce. Colonel Thomas Green, his sons Abner and Thomas Maston, and son-in-law Cato West had become well established land owners in Adams County (Natchez). Colonel Green had serious problems earlier with Spanish authorities when he demanded they surrender the region north of the thirty-first parallel. His land, slaves and property were confiscated and he was imprisoned in New Orleans. However, he was released and appeared to accumulate more property as did his sons and West. Thomas M.

Green was described as "a man of wealth and remarkable for his pride and fastidiousness in selecting friends and acquaintances."[75]

The Greens and West were prominent men in the Natchez District according to legal records. They appraised estates, witnessed deeds and signed sureties for family and friends. Many of their land and slave transactions were in cash. In December 1784, Thomas M. Green paid $700 in cash for 200 acres on Coles Creek. Cato West, in January 1787, paid $2,000 in cash for 600 acres on Coles Creek. West paid $350 in cash for a fourteen-year-old slave boy in May 1788.[76]

There was one other possibility that the Jacksons were married in Mississippi. Jackson's good friend and Bayou Pierre neighbor, Peter Bruin, was named an alcade by the Spanish government.[77] An alcade, in the Spanish governmental structure, had authority equal to that of an American civil magistrate or a justice of the peace.[78] Bruin could have easily married them and said nothing about it. The feisty Irishman, given his history, would have relished doing something so unorthodox.

Perhaps it will never be known if Rachel Robards applied for and received a Spanish divorce or if there was a Mississippi wedding but it would certainly explain Andrew Jackson's strong reluctance to their repeating their vows.

If they were married by a Protestant minister in Mississippi, he would have been extremely wary about keeping a record of such an event and would have feared for his life since Spanish officials, while generously welcoming settlers, took a dim view of their practicing any organized religions other than Catholicism. The Mississippi Department of Archives and History, in an email to the author on February 13, 2017, cited the reason why: "There is one case where a Protestant minister was arrested by the Spanish government for performing marriages."[79]

That minister was Richard Curtis, Sr. Curtis and his group of settlers left South Carolina in 1780, built three flat boats alongside the Holston and raised a crop of corn before traversing the Tennessee River to the Ohio and down the Mississippi to Natchez. It is possible Curtis knew about the voyage of John Donelson and his family from Holston inhabitants. Curtis organized a Baptist church at Coles Creek, thirty-six miles southwest of Bayou Pierre. He died in 1784, and was succeeded by his son Richard Curtis Jr., who was later told by the Spanish he would lose his property and be driven from the colony if he continued preaching. Then he did the unpardonable, conducting a marriage ceremony, contrary to Spanish law. To avoid being shipped to Mexican silver mines to perform hard labor for a lifetime, Curtis escaped back to South Carolina.[80]

Curtis was not an exception to how Protestant ministers were treated by the Spanish in Mississippi's Natchez District. Congregational minister

Reverend Samuel Swayze began holding secret church meetings in 1779. Spanish officials learned of his activities and burned all his Bibles and religious tracts. The Reverend Adam Cloud, an Episcopal minister, came to Mississippi in 1792, was allowed to preach occasionally and then was arrested, sent to New Orleans in irons and banished from the colony. Methodists did not arrive until 1799 and Presbyterians followed in 1801. Religious communities gained their freedom after Mississippi became a United States territory in 1798.[81]

It would be ludicrous to say that there were no Protestant couples were married in Spanish Mississippi from 1788 to 1798. Rachel and Andrew Jackson, since Bayou Pierre was at the northern edge of the Natchez District, could have done what Phoebe Jones, Curtis's niece, and her fiancé David Greenleaf did in 1795. Greenleaf went outside the Natchez District to obtain a marriage license and the Reverend Curtis conducted the marriage ceremony, after much subterfuge, in the home of William Stampley in the middle of the night to avoid attracting notice of the Catholic Church and Spanish officials.[82]

The conundrum was that no recorded proof of the Jacksons' Natchez marriage or Rachel's Spanish divorce has ever been found. The Jacksons said they were married; the Donelson clan agreed and accepted them as a married couple as did their close friends and associates. There were others who stored that information away to use another day. It is possible Rachel Donelson Robards and Andrew Jackson, given their situation, made a conscious decision—some might say an agreement with the devil—to bluff their way to matrimonial harmony. In doing so, they gave Lewis Robards the vital evidence, desertion and adultery, he needed for a divorce. Both Rachel and Jackson paid an enormous price for the decision they made that flaunted not only social norms but the very laws and legal opinions that he, as an attorney, was sworn to enforce. Rachel had no other escape from an abusive husband than to give him a reason to divorce her and, if that was her decision, it took an enormous amount of determination and courage.

7

Landed Gentry

When Rachel Donelson Robards and Andrew Jackson were married in January 1794 they continued in the landed gentry's lifestyle to which she had become accustomed. He had acquired 4,970 acres of land and seven slaves—Nancy, George, Molly, Tom, Aaron, Peg and Roele—and, along with her personal estate inheritance from her father, the couple was firmly established with the status of landed gentry.[1] At that time they were living in a home on the 630-acre Poplar Grove plantation Jackson had purchased in February 1792 from her brother John for £100.[2]

Jackson purchased Hunter's Hill, with its elegant plantation house, in March 1796 before his first trip to Philadelphia to sell land and purchase merchandise for his store.[3]

Landed gentry was a term imported into Virginia from Britain, Albert H. Tillison, Jr., wrote in *Encyclopedia Virginia*. He explained it referred to men in England and Ireland, not members of nobility, who owned extensive country estates and lived off the rental income of their tenants. "Their land ownership entitled them to a share of political power and their leisured lifestyle supposedly facilitated the cultivation of refined standards of personal conduct and cultural appreciation."[4]

Tillison's definition applied to Rachel and the Donelson family more than Jackson's hardscrabble youth and early years. The Donelsons, however, broke the mold of the old Virginia families by moving west, acquiring vast amounts of land, some by questionable means. They created their own Tennessee dynasty within the Virginia definition.[5]

The Donelsons, Natalie Inman wrote in *Brothers & Friends: Kinship in Early America,* made their initial fortunes not from plantations and slaves—that came later—but from land speculation built on a family network of surveyors, lawyers and judges. "The Donelson family integrated land speculation, legal careers and other economic ventures to take advantage of the interconnecting opportunities for vast profits based on the booming land market." The Donelson family network, Inman pointed out, owned land in

Davidson, Wilson, Williamson, Maury, Knox, Grainger, Sevier, Robertson, White, Sumner, Montgomery, Campbell, Blount and Greene Counties between 1796 and 1815, in addition to land speculations in parts of Georgia, Alabama, Florida and Mississippi.[6]

The acreage the Donelsons amassed, not including that owned by Jackson, was indeed impressive.

The late John Donelson II, head of the clan, held patents on at least 2,500 acres in Davidson County at one time.[7] In Kentucky, he had entries for 55,000 acres.[8] Those lands were in addition to acreage he held in Virginia and in what is now Alabama.

In Tennessee alone, John Donelson III held patents for 55,485 acres.[9] The two John Donelsons were pikers compared to the land holdings of their son and brother, Stockley. Individually and with other partners, Stockley Donelson entered 1,270,567 acres in North Carolina/Tennessee land records.[10]

Inman credited this vast accumulation of lands to the family's involvement in every aspect of the young government. Negotiating treaties with Indian tribes involved John Donelson II and his son-in-law John Coffee. Of Donelson's eleven sons and sons-in-laws, nine held military titles: Andrew Jackson, Robert Hays, Stockley Donelson, Alexander Donelson, John Donelson III, Samuel Donelson, John Caffery, John Coffee and Thomas Hutchings. Three Donelson sons, John, Stockley and William, were surveyors as were sons-in-law Robert Hays and Thomas Hutchings. In addition, Jackson, Samuel Donelson and Robert Hays were attorneys. In the 1790s, members of the Donelson clan were justices of the peace in Davidson County. Jackson was a Superior Court judge from 1798 to 1804. Stockley Donelson was appointed by George Washington to the Upper House of the Territorial legislature for the Territory South of the Ohio River.[11]

In 1797, the Nashville population ranged between 150 and 300 and thirty-nine of them were Donelsons.[12]

What about the Donelson women?

"Through this view of marriage," Inman wrote, "the women almost disappear entirely from the narrative, serving only as the means to tie men together for business deals and political alliances. In this case, the surviving sources deceive the readers into believing the Cumberland settlements were essentially masculine with women serving little purpose other than being the means to forge together important men, bearers of the heirs and keepers of the household."[13]

Married frontier women were little more than their husbands' chattel. They could own no property, had no control of their money—if they had any—and were unable to make important decisions concerning their own children if they became widows. However, they played their own roles both as housekeeper and overseer when their husbands were away.

Rachel Jackson was an exception, somewhat of a rebel who thumbed her nose at conventional mores. She found herself in an unhappy, abusive marriage with no acceptable foreseeable exit. The headstrong, beautiful twenty-four-year-old created her own strategy by leaving Lewis Robards and, in the process, enabled him to initiate the first step in their divorce proceedings by living with Jackson. The Donelson family later attempted to whitewash her actions by pointing to Overton's word of mouth information from the Widow Robards who had been informed by her son that he had divorced Rachel.[14]

Rachel's family insisted she and Jackson were married in Natchez by a Catholic priest. "Natchez was missionary country where priests had extraordinary powers," wrote Pauline Burke, "and if the ceremony was performed as stated the priest acted in the capacity of a civil magistrate."[15]

There were those words, civil magistrate, again.

The Robards' marriage was obviously an unhappy one, perhaps even unhealthy, but many women who found themselves in similar situation often remained with their husbands because they saw no alternative. State divorce laws, if they existed, were different. In Rachel's case, the landed gentry's social mores, which included the Donelson family, would certainly have frowned on one of their own seeking a divorce in the 1790s, even from an abusive husband such as Robards. However, some Mississippi women chose that option. Rachel spent several months in Natchez in the early 1790s and was undoubtedly aware of women receiving divorces.

In the mid-1790s, Natchez, Mississippi, resident Wilhelmina Aubaye, her clothes ripped from her body, fled from her husband Joseph as he pursued her with a drawn sword and cocked pistol, Joyce L. Broussard wrote in *Stepping Lively in Place, The Not-Married, Free Women of Civil War-Era Natchez, Mississippi*. Wilhelmina hid out with friends and began earning a living as a merchant while fearing Aubaye could attach her earnings because she was a femme covert. She petitioned the territorial legislature to dissolve her marriage. "After investigating her case and interviewing witnesses," Broussard wrote, "the legislature by a two-thirds vote granted Wilhelmina a permanent divorce in 1806, which restored her *femme sole* status and thereby prevented Joseph from legally claiming (then and forever) her assets or her body."[16]

Rachel, cosseted from many of the hardships of pioneer life, the flatboat voyage notwithstanding, flaunted those landed gentry social conventions determined to have her way and to have Andrew Jackson although she was married to another man. It is doubtful if she ever had to milk cows, grind corn into meal or preserve meat as Rebecca Boone did. The Donelsons had slaves for those chores. John Donelson had the foresight to move his family from Cumberland to Kentucky and avoided the Indian carnage he saw coming.

After the siege of Bryan Station and the Battle of Blue Licks, Kentuckians, for the most part, began to live in communities not forts and stockades.[17]

Catherine Sevier, the second wife of John Sevier, provided for her family of ten stepchildren and eight of her own while her husband was away fighting either the British or the Indians. She managed not only her household but their farm.[18]

Charlotte Robertson, who accompanied the Donelsons on their river voyage to join her husband, James Robertson, at Cumberland, remained in the fledging settlement. Charlotte endured the agony of seeing the headless body of one son killed by Indians and a second murdered. Robertson and another son were wounded in skirmishes with Indians.[19]

Rachel, due to her family's power and influence, was sheltered from most of the horrors other adult pioneer women experienced. Rachel Stockley Donelson, her mother, was held in high esteem by the community and her approval of the Jackson marriage was accepted by most Nashville/Davidson County residents. Her blockhouse was the scenes of militia meetings, community events and evening gatherings of her large family who lived nearby.[20]

In the mid-1790s, Rachel had the husband she wanted settled in a comfortable home amidst her family. There were slaves to do the heavy work but something was missing. Both Rachel and Jackson wanted children but none were forthcoming. Burke wrote of a family scene when one of Rachel sisters-in-law came to spend the day with her baby. "The ladies sat chatting while Jackson played with the baby under the trees, now stroking its curls, now kissing its hands and feet, now delighting it with that never failing source of infantile ecstasy. 'This little pig went to market, this little pig stayed home, this little pig went squeak, squeak.'[21]

"Mrs. Jackson broke into tears, sobbing, 'Oh, husband how I wish we had a child.' Returning the baby gently to its mother, he embraced her saying tenderly, 'darling, God knows that to give and what to withhold; let's not murmur against Him.'" Burke said that shortly before her death Rachel referred to that scene saying, "he would have given his life for a child; but knowing how disappointed I was at never being a mother, he, pitying me, tried to console me by saying God denies us offspring that we may help those who have larger families and no means to support them."[22]

Rachel, with no children to care for, became the plantation manager as Jackson's frequent trips took him away from home for months at a time. Certainly there was an overseer but she made the final decisions. In 1795, Jackson began operating a Nashville store in partnership with her brother Samuel. The store carried a wide range of merchandise including horse harness, books, cutlery, tools, tobacco and wines, shoes, groceries and a wide range of fabrics, trim and sewing implements. A partial listing of the Jacksons' purchases in August 1795 gave an indication of their lifestyle.[23]

Rachel chose serviceable fabrics for her clothes and décor. There was an occasional indulgent item such as silk hose, ribbons and a ladies' fan. She purchased four yards of vellum used for dress and quilt patterns; eleven and one-half yards of linen probably used for bedding, draperies or towels; five yards of corded muslin, and six yards of stripped durant, a woolen fabric. Sewing implements included a pair of scissors, seven dozen needles and two papers of pins.[24]

Rachel, even with Jackson traveling, had little time to do the sewing herself. She either engaged the assistance of a seamstress or had a slave to do most of the work.

A year earlier, Jackson began a land speculation partnership with John Overton. In the spring of 1795, Jackson went to Philadelphia to sell land and purchase merchandise for the store and items for their Poplar Grove home.[25]

Traveling by stagecoach, he made the 1,100-mile trip to Philadelphia in three to four weeks.[26] He was there for more than a month. With another month of return traveling time, Jackson was away from Poplar Grove for more than three months. During this time, Rachel not only was overseeing work on the plantation during the planting season but other facets of their businesses.

Wives overseeing their husbands' business was not unusual, since men were often away at war, surveying or hunting. Martha Dandridge Custis ran her late husband's five plantations and corresponded with the English factor handling their tobacco crops before marrying George Washington in 1759.[27]

"In the south, women who ran plantations in their husbands' absences were not that uncommon," Maxine L. Margolis wrote in *Mothers and Such: Views of American Women and Why They Changed*. "A study of test cases showed that women during the colonial period had intimate knowledge of their husbands' businesses."[28]

On September 17, 1799, while Jackson was in Knoxville presiding as judge of the Tennessee Superior Court, he wrote Rachel that he had received her letter written two weeks earlier where she informed him the carpenters were busy working but that she was not well. "One thing I do request of you, not to fatigue yourself. Let the business stop rather than you should either fatigue yourself or fret yourself. Recollect my love how precious health is and how carefully we ought to be to acquire it."[29]

Jackson's letter clearly indicated Rachel's involvement in their business enterprises. Among her responsibilities were making sure their cotton, and that of their customers, was ginned, baled and ready for shipment; wheat and corn were grounded into flour and meal; meat was cured, and money was collected from their debtors. Rachel was the medical caretaker not only on the plantation but also tended to neighbors' maladies.[30]

Rachel's correspondence confirmed her involvement in supervising their plantation. In a letter to Latitia D. Chambers on February 24, 1824, she bragged, "We have the finest crop of cotton, corn and potatoes I ever saw and all the country round as far as I have heard." At that time Jackson have been absent from home for seven months, which Rachel complained about in her letter.[31]

Jackson's 1795 business trip to Philadelphia almost bankrupted them. Jackson made the trip to sell land he and John Overton owned and to purchase supplies for the Nashville store. Overton warned Jackson, before he left Nashville, not take any notes for the sale of the land. While in Philadelphia, he met David Allison, a land speculator with connections to William Blount. Ignoring Overton's advice, Jackson sold Allison 50,000 acres of land he and Overton owned and 18,000 acres owned by Joel Rice and accepted the buyer's notes.[32]

Jackson used Allison notes to pay for merchandise and supplies he purchased from Meeker, Cochran and Company and John B. Evans and Company. The cost to ship Jackson's purchases to Limestone, Kentucky, by boat, where Samuel Donelson awaited, was $645.[33] The shipment must have been considerable since $645 in 1795 money translated to an economic value of $433,000 in 2017.[34]

There were gifts for Rachel within those purchases. Marsha Mullin, The Hermitage's curator, said there are several pieces of silver from Philadelphia that date to the 1790s. "There are no receipts or documents to prove that is when Jackson acquired them," she said. "But it suggests he brought those things home to Rachel."[35]

On one of his trips to Philadelphia, Jackson purchased a settee and perhaps other furnishings for his wife.[36]

Jackson brought something else home to Rachel, a debt that would almost wreck their livelihood and his anticipated political career. David Allison defaulted on the $40,500 in notes (three notes of $13,500 each) he gave Jackson in payment for the 68,000 acres of land. Jackson used the notes to pay for his Philadelphia purchases and was surprised to learn from Meeker, Cochran & Company in August 1795 and from John B. Evans & Company in January 1796 the notes were not acceptable.[37]

"We take this early opportunity to make known to you that we have little or no expectations of getting paid from him [Allison] and we shall have to get our money from you." John B. Evans & Company wrote five months later, "we think it but right to inform you that our friend David Allison's affairs having for some time past been much damaged he has been under the necessity of letting his notes lay over, his note therefore that we received from you for the goods which is due on the 13th of next month in all probability will not be paid by him we therefore request you will make provision for same."[38]

Suddenly, the Jacksons were faced with a $40,500 debt they had no cash to pay. In 2017 dollars, that $40,500 had the economic power of $1.18 billion.[39] Jackson began selling and/or swapping land, sold his store to Elijah Robertson, James Robertson's brother, sought assistance from John Overton and William Blount, gave up his law practice for the salary of judge of the Superior Court and eventually sold Poplar Grove. Allison was thrown into debtor's prison in Philadelphia and died there in September 1798.[40]

Jackson bought Hunter's Hill from John Shannon of Logan County, Kentucky, in March 1796 for $700. The 640-acre property was originally owned by Lewis Robards. "The fine house at Hunter's Hill," Marquis James wrote, "stood high commanding a view of the beautiful river where Jackson had his store, his private landing and a ferry."[41]

From 1795 to 1797, Jackson was seldom at home. There was another trip to Philadelphia and elections to the House of Representatives and the United States Senate.[42]

Rachel Jackson had no choice but to keep the Jackson's ever-changing plantations and various businesses going while her husband was away to keep them solvent. She probably had advice from the Donelson men and Overton but day-to-day decisions fell on her. Rachel's lot was like many other women after the Revolutionary War when the nation began to recognize women made their own contributions to the nation's struggle. "I expect to see our young women forming a new era in female history," women's rights advocate Judith Sargent Murray was quoted as saying in 1798. She was talking about women exercising their newfound intellectual strengths and capabilities.[43]

Rachel appeared to be out of her comfort zone in such a demanding position and complained to her husband. In May 1796, Jackson wrote her from Knoxville while they were still living at Poplar Grove, attempting to assuage her situation. "Tho, I am absent," he wrote, "my heart rests with you. With what pleasing hopes I view the future period when I shall be restored to your arms there to spend my days in domestic sweetness with you the dear companion of my life, never to be separated from you again during this transitory and fluctuating life."[44]

Then, Jackson made her a promise that he would break repeatedly. "I mean to retire from public life and spend my time with you along in sweet retirement, which is my only ambition and ultimate wish." He went on to write, "Could I only know you were contented and enjoyed peace of mind what satisfaction it would afford me whilst traveling the lonely and tiresome road. I would relieve my anxious breast and shorten the way—may the great 'I Am' bless and protect you until that happy and wished for moment arrives when I restored to your sweet embrace which is the nightly prayer of your affectionate husband."[45]

Rachel was not contented and her situation worsened. Jackson heaped more responsibility on his wife by building two distilleries. Normally a distillery was a profitable enterprise but an excise tax, which was confusing to most small distillers, was levied in 1791 by Washington and his Secretary of the Treasury Alexander Hamilton on distilleries. The tax was to pay for the states' Revolutionary War debts which the federal government had assumed.[46]

Marquis James, one of Jackson's early biographers, wrote that Rachel's comfort zone, aside from having her husband at home, involved her large family of siblings, nieces and nephews and long-standing friends like the Robertsons, the Manskers and the Overtons, who gathered to socialize at her mother's blockhouse.[47]

Rachel's comfort zone was further disrupted when her brother Stockley became involved in one of the biggest land fraud scandals of the new nation and its exposure was perpetuated by her own husband, whose intent was to wound a political rival, John Sevier.

While the rest of the Donelson family was on their river trip to Cumberland in 1780, Stockley Donelson was busy surveying and buying land.[48] The Glasgow Land Fraud, which occurred from 1783 to 1800, involved public officials, land speculators and surveyors forging Revolutionary War veterans' bounty grants for land in Tennessee. During that period, it resulted in 3,723 warrants being issued for 2,798,224 acres in what is now Tennessee. "Martin Armstrong, the entry taker for the Mero District [Nashville] land office, and Stockley Donelson, who was responsible for surveying the land designated for bounty land grants, invited North Carolina Secretary of State James Glasgow to partner with them in buying military land warrants for the purpose of reselling them," Jason E. Farr wrote in his 2010 University of Virginia master's thesis.[49] "Armstrong and Donelson insisted their scheme was legitimate but told Secretary Glasgow that they should nevertheless 'keep matters secret nor the right hand should know what the left hand is doing.'"[50]

The more prominent names involved included Glasgow, his two sons-in-law Willoughby Williams and Stockley Donelson and the Blount brothers—William, John Gray and Thomas. Charles R. Holloman, in the *North Carolina Encyclopedia*, described Stockley Donelson as being "certainly the most active, charming, accommodating, cunning and indefatigable practitioner of fraud and deceit to be found in state service."[51]

"He was barely twenty-one years old when appointed by the General Assembly in October 1783 (through the influence of the Blount family) as a field surveyor under the Armstrong office," Holloman continued. "Within ten years he [Stockley] had accumulated more than 200,000 acres of western and eastern lands of North Carolina (including the area that became Tennessee). In April 1787, he procured, by what later was perceived to be fraud and deceit, a marriage with Elizabeth Glasgow Martin, the very wealthy widowed daughter of Secretary Glasgow and the mother of two small sons by her deceased husband, John Martin, of Snow Hill, Md., and Snow Hill, N.C. James Glasgow became Donelson's adversary at the time he was trustee for his daughter's prenuptial deed of marriage agreement."[52]

Rachel's new sister-in-law Elizabeth Martin Donelson, like herself, suffered from the lack of protection for married women's property rights. That she was a femme sole hardly mattered. The difference was that Elizabeth Glasgow Donelson did not have an Andrew Jackson to run interference for her.

Stockley Donelson and William Terrell, a clerk in the secretary of state's office, were indicted in North Carolina but escaped into Tennessee whose legislature refused to return them. Also indicted and apprehended for land fraud were William Glasgow, John Gray and Thomas Blunt, John Bonds, a Nash County, North Carolina, legislator and Wynn Dixon, a Caswell County land speculator.[53]

The two Blount brothers walked but their political careers were over. Glasgow was stripped of his office, found guilty of fraud and fined £1,000. Williams was fined £500 and Bonds £100. Armstrong, kicked out of the land office, kept his 200,000 acres of land and Tennessee made him surveyor general. Stockley Donelson managed to salvage 562,000 acres of land from the fraud and kept his position as surveyor due to the Blount brothers' influence.[54]

Jackson's whistleblower role came when Charles Love from Salisbury, North Carolina, told him of a conversation he overheard while lodging at the home of William Terrell Lewis in Nashville. Lewis was William Terrell's nephew. Jackson, despite promising Rachel he would settle down and clear their debts, was elected to the U.S. Senate in 1797, and was en route to Philadelphia when he met Love. He immediately saw a connection between Glasgow and John Sevier he could promote to his advantage. When Jackson arrived in Philadelphia in December 1797, he relayed Love's information to North Carolina Congressman Alexander Martin, who requested the senator to put the particulars in a letter to Governor Samuel Ashe of North Carolina.[55] The land fraud dominos fell but John Sevier essentially escaped despite having an advisory relationship with Glasgow about how to scalp loyalists, those who supported the British during the Revolutionary War, of their confiscated lands.[56]

Farr saw Jackson's statement to Governor Ashe, where he repeated Love's narrative of William Terrell and William Terrell Lewis plying Major John Nelson with alcoholic beverages to obtain his signature on 500 blank military land warrants, as accelerating his political career.[57]

"When you set a bear trap, you never can tell what particular bear is going to blunder into it," John Finger quoted Jackson as saying.[58]

In a letter to Rachel six weeks after his report to Governor Ashe, Jackson made no mention of the land fraud matter. He expressed concern about her health and was disappointed that his Nashville friends had not kept him informed about her. Despite his concern, Jackson asked Rachel to attend to the receipt he sent her. "I hope Mr. Hammonds does everything to make you comfortable; it was my only and last charge and if he does this I will amply reward him," Jackson wrote. Eli Hammond, a federal tax collector and later a Davidson County justice of the peace, obviously had some distilling experience.[59]

However, it was not in his job description to make Rachel feel comfortable with their distilling operations.

The Jackson distilleries were in operation only a few years. In 1799, there were sixty-one distilleries for the 4,000 residents of Davidson County according to John Overton, who President George Washington appointed supervisor of revenue for the District of Tennessee, Territory South of the Ohio River.[60]

Congress's excise tax on whiskey, instituted in 1791, was retired after Thomas Jefferson was elected president. However, a complicated tax structure remained that often confused smaller distilleries. The tax on a distillery with a capacity of less than 400 gallons could be figured at varying rates: fifty-six cents per gallon for each month the still operated; seven cents for each gallon produced, or ten cents per gallon of capacity for each month the still was active.[61]

In June 1796, Washington elevated Overton to the position of district inspector of the revenue, a position he held at the time of Jackson's letter to Rachel on January 26, 1798.[62]

Jackson indeed took care of advancing Hammond's career according to a letter John Sevier wrote him on March 27, 1799. "Be assumed that I shall take the earliest opportunity in recommending Mr. Eli Hammond to the Secretary of War and shall also name him in a particular manner to the Secretary of State and the Commander in Chief and under these considerations, I shall have no doubt of success."[63]

There was extensive correspondence between Jackson and Sevier during 1798–99, despite the land fraud scandal.[64]

Overton, however, was unhappy with his pay as supervisor of revenue for the Tennessee district south of the Ohio River. On February 3, 1798, Jackson wrote Overton addressing a requested raise in his salary. He explained the president could not raise the salary of one without altering the rules throughout. "But, sir, you can by a strict construction of the law make your salary much better than it is at present—*agreeable to the construction of the comptroller*, I expect you are furnished with a copy of the executive rules or law on this subject—and when I have the pleasure of seeing you will give you this construction." Jackson said Overton, as a result of such actions, would not be relieved of his job unless Congress interfered, which he doubted.[65]

In December 1802, the Jacksons' distilleries and their taxes became a mute issue. Both stills—one had a capacity of 127 gallons and the other 70 gallons—burned, destroying not only the equipment but more than 300 gallons of whiskey.[66]

Although Jackson left his Senate seat in 1798, he was not destined for the domestic life Rachel wanted. In December of that year he was elected judge of the Tennessee Superior Court, which meant he had to travel a court circuit.[67]

His letters to Rachel again demonstrated his dependence on her to supervise the plantation. In a letter on March 22, 1803, he asked Rachel to have their overseer, Henry Gowyer, plant the cotton between April 15 and 25. "I hope it has been in his power to make your time more agreeable with the Servants," he wrote. "I also hope that he has brought Aston to a perfect state of obedience."[68]

Her husband remonstrated that he had not heard from Rachel since he left home. "I hope you have enjoyed and are now enjoying health—and may health and happiness surround you until I have the pleasure of seeing you is the sincere wish of your affectionate husband."[69]

Finally, it was Rachel's turn to travel and leave behind the supervision of their plantation and businesses. In the summer of 1800, Jackson took his wife and her niece Rachel Hays for a month-long vacation at the Warm Springs Spa in Bath County, Virginia. For his service in the French and Indian War, Colonel George Washington awarded Captain Thomas Bullitt with a land grant of 300 acres which contained seven mineral springs. Bullitt opened an eighteen room wooden hotel, the Homestead, there in 1764. The Jacksons, however, stayed in a cabin at nearby Warm Springs, which opened the first gentlemen's bathhouse in 1761.[70]

Their cabin was not furnished when they arrived and where they spent the night is not known. The next day, the cabin was outfitted for their comfort and they were furnished with food to cook. Apparently, both Jacksons partook of the springs as he mentioned refreshing showers they enjoyed. Jackson's description of the springs, while graphic, left much to be desired. "The springs," he wrote Robert Hays, "are situated between two lofty mountains where Providence has scooped out a valley to convey the water of the river and where the wind cannot blow."[71]

A spring whose water flow was warmer than 100°F was classified as a hot spring. If the temperature was lower than that it was a warm spring. To reach these surface temperatures, water would have to begin to circulate at a depth of 26,000 feet or almost five miles below ground.[72]

Rachel spent so much time in the spa's springs that when they began to cross the mountain she was unable to ride in the carriage and got on a horse and rode during a rainstorm. "Just being from a warm bath," Jackson said, "gave her a violent cold. She has got over it but its elects as yet remains."[73]

Despite his deep involvement in the Glasgow Land Fraud, Rachel gave the sanctuary of Hunter's Hill to her brother Stockley in March 1801, when he was avoiding North Carolina litigation. He was grateful to both the Jacksons for what he called their unbounded friendship. His letter to Jackson made no mention that his wife and stepsons were not with him.[74] They separated in 1803 but reconciled before Stockley died in 1805.[75]

Elizabeth Glasgow Donelson, despite Rachel's sympathy and support, was not treated kindly by some in the Donelson family who objected to her moving to Nashville. "If you only heard half the ill-natured things which I have heard of Col. Donelson's family saying of me you would not blame me for not wanting to be in the way," she told Jackson in a letter on January 2, 1802, regarding his offer to help the couple.[76]

After his 1798 trial, James Glasgow loaded his twenty-two slaves, possessions and family members—including several unmarried daughters—into an extensive wagon train and headed for what is now Roane County, Tennessee. William Willoughby, who was married to Nancy Glasgow and was also found guilty in the scandal, died while they were encamped at Dandridge. When he left North Carolina, Glasgow owned the 3,000-acre Nahunta plantation. In 1810, Glasgow was living on a plantation seven miles from Nashville.[77]

Glasgow was far from poor. From 1781 to 1793, he entered 43,340 acres in Tennessee land records which included 8,740 acres in Davidson County. Some of the land he owned with others was located in Sumner, Washington, Sullivan and Hawkins counties.[78]

While Rachel extended the hand of friendship to Elizabeth Glasgow Donelson, other members of her family wanted nothing to do with the Glasgows. That changed with the third generation of Donelsons. Once settled near Nashville, the unmarried Glasgow daughters made some advantageous but not necessary happy marriages. Phereby Sheppard Glasgow married Robert Whyte, who was appointed to the Tennessee Supreme Court of Errors and Appeals by Governor Joseph McMinn in 1816. Their daughter Elizabeth married Lemuel Donelson, a son of John Donelson and Mary Purnell Donelson. Lemuel's sister Catherine married James Glasgow Martin, one of the sons from Elizabeth Glasgow Donelson's first marriage.[79]

Nancy Glasgow Willoughby left her widow weeds to marry Governor McMinn in 1815. She later accused her husband of leaving her alone for weeks at a time while he chose to live with an Indian tribe. McMinn petitioned the Tennessee House of Representatives for a divorce. Nancy retaliated by hiring the immensely successful attorney Felix Grundy to represent her. It was said Grundy could stand on a street corner and talk the cobblestones into life. The legislature voted 20–19 to deny McMinn his divorce. Nancy lived in fashion in Nashville while her husband lived on his farm near Cleveland.[80]

While the Glasgows were settling in and around Nashville, Jackson's harbored resentments against John Sevier for the land fraud scandal boiled over in 1803 in Knoxville, then the state capital. Governor Sevier was speaking of his public service to the state and, according to biographer Marquis James, Jackson interrupted, citing his own record of service. "Service?" Sevier asked. "I know of no great service you rendered the country except taking a trip to Natchez with another man's wife." Jackson lunged at Sevier with his cane shouting, "Great God, do you mention her sacred name?" The crowd separated them with Jackson challenging Sevier to a duel. Sevier, nearly two decades older than Jackson, pleaded his advanced age, pressing state business, his proven courage on the battlefield and his family's likely poverty if he were killed. None of those pleas were recognized in the Code Duello.[81]

Jackson ignored Sevier's excuses. Rachel's honor had to be avenged.

The next day, Jackson wrote Sevier, who was in no hurry to engage in the duel, a colorful letter. "The ungentlemanly expressions and gasconading conduct of you relative to me on yesterday was in true character of yourself and unmasked you to the world. I request and interview and my friend who will hand this will point out the time and the place where you and I shall expect to see you with your friend and no other persons. My friend and myself will be armed with pistols. You cannot mistake me or my meaning."[82]

When the governor continued to disregard the challenge, Jackson wrote a newspaper article calling him a coward and poltroon. What followed between the two men matched the folly a few years later of Henry Clay and Humphrey Marshall dueling over whether members of the Kentucky legislature should be prohibited from wearing clothes manufactured by the British as opposed to homespun apparel. The two men had three chances at each other. Clay's pistol misfired twice but his first fire grazed his opponent's stomach. Marshall missed Clay twice and finally shot him in the thigh. Clay wanted a fourth chance but their seconds agreed enough was enough.[83]

Stockley Donelson Hays, Rachel's nephew, wrote Jackson from Lexington about the Clay-Marshall duel, saying it was observed by 3,000 spectators, which was unlikely. He described the duel as being "a circumstance pregnant with curiosity." Jackson had instructed Hays to inquire of Clay about a legal fee.[84]

After a lengthy delay, Jackson and Sevier finally met at Southwest Point near present day Kingston in October 1803. Jackson and his second, Dr. Thomas Carlyle, waited five days for Sevier to appear. He arrived with a band of armed men. After the men drew their pistols, an attempt was made to settle the dispute. Sevier put his pistol in his saddle bag. Both men began loudly berating each other. Sevier's horse, spooked by the shouting, ran away with the governor's pistol. Jackson still had his pistol. Sevier hid behind a tree daring Jackson to shoot an unarmed man. Their seconds defused the situation but both men left the dueling grounds still shouting at each other.[85]

Rachel was aware of Jackson's intent to force Sevier into a duel over what he considered a public impugning of her character. Rachel begged her husband to come home. From all indications, Jackson was too busy attempting to force Sevier to meet him on the field of honor to keep her informed of his actions. Finally, Rachel received word from her nephew, Jack Hutchings, that Jackson was well and all was quiet on the Sevier front. Jackson wrote her that he would like nothing better than to "Return to your arms to dispel those clouds that hover over you [but] the questions occurs would it bring contentment to my love or might it not involve us in all the calamity of poverty—an event that brings horror to my mind."[86]

Jackson was doing all he could to stave off that poverty. From 1801 to 1803, while serving as a judge and major general of the militia, his business in buying and selling land involved 36,553 acres of land changing hands. During that period, he sold 15,307 acres of land in nine Tennessee counties and purchased 21,246 acres.[87]

He was ready to leave his judgeship and the military if he could be appointed governor of the Louisiana Territory after President Thomas Jefferson's purchase in 1803. That appointment went to Virginia-born William C. C. Claiborne, who replaced Jackson in Congress.

8

The Hermitage Begins
and Children Cometh

Jackson was forced to sell Hunter's Hill to Edward Ward in July 1804 for $10,000. He had paid $700 for the property in 1796. In August, he purchased 425 acres with a log farmhouse from Nathaniel Hays for $3,400. The property was originally called Rural Retreat.[1]

Jackson's selection of The Hermitage as the name of their plantation and home could have originated from his early days in Bayou Pierre, in Claiborne County, Mississippi. One of the Hermitages there, built by George W. Humphreys, was one and a half story house with a broad front gallery and wide central hall. Jackson was said to have visited there while living in Bayou Pierre. Humphreys' son Benjamin was at West Point in the mid-1820s when some of Jackson's wards were there. The other Hermitage, built by William McCaleb across from Bayou Pierre, was also one and a half stories with a wide front gallery.[2] Perhaps, Rachel had a glimpse of the houses during her short time in Bayou Pierre.

The Jacksons' first Hermitage bore little resemblance to the Mississippi homes.

Hays, a skilled craftsman, built the farmhouse from tulip popular, oak and red oak. The foundation and the chimney were constructed of blue limestone. The building's dimensions were 24 by 26 feet. The first floor consisted on one large room with a corner staircase; the second two bedrooms and stairs to the attic. Before they moved from Hunter's Hill, Jackson hired a local French craftsman to spruce up the first floor's interior with French wallpaper and painted trim. About 40 feet from the farmhouse was another log building, a thirty by eighteen foot kitchen and slave quarters with large chimneys at each end. Later outbuildings included guest cabins. The Jacksons lived in the farmhouse until 1819.[3]

Rachel had to downsize from the commodious Hunter's Hill to basically a three-room house. It would be interesting to know how she used family

The Albert Ward watercolor drawing of the first Hermitage, where the Jacksons lived from 1804 to 1821. It was basically a three-room log house with an attic. The exterior kitchen was built in 1808. After the Jacksons moved out it was used as slave quarters (Andrew Jackson's Hermitage, Nashville, TN).

pieces she inherited, the furniture Jackson had purchased in Philadelphia and possibly the Donelson mirror in the one large first floor room. "In the middle of the room," Patricia Brady wrote, "was a long dining table, which could easily seat twelve to fourteen people. At Andrew's request, it was always set, ready to entertain their many guests at a moment's notice."[4]

The Jacksons' hospitality was not confined to guests; it extended to children who had lost one or both parents and to those in need of a guardian. Rachel had grown up in a large family with ten siblings and deeply felt the inability to have a child of her own. She lavished love and care on her nieces and nephews. Jackson's father died before he was born in 1767, and his brothers, Hugh and Robert, died during the Revolutionary War. He lost his mother to disease in 1781, lived with relatives for a short while. He found a real family, in all aspects, when he bonded with the Donelsons.[5]

Had there been one or two instances of Jackson's wards, or their spouses, becoming associated with him in the military or in politics nobody would have noticed. However, it occurred so often that what might have been coincidences turned into a bold pattern where the recipients, either with gentle prodding or an outright push, yielded to the benefactors wishes and requests.

Not all the Jacksons wards lived at The Hermitage. Samuel Hays, who

There were two natural springs on the Hermitage property when Andrew Jackson purchased it in 1804. He later built the limestone springhouse to prevent contamination of their drinking water supply. The springhouse also kept food products cool. Water was carried in pails from there to the mansion for cooking, bathing and other uses (Andrew Jackson's Hermitage, Nashville, TN).

had a trading station on Stones River, was killed by Indians in 1793 outside William Donelson's house. He left four children—Andrew, Campbell, Charles and Hugh Hays. Jackson was appointed their special guardian controlling their estate but the children continued to live with their mother Elizabeth Hays.[6]

In 1803, Jackson's close friend Edward Butler who lived in Robertson County died, leaving four children—Edward G. W., Anthony Wayne, Caroline and Eliza. Their mother, Isabella Fowler Butler, was the daughter of Captain George Fowler who fought against the Americans at Bunker Hill. She knew of the close relationship between her husband and Jackson and wrote him a poignant letter:

> You have no doubt heard of, & felt for the loss, myself & little family have sustained by the death of the *best of husbands* & of fathers. It has pleased Providence when, I thought I was at the summit of happiness to deprive me of what I held most Dear in this life by taking *my much loved Edward* when he had determined to sit down in retirement with his little family & after sparing him many times in the field of battle. It now becomes necessary for me to double my attention to those that were dear to him. In doing so, I must beg your assistance. My dear children want a guardian & you are their choice & my own. I fear a confidence you will comply with our wishes, if it

is consistent with your other duties. Carolina and Eliza join me in affection regard to your worthy companion. Accept their & my best wishes for both your happiness.[7]

Anthony Butler was born the year his father died and Edward was three years older. Although Jackson was the Butler children's legal guardian, some questioned if the Butler boys lived with the Jacksons. According to Burke, they did. The Hermitage's curator, Marsha Mullin, agreed and confirmed receipts indicated they were there in 1814 and 1815.[8]

Not only did Rachel and Jackson raise the Butler boys, they educated them. Jackson had an agreement with Colonel Richard Butler to pay for Anthony's education and he would do the same for Edward. Anthony wanted to go to Princeton but Jackson suggested Yale and that was where he went. Jackson arranged for Edward's appointment to West Point. Although Anthony received $750 dollars per year from his cousin (in 2017 the relative value of that figure was $18,100), Jackson allowed him access to his account. Anthony abused his generosity while Edward apologized for having to request funds.[9]

Jackson finally had to refuse Anthony Butler's request for funds. He said his fund were exhausted from helping both Butlers, Samuel Jackson Hays, Daniel Smith Donelson and Andrew Jackson Donelson.[10]

Edward Butler had a stellar career in the U.S. Army, married a grand-niece of George Washington, resigned his commission in 1831, and became the owner a profitable sugar cane plantation, Dunboyne, in Bayou Goula, Louisiana. The Civil War ruined his business and Butler and his wife moved into a rental cottage in Pass Christian, Mississippi, owned by his daughter's father-in-law, Edward J. Gay.[11]

Anthony Butler, a Phi Beta Kappa at Yale, lived beyond his means demanding loans from friends, chased the ladies, wrote poetry and planned to be a lawyer if he could find someone to pay for his law school education. At only twenty-one-years of age, he became ill aboard *The Virginia* on a trip from New Orleans to New York and died in 1824.[12]

Rachel had a maternal instinct and loved children but how she reacted to Jackson paying for their wards' education was not known. The more money he spent the harder she had to work managing their plantation and other businesses when he was away.

There was a bedroom for the two Butler boys but sleeping arrangements became complicated when Rachel's favorite brother, Samuel, died in December 1804. Samuel and Mary "Polly" Smith Donelson, whose elopement Jackson assisted with, lived on Drake's Creek across the Cumberland River about three miles from the Jacksons. Her father, Daniel Smith, a large landowner and a U.S. senator, also lived on Drake's Creek. Samuel was the brother who cared enough for Rachel to deliver her from Robards' abuses and bring her back home to Cumberland. That winter he had been visiting the Jacksons and, after snow began falling, attempted to return home. He caught pneumonia and on his deathbed asked Jackson to take care of his three sons: John Samuel, age six; Andrew Jackson, age five; and Daniel Smith, age three. Samuel Donelson, like other members of his family, was on his way to being a large landowner—1,174 acres in Sumner and Davidson counties. He was a lawyer with a bright future but he would leave no will.[13]

Polly lost little time after Samuel's death in accepting the attentions of James "Jimmy Dry" Sanders, from Sumner County, a wealthy planter friend of her father. The older boys, John and Andrew, deeply resented their mother's second marriage in February 1806. Polly defended her actions by saying her father advised the marriage since he deemed it best for she and her sons.[14]

Jackson hired tutors for Samuel Donelson's sons and he and Rachel raised them in their home according to Rachel Meredith in her 2013 Middle Tennessee State University thesis, *There Was Somebody Always Dying and Leaving Jackson as Guardian: The Wards of Andrew Jackson.* John Samuel served under Jackson in the Creek War, became a surveyor and died in 1817 while surveying land in Alabama.[15]

Later, Sanders refused to allow Polly to give her sons the land Daniel Smith left them in his will. He claimed the land was his and it actually was. With Jackson's assistance, John and Andrew took legal action against Sanders. Both sides agreed to have two local lawyers, William L. Smith and Henry Crabb, arbitrate the issue. The attorneys not only ruled in favor of the Donelson brothers but did something rather unusual in the 1820s. Smith and Crabb gave Polly Donelson Sanders sole control over her will "without the consent and cooperation of her husband."[16]

Jackson sent Andrew Jackson Donelson to Cumberland College in Nashville, the United States Military Academy at West Point and to law school at Transylvania College in Lexington, Kentucky. Donelson married his first cousin, Emily Tennessee Donelson, daughter of Rachel's brother John and Mary Purnell Donelson. AJD, as he was called, was Jackson's aide-de-camp during the Seminole campaign, served as his private secretary during most of his two presidential administrations except for the time he and Emily spent in exile in Tennessee for their failure to socially accept Margaret Timberlake Eaton, wife of Jackson's Secretary of War John H. Eaton. AJD spent nearly twenty years serving Jackson in some capacity. He was listed as the owner of the Thoroughbred horses Andrew Jackson raced in Washington, DC, and in Maryland while president.[17]

Like a number of third generation Donelsons, AJD was not a good financial manager. "His plantations never turned the profit he predicted," Mark Cheatham wrote in his biography of AJD, "an outcome he blamed on every conceivable reason except his own financial ineptitudes and an ignorance of farming. Donelson not only borrowed money from family, friends and politicians to maintain his plantations [in Tennessee, Mississippi and Arkansas] but also avoided repaying the loans, repeatedly ignoring requests for repayment until he had exhausted his creditors' patience."[18]

Daniel Smith Donelson also graduated from West Point but resigned his commission a year later in 1825. He married Margaret Branch, daughter of Jackson's first Secretary of the Navy John Branch, a former North Carolina governor and U.S. senator. Branch left the Jackson administration over the Eaton affair. Donelson developed a Florida plantation but returned to Tennessee and served three terms in the Tennessee General Assembly and was a brigadier general in the militia for five years.[19]

Daniel Smith Donelson achieved more financial success than his brothers.[20]

Rachel must have experienced pride for her part in raising Samuel Donelson's sons. She considered herself their second mother.[21]

Edward Butler's brother Thomas who also lived in Robertson County, was in Jackson's circle of friends. When he died in 1805, Jackson became the legal guardian of his children—Thomas Jr., Robert, Lydia and William. Thomas Jr., was already practicing law and married Rachel's niece Rachel Hays, daughter of Robert and Jane Donelson Hays. Two of Robert's siblings, Lydia and William, married a brother and sister of Rachel Hays, Stockley Donelson Hays and Martha Hays. Robert was later Jackson's adjutant general during the War of 1812.[22]

Rachel Meredith wrote that being a child's guardian was a time-consuming effort both financially and emotionally. Sometimes years were involved in the business arrangements of settling an estate. "In addition to the duties of paying off the debts of their ward's estate," Meredith wrote, "a guardian was also required to appear before the courts annually to present an account of a ward's estate and an annual orphan's court was held at the beginning of the year for this purpose. Records of Jackson giving an annual account seem to be nonexistent."[23]

She had slaves to help but undoubtedly Rachel was the person the children looked to for love, care, and adjudicating their conflicts. There were clothes to make, shoes to buy, ponies to ride and a number of other requirements the boys needed that Rachel and Jackson were unaccustomed to providing.

Rachel had time to devote to the boys because Jackson was home more attending to their business affairs. Part of her time was devoted to entertaining visiting politicians such as former vice president Aaron Burr in 1805, as well as their own friends and neighbors. When Burr returned to Nashville in 1806, he was accorded a cool reception from Rachel and he found lodging at the Clover Bottom tavern and a home in Nashville.[24]

The Jackson's wards and children who needed a home were always welcome at The Hermitage. Jane Gillespie Hays lived there before her father sold the house and land to Jackson. After the death of Jane's parents, Nathaniel and Elizabeth, Rachel and Jackson offered to care for her.[25]

When the Jackson's neighbors Jacob and Sally Lloyd Watkins died in 1806, they left six children. Rachel and Jackson took in two of them, Margaret and Jane. Other neighbors stepped up and raised the other children. In 1814, Margaret was still living at The Hermitage where she helped Rachel entertain visitors and assisted her with various chores. When she married John Allen, who had a store on Stones River, Rachel gave her a cow and a bedstead. Jane Watkins' stay with the Jackson appeared to be lost in time.[26]

When William Terrell Lewis, an owner of vast Tennessee lands and former North Carolina legislator, died in 1813, he placed his daughters, Margaret and Myra, under Jackson's care but not his sons, Kinchen and Jesse. The girls both married the same year. Margaret married her cousin William Berkley Lewis, who was Jackson's quartermaster in the War of 1812. Their daughter Mary Anne spent some time at The Hermitage and was a favorite of Rachel's. She later married Alphonse Pageot, a French diplomat, in a President's House ceremony arranged by Jackson. Lewis remained a lifelong supporter of Jackson. Myra married John Henry Eaton who came to Williamson County from North Carolina in 1809 to practice law and develop land owned by his father. Marrying a Jackson ward smoothed Eaton's entry into politics where he was a Tennessee legislator in 1815 and '16, and U.S. senator from 1818 to 1829. Myra Eaton died two years after their wedding and her husband remained a widower until his 1829 marriage to Margaret O'Neal Timberlake, a Washington innkeeper's daughter deemed unacceptable by Washington society. Jackson's efforts to force Mrs. Eaton's social acceptance upon his cabinet and administration sent his President's House hostess Emily Donelson back to Tennessee, broke up his cabinet and resulted in Eaton's losing his U.S. Senate seat.[27]

The oldest Lewis daughter, Sarah, married Thomas A. Claibourne, a Virginia physician who settled in Nashville. They had three children—William Ferdinand, Mary Lewis and William Lewis Claibourne. Jackson's guardianship of William was not officially confirmed but Meredith pointed out legal records exist indicating he was William's guardian.[28]

When Jackson drew up the 1817 will of Rachel's nephew John Hutchings, he had no idea of the problems five-year-old Andrew Jackson Hutchings would eventually create for him. John Hutchings was the son of Rachel's sister Catherine Donelson and Thomas Hutchings. John Coffee, Jackson's close friend whose Hickory Hill plantation was near Florence, Alabama, was an executor of the will. He agreed to supervise the Hutchings plantation near Huntsville, Alabama, for the young boy. Thomas Hutchings, Jackson and Coffee were once partners in a mercantile business at Clover Bottom. Rachel signed as a witness to the will Jackson drew up and the young boy came to live with them at The Hermitage.[29]

Andrew Jackson Hutchings had a loathing for education. He was kicked out of the University of Nashville for throwing a chair at a professor. Jackson arranged for him to study with private tutors without success and eventually became so frustrated he only communicated with his ward through his brother-in-law William Donelson. Donelson asked Hutchings what he expected to do with his life. "I want to be a damn rich old farmer like the rest of my kin folks," he replied.[30]

Jackson also wrote his good friend John Coffee and asked him to check on Hutchings' problem with education. "He is an orphan," Jackson wrote, "and, although strong headed and ungovernable boy, I have his good name and prosperity at heart. I am fearful to leave him without some person to control and counsel him and I am happy I did not bring him with me as here [Washington, D.C.] he would have been ruined. I must send Samuel Hays from here and, when I can find a good place, my son also. They must be separated or both ruined by idleness."[31]

Hutchings married Coffee's daughter Mary.[32]

Another of Jackson's wards, Samuel Jackson Hays, gave him as much trouble as John Hutchings but with a different outcome. Hays was the son of Rachel's sister Jane and Robert Hays. Hays, who died in 1819, experienced financial hardship and Jackson basically supported the family for years. Their daughters Rachel and Narrcisa spent time at The Hermitage and often traveled with Rachel.[33]

Like Hutchings, young Hays preferred idleness, frolic and chasing women to going to school.[34] Hays, at some point, gave up his gay blade ways and became a lawyer. Despite all the trouble he caused his guardian, Jackson shaded the facts a bit when he replied to inquiry of James Hamilton, Jr., guardian of Frances Pinckney Middleton, about Hays' worth as a husband. "I assure you," Jackson wrote, "that Mr. Hays is a young man of unblemished character and good morals and that his family is respectable. His father once had a fortune but like many others died insolvent. His mother, one of the most amiable of her sex, has by her industry and prudent management obtained an independence and lives comfortably on a farm in west Tennessee which she owns. So you will perceive her son is not a man of fortune being independent upon his profession as a lawyer and the share he will have in his mother's estate. I have taken some pains with his education in aid of his amiable mother and trust that it will secure success in his profession." Jackson added that he hoped Hays had already informed the young lady of his financial status. Frances Pinckney Middleton had impressive relatives of her own. She was the niece of Arthur Middleton, a wealthy South Carolina planter who was a signer of the Declaration of Independence. Hays married

Frances and became a rich South Carolina planter and the owner of more than 1,000 slaves.[35]

Some of the Jackson wards achieved success but others faltered and none more so than Andrew Jackson Donelson, one of the twin infant sons of Rachel's brother Severn and his wife, Elizabeth Rucker Donelson. He was the son Rachel and Jackson said they adopted in 1808 and renamed Andrew Jackson, Jr. From the existing correspondence between Rachel and Jackson, they were so elated to have a child they could call their own that they spoiled him to an excess by giving him everything they could afford, which was considerable. Consequently, despite being educated at Cumberland College and its successor, the University of Nashville, Andrew Jackson, Jr., was devoid of any degree of financial responsibility—something that must have deeply troubled both Jacksons.[36]

Once he discovered Jackson would bail him out of financial difficulties he continued to spend indiscriminately. In 1829, he married Sarah York, the daughter of Philadelphia ship's captain Peter York and Mary Haines Yorke. Sarah was related to many of Philadelphia's richest and most prominent families—the Robesons, Potts, Claypools, Lippincotts, and Farquhars. York died in 1815, leaving his wife and three daughters—Marion, thirteen; Sarah, ten; and Jane, seven. Mary Haines Yorke's mother, Margaret Haines, left her estate to her daughter and the three girls. When Mary Haines Yorke died in New Orleans in 1820, her daughters were raised by Peter Yorke's sisters Eliza Yorke Farquhar and Martha Yorke Wetherill.[37]

Whatever Sarah Yorke brought to the marriage, monetarily, was not known. She did bring impeccable social and business connections from a host of wealthy relatives and friends in Philadelphia. One of those connections was her cousin Emma Farquhar, who married Thomas Jefferson Donelson, her husband's twin brother. Her guardian, Martha Yorke Wetherill, insisted the wedding be held at The Hermitage and Jackson attended. Initially, the couple apparently lived at The Hermitage for a while.[38]

Thomas achieved financial stability, otherwise he would not have been able to loan his twin brother $800 for six months in 1839.[39] In Philadelphia, Thomas and Emma Donelson's daughters made advantageous marriages. Eliza Yorke Donelson married Bernard Adolphus Hoopes, a noted essayist and member of an old Philadelphia family. Frances Donelson did even better. She married Edward Gratz from a wealthy family of financiers, merchants, philanthropists and patrons of the arts. During the War of 1812, Simon and Hyman Gratz supplied great quantities of saltpeter from Mammoth Cave for the manufacture of gunpowder.[40]

Thomas Jefferson Donelson was mentioned in Jackson's will but only as a witness. The only United States president to pay off the national debt, Jackson died with a personal debt of $16,000, plus interest, that he borrowed in hopes of once again bailing his adopted son out of his constant fiscal mire. Regardless of his past history, he turned around and made Andrew Jackson, Jr., the will's sole executor with no security required. Jackson told his friend Major William B. Lewis he had made a new will leaving everything to Andrew Jackson, Jr. Lewis suggested he leave something to Sarah Yorke Jackson in case her husband's investments continued to be unsuccessful. Jackson was quoted as saying, "No that would show a want of confidence. If she (pointing to Rachel's tomb) were alive, she would wish him to have it all and to me her wish is law."[41]

9

Drum Tap at the Post

"If I were to begin life again, I would go to the turf to get friends," Lady Harriet Ashburton wrote Lord Houghton, Richard M. Naines. "They seem to me the only people to hold close together. I don't know why; may be that each knows something that might hang the other but the effect is delightful and most pecular."[1]

Some of Rachel and Andrew Jackson's friends and associates in Thoroughbred racing certainly matched the personalities described by Lady Ashburton. Despite that fact that Jackson hated the British, he accepted the fact they established organized racing in the colonies and, after the Revolutionary War, embraced all aspects of the sport with great enthusiasm and even greater spending. Jackson's early racing years were intercepted by the Creek War, a deadly duel, a brawl that almost killed him and the War of 1812.

"Presumably, organized racing began in such countries as China, Persia, Arabia and other countries in the Middle East where horsemanship early became highly developed," according to the *Encyclopædia Britannica*. "Thence came to the Arabian, Barb and Turk horses that contributed to the earliest European racing. Such horses became familiar to Europeans during the Crusades (11th–13th centuries) from which they brought those horses back."[2]

The first known racing purse, £40, was offered in England during the reign of Richard the Lionheart (1189–99) for a race over a three-mile course. Henry VIII (1509–47) imported horses from Italy and Spain and established studs in several locations. It was Charles II (1660–85) who was known as the "Father of the English Turf." He inaugurated the King's Plate races, created the earliest racing rules, established Newmarket as the headquarters of English racing, imported forty mares and began the importation of three stallions—Darley Arabian, Godolphin Barb and Byerley Turk—from which all Thoroughbred are said to descend.[3]

Thoroughbred racing began early in the colonies. In 1664, Colonel Robert Nicholls, commander of British troops in New York, laid out a two-mile course on Long Island and established organized racing in America. A silver cup was awarded to the best horses in spring and fall meets. The earliest races were match races between two, or at the most three, horses with owners providing the purse.[4]

Only the wealthiest or those with titles were allowed to participate in the sport in the colonies' races. In 1674, a Virginia tailor wagered 2,000 pounds of tobacco that his mare could beat his neighbor's horse. The York County court fined the tailor 1,000 pounds of tobacco declaring, "It being contrary to law for a laborer to make a race being only a sport for gentlemen."[5]

That concept became known as "The Sport of Kings."

Arabian-blooded horses were introduced into Virginia in 1730 according to the August 1997 issue of the *Colonial Williamsburg Journal*, when Bulle Rock, then twenty-one years old, was imported by Samuel Gist of Hanover County. Bulle Rock was sired by Darley Arabian out of a Byerley Turk mare. By 1774, fifty English stallions and thirty mares had been imported into Virginia. In 1798, John Hoomes of Bowling Green, Virginia, purchased the 1780 Epsom Derby winner Diomed from Sir Charles Burbury, a member of Parliament from Suffolk, who decided he was a failure at stud. Diomed was a big success in Virginia, siring not only Andrew Jackson's Truxton but Sir Archy, who along with his get, had an overwhelming influence on the development of the American Thoroughbred.[6]

British horse races held in the colonies most likely followed the English turf rules of racing clockwise if there was an enclosed course. Many of the early races were straight chute races. After the Revolutionary War, the direction American horses raced on enclosed courses was changed. William Whitney, a crusty old Indian fighter who hated the British with a passion, built a racetrack at his Sportsman Hill home near Crab Orchard, Kentucky, in 1788. All horses who race at Whitney's track ran in a counterclockwise direction. To this day, all American sports, using an enclosed track, run in a counterclockwise direction.[7]

American Thoroughbred rules for racing were initially controlled by the various jockey clubs who instituted rules of racing in their regions and decided which silks were worn by the jockeys. Earlier silks were solid colors. In 1766, the Pennsylvania Jockey Club approved seven colors for silks: two different shades of blue, a dark blue, two shades of red, a green and a yellow to be worn with a black velvet cap. By 1844, the New York Jockey club was enforcing riders' colors according to the secretary's book.[8]

The Jacksons' racing silks were a solid maroon.[9]

Those silks were probably worn by jockeys such as Alston Gibson, who was said to have ridden Truxton against Plowboy and William "Billy" Phillips who allegedly rode for Jackson at his Clover Bottom track. In 1904, Gibson, according to a Michigan magazine, *The Gateway,* was the oldest living jockey at that time. He sent out a letter to horsemen inviting them to celebrate his 115th birthday.[10]

Phillips was taken to Washington by Tennessee Senator George W. Campbell as a clerk or secretary but instead became one of President James Madison's twelve select express couriers who spread the word about the War of 1812 as rapidly as possible. A North Carolina minister, Thomas Raymer, described Billy Phillips' ride through his hometown of Lexington. "I have to inform you that just now the president's express rider, Bill Phillips, has tore through this little place without stopping. He came and went in a cloud of dust his horse's tail and his own hair streaming alike in the wind as they flew by. But, as he passed the tavern where some had gathered, he swung his leather wallet by its strap above his head and shouted, 'Here's the stuff! Wake up! War! War with England! War!' Then he disappeared in a cloud of dust down Salisbury Road like a streak of greased lightning."[11]

The Jacksons shared an interest in Thoroughbred racing since their days in Bayou Pierre. Both learned to ride early in life. Jackson in the Waxhaw Settlement, North Carolina, where, aside from learning about horses he acquired a lifelong practice of wagering on equines, cocks and a roll of the dice. Marquis James wrote about Jackson being in debt to his landlord when he walked into a tavern where a high stakes game of rattle and snap was in progress. Invited to join the game, Jackson wagered his horse against a $200 bet. He rolled the dice, kept his horse and paid the landlord.[12] Rachel developed a love for horses in Pittsylvania County, Virginia, where she started riding a pony before graduating to a horse. It was said she was the most dashing horsewoman on the frontier.[13] It was a natural progression that she would be involved in the sport's early days at their Clover Bottom track.

Rachel attended the Clover Bottom race in 1804 with her niece Rachel Hays and Jackson. The Jackson's mare, Indian Queen, was racing against Dr. Redmond D. Barry's Polly's Medley by Grey Medley out of the Mark Anthony mare.[14] Polly's Medley went back to Godolphin Arabian on both her sire and dam's lines.[15]

Rachel was concerned that Polly's Medley was too small to race against their entry, Indian Queen. "Horses are like people, the smallest are generally the smartest," saucily remarked newlywed Polly Alexander Hull, the sister of Mrs. Barry for whom the horse was named.[16]

Their discussion was interrupted by a preacher who came by searching for his stray cow. The bovine was soon forgotten when the horses lined up and a drum tap started the race. Polly's Medley took a commanding lead. The horses' backers were enthusiastically urging their equines to run faster. The preacher was caught up in the excitement. He jumped on the fence, waved his hat, shouting, "Look at Polly's Medley! Look at Polly's Medley! She leaves [expletive deleted] a blue streak behind her." In the minister's excitement, the

wandering cow was forgotten. When his parishioners heard about his attending a horse race, a church trial was convened and he was suspended from the
pulpit.[17]

After the race, Redmond and Jane Alexander Barry gave an elaborate
ball at their two-story brick mansion in Sumner County. "Gen. Jackson, the
most graceful dancer and most courtly gentleman of his day, opened the ball
dancing with the beautiful bride [Mrs. Hull] as his partner," James Anderson
wrote in his history of Thoroughbred racing in Tennessee.[18]

Once he arrived in Nashville, Grey Medley stood his first season at stud—
fee was eight dollars or twelve dollars in cotton—at the Gallatin Road farm
of William Donelson, one of Rachel's brothers. Barry later moved the horse
to his 11,000-acre farm in Sumner County. The circuitous route Grey Medley
followed from North Carolina, where Barry practiced medicine, to Nashville,
where he studied law, was the real story of how that section of Tennessee, for
a short time, became the breeding center of America's Thoroughbred world
where Jackson was the dominant figure. When Barry moved to Nashville, he
left his slave and trainer, Altamont, to ride the horse across the mountains.
After a year, Barry decided his horse and slave were lost. A few months later,
Altamont and Grey Medley arrived in Nashville, much to Barry's surprise. He
was even more astounded when Altamont handed him $2,000 in stud fees he
had collected on the way. Barry gave Altamont his freedom and he continued
to train Grey Medley and his other horses. Grey Medley was such a vicious
animal that only Altamont could control him.[19]

Jackson soon found his own Altamont after he purchased a bay stallion,
Truxton, in 1805 from Virginian John Verrell for $1,500. Truxton was almost
past his racing prime at age five but Jackson saw him as stallion bringing in
stud fees and felt he had a few more races in him. Sired by the great Diomed
out of the Nancy Coleman mare, Truxton's pedigree was heavy with Godolphin Arabian lineage.[20] A year after purchasing Truxton, Jackson paid Verrell
$800 for his trainer Dinwiddie. Dinwiddie trained Jackson's stable of horses,
with the rare occasions when Jackson took over their training, for four decades and died at The Hermitage in the mid-1840s.[21]

Jackson often lent Dinwiddie out to train other owners' horses. In 1810,
while working for Dr. William Purnell, Dinwiddie was accused of poison-
ing one of his horses. There was a veiled threat in Jackson's response. He demanded to know all the conditions related to the horse's death and said the
villain should be punished. If Dinwiddie, however, had been falsely accused,
Jackson said the accuser deserved punishment. Purnell fell all over himself
retracting his accusation and even provided an affidavit that exonerated
Dinwiddie.[22]

Despite Truxton's defeat by Lazarus Cotton's Greyhound, sired by Spread
Eagle out of the Pandora mare, at an 1805 Hartsville race, Jackson decided

horse had not been properly trained.[23] He asked for a rematch and began an arduous training regimen for Truxton. Jackson raised $5,000 for a side bet. "Interest in the race was so high that people were literally betting their shirts," John Durant wrote in *Sports Illustrated* in 1956. "Jackson accepted $1,500 wagers in wearing apparel and his friend, Patton Anderson, put up money, his horse and fifteen horses belonging to other people. Many of the fifteen had ladies' saddles on their back and Jackson, making a fine moral distinction, commented, 'now I would not have done that.'" Durant speculated that the horses belonging to Rachel and niece Rachel Hays were in that group. "Fortunately for Jackson, Truxton beat Greyhound handily."[24]

Patton Anderson treated the entire crowd to cider and ginger cakes after the race.[25]

"He had wagered all his money," William H. P. Robertson wrote about Patton Anderson, "plus fifteen fine horses standing on the grounds and only after Truxton won did anybody notice that most had ladies saddles on their backs and didn't belong to Anderson in the first place." Robertson said, with cash relatively scarce, it was Jackson who wagered $1,500 in wearing apparel. "After the race, Jackson described himself as 'eased in finances and replenished in my wardrobe.'"[26]

It was not known if Rachel and Rachel Hay's horses were returned to them. Or, if the other owners claimed their horses from Patton Anderson's wager.

"No contest on the soil of Tennessee has even been so exciting or caused so much betting considering the means of the people as this race," Anderson wrote. "The old pioneers, who were accustomed to quarter-racing and had witnessed the indomitable game and great success of Greyhound, bet their hoses and land upon him with the utmost confidence. When the race was over there were general inquiries of 'will you carry my saddle home for me' or 'does your horse carry double?'"[27]

In the fall of 1805, Jackson had Truxton, Greyhound, whom he purchased after the match race, and fourteen other horses in his stable. Wealthy planter and cotton factor Joseph Erwin also had an impressive stable on his Peach Blossom plantation. Erwin offered to race his horse, Tanner, against all comers with a $5,000 side wager. Out of the horses training in his stable, Jackson picked Greyhound to race against Tanner. Greyhound won in three heats over the Clover Bottom course.[28]

There appeared to be no recorded comments from Rachel about her husband's outrageous wagering but she must have been concerned. The Second Great Awakening was sweeping through Tennessee in the early 1800s and swept up Rachel and her sisters along with many others. The Reverend Thomas B. Craighead arrived from Scotland in 1801 to minister the Presbyterians in Cumberland. In 1814, the Reverend Gideon Blackburn, who Rachel considered her minister, legally chartered the First Presbyterian Church, which had been in existence for more than two decades.[29]

A month after the Greyhound-Tanner race, Truxton was at the center of a dispute that almost made Rachel a widow. Erwin, having suffered a loss with Tanner, proposed a race between another of his horses, Ploughboy, which he owned with his son-in-law Charles Dickinson, and Truxton. Ploughboy's lineage included Godolphin Arabian on both the sire and dam's pedigrees. Jackson and Erwin agreed on a $3,000 stakes with cash notes and a $800 forfeit. Before the race, Jackson sold a quarter interest in Truxton to Kentucky sportsman Thomas Pryor.[30]

Ploughboy came up lame and Erwin and Dickinson paid Jackson the forfeiture out of promissory notes previous agreed upon. They would have simply rescheduled the race for some future date had a busybody lawyer, Thomas Swann, not inserted himself into the situation, causing tension between the parties. Swann told Erwin and Dickinson that Jackson had impugned their integrity. Jackson called Swann a "damned liar" and Swann challenged him. Jackson refused the challenge, Robert Brammer wrote in his Library of Congress blog, because he believed Swann was acting on Dickinson's behalf. Brammer called attention to a letter Dickinson wrote to Jackson on January 6, 1806. "The letter recounts the dispute over the forfeit and illustrates the role that Swann played in fanning the flames of the conflict, driving it towards its tragic conclusion."[31]

One version of what pushed Jackson to challenge Dickinson to a duel had nothing to do with the aborted horse race but everything to do with an alleged disparaging remark Dickinson made about Rachel. Dickinson, also a lawyer, was said to have apologized, citing his drunken condition at the time. When Dickinson did the same thing a second time in a Nashville tavern, Jackson advised Erwin to get control of his son-in-law. James Parton, in his *Life of Andrew Jackson, Volume I*, cited Sam Houston as the source for Dickinson's remarks about Rachel.[32]

Houston was an unlikely source for Dickinson's remarks about Rachel as he was thirteen at the time and his family was living in Virginia. Houston's father died in 1806 and his mother moved their family to Blount County, Tennessee, in 1807. Sam Houston and Jackson became friends during the War of 1812.[33]

Harold D. Moser and Sharon Macpherson, editors of the second volume of *The Papers of Andrew Jackson*, wrote,

> Most Jackson biographers have claimed the duel [between Jackson and Dickinson] was the result in part of the insolent remarks Dickinson had made about Rachel, But, unlike Jackson's controversy with John Sevier, there is in the extant Jackson-Dickinson documents, published or unpublished, no reference to her. Whether Rachel was part of the Jackson-Dickinson disagreement or not, she was

aware of the future action as both parties wrote letters to each other. Beyond that, the future combatants took their quarrel to broadsides in Nashville newspapers. The elderly James Robertson, who founded Nashville with Rachel's father, wrote Jackson in an effort to prevent the duel. Jackson failed to follow his sage advice. Obviously, there was going to be a duel to the death but that would have to wait. Dickinson went to New Orleans to sell some slaves in March 1806, before the Truxton-Ploughboy race.[34]

As interest grew in the upcoming Truxton-Ploughboy contest, the *Imperial Review* warned those attending the race to leave their dogs at home. "All persons are requested not taking their dogs to the field as they will be shot without respect to the owners." Erwin posted his own advertisement. "The present engagement with this horse [Ploughboy] is such that he cannot be put to mares any sooner than the above stated time. He is now engaged in a match of $3,000, half forfeit against Gen. Jackson's celebrated Truxton. In a few days after the race, he will be ready to receive mares. Gentlemen who wish to breed fine horses would do well not to put their mares to horses until after the race as at that time it will be seen (barring accidents) whether or not he be the true bred racer."[35]

Called the greatest and most interesting match race ever run in the Western Country, Truxton and Ploughboy met on April 3, 1806, for the rescheduled race. Six-year-old Truxton, who had a thigh injury, was assigned to carry 124 pounds and eight-year-old Ploughboy was assigned 130 pounds. The horses were to run two-mile heats for the $3,000 purse. Truxton won both heats but came up lame, basically ending his racing career. He was retired to stud at John W. Clay's farm after the race.[36]

When Dickinson returned from New Orleans in early May 1806, the two antagonists took up where they left off the previous January. Dickinson issued the challenge and Jackson responded on May 23. Hanson Catlett, a physician, was Dickinson's second and Thomas Overton, a brother of his close friend John Overton, was Jackson's second. Catlett and Overton made arrangements to meet on the Red River at Harrison's Mill in Logan County, Kentucky, just across the Tennessee state line on May 30, 1806, at seven o'clock in the morning. The seconds agreed to abide by dueling rules.[37]

Rachel was unable to dissuade her husband from fighting the duel. In recent months, she had lost two brothers, Stockley in September and Samuel in December 1805, and now had to deal with the very real possibility of losing her husband. Both she and the pregnant Jane Dickinson knew one or the other would be a widow the next day. "Goodbye, darling," Dickinson supposedly told his young wife, "I shall be sure to be at home tomorrow evening." Jackson kissed Rachel on the morning of May 29, and she was not sure he would survive as she knew Dickinson was known to be the best shot in Cumberland while her husband's talents were only ordinary. It was said that Dickinson was so confident he would kill Jackson that he wagered $500 (some said $3,000) on the outcome.[38]

"Rachel would not forget to her dying day," Pauline Burke wrote, "those hideous hours of suspense when she waited and prayed that spring morning after her husband had tenderly bade her goodbye. It is not to be doubted that her sister-in-law, Mary Purnell [who married her sibling John Donelson] was there to comfort her during those hours of anxiety."[39]

With the sun streaming through an umbrella of budding spring trees, Jackson and Dickinson took their place at the line, 24 feet apart. Overton gave the command to fire. Dickinson raised his pistol in a smooth, experienced motion and fired. A puff of smoke arose from Jackson's chest under a loose-fitting coat but he did not fall. Dickinson was astounded. In disbelief he stumbled back from the line saying, "Great God! How did I miss him?" Overton, hand on his pistol, ordered him back to the line. Dickinson complied. Jackson, with his left hand over his chest, raised his pistol to fire. Nothing happened because the weapon was only half-cocked. Jackson re-cocked his pistol, took careful aim, hit Dickinson in the abdomen and he crumpled to the ground.[40]

Jackson could have shot Dickinson in the arm, shoulder, leg, and hip or fired into the air. Instead, he took careful aim and chose a target, Dickinson's abdomen, that he knew would be fatal.

Andrew Jackson's dueling pistols are displayed by Grace Stockman at the National Museum in this 1926 photograph. It is not known if one of the pistols was used by Jackson to kill Charles Dickinson in their duel in Logan County, Kentucky, on May 30, 1806, following a disagreement over how the forfeit would be paid when a horse race was cancelled. Dickinson shot Jackson in the chest, near his heart, breaking two ribs. When Jackson attempted to return fire, his pistol was only half-cocked. According to dueling rules, that accounted for a shot. Instead, Jackson re-cocked his pistol and fatally shot Dickinson in the abdomen (Library of Congress, Prints and Photographs Department).

Jackson was able to mount his horse before Overton and his physician knew the extent of his wounds, and rode away not wanting Dickinson's friends to know how close he was to dying. When they reached the tavern where they had spent the previous night, Jackson's boots were full of blood. Dickinson's aim was not far off the mark. His bullet was embedded in Jackson's breastbone only a few inches from his heart. The loose-fitting coat had thrown off Dickinson's aim. In addition, Jackson had two broken ribs. After his wounds were cleaned and dressed, he dispatched a messenger to Dr. Catlett to ask if he needed any assistance. Catlett send back word that Dickinson was past surgery. A rider was sent to bring Jane Dickinson to Logan County but her husband died before she arrived.[41]

Burke, a Donelson descendent, subscribed to the theory the duel was all about Dickinson's remarks about Rachel and not about the horse race. She gave this account of Jackson's homecoming supposedly heard by seven-year-old Andrew Jackson Donelson and related by his daughter, Rachel, ninety-two-years later.

"You are wounded," Rachel cried when she saw Jackson's bloody clothes. "Yes," Jackson was said to have replied, "only slightly but Dickinson will insult no more innocent women. I meant to keep my promise [made to Rachel to spare his life]. On the road, I saw signs of his skill—small circles on trees and fences black with shot and then heard his message. 'Tell Jackson I will pepper his craven breast like that disk.' Even when we took our places on the ground and waited for the second to give the word, I still intended to fire into the air but when I felt his bullet plowing through my body and heard him shriek, 'Great God have I missed the damn scoundrel,' the demon in me woke. I fired and he fell." Burke said Rachel almost fainted, fell on her knees, praying, "Oh God, have pity on the babe in her womb."[42]

Jackson was more than slightly wounded. His recovery, even with Rachel's careful nursing, took several weeks and he carried Dickinson's bullet in his chest the rest of his life. Although Dickinson was dead, Jackson was unable to let the matter go. He was offended that a Nashville newspaper, carrying Dickinson's obituary, draped their edition in mourning black. Jackson continued, much to Rachel's distress, to pick at the matter like someone refusing to allow a wound to scab over.[43]

There was speculation that Jackson had murdered Dickinson by firing twice—first when his pistol was half-cocked and did not fire and second when he took another shot. That assumption was correct and it was puzzling that Jackson's enemies did not pursue that fact with more gusto. The Irish Code Duello, adopted in the colonies in 1777, was followed until dueling was outlawed by the various states. The Code Duello contained twenty-six commandments. Jackson clearly violated Commandment XIX, "In all cases, a misfire is equivalent to a shot and a snap or non-cock is to be considered a misfire." Thomas Overton, Jackson's second, was certainly familiar with the code. When Dickinson stumbled back from the line after firing, Overton ordered him back to the line as prescribed by Commandment XVI, "Neither party can advance or retreat on measured ground. Seconds must enforce this rule."[44]

Overton saw the very real possibility Jackson might be charged with murder and took evasive action. On June 20, three weeks after the duel, Overton contacted Catlett, Dickinson's second, and asked him to make an affidavit that the two men followed the Code Duello commandments. Catlett's affidavit, curiously dated that same day, was interesting in its wording. "I do hereby certify that the affair of honor which took place between Gen. Andrew Jackson and Mr. Charles Dickinson was conducted agreeably to what was agreed upon as far as any agreements were made." Catlett's phrase, "as far as any agreements were made," appeared to indicate neither the principals nor their seconds discussed Code Duello Commandment XIX during preparation for the duel. Apparently the Jackson supporters felt Catlett's affidavit was lacking even though Overton signed the document. Five days later, Catlett made a second affidavit, "I do certify that every circumstance in the affair which lately took place between Gen. Jackson and Mr. Dickinson was agreeable to the impressions that Mr. Dickinson and myself were under." Overton's affidavit read, "I do hereby certify that every circumstance to the affair which lately took place between Gen. Jackson and Mr. Dickinson was agreeable to the impressions Mr. Jackson and myself were under."[45]

Nevertheless, Dickinson was dead, Jackson's reputation suffered and Rachel attempted to deal with it all. Dickinson's funeral at Erwin's Peach Blossom plantation drew a large crowd. Jane Dickinson gave birth to Charles H. Dickinson and later married John B. Craighead, a Nashville attorney. In 1807, Erwin moved to Iberville Parish, Louisiana, where he developed an extensive plantation, first with cotton and then sugar cane. His grandson Charles H. Dickinson later joined him in Louisiana.[46]

Erwin suffered severe financial losses in the economic crisis of 1819 according to Nathan A. Burman in his 2012 Louisiana State University dissertation. "Debts of such speculation overcame him and he took his own life at the home of his daughter in 1829," Burman wrote. He said Dickinson was goaded by Erwin into the duel with Jackson. William F. Clement, in *Plantation Life on the Mississippi,* said Erwin was haunted by his guilt in the Dickinson–Jackson duel. Erwin's daughter Eliza Wilson wrote her brother-in-law Andrew Haynes in 1829 that her father was living with her and he was the most miserable person she had ever seen. "He is now once more completely deranged. His suffering is beyond recognition. It is most pitiful and truly distressing to hear his agonizing complaints." In April 1829, she wrote Haynes that Erwin was dead. "Yesterday morning he was found wrapped up in his cloak with his head in a water jar."[47]

Rachel, as her husband recuperated from his injuries sustained in the Dickinson duel, had him home at The Hermitage for a while. With various young wards running about, she experienced some degree of domestic contentment as their finances had improved. Rachel and Jackson visited the North Carolina spa and resort at French Broad Springs.[48]

Nothing, however, distracted Jackson from his racing stable.

In the fall of 1806, Rachel and Jackson attended the races at the Gallatin Jockey Club where their horse, Escape, trained by Green Barry Williams, lost to Post Boy in a three-mile heat. They were more successful in the spring of 1807, when the Bibbs mare, sired by Diomed, won a three-mile heat against Henrietta, trained by Williams. Jackson, who was at the Burr treason trial in Richmond, Virginia, sent instructions to Patton Anderson. "At the race, I hope you will tell Mrs. Jackson not to be uneasy. I will be home as soon as by obedience to the precept of my country will permit." Jackson was certain the Bibbs mare would win and she did, adding $1,000 to their coffers.[49]

Patton Anderson's association with Rachel and Jackson was destined to soon end. Newton Cannon, a Williamson County plantation owner, had some success with his Thoroughbred Expectation, by Sir Peter Fox out of an Eclipse mare. Cannon was out of his element in dealing with Jackson when he agreed to a $5,000 match race between his horse and Jackson's Doublehead by Diomed out of Polly's Medley. When the four-mile heats were over at the Clover Bottom Course, Doublehead was the winner. Cannon and his friends had bet heavily on Expectation and he was almost bankrupt.[50]

Patton Anderson was up to his usual antics and Jackson saved him one last time.

As dusk was falling on the Clover Bottom course, Jackson left Rachel and walked back to the stables to see that Doublehead was properly cooled down. En route, he met Anderson being chased by a group of angry men. Jackson stalled them while Anderson made his escape in the near darkness but they continued their pursuit. Jackson stood at a fence stile and dared the first man to cross it. Unarmed, biographer Marquis James wrote, Jackson took out a tin tobacco box from his coat pocket, opened it and then clicked it shut. That click sounded like a pistol being cocked. No one dared to defy Jackson and the crowd dispersed.[51]

Patton Anderson once again escaped unscathed but his luck was running out.

A few weeks later, Anderson became involved in a heated argument in Shelbyville with David Magness, his father Jonathan and brother Perry as part of a long-running feud between the Anderson and Magness families. During a confrontation, Anderson drew his dirk, advanced on David Maness and attempted to stab him but bystanders separated them. Nobody left the town square as both sides continued to verbally abuse the other. Suddenly, David Magness drew his pistol and shot Anderson, mortally wounding him. Magness was arrested and charged with murder. Both sides lawyered up.[52]

Magness' trial was moved to Franklin, Tennessee, where he was represented by Felix Grundy, one of the South's premier attorneys. Assisting Grundy was one of Rachel nephews, Stockley Donelson Hays. At the prosecution's table were former judge John Haywood, U.S. Senator Jenkin Whiteside, Thomas Hart Benton and Andrew Jackson.[53]

J. Roderick Heller, in his biography of Grundy, described Patton Anderson as "a sporting man of uncontrollable passions." He said Anderson was a partner of Jackson's in a cockpit and the Clover Bottom course. There were charges that Grundy packed the jury with men such as Newton Cannon and others who were personal enemies of both Anderson and Jackson. Forty-two witnesses testified, including Jackson, during the nine-day trial. During his testimony, Grundy pressed Jackson about Anderson's temper. "Sir," Jackson was said to have replied, "my friend Patton Anderson was the natural enemy of scoundrels." Grundy thanked him for his honesty. Grundy did his legal magic and the jury found David Magness not guilty of murder but convicted him of manslaughter. He was sentenced to eleven months in prison and had the letter M branded on his hand.[54]

In December 1808, after the fall racing season was over, Rachel's brother Severn and his wife Elizabeth became the parents of twin boys, Andrew Jackson and Thomas Jefferson Donelson. Did the new parents offer the Jacksons one of their sons or did Rachel and Jackson ask for the child? To this day the arrangements that followed remain murky. The Donelson version was that the Jacksons chose one of the boys immediately after birth, named him Andrew Jackson, Jr., and legally adopted him. "The third day," Burke continued, "they brought the infant son to The Hermitage, reared him with the tenderest of care, educated him and the devotion of this father and son is well known."[55]

Burke's account left a number of questions unanswered.

Taking a three-day-old infant from his mother meant that Rachel had to make previous arrangements for a woman, possibly a slave, to wet nurse the child. Elizabeth Rucker Donelson was possibly unable to care for two infants but they only had one other child, Rachel, at that time. Perhaps the couple was unable to afford to care for two infants at the same time. During the next seven years, Severn and Elizabeth had three more children.[56]

No records of Rachel and Jackson adopting the infant have ever been found. "There was at that time no provisions in Tennessee for judicial adoptions," Harold Moser and Sharon Macpherson, editors of the second volume of the *Papers of Andrew Jackson*, wrote. "Moreover, the Tennessee legislature was not in session when the adoption was supposed to have been considered and a careful search of records for subsequent years has failed to turn up any reference to the matter. Whether officially sanctioned or not, Jackson always contended that Andrew Jackson, Jr., was his adopted son."[57]

Having an infant in the household did not deter the Jacksons' racing interests. Green Berry Williams was no longer their trainer and was searching for horses to beat their entries. Williams did not have to look far when in 1810, he found Maria (sometimes referred to as Haynie's Maria) in Sumner County. Jesse Haynie, as prosperous plantation owner, liked the looks of the filly and paid $100 for her. Maria was among Diomed's last crop of foals out of the Taylor Belair mare. Haynie and Williams began training Maria when she was two but did not race her until she was a three year old.[58]

Colonel George Elliott, who owned Wall Springs plantation in Sumner County, supplied Williams and Haynie with the missing piece in their Maria picture. One of Elliott's slaves, Monkey Simon, was one of the most successful and most vocal of the early slave jockeys. Elliott charged $100 per ride for Simon's services and divided the fee with his tiny hunchback rider. Simon was said to have been a prince in his native Africa.[59]

Maria broke her maiden in the fall of 1811 at the Nashville course where she defeated five other horses in two-mile heats. Among the losers was Decatur, the best son of Truxton, owned by the Jacksons. In the fall of 1812, Rachel and Jackson backed Dungannon, which they owned in partnership with Edward Bradley, in another race on the Nashville course against Maria. They lost again.[60]

Whatever Jackson wagered was a princely sum as he was determined to beat Maria. The

Born Andrew Jackson Donelson, along with a twin brother, Thomas Jefferson Donelson, in 1809 to Rachel's brother Severn and his wife, Elizabeth Rucker Donelson, the infant ended up with Rachel and Andrew Jackson who raised him as their son. The Donelson family claimed Rachel and Andrew Jackson adopted the child but there are no records to sustain that. The boy, renamed Andrew Jackson, Jr., was painted by The Hermitage artist Ralph E. W. Earl in oil on canvas circa 1820 (Andrew Jackson's Hermitage, Nashville, TN).

$20,000 he won with and for Truxton's stud fees was probably lost betting against Maria.[61] Rachel, her niece Rachel Hays and friends from Davidson County had their own betting pool on Dungannon against a group of ladies from Sumner County led by Clarissa Bledsoe, daughter of Colonel Anthony Bledsoe, a pioneer settler. The ladies were wagering wearing apparel—hats, jewelry, scarves, shawls and gloves. Just before the drum tap sounded, Clarissa was concerned that all she had left to wager was a pair of fine gloves. She threw them in the pot and, of course, soon reclaimed them.[62]

Jackson was, without a doubt, an intimidator but that tactic failed to work with Monkey Simon. Before one of Maria's races at the Clover Bottom course, Jackson warned the jockey not to spit tobacco juice in the eyes of his rider or his horse. "Well General," the four-foot-five-inch hunchback replied, "I've rode a great deal against your horses but [expletive deleted] none were ever near enough to catch my spit."[63]

Jackson, while fighting the War of 1812, was still looking for a horse to beat Maria. Dinwiddie was running his stables and preparing his horses for competition. "The saying, 'that all men are equal on the turf and under it,'" Robertson wrote, "was never better illustrated than by the experience of Andrew Jackson. The successful Congressman, U.S. Senator, justice of the Supreme Court of Tennessee, general and President of the United States was balked in his fondest ambition."[64]

"While masterminding his Natchez campaign," Robertson continued, "he commissioned W. B. Johnson to acquire for him 'the best four-mile horse in Virginia without regard to price.' Johnson, who owned the most prominent racing stable in Virginia at the time, filled the bill with Jackson's Pacolet, sired by Citizen out of Mary Grey, whom the absent owner matched against Maria for the Nashville fall meet in 1813." Pacolet, whose sire line was heavy with Godolphin Arabian influence, wrenched an ankle and Jackson paid a $500 forfeit. Robertson said Jackson, after paying $3,000 for Pacolet, purchased three other horses in unsuccessful efforts to defeat Maria.[65]

Rachel, according to available documents, faded from the equine scene. She had a baby to care for, a plantation to run and her husband was bleeding their funds by buying horses and wagering on them. In addition, he was expending their own funds to equip 2,000 troops for a march to Natchez and, after the War of 1812, managed to get himself critically wounded in the Benton Brawl.[66]

On December 17, 1811, Jackson wrote Rachel he had reached Natchez two days earlier but had been detained by the loss of his horse and spent two days with Abram Green's family near Port Gibson. He was bringing back some slaves and thought it would take several days in Bayou Pierre to prepare them for the trip through the wilderness. "I shall bring home with me from twelve to twenty. I hope to be able to sell some of them on the way at a good price but many of them I shall be obliged to bring home as most of that number will be females. I leave it to you to point out to Mr. Fields where to have the house built for them."[67]

In a letter to Rachel on January 8, 1813, Jackson acknowledged their financial plight. "Say to Mr. Fields [their plantation overseer] I have sent him all the money I could spare and that I shall not leave Nashville with more than thirty dollars." Before he left, Rachel had Dinwiddie deliver a letter and a miniature of her to him before he left for Natchez. "I shall wear it near my bosom," he told Rachel, "but this was useless for without your miniature my recollection never fails me of your likeness."[68]

Rachel's February 8 answer to Jackson's letter was filled with sadness that tears at one's heart. Her joy radiated from having received his letter but acute pain cried out from her words. She told him he was everything to her and she rejoiced in knowing he was safe. "To hear you were in [good] health it was my nightly prayer to the Almighty God. My thoughts forever on where ever I go, where ever I turn my thoughts, my fears, my doubts distress me. Then, a little my hope revives again. That keeps me alive; was it not for that I must sink. I should die in my present situation. But my blessed Redeemer is making intersection with the Father for us to meet again, restore you to my bosom where every vein, every pulse beats high for your health, your safety, all your wishes crowned.[69]

"Do not my beloved husband," she beseeched, "let love of country, fame and honor make you forget you have me. Without you, I would think them all empty shadows. You will say this is not the language of a patriot but it is the language of a faithful wife, one I know you esteem and love sincerely, but how many pangs, how many heart-rendering sighs you absence has cost me. My time passes heavily not in good health but I hope to see you once more on their globe and, after this frail life ends, be with you in happier climes where I shall experience no more painful separation and then I'll be at rest. I feel a forecast of the joy that is to the virtuous souls. Gracious God help me pray for your happiness."[70]

In discussing their finances, Rachel wrote that she had paid Fields "every cent that I did not send you in my letter. He was not satisfied; then borrowed thirty dollars as he was going about trying to sell you note. I have made nearly enough to pay him off." A week later, Jackson wrote Rachel he was two miles from Natchez and complained about the cold weather and the ice they encountered on the Ohio and Mississippi rivers.[71]

Jackson replied to Rachel's February 8 letter on March 1 in a rather high-handed manner, ignoring the many concerns she had expressed so eloquently. "My Love," he opened his letter saying, "I have no doubt by my presence at home would be agreeable to all and beneficial to our interests. But, my love, if you can enjoy health and calm your mind and our little Andrew be spared to us and I to return and find you in health I shall be thankful for the blessing." Jackson advised her to sell a slave, Sandy, to Thomas Watson for $500, but to seek the advice on the transaction from the Bank of Nashville's John Anderson, who had married Elizabeth Glasgow Martin Donelson, Stockley's widow. He bragged about the reception he and his troops had received from Mississippi citizens, discussed the price of meal and flour, and related that Abram Green, a friend from their Bayou Pierre days, said her sister Mary Caffery was in ill health.[72]

A week later, Jackson wrote Rachel that he had been laboring from a violent cold but assured her he was restored to health. Abram Green, he said, planned to move to Tennessee in a few weeks. Jackson was proud of how George Washington Martin, Stockley Donelson's stepson was performing in John Coffee's troop of cavalry. Stockley D. Hutchings, Rachel's nephew, was doing a fine job as a quartermaster sergeant. Jackson expressed his disgust with the Donelson family for ignoring Mary Caffery's illness. "Your sister Caffery, he [Abram Green] tells me is in bad health [and is] anxious to get up to Tennessee. Should I return direct to Tennessee, will take her with me. If I should not will, if possible, aid her in getting up. Certainly there can be but little family affection existing if one sister cannot be taken from the jaws of sickness and (of course before long if left where she is) the grave."[73]

After Jackson and his troop reached Natchez, he refused to place them under the command of General James Wilkinson and was ordered to return to Nashville without rations or provisions. He wrote Rachel on March 15 of his bitterness that the government had not provided adequate conveyances and supplies for their return. Field, their overseer, had a disagreement with Rachel. "You may tell him that I will soon be home and expect my farm and stock in good order." Rachel replied on April 5 of her joy that he was returning home but was concerned that he would be leaving again. "I should shortly be blessed with my dearest self once more with you in this life—never another painful separation. But, I saw the letter you wrote General Overton wherein you expressed a wish to go to the northwest. Oh, how hard it appeared and the one to Col. Ward of the same tenure. How can you wish such a perilous power but for the love of country, the thirst for honor and patriotism is your motive."[74]

Apparently, Rachel was not aware of a third letter Jackson wrote to William Berkley Lewis on April 13 about organizing a force to help America defend Detroit against the British. General William H. Harrison had been defeated by the British and Indians in the Battle of the River Raisin, twenty-six miles south of Detroit, the previous January.[75]

Rachel also wrote of the death of Mary Smith, the wife of her nephew Johnny Hutchings and her sorrow that rain-swollen rivers and creeks preventing her from reaching their house. She said the farm looked well and wished him a safe return. "I could write you all day long but such a pen I fear you never can read it. Pray, my dear, write me on the way home—and may the Lord bless your health [and] safety restore you to my arms in mutual love is the prayer of your affectionate wife."[76]

After Jackson returned home, he sent his principal aide, Thomas Hart Benton, to Washington, to request reimbursement for the personal funds he expended on moving his troops to Natchez and back. While Benton was away, his younger brother Jesse managed to get himself entangled in a duel with Major William Carroll, who also served under Jackson. In a rash moment, Jackson agreed to be Carroll's second. Neither Carroll nor Benton were good shots and the distance agreed upon was 10 feet. When the command was given, Carroll turned to fire and found Benton in a squatting position. Benton was seriously wounded in his rear end and Carroll was only grazed.[77]

Benton, on his return from Washington, took exception to Jackson's involvement in the duel and sent him an extended letter on June 25 outlining his objections. Jackson threatened to horsewhip him. Things came to a head with the Benton Brawl on September 4 when both Bentons, armed to the teeth, showed up in Nashville. They met Jackson, John Coffee and Stockley Hays, one of Rachel's nephews, in front of Talbot's Tavern. Both Coffee and Hays were tall, well-built men while Jackson was rather slender. Jesse Benton disappeared inside the tavern. Jackson advanced on the older brother, backing him into the building, and shouted, "Now, defend yourself, you dammed rascal." Jesse Benton, who had been waiting inside, shot Jackson in the left shoulder at the same time Jackson fired at his brother. Jackson, bleeding profusely from a severed artery, fell to the floor. Coffee charged through the cloud of acrid Sulphur-laced smoke, fired at Thomas Benton, missed and began clubbing him with his pistol. Jackson was still on the floor bleeding. Hays, after making sure Jesse Benton fell in his still-inured rear end, began slashing at him with a sword cane. The only thing that saved Jesse was Hays' weapon breaking when it hit a button on his coat. Jesse still had a gun, placed it against Hays' chest and fired. The weapon failed to discharge. By this time, Rachel's brother, William Donelson, joined the fray. Thomas Benton had been stabbed five times. The brawl ended when somebody yelled that Jackson, still bleeding profusely, might need medical attention for his shattered left shoulder and a bullet embedded there. The fighting ceased and Jackson was carried to a nearby hotel where he soaked two mattresses with blood. He refused to allow surgeons to amputate his left arm.[78]

Rachel nursed her husband as best she could at The Hermitage but, far from being recovered, he was off on another military exercise. On October 7, just over a month after the Benton Brawl, Jackson, still weak from his wounds and the loss of blood, began organizing and moving troops in response to

DREADFUL FRACAS ATWEEN THE GINERAL AND THE BENTONS AT NASHVIL

While Thomas Hart Benton, a military aide to Andrew Jackson, was in Washington, his brother Jesse became involved in a dispute with William Carroll. There was a duel, with Jackson as Carroll's second, and Jesse Benton somehow managed to get himself shot in the rear. His brother blamed Jackson. A confrontation occurred at Nashville's Talbot's Tavern on September 4, 1813, between the Bentons and Jackson, John Coffee, and Stockley Hays, one of Rachel's nephews. Jesse Benton shot Jackson in the left shoulder, severing an artery, and he fell to the floor while the other four men shot, pistol-whipped and stabbed each other (Library of Congress, Prints and Photographs Division).

Governor Willie Blount's orders to proceed against the Creek Indians for their August 30 attack on Fort Mims in the Mississippi Territory that killed 250 settlers.[79]

Rachel received a letter from her husband on October 11 with instructions for Robert Hays and John Hutchings to fire the new overseer, a man named Nollyboy, and bring back John Fields, the former overseer. "You shall not be pestered by him anymore," Jackson wrote. He said Hays would provide her news of their camp and that his shoulder was giving him more pain than his arm. Two days later, when Jackson and his troops had reached Fort Coffee, near Huntsville, Alabama, Jackson wrote he was in good health and his arm was mending. Another letter assured Rachel that his arm was mending and he was sufficiently strong to penetrate to Pensacola. He ended the letter saying, "With fervent prayers for your health, our little Andrew and all friends, believe me to be your affectionate husband."[80]

Jackson kept reassuring Rachel that he was in good health and his arm was mending fast. In another short letter, dated October 18, he wrote that his arm was still mending. On November 4, he wrote Rachel about a young Indian boy, Lyncoya, who was found in the embrace of his deal mother after Coffee captured the town of Tallahatchie. "I send on a little Indian boy for Andrew at Huntsville with a request to Col. Pope to take care of him until he is sent on."[81]

Jackson realized, in a November 21 letter, he had not addressed Rachel's concerns about her sister, Mary Caffery. "Have a house put up for her on any part of the track where she will be convenient to us and where you choose or let her live in the house with us as your please. We can always raise a supple for her as well as ourselves. Present her with my best wishes."[82]

Rachel was overwhelmed with responsibilities in Jackson's absence— changing plantation overseers, running the gin for their cotton and that of their customers, providing medical care for their slaves, family and friends, collecting debts and running the household. Jackson now wanted her to oversee building a dwelling for her sister. Certainly, there were slaves to do the work but the final responsibility was on Rachel's shoulders.

All of these activities called for Rachel to be outdoors all the year and that was not good for her complexion. Being lonely, she did what millions of women have done when their husbands were absent from home—ate too much and gained weight. Rachel begged Jackson to let her join him in the field. She told him of crying throughout the night and how their son consoled her.[83]

"I would to God," Jackson wrote Rachel on December 4, "I had a place I could bring you to; I would certainly send for you and my little Andrew. And, if Gen. Pinckney, under whose command I am, will direct me to take a stand at any stationary point—for any specific time I will send for you. My heart is with you; my duty compels me to remain in the field whether we will have men enough to progress with the camping I cannot say." Jackson went on to say that it might not be long before he could send for her or see her at home. "But, you know my motto, I know you approved of it—that is death before dishonor."[84]

He acknowledged in a December 19 letter to Rachel that the supplies she had shipped had arrived. "For a few days, we had ample supplies of bred and meat," he wrote. In another letter, ten days later, Jackson expressed disgust with his troops for leaving when their enlistments were up. He added that he had not been able to get his injured arm into the sleeve of his coat. "I hope I will be able to wear my coat sleeve on it soon."[85]

Rachel and the Donelson family were devastated when they heard the news that Alexander "Sandy" Donelson, the son of Rachel's brother John and Mary Purnell Donelson, had been killed and John Coffee wounded. "I was prepared my troops, tho raw, met their bold and ferocious attacks with firmness and undaunted resolution," he wrote Rachel on January 28, 1814. "On our side four were killed and several wounded. Amongst the killed was our friend Major Alexander Donelson, who fought bravely and bravely fell."[86]

Rachel hurried to her brother's house and later wrote her husband of her grief and her fear he would meet the same fate. She said she had not slept one night since Sandy's death. "I deplore his untimely end. My dear, pray let me conjure you by every tie of love and friendship to let me see you before you go again. I have borne it until it has thrown me into fevers. I am very unwell. My thoughts are never directed from that dreadful scene. Oh, how dreadful to me. Oh, mercy and goodness of heaven to me [that] you are spared perils and dangers so many troubles my prayers are increasing. How long, oh Lord, will I remain so unhappy, no rest, no ease; I cannot sleep. Had it not been for Stockley Hays, I should have started for Huntsville. Let me know and I will fly on wings of the purest affection. I must see you. Pray, my darling never make me so unhappy for any country." She ended her missive saying, "The blest blessings of heaven await you. Crown you wishes with health and happy days until we meet. Let it not be long." Jackson replied that he was grieved to know the pain his absences had caused her and added that he could not retire when he pleased. He pointed out that he was protected by the same providence whether he was in the Creek Nation or at home.[87]

The war ended on March 2, 1814, when Jackson, with reinforcements, defeated the Creeks at Horseshoe Bend on the Tallapoosa River, which ran from Georgia, through Alabama to the Gulf of Mexico. Jackson negotiated a treaty with the Creeks that gave the United States 23 million acres of land in what is now parts of Georgia and Alabama. Cherokee Chief Junaluska, who led 500 men to assist Jackson and who saved his life, said, "If I had known Jackson would drive us from our homes, I would have killed him at Horseshoe."[88]

Jackson survived and Rachel's delight was immeasurable when she and young Andrew met him in Nashville on May 13. It was a grand reunion for a returning hero. Her husband's past misdeeds appeared to have been forgotten and forgiven.[89]

Assuming her husband would be home for a while, Rachel was probably shocked when the news came five days later that Jackson had been commissioned a major general in the U.S. Army with a salary of $6,500 a year, a very comfortable salary in modern terms.[90]

As involved in their finances as she was, Rachel knew the Creek War had not stopped Jackson from buying and betting on horses. Still determined to defeat Maria, Jackson ran Tam O'Shanter against Maria with a $1,000 side bet and lost the four-mile heat in the fall of 1814. In the same time frame, he sent DeWitt mare (also a daughter of Diomed) out to challenge Maria in a mile dash and lost another $1,000. In 1815, Jackson decided that DeWitt Mare's early speed could help her in another race against Maria. Side bets of

$1,500 were broken up accordingly: $500 due at the quarter pole, $500 at the 600-yard post and $500 at the finish line. Jackson's divided wagering was not helpful and Maria won again. Not willing to accept defeat, Jackson thought up another angle to beat Maria. He demanded Jesse Haynie, Maria's owner, concede 120 yards to DeWitt mare in a two mile heat with a $1,000 side bet. Haynie agreed and Maria won again.[91]

When Haynie offered to run Maria against any and all comers for $5,000, Jackson suggested, "Make the race for $50,000 and consider me in with you. She can beat anything in God's whole earth."[92]

There are no records that Rachel attempted to curb Jackson's wagering but there was one person who accomplished that task. Jackson was attended the races with his close friend John Coffee. Jackson was placing wagers as fast as he could on a horse that Coffee knew something about that his friend did not. Quite concerned, Coffee said, "Mr. Jackson come here. I must speak to you." Jackson replied, "Don't bother me now, John, I'm busy." Realizing speech was useless and determined to save his friend from a monetary loss, Coffee plunged into the crowd, picked Jackson up, threw him over his shoulder and carried him off. Turned out that Coffee was right about the horse.[93]

Jackson took his passion for Thoroughbred racing to the President's House with him in 1828, and he became actively involved in the sport in the Washington area. In 1830, Jackson helped revive the Maryland Jockey Club which built a new race track, the Central Course, in Baltimore. When Dinwiddie was in Washington, the Reverend Hardy M. Cryer, known as the "racing parson," looked after his Nashville stable.[94]

Jackson kept his horses at the Clover Bottom track or boarded them with fellow racing acquaintances but never on The Hermitage plantation. When he learned in 1832 that Andrew Jackson, Jr., who was in charge of The Hermitage while he was in Washington, not only allowed a track to be built on the plantation but was training horses there, Jackson went ballistic. He accused his adopted son of injuring his reputation. "I have been mortified," Jackson wrote him, "with the course pursued with the colts. Steel [The Hermitage overseer] well knew that I was opposed to have any horse trained or a track on my plantation."[95]

Jackson razed the old building and built new stables just east of the President's House in 1834. The new stables were built of brick and trimmed with Aquia limestone and remained in use until 1857. He raced his horses at the Washington and Maryland tracks in the name of Rachel's nephew, Andrew Jackson Donelson, who was also his secretary.[96]

10

New Orleans

To go along with Jackson's new rank of major general, Rachel insisted that he order a new uniform. The order called for "one suit of full dress uniform, one pair of gold epaulettes, chapeau, one pair of military boots with spurs—all the best quality for Maj. General Andrew Jackson." Jackson ordered, at his own expense, "one full dress coat, embroidered on the cape. One pair large gold epaulettes price seventy or eighty dollars; one large yellow mounted saber; belt and sword knot, one chapeau, one pair of military boots and spurs for his adjutant general, Col. Robert Butler."[1] The order was sent to Murfreesboro tailor Joel Childdress.[2]

Much of the Jacksons' 1814 correspondence concerned his absences, her fears for his health and Rachel joining him in either Natchez or New Orleans. From his February 17 letter it was apparent that Rachel was becoming exceedingly tired of him being from home. He wrote apologizing for the pain his absences have caused her. "But, when you reflect that I am in the field and cannot retire when I please without disgrace," he wrote, "I am in hopes that your good sense will yield to it a little while with resolution and firmness and, my love, as it respects my safety when you reflect that I am protected by the same overruling providence when in the Creek nation as I am at home His protecting hand can shield me as well from danger here as there."[3]

Jackson made his often repeated promise to retire as soon as he had supplies and could end the Creek War. "As soon as this is done and I can honorably retire, I should return to your arms on the wings of love and affection to spend with you in peaceful domestic retirement."[4]

In his May 8 letter, Jackson told Rachel he was unsure when he could meet her in Mobile. Two months later, he told her if he did not return to Nashville, he would send a boat for her to meet him in Natchez.[5]

On August 27, three British warships landed at Pensacola in Spanish Florida only fifty miles from Jackson and his force of less than 2,000 troops at Mobile. By November, Jackson's army occupied Pensacola and moved on to

New Orleans where he engaged the British from December 1814 to February 1815 and emerged victorious.[6]

On September 22, Jackson wrote apologizing for the delay in her traveling. "I hope you will reconcile yourself to our separation as well as possible—the very moment that the situation of this lower country would make it prudent, I shall direct you to join me. Until this happens and I have a sufficient force to guarantee its security and defense it would be imprudent for me to descend the river."[7]

Three weeks later, Jackson began listing provisions Rachel should bring with her and preparations for her trip. He wanted flour, bacon and other food items. She was to find someone to help Fields, the overseer, supervise the plantation. He suggested she either get their carriage repaired or buy a new one. John Hutchings, he told her, would get a good pair of carriage horses. In addition to all the other responsibilities Rachel has, she is taxed with even more work. Then, he gives her advice as to her clothing. "You must recognize," he wrote on October 9, "that you are now a Major General's lady—in the service of the United States and as such you must appear elegant and plain, not extravagant but in such style as strangers expect to see you."[8]

He loved her in homespun garments but his standing as a major general, he felt, demanded she appear in silks and satins. When would she have time to select those fabrics, patterns and turn them over to a seamstress with all her responsibilities which increased before her departure?

On November 15, Jackson told Rachel she could start for New Orleans and he would send men to accompany her. He wanted her to bring the uniform Joel Childress had tailored for him. Two days later, he wrote Rachel to bring as many servants a possible, two dozen Windsor chairs plus other furniture previously mentioned, smoked pork and beef. He told her they could buy silver and china in New Orleans. Six days later, Jackson sent her a blank bank draft for her clothes and passage down river. He still did not know if he would meet her in Natchez or New Orleans.[9]

Finally, Rachel assembled all Jackson's requests on the Nashville wharf and Burke said they were loaded on a keelboat (flatboat) called the *Cumberland*. The passengers included Rachel and Andrew Jr., her niece Rachel Hays Butler and her son, and Harriet Winter Overton, wife of Major Wade Hampton Overton. Their trip began on January 19, 1815, and ended twenty-five days later in New Orleans. Burke made no mention of a crew.[10]

From all indications, the *Cumberland* encountered none of the trials Rachel experienced on another flatboat, *Adventure,* thirty-five years earlier. The trip must have reminded her of the journey she took with Jackson on Captain Stark's flatboat when they fled to Natchez in 1790 to escape alleged threats made by Lewis Robards, her husband at the time.

Rachel's carriage was unloaded at Natchez for the return trip overland.[11]

Waiting in New Orleans to greet Rachel and her assemblage were Jackson, Colonel Robert Butler, General John Coffee, Colonel George Smith, Jackey Caffery, Stockley Donelson Hays, John Hutchings, Billy Donelson and Captain John Donelson. It was a regular Donelson family gathering. Rachel probably took one look at her husband's wasted appearance and wonder if she was close to becoming a widow once again. Jackson suffered from dysentery and had worked constantly for the last two months. "Of all men on earth," she wrote Robert Hays, "he does the most business from daylight to ten at night and devotes little time to pleasure."[12]

The joy of Rachel and Jackson's reunion, Brand wrote, certainly repaid some of the pain of separation. "Although like most intimate moments in history its details went unrecorded. And like most reunions, this one was both more and less than the partners had participated. Rachel had not realized what a hero her husband was to the Americans in the city or how he annoyed the French and other Europeans."[13]

Rachel should not have been surprised at what her husband had been through since she had also been laboring similar hours for years. "Rachel was full of gratitude," Burke wrote, "because of the deliverance of her husband. Rachel was forty-eight years old and plump, her complexion had lost its fairness from long hours in the warm Tennessee sunshine, in her beloved garden or riding horseback about their plantation."[14]

Neither Rachel nor the Nashville seamstresses she employed had any concept of New Orleans fashions. Edward Livingston's wife, Louise Davezac, kindly took Rachel in hand with bolts of fabric, trim and a corps of French dressmakers. She helped Rachel select fabric for the deep violet velvet gown she wore to the February 22 celebration of Washington's birthday.[15] "There was no gray in her black hair," Marquis James wrote, "her generous lips ready for a warm smile revealing teeth that would have been the pride of a duchess." Regardless of her size, James said Rachel's simplicity and unaffected kindliness won the admiration of the women of New Orleans.[16]

Meade Minnigerode, a London-born Yale graduate known for his biographies of Herman Melville and Aaron Burr, agreed with James' assessment of Rachel and the ladies of New Orleans. "They helped her, of course," Minnigerode wrote, "those fine Creole ladies; they told her what to do, they brought her clothes to wear; with gentle and ministering hands they set the seal of their own splendidly generous loyalty upon her going outs and comings in." Minnigerode was vilified in Nashville for an article he wrote about Rachel in the May 21, 1925, issue of *The Saturday Evening Post*.[17]

However, in his 1926 book, *Some American Ladies: Seven Informal Biographies*, Minnigerode was complimentary of Rachel. "They would have done this for any *Madame La Generale*, punctiliously and coldly; for Rachel they did it warm kindliness because they liked her. They stood in a stately row behind her chair and watched approaches to her dignity, guarded the portals of her negligent tongue." With Louise Livingston at her side, Minnigerode added, Rachel could do no wrong and made them all laugh heartily.[18]

Rachel wrote a vivid description of the New Orleans dinner on the evening of March 5 to Robert Hays, her brother-in-law:

> This being the first moment I could call my own ever since my arrival at this place. I gladly snatch the opportunity of writing you a few lines. In the first place, we had a tolerable passage in 25 days. We arrived at this place in time for the ball and celebration of Washington's birth night. To give you a description is beyond the power of my pen. The splendor of the brilliant assemblage, the magnificence of the supper and the ornaments of the room with all out great characters in large letters of gold on a long sheet of glass about four inches wide with lamps behind that they be read as we sat in supper. I was placed opposite the motto, "Jackson and Victory," at one [end]. On the table a most elegant pyramid, on the top was Viva Jackson in large letters and on the other the immortal Washington. There was a gold ham on the table. Suffice to say, nothing could excel the ornaments and supper—neither tea nor coffee was on the table.[19]

Brady wrote, "The supper was served on the ground floor of the French Exchange Building, which was decorated with flowers, colored lamps and transparencies with inscriptions hung between the arches. At the ball on the second floor, the Jacksons led out the first dance."[20]

Biographers described the Jacksons' dancing at the elegant dinner as seen through the words of a German caricaturist, Vincent Nolte. "After supper we were treated to a most delicious *pas de deux* by the conqueror and his spouse, an emigrant of the lower classes, whom he had from a Georgia planter and who explained by her enormous corpulence the French saying, 'She show how far the skin can be stretched.' To see these two figures, the general a long, haggard man with limbs like a skeleton and Madame la Generale, a shot, fat dumpling, bobbing opposite each other like half-drunken Indians to the wild medley of *Possum Up de Gum Tree* and endeavoring to make a spring into the air, was very remarkable and a far more edifying a spectacle than any European Ballet could have possibly furnished."[21]

Nolte sought attention for himself by ridiculing famous people. He once described British Queen Victoria as waddling like a duck as she walked and said she had a rabbit mouth—two front teeth protruding over her lower lip. Nolte, however, failed to call attention to his own misdeeds which were far more serious than Rachel Jackson's dancing or Queen Victoria's walking gait. He came to America in 1805 as a representative of a commercial house in Amsterdam. At various times thereafter, Nolte was imprisoned in London and New Orleans for debt.[22]

If Rachel was aware of such critics as Nolte, she never gave any indication in any of her letters that survived. Rachel had not lost the twinkle in her eyes or her maternal concern and the women of New Orleans realized this. An expression of their affection for her was the set of topaz jewelry they gave her.[23]

New Orleans life, however, was not for Rachel.

"In fact," Rachel continued, "I have seen more already than in all my life past. It is the finest county for the eye of a stranger but [in] a little while he tires of the dissipation of this place—so much amusements, balls, concerts, plays, theatre, etc., etc., but we don't attend half of them. I heard the full band of music a few evenings ago since we are living in a very comfortable house near the general's headquarters which is a large elegant building. We dined with General Gaines yesterday. He lives very stylish. Tomorrow we dine with General Carroll. Say to her [Mrs. Carroll] she must not grieve so much, he enjoys himself."[24]

Rachel, who was reunited with Jackson after all her unrepressed protests, had advice for the absent spouse of one of his generals.

"I've have given you some of the flowers; now the thorns," she wrote Hays, "Major [John] Reid tells me this morning nearly one thousand have died lately. Doctor Fore is no more. Gen. Coffee had him decently interred in the burying grounds. Mr. Webb, our near neighbor, is dead; married Mrs. F. Sanders' relation. We entertain great hopes of peace and that our troops may be once more at rest. Coffee's men have done so much and suffered more than all the army. Mr. J. says his troops should never be forgotten by their country. I am not very well. Col. Butler is well and Rachel and little Robert have been unwell. The General looks better in health than when I came here." She added that they would start for home in a few days.[25]

There were, however, more celebrations to attend. Jackson's forty-eighth birthday, March 15, 1815, called for a banquet in his honor. Finally, the Jacksons and their party, including Major Reid, left New Orleans taking a boat to

Rachel Jackson's letters were usually legible despite her having little, if any, formal education. In the late 1700s, when Rachel was growing up, her father, John Donelson, placed a higher value on educating his sons rather than his daughters. Regardless, Rachel usually got her point across in the correspondence that exists (Andrew Jackson's Hermitage, Nashville, TN).

Natchez, where Rachel's carriage awaited for the overland portion of the trip to The Hermitage.[26]

Brand wrote that it took the Jacksons and their party two weeks to reach Natchez because everyone on the Mississippi wanted to see the man who saved them from the British. In Natchez, Rachel and Jackson were feted with a supper and a ball. There were dinners for Jackson in and around Natchez.[27]

Did they recall Natchez horse races on the bluff or the soft summer nights in Bayou Pierre of twenty-five years earlier when they were young, in lust and in the first blooms of love? There must have met people there who were reminders of that time. Now, they were the general and his lady. When Jackson looked at Rachel did he see the results the years and his absence from home had wrought? Rachel undoubtedly looked forward to Jackson being home for a while to share the domestic bliss missing from their marriage. "It was a mark of Jackson's devotion to Rachel that he never uttered a negative word about the figure she cut," Bland wrote, "or intimated in the slightest manner that she didn't perfectly fit into any setting she found herself."[28]

"The celebration increased as they neared Nashville," Bland continued. "Militiamen who had preceded him home made an escort for the final miles. Politicians past, present and prospective crowded to share his aura. Senator Felix Grundy conveyed the gratitude of the state and republic. Governor Blount hosted the finest dinner Tennessee had ever laid on. The procession didn't end till his supporters deposited him at The Hermitage."[29]

Upon their arrival, Jackson received a message from the War Department that he would share the command of U.S. Armies with General Jacob J. Brown. Brown would command the Division of the North and Jackson the Division of the South. The command was something Jackson coveted and it assured Rachel he would be home for a while since he designated The Hermitage as his headquarters. Jackson had been away from home twenty-one months. During that time an enormous amount of responsibility fell upon Rachel.[30]

The Hermitage was filled to overflowing with Jackson's staff some of whom had been his wards. Rachel and Jackson were not in good health when they left New Orleans and the next four months they spent together at The Hermitage was balm to their bodies and soul. The plantation and their business interests demanded attention.[31]

Whether heady with his victory in War of 1812 or influenced with the adulations he received there and en route to Tennessee, Jackson envisioned the highest political office when his commission expired. He began accumulating a personal archive for a biography. "The smoke from the Battle of New Orleans had scarcely lifted before proposals were made to write the life of Jackson," John McDonough, a specialist in the History of the Nationalist Period at the Library of Congress, wrote. "Beginning with the Creek War days,

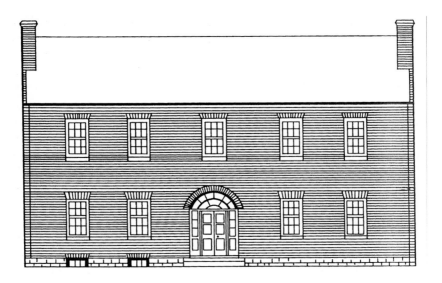

An architectural rendering of the south façade of the second Hermitage as it appeared while Rachel lived there prior to her death in 1828 (Andrew Jackson's Hermitage, Nashville, TN).

however, Jackson carefully accumulated his papers, often noting on a letter the name of the writer, a summary of contents and the date and nature of his reply."[32]

Originally, David Ramsey, a Revolutionary War veteran and South Carolina historian, was going to write the Jackson biography as soon as Major Reid completed information on the general's early life. In March 1815, a deranged tailor shot Ramsey in the back and writing the biography fell to Reid, who was also serving as his aide de camp. That summer, Reid said he was "diving into four chests" of Jackson papers. In June 1815, Reid wrote to his wife, "The General today removed his papers to his own house whither I shall accompany him." During the summer and early autumn of 1815, Reid's time was divided between performing his duty for Jackson and accumulating research and writing the biography.[33]

When Reid was ill at his home in Franklin, Tennessee, Jackson wrote him on June 13 to complain of his absence. "I have had a laborious siege of it," Jackson wrote, "and wanted your aid very much. The various communications to be made has kept me very busy."[34]

None of this would have escaped Rachel's notice. She knew everything that occurred at The Hermitage, looked upon her husband's young officers as surrogate sons and they returned that affection.[35] Jackson had previously served in the U.S. House of Representatives and Senate and she hated his absences even when he was a traveling circuit judge. The woman was not dumb.

She knew there was only one office that he husband had not yet reached but desired. She made the connection that her husband's published biography was a stepping stone to the presidency. Jackson's decision to go to Washington, where he could cultivate contacts, was further confirmation but the purpose of the trip was not exactly his decision.

Officials in Washington had questions about Jackson's declaring martial law in New Orleans, his treatment of some city residents and they wanted answers. Rather than carry out a lengthy long distance correspondence, Jackson decided to answer his critics in person. In mid-October, Jackson, Rachel, young Andrew and his nurse, Rachel's nephew Lemuel Donelson, Major Reid and house servants left The Hermitage for the nation's capital. Robert Butler was left in charge of the plantation, their businesses and their wards.[36]

Their journey was delayed by those showing their appreciation for Jackson's victory at New Orleans. In Knoxville, a parade and celebration banquet delayed their progress. Lynchburg, Virginia, celebrated their arrival with a banquet on November 7 attended by 300. One of those attending the banquet was former President Thomas Jefferson. Nine days later the Jackson entourage arrived in Washington.[37]

Rachel and Andrew Jackson must have been shocked when they saw the burned-out shell of the President's House, the Navy Yard obliterated of weapons and ammunition and other government buildings the British torched in August 1814. The center portion of the capitol had not yet been built. A covered, hundred-foot-long wooden walkway connected the Senate and House chambers which were burned, looted and gutted. The British claimed the burning and looting of Washington was in retaliation for the Americans looting and burning public and private buildings in York (now Toronto), the capital of Upper Canada.[38]

The invading forces might have completed their intended obliteration of the nation's capital except for a tornado that formed in the center of the city and headed straight for the British on Capitol Hill. Buildings were toppled, trees torn out by their roots and British cannons tossed around by the wind. Several British soldiers were killed. The rain continued for two hours, drenching the flames while the British scooted back to their ships.[39]

Jackson may have been the face of victory over the British at New Orleans, but the heroes of their looting and burning of government buildings in Washington were not President James Madison, President of the Senate Elbridge Gerry or Speaker of the House Henry Clay. They were clerks in the Senate, House and State Department. Senate clerks John McDonald and Lewis Machen commandeered a wagon, loaded the most valuable Senate documents including the only copy of the Senate's quarter-century executive history and the names and positions of all American military forces. The wagon lost a wheel before the conveyance got out of the district. Machen stole a wheel from a nearby blacksmith's shop. Then, the wagon overturned, documents were unloaded, repairs completed and the records were reloaded. The wagon was left for safekeeping with a Quaker village in Montgomery County, Maryland.[40]

House clerks J. T. Frost and Samuel Burch secured a cart with four oxen, loaded the most important House documents in it and drove nine miles into the countryside to a place of safety. Unfortunately, none of the 3,000 documents and rare books in the Library of Congress were saved.[41]

Secretary of State James Monroe was not in Washington. He was outside the district spying on British troop advancing into the city. He sent a message to his staff to secure precious national documents and department records. A State Department clerk, Stephen Pleasonton, rushed out to buy a quantity of coarse, durable linen and had it made into book bags. While Pleasonton was carefully placing the Declaration of Independence, the Constitution, international treaties and George Washington's correspondence including his commission resignation into the bags, Secretary of War John Armstrong rebuked Pleasonton for being an alarmist. The clerk ignored him, loaded the cart and drove it to a vacant house in Leesburg, Virginia. Pleasonton placed the documents in the house, locked the doors and gave the key to the local sheriff. All documents and records were later returned to their rightful place.[42]

First Lady Dolley Madison had the Gilbert Stuart portrait of George Washington cut from its frame. With the help of fellow Quaker Jacob Barker and his friend, Robert De Peyster, the portrait was taken to a farmer's house where they lodged overnight. In only twenty-six hours the British had looted and burned the Washington that Andrew and Rachel Jackson saw.[43]

What went through Jackson's mind as he looked at the destruction that was Washington must have been profound? Major Reid recalled at the meeting with Madison that "Gen. Jackson, who whenever the conversation flagged, was looking—with a melancholy air out the window on the ruins of our public buildings."[44]

It was Rachel's first look at the nation's capital and the largest city she had ever seen. Reconstruction of the President's House had not yet begun so the president and Mrs. Madison entertained the Jacksons in the Octagon House, built from 1798 to 1800 by Virginia plantation owner Colonel John Tayloe, who offered the residence as temporary quarters for the Madisons.[45]

The next day after their arrival in Washington, Jackson called on President Madison and the cabinet. Historian James Parton pointed out that his visit to Washington was couched in the language of an invitation from Secretary of War John Armstrong to arrange the posts and stations of the Army.[46]

Washington society, notwithstanding the city being in ruins and the bitterly cold weather, entertained lavishly for the Jacksons. A highlight was a visit to Mount Vernon, George Washington's plantation. The nasty weather took its toll on Rachel, young Andrew, and Lemuel. Just as they were recovering, Jackson became ill with, among other ailments, a massive infection in his left arm. His illness prolonged their departure from Washington until December 24.[47]

Postponement of their departure from Washington gave Reid time to work on the manuscript, which he carried with him in a trunk. After leaving Washington, Jackson's party stopped at New London, Virginia, at the home of the major's father Nathan Reid. When the Jacksons left New London on January 2, 1816, Reid remained behind to work on the first four chapters of the biography. Jackson left him a mare, Fanny, to ride back to Tennessee. Before Rachel, Jackson and their party arrived at The Hermitage on February 1, Reid had suddenly became ill and died on January 18.[48]

Rachel and Jackson were shocked when they received Nathan Reid's letter informing them of his son's death. Jackson wrote Nathan Reid of his heartache at the major's death. Upon the immediate receipt of Nathan Reid's letter, Jackson sent Major Abram Maury, Betsy Reid's father, to notify his daughter of her husband's passing. Jackson told Reid that the book must be finished for the benefit of his son's family and to consider the horse, Fanny, he left behind a gift. Jackson said he would pay for the shipment of the Reid's trunk and its contents.[49]

Rachel wrote Sophia Thorpe Reid, the major's mother, of her sympathy on her loss. The letter was not dated until April 27, 1816, three months after John Reid's passing, but it was in reply to a letter from Mrs. Reid. "Madam," Rachel wrote, "I received your friendly and affectionate letter of March 26th. I never wished more sincerely for anything than to hear from you at the time your letter came to hand. You perhaps will believe me when I declare to you that I was as much distressed the day I left your house as if you had alone been my nearest relations. Oh my, will you pardon me for not writing to you. I fully intended it the next day & nothing prevented it but my writing so bad a hand. Mrs. E. Reid [Elizabeth Branch Maury Reid, the widow] did not call on me. She passed about some distance, say 20 miles. How sincerely I have sympathized in your sorrows."[50]

Rachel told her that no one was exempt from trouble. "The great disposer of all who holds the destiny of nations in his hand see and knows what is best for us. Let us, my friend, resign to His will. Your son was an honour to his friends and country—a bright gem plucked from among them. But, alas, he has gone the ways of all earth. I cannot describe my feelings on the day I left your house." Rachel said she had written Reid's wife but have received no answer as yet.[51]

Jackson kept his word about the proceeds from the book. Reid's first four chapters and John Henry Eaton's seven chapters were published in

Philadelphia in 1818. The proceeds went to the estate of John Reid, which was administered by Major Abram Maury, his father-in-law.[52]

Eaton wrote a revision of the earlier biography in 1824, prior to the presidential election. "Since 1824, no presidential election year has passed without a campaign biography printed about the time a candidate is nominated, chiefly for the purpose of getting him elected," Jill Lenore wrote in *The New Yorker*.[53]

11

Florida in Her Future

Rachel and Jackson barely had time to reestablish a routine at The Hermitage after they returned from Washington. He left on February 24, 1816, to tour Gulf Coast installations. Rachel fell back into the familiar pattern of once again running the plantation as her husband would leave dozens of times to fulfill his military duties, further his political ambitions and acquire land.[1]

Rachel was lonely when he husband was absent. She had their eight-year-old adopted son and four-year-old Lyncoya to mother and various wards—many of whom were leaving the nest as well as numerous nieces and nephews who were always around. Surrounded by family and friends, she still probably suffered from depression. Her concern that young Andrew was growing up without the attention and influence of a father was legitimate. The boy was three when Jackson set off on his first expedition, Brady wrote, and he was seven when they were reunited in February 1815, and just learning his letters and figures. "In some ways, the Jacksons were more like grandparents than parents," Brady continued, "spoiling and coddling the little boy. Discipline never played a large role in their relationship with him and the results showed in later life."[2]

Rachel voiced her concern about his absences from their son in a letter to her husband. Replying to one of her letters on March 13, 1816, Jackson told her to tell their son, "if he will learn his book well his sweet papa with bring him a pretty from New Orleans. Kiss him for me and say to him I send my blessing." As usual he had messages for her to pass on to John Coffee. He added that he was sorry he had to leave her brother Lemuel who was supposed to accompany him, behind in Franklin.[3]

It was a common practice for Jackson to send messages to his officers and his political associates through letters to Rachel. The practice enabled Rachel to have an unusual knowledge of Jackson's political and military plans. He trusted Rachel to be the custodian of his personal and legal documents. When his good friend General Thomas Overton died in 1824, Jackson had his will. After Overton made some changes in his will, Jackson thought Overton returned the document to him. "If he did," he wrote Andrew Jackson Donelson, "you will find it in Mrs. Jackson's little trunk in which my valuable papers are. Ask your aunt to look into it and if the general's will is found there make it known to Judge Overton."[4]

When questions arose over Jackson's major general's commission while he was serving in the Senate, he again directed Donelson to check with Rachel although he did not want the documents forwarded. "My commissions will be found in a red pocketbook, I think, in your aunt's small trunk or my paper trunk in her room."[5] Rachel, as the archivist of her husband's documents, knew much more about her husband's activities than many writers conceded.

Jackson returned to The Hermitage on May 8, left again on August 20 for the Chickasaw-Cherokee Treaty negotiations and returned on October 11. Before returning, he wrote Rachel about their son. "Tell him that his sweet papa hears with pleasure that he has been a good boy and learns his book. Tell him his sweet papa labors hard to get money to educate him. But, when he learns and becomes a great man his sweet papa will be amply rewarded for all his care, expense and pains."[6]

Lyncoya had been living with the slaves. Jackson told Rachel how thankful he was that she took the child home and clothed him. "I have been much hurt to see him there with the Negroes, like a lost sheep without a shepherd." He instructed her to tell their overseer, Harrison Saunders, to sell nothing without her expressed orders or he would make him answered for more than the value. Jackson added a postscript saying, "I thank you for your admonition. I hope in all my acts and conduct through life they will measure up with propriety and dignity or at least with what I believe true dignity consists, that is to say honesty, propriety of conduct and honest independence."[7]

Some questioned if Jackson was endowed with all the moral characteristics he saw in himself and wanted Rachel to see.

When he returned home in October, Jackson and his fellow commissioners—David Meriwether, a former Georgia congressman, and Jesse Franklin, a former North Carolina governor and Congressman—had concluded their assignments with less than stellar means.[8]

Their work was succinctly described by Ronald M. Satz in the *Tennessee Encyclopedia of History and Culture*:

> As the economic distress in the East drew attention to western lands, the United States established a trading house near Fort Pickering in the Lower Chickasaw Bluffs in 1802. American officials encouraged the Chickasaws to buy goods on credit so as to establish individual debts that might later be paid off in tribal lands. Negotiations with mixed bloods who controlled tribal affairs paved the way for land cessions. In the treaties negotiated in 1808, 1816 and 1818, General Andrew Jackson and other treaty commissions used threats, economic coercion and bribery to acquire nearly

20,000,000 acres of land in Tennessee from the Chickasaws and open vital lines of communications through areas lying within the tribal domain.[9]

Six weeks later Jackson and John Hutchings purchased the Melton's Bluff plantation on the Tennessee River in the Northern Mississippi Territory. The plantation was established by John Melton who obtained his fortune by robbing pioneers' flatboats coming down the Tennessee River. Jackson and Hutchings farmed the plantation until 1827.[10]

The plantation's location was reminiscent of Jackson's Bayou Pierre location where he and Rachel lived together for a short time. Both were pivotal shipping locations with exotic settings. "No language can convey the beauties of Melton's Bluff," Anne N. Royall, a Washington newspaper correspondent, wrote in 1818. "I can sit in my room and see the whole plantation: the boats gliding down the river, the ducks, the geese and swans playing on the bosom of the stream with a full view of many islands." Royall described the large mansion as being built of logs with a shingled roof. "All the trade of East Tennessee passes by the Bluff and halt here to take on their pilots."[11]

Rachel and Jackson left The Hermitage October 27, 1817, for Melton's Bluff. John Hutchings, Rachel's nephew, was ill and Jackson drew up his will. Rachel was one of the witnesses. Hutchings died on November 20, leaving his estate to his son Andrew Jackson Hutchings with Jackson as the child's guardian. Young Hutchings' life was spent with the Jacksons at The Hermitage with General John Coffee overseeing his plantation near, Florence, Alabama.[12]

While the Jacksons were returning home from Hutchings' funeral, Indians attacked a supply boat ascending the Apalachicola River killing Lieutenant Richard W. Scott and forty-three men, women and children. The raid was apparently in retaliation for U.S. soldiers attacked in the Seminole village of Fowltown, along the Flint River. Jackson again left Rachel at The Hermitage and raced off to fight the First Seminole campaign. The Seminoles and Black Seminoles were allied with the British during the War of 1812 and were targets of frequent raids by militia from Georgia who sought runaway slaves as well as land and cattle.[13]

The United States had long wanted to acquire Florida, divided into East (capital at St. Augustine) and West (capital at Pensacola) sections. Florida was divided when the British controlled the territory from 1763 to 1784. West Florida stretched from the Apalachicola River to the Mississippi River including parts of what is now Alabama, Mississippi and Louisiana. After the Revolutionary War, Spain regained control of the territory it first settled in 1513.[14]

Rachel's husband managed to make himself the focal point of the First Seminole War and it almost wrecked his future political plans and, from some of her letters, she not only was aware of the charges against him but

exhibited deep hostility toward those who accused him of questionable decisions. Rachel was especially angry over allegations lodged against Jackson
for his conduct of the First Seminole war.

"President [James] Monroe sent General Andrew Jackson, the hero of
the Battle of New Orleans, to the Florida border in 1818 to stop the incur-
sions," wrote Daniel Preston, editor of The Papers of James Monroe at the
University of Mary Washington. "Literally interpreting his vague orders,
Jackson's troops invaded Florida, captured a Spanish fort at St. Marks, took
control of Pensacola and deposed the Spanish governor." Preston added that
Jackson also executed two British citizens whom he accused of having incited
the Seminoles to raid settlements in Georgia.[15]

"The invasion of Florida caused quite a stir in Washington, DC," Preston
continued. "Although Jackson said he had acted within the bounds of his instructions, Secretary of War John C. Calhoun disagreed and urged Monroe to
reprimand Jackson for acting without specific authority. In addition, foreign
diplomats and some congressmen demanded that Jackson be repudiated and
punished for his unauthorized invasion. Secretary of State John Q. Adams,
who saw a chance to add the Florida territory to the United States, came to
Jackson's defense stating that Jackson's measures were, in fact, authorized as
part of his orders to end the Indian raids. Monroe ultimately agreed with
Adams." Preston wrote that Monroe, before his death in 1831, wrote a letter
disclaiming any knowledge of the secret instructions that Jackson claimed he
had received.[16]

The irony of Adams' support of Jackson, in this instance, was the two
men became bitter political enemies over the final result of the 1824 presidential election.

Samuel T. Morison, Appellate Defense Counsel, Department of Defense,
had a much stronger condemnation of Jackson's actions in the First Seminole
War, which he called "one of the most notorious episode in the history of
American military justice."[17]

"In 1818," Morison wrote,

then Major General Andrew Jackson led an armed invasion of Spanish Florida,
thereby instigating what historians have since designed as the First Seminole War.
In the course of the conflict, his troops captured two British citizens, Alexander
Arbuthnot [a seventy-year-old Scottish trader], and Robert Ambrister [a British
soldier of fortune] who had been living and trading in Indian Territory before the
outbreak of the war. In his inimitable style, Jackson managed to precipitate a major
international incident as well as the first full-scale congressional military investigation in the nation's history when he impetuously ordered the summary trial and
execution of these men allegedly for "inciting" the Seminoles and their black allies to
engage in "savage warfare" against the United States. If the jingoistic overtone does
not seem a promising beginning to the story, it gets worse. William Winthrop, who is
widely acknowledged to be the leading authority on the American military, actually

concluded that Jackson himself was guilty of *murder* for ordering the execution of Ambrister contrary to the court martial verdict.[18]

"In any event," Morison continued, "Jackson's forces quite literally blew up Negro Fort by deliberately firing a cannon ball into the fort's ammunition depot. Some 270 men, women and children were killed in the explosion and the ensuing battle. The Americans reportedly took sixty-four prisoners, including two men who were identified as the resident Negro and Choctaw chiefs. In a nascent version of extraordinary rendition, they were turned over to a friendly Creek Indians who had been recruited to fight alongside the U. S. Army. The two men were immediately executed in retaliation for the death of an American prisoner, although not before the Choctaw chief was scalped alive." In a citation from the American State Papers: Foreign Relations 4:555, Morison noted that in exchange for assisting in the attack on the Negro Fort, the Creeks were promised booty seized there and a bounty of fifty dollars for each American-owned slave they captured.[19]

On March 26, 1818, Jackson wrote Rachel a long letter from Fort Gadsden, on the Apalachicola River. He spent most of the letter complaining about constant rains, bad roads, high waters, lack of supplies but assured her he was in good health. Jackson failed to mention in his letter that he, John Coffee, John Childress, James Jackson and Rachel's nephew John Donelson signed an agreement to purchase land in Alabama for Philadelphia investors.[20]

Just as the War of 1812 did not curtail his horse racing interests, the First Seminole War failed to keep Jackson from speculating in land. On April 10, he wrote Rachel about a letter he received from Rep. Thomas Claibourne regarding his earlier congressional appeal for land due her father for his work as commissioner in the Big Bend of the Tennessee River, in Alabama, shortly before he was killed. "It affords such prospects of relief to Mrs. Caffery [Rachel's sister Mary] and Mrs. Hays [her sister Jane] in procuring a permanent settlement of land and aiding Mrs. Hutchings [her sister Catherine] in paying for what she has bought."[21]

On April 16, Jackson reached Bowlegs Town, 100 miles into the Florida interior, experienced a brief skirmish, and ordered the town looted. Ambrister wondered into their camp at midnight. He already had Arbuthnot in custody. In a hurry to get back to Tennessee, Jackson told Calhoun his presence in Florida was no longer needed. However, there was the matter of the two British citizens. On April 26, Jackson ordered a "special" court martial convened. "The proceedings then moved with breathtaking alacrity," Morison wrote, "over the course of the next seventy-two hours, the defendants were formally charged, tried, convicted and executed."[22]

Arbuthnot contested his charges but Ambrister threw himself on the mercy of the court. "The panel had initially sentenced both men to death but upon reconsideration reduced Ambrister's sentence to fifty lashes and one year's confinement at hard labor," Morison wrote. The military court adjourned *sine die*. "Never a stickler for legal formalities," Morison continued, "Jackson was not inclined to let a mere verdict stand in the way of exacting vengeance. As such, he presumed as the convening authority to approve the findings and sentence with respect to Arbuthnot but disapproved the reconsideration of the sentence given Ambrister and re-imposed the death penalty. Shortly thereafter, Arbuthnot was hanged from the yardarm of his schooner while Ambrister was given the military honor of being shot by a firing squad."[23]

In March and April, the Cypress Land Company was formed with Jackson as a stockholder owning shares in nine lots. He acquired land in Lauderdale County, Alabama. On June 2, he wrote Rachel from Fort Montgomery bragging, "I have destroyed the Babylon of the south, the red hot bed of the Indian war and depredations on our frontier by taking St. Marks and Pensacola." He asked her to meet him in Nashville on June 25, but he arrived three days late.[24]

While Jackson was concluding the Chickasaw treaty and buying town lots in Marathon, Alabama, a section in Franklin County and hiring William W. Crawford to manage the plantations there, Rachel wrote her nephew, Andrew Jackson Donelson, at West Point, in an interesting and revealing letter. Her October 19 missive told him how proud she was of his accomplishments thus far in life. "May you go on and prosper in every laudable undertaking is the sincere wish of a second mother," she wrote. She lamented the loss of family members—Severn Donelson, John Hutchings, John Samuel Donelson and his maternal grandfather Daniel Smith—in less than three years. "Your uncle Jackson has been from home going on five weeks. I hope he will be home next week."[25]

"I am sincere, I am in earnest and I speak as one that has authority," she told him. "That is experience convinces me that pure and undefiled religion is the greatest treasure on earth and that all the amiable qualities hang on this." Toward the end of her letter she again wrote, "I am looking for your uncle next week."[26]

This was a more assertive and less whiny Rachel as compared to her expressed woes during her husband's earlier absences. Patricia Brady attributed the change in Rachel as she aged to the responsibilities she had to assume during those days and her religion. "With Andrew away from home for months on end," Brady wrote, "she spent much of her free time in Bible study and in the company of ministers and the devout women of the First Presbyterian Church. Having seen the light herself, she could no longer be intimidated by people she considered ungodly—and Catholics were not among the godly as far as Evangelical Protestants were concerned."[27]

Jackson arrived at The Hermitage on November 12 but left on January 7, 1819, for Washington carrying records of his orders and correspondences to explain his conduct of the First Seminole War to the House Committee on Military Affairs. Jackson denied allegation that he invaded Pensacola to protect the land investment of he and his friends. On February 6, he replied to Rachel's January 20 letter, saying he regretted to learn she was indisposed and elaborated on his good health. "The Seminole war is still before the House. When a question may be taken, I know not as I never have been in Congress hall since I have been here nor do I mix with the members determined that my enemies shall not have it to say that I attempted to influence their vote. I am told there will be a great majority in my favor—and the *insidious* Mr. Clay will sink into that insignificance that all those who abandon principle and justice and would sacrifice their country for self-aggrandizement ought and will experience."[28]

Jackson accusing Clay of self-aggrandizement was hardly the point. Clay made it abundantly clear that Arbuthnot's actions were not wrong in any event as they merely "consisted in his trading without the limits of the United States with the Seminole Indians in the accustomed commodities which form the subject of the Indian trade; and that he sought to ingratiate himself with his customers by espousing their interests in regard to the provisions of the Treaty of Ghent, which they may honestly have believed them entitled to the restoration of their own lands"[29]

Clay contended that even if one assumed Arbuthnot and Ambrister were individually waging a private war they were not the proper subject of Jackson's military tribunal but should have been turned over to the civil authority. "Conversely," Morison wrote, "Clay's analysis continued if one assumes that Arbuthnot and Ambrister abandoned their neutral status by directly joining the Seminoles' cause, they were no more subject to immediate execution than the Seminoles themselves."[30]

"Over and above the execution of two British citizens," Morison continued, "Jackson's decision to occupy the Spanish garrisons at St. Marks and Pensacola without clear justification caught the Monroe administration in a diplomatic bind and the cabinet was sharply divided on the appropriate response. Behind closed doors, Jackson's staunch defender was the secretary of state [Adams] who saw the dislocation caused by the invasion as an opportunity to gain leverage in his negotiations with Spain over the final disposition of Florida. For these unrelated political reasons, Adams therefore urged the President to defend the invasion as an act of preemptive self-defense and the executions as legitimate acts of retributive justice."[31]

Morison said that Secretary of War John C. Calhoun, Secretary of the Treasury William H. Crawford and Attorney General William Wirt argued that Jackson waged an undeclared war against a nation in amity with the

United States in violation of Calhoun's explicit orders. "For that reason they secretly urged Jackson's censure and roundly called for an investigation." President Monroe refused to issue a public censure of Jackson, Morison added, because of his own involvement.[32]

The Senate Committee on Military Affairs' statement on Jackson's execution of the two British subjects was a tap on the hand. "In reviewing the execution of Arbuthnot and Ambrister, your committee cannot but consider it as an unnecessary act of severity on the part of the commanding general and a departure from that mild and humane system towards prisoners, which, in all our conflicts with savage and civilized nations has heretofore considered not only honorable to the national character but comfortable to the dictates of sound policy."[33]

Two days later, Jackson was exonerated by the congressional committee. He left Washington on February 11 for a tour of the east arriving in New York on February 20.[34]

Meanwhile, Rachel was dealing with yet another death in her extended family. Her niece Jane Caffery had married Ralph E. W. Earl, an artist who came to Nashville in January 1817 by way of England, Paris and Savannah. The couple frequently visited at The Hermitage. Jane and her infant son died in childbirth a year later. Rachel wrote Earl, then living in Nashville, on February 23 to check if she had any mail from Jackson who was still in the east. "I can't help feeling so much anxiety but hope has supported so often and still does," she wrote.[35]

"Let me as a real and sincere friend persuade you to try and reconcile the solemn dispensation for be assured my friend you have not to weep as those who have no hope. Angels wafted her on their celestial wings to the blooming garden of roses that have no thorns where honey has no sting. Look forward to that happy period when we shall meet all our dear friends in heaven where the parting sigh will be no longer heard. All tears will be wiped from our eyes."[36]

"I can say with truth that a more correct young man I never knew therefore put your trust in the Lord. He will never desert nor forsake those that chose him."[37]

While Jackson was being wined and dined in the east, sitting for portraits in Philadelphia and Baltimore he apparently was not keeping in touch with Rachel. A March 18 letter to William Davenport, a career army officer from Pennsylvania who had been in Nashville the previous March, indicated Rachel was trying to get news of Jackson. "I must repeat the thanks I owe you for writing to me at the time you did. It was relieving my mind from doubts and fears for the welfare of my dear husband. I am indeed gratified at the attentions the citizens of Philadelphia and New York have manifested toward the general in as much as the insidious base enemies that envy, even to the green-eyed jealousy—what a combination of villainy. Indeed, I did think hard, that after all the fatigues and hardships of so many campaigns after all arraigned and called in question by a set of reptiles. Well, let us forgive them. How shall I relate the scenes of sorrow I have experienced since you left us?" Rachel lamented the passing of her brother Severn, her friend Mary Hamlin and her niece Jane Earl.[38]

Rachel's use of terms such as *insidious base enemies, green-eyed jealousy* and *a set of reptiles* to describe Jackson's adversaries in Washington were certainly an indication she knew about the accusations against Jackson arising from the first Seminole War. Her religion required that she forgive those who accused Jackson and wanted him held accountable. But, how did she defend him, in the light of her religion, for the executions of the two British citizens who many considered innocent?

Then, there were the soldiers that Jackson ordered executed in Alabama. If Rachel was unaware of their deaths at the time, she certainly learned about the incidents a few years later.[39]

The day after Rachel wrote Davenport inquiring about her husband, Jackson left for Tennessee. He arrived at The Hermitage on April 2. Rachel once again attempted to minister to her husband's ill health from May 2 through May 12. In the spring and summer of 1819, Jackson dabbled in politics, was in and out of his sick bed, engaged in Indian treaty negotiations and entertained President James Monroe and his entourage at The Hermitage.[40]

Monroe arrived at The Hermitage on June 5, and remained there until going into Nashville to attend a public dinner at the Nashville Inn on June 9. The next day he toured and spoke at the Nashville Female Academy, a finishing school which attracted students from Texas, states east of the Mississippi River and from Europe. The imposing structure on Church Street, its curriculum and faculty were points of pride for Nashvillians. Prominent men on its board of trustees included Felix Grundy, James Trimble and John P. Irwin. On June 10, Monroe was honored by Masons with a public dinner at the Nashville Inn. After a ball at the Nashville Inn the next day, Monroe returned to The Hermitage and remained there until he and Jackson left for a tour of Kentucky on June 14. Jackson returned to The Hermitage on July 11, and a month later left to take of business on his plantation in Florence, Alabama.[41]

Undoubtedly, Monroe and Jackson discussed the territorial governorship of Florida during his extended stay at the Hermitage.

Rachel, of course, was once again left in charge of the plantation, their cotton gin and other businesses. Monroe's visit probably also made it clear to the Jacksons they need a larger home. The small log farmhouse had outlived its usefulness and the Jacksons, with his army pay and land deals, decided they could afford to build a new home. Rachel selected the site in a large flat field near where an old blockhouse once stood and Jackson refused to change it. "Mrs. Jackson chose this spot," Jackson said, "and she shall have her wish. I am going to build this house for her." In August 1819, Jackson contracted with Benjamin Decker for carpentry and construction of a new Hermitage.[42]

The structure, build of brick fired on the property, and oak timbers was about 85 feet wide, Marquis James wrote, and about the same in depth. A small front porch led into a wide first floor hallway with two parlors, a dining room and the Jackson's bedroom. The second floor had four bedrooms off another wide hall. There was a summer kitchen in the basement. The house had nine fireplaces. The kitchen and house servants' quarters were in the rear and Jackson's office was on the west side of the new house.[43]

Shortly after contracting with Decker to build the new house, Jackson again became ill and Rachel was there to nurse him through the illness due to his failure to take care of himself during the First Seminole War. A lingering illness did not keep Jackson at home. He was away again looking after his Evans Springs plantation in Florence.[44]

The Jacksons were not exempt from the financial panic of 1819, which was the nation's first financial downfall resulting from the re-charter of the Second Bank of the United States and ended the post–War of 1812, economic expansion.[45] In a single legal action, Jackson sued 129 people who owed him money.[46]

An engraving of the second Hermitage showing Andrew Jackson's office and horses in a pasture. The second Hermitage was where Rachel Jackson lived out her final years before passing away in 1828 (Library of Congress, Prints and Photographs Division).

Construction continued on the new Hermitage, however. On January 7, 1821, the Jacksons attended a Nashville ball honoring his victory at the Battle of New Orleans.[47]

President Monroe had to make a decision. The War Department, after the War of 1812 and the First Seminole War, supposedly wanted to downsize the Army so there would be no need for two major generals. General Jacob Brown had seniority. The idea of eliminating Jackson's position as major general, according to Morison, had been discussed as an alternative to censure during House debate. The House of Representatives exonerated Jackson on all charges in the Florida invasion during the First Seminole War including land speculation there by Jackson and his friends.[48]

"Tellingly," Morison wrote, "once the political crisis had passed, the next Congress (including eighteen members who had taken Jackson's side in the censure debate) quietly voted to eliminate his position as a major general under the guise of reducing the size of the Army in a cost-cutting measure." Morison pointed out the action had the assent of Monroe and Calhoun.[49]

Jackson, on January 31, 1819, wrote Andrew Jackson Donelson, then at West Point, after he arrived in Washington to await the verdict on his actions in the First Seminole War. "I fortunately arrived here in time to explode one of the basest combination every formed, the object not to destroy me but the President of the United States and to wound my reputation and feelings. The virtue of a majority will defeat the hellish machinations at the head of which is Mr. Wm. H. Crawford and Mr. Speaker [Henry] Clay the latter's speech is in print and noted by me for the purpose of commenting on it as soon as the debate is ended—and if necessary I shall wait until the 4th of March when Mr. Clay has no congressional privileges to plead." Jackson sounded as if he intended to challenge Clay to a duel. He had already challenged General Winfield Scott to mortal combat for comments he made about Jackson's conduct of the First Seminole War. Scott, according to Jackson, refused the challenge on account of religious scruples.[50]

After the Adams-Onis Treaty was signed on February 22, 1819, where Spain ceded Florida to the United States for $5 million, the territory needed a governor. Monroe offered Jackson the territorial governorship of Florida. Jackson waivered back and forth on his decision. Rachel was hostile to the idea and urged him to refuse. However, there was an annual salary of $5,000, plus expenses, attached to the offer and Jackson accepted. He later wrote Andrew Jackson Donelson, "I sincerely regret that I did not adhere to my first determination not to accept the governorship of Florida. Your aunt appears very reluctant to go to the climate and really I am weary of public life."[51]

Nonetheless, Rachel, Jackson and their son along with her niece Narcissa Hays, servants and staff boarded a steamboat in Nashville for the trip.

On April 27, 1821, Rachel complained about the crowded conditions aboard the steamboat in a letter to her friend in Nashville, Eliza Kingsley, whose husband served under Jackson in the Battle of New Orleans. "We had not a very pleasant passage thither owing to so many passengers, nearly 200, more than half of them Negroes. How thankful should we be to our Heavenly Father." Perhaps there would have been more space on board if the Jacksons had not shipped their newly refurbished carriage on the steamboat. "On board," Marquis James wrote, "was their carriage, newly glassed, curtained with broad lace and upholstered in Morocco skins at an expenditure of $163.00 ($3,650 in 2017 dollars)."[52]

Before Rachel and her party reached the junction of the Mississippi River, news arrived about the explosion of the steamboat *Robertson* on the Cumberland River, near Eddyville, Kentucky. "There is not an hour of our lives but we are exposed to danger on this river," Rachel wrote her friend. "Oh, how can I describe to you my feelings when that sad and melancholy news reached us of the Robertson steamboat? Oh, how dreadful! Poor Sally McConnell! She traveled far to find a watery grave. Oh, Lord, thy will be done in all thy appointments."[53]

Rachel was referring to the April 17 tragedy aboard the steamboat *Robertson* where a boiler explosion took out one side of the boat and claimed a number of lives. Sally McConnell was scalded to death and a number of other Nashvillians perished.[54]

"I will give you a faint description of this place [New Orleans]," Rachel continued. "It reminds me of those words in Revelations, 'Great Babylon is before me.' Oh, the wickedness, the idolatry of this place! Unspeakable the riches and splendor. We were met at Natchez and conducted to this place. The house and furniture are so splendid I can't pretend a description."[55]

The letter writer was not the naïve Rachel who was overwhelmed by the New Orleans she first encountered seven years earlier. She was now steeped in her religion which offered little allowances for the frivolity and what she determined to be the excesses of society.

However, Rachel was more than happy to avail herself of the fine furnishings, linens, silver, Spanish cigars and adult beverages the city offered. She and Jackson purchased seven cases of furnishings in New Orleans for their new home. The freight bill for shipping back to Nashville was $273.25 ($6,190 in 2017 dollars). The purchases included a fine fluted mahogany bed for $100 ($2,240); mattress in fine ticking, $45 ($1,070); muslin for bed linens was $16 ($358), and $24 ($537) for a fine knotted Marseilles counterpane. They also purchased a new sideboard.[56]

Their purchases of adult beverages was indeed impressive given Rachel's religious proclivity. They spent $45 ($1,070) for eighteen gallons of brandy; $275 ($6,150) for a half pipe (56 gallons) of Madeira; $72 ($1,610) for six boxes of claret; $28 ($626) for a cask of porter; $30 ($671) for old whiskey; $16 ($358) for two boxes of brandied fruit, and $24 ($537) for six boxes of cigars. Rachel had developed a taste for Spanish cigars.[57]

"We were met at Natchez and conducted to this place," Rachel wrote. "The house and furniture is so splendid I can't give a description."[58] She neglected in this letter to tell her friend about their furniture and other purchases in New Orleans.

Rachel Jackson's Psalter, *Palms, Hymns and Spiritual Songs*, was actually two volumes bound together and apparently held in place with a needlepoint cover. They were edited by Isaac Watts and published in Philadelphia in 1818. Watts, a dissenter in England, wrote more than 500 hymns and songs including, "O God, Our Help in Ages Past" and "Joy to the World." (Andrew Jackson's Hermitage, Nashville, TN).

"The attention and honors paid to the General far exceed a recital by my pen," Rachel wrote. "They conducted him to the Grand Theater; his box was decorated with elegant hangings. At his appearance the theater sang with loud acclamations, 'Vive Jackson.' Songs of praise were sang by ladies and in the midst they crowned him with a crown of laurel. The Lord has promised his humble followers a crown that fadeth not away. The present one is already withered and the leaves are falling off. St. Paul says, 'all things shall work together for good to them who are in Christ Jesus.' I know I

A mahogany card table, circa 1821, was probably purchased from Francois Seignouret, in New Orleans. Seignouret, a furniture maker and wine merchant, was one of the leading craftsmen of his era (Andrew Jackson's Hermitage, Nashville, TN).

never was so tried before, tempted, proved in all things. I know the Redeemer liveth and that I am His by convent promise."[59]

She urged Eliza Kingsley to read the 137th Psalm and said that not a day or night passed that she did not repeat it. "Oh, for Zion! I wept when I saw this idolatry. Think not my dear friend that I am in the least unfaithful. It has a contrary effect. I have written you this through the greatest bustle and confusion. The nobility have assembled to escort the General with a full band of martial music to review the troops. Remember me to your dear husband, Mrs. Foster, Mrs. McLemore, Mrs. Martin and all my Christian friends. Say to my father in the gospel—Parson Blackburn—I shall always love him so much. Often I have blessed the Lord that I was permitted to be called by his ministry. Oh, farewell! Pray for your sister in a heathen land far from my people and church. Present me to all friends. I scarcely can hear for confusion."[60]

"I was much gratified, my dear Mrs. Jackson," Eliza Kingsley replied on May 15, "to hear of your safe arrival in New Orleans with that of your other friends and am truly thankful that you were so good as to remember your unworthy friend amidst all the honors and attentions paid you by the respectable citizens of that place and am still more pleased to know that although you are surrounded by circumstances which are calculated to fix our attention on earth. And, in too many instances, to draw our attention from God. You are firm and steadfast and have a view of the hills from whence all our comfort flows. Yes, we are the monuments of redeeming mercy, protected from many evils and preserved through many dangerous scenes while many are hurled from this footstool of mercy in the twinkling of an eye called to appear before the awful Judge."[61]

On June 21, Rachel replied to Eliza's letter from West Florida. "I will now give you an account of our journey to this place. We took shipping on Lake Pontchartrain, crossed the Gulf Stream and landed at Mobile Bay at a town known by the name of Blakely. There we tarried nine days. From thence we went to Montpelier, Alabama. There we tarried *five weeks* awaiting the arrival of the Hornet that went with dispatches of the Governor General of Cuba on this Florida business."[62]

Rachel was no happier in Montpelier than she was in New Orleans. She complained that the Spanish as well as American soldiers profaned the Sabbath. She reminded Jackson that he should have taken her advice and turned down the governorship.[63]

"At length," Rachel continued, "she [the Hornet] arrived and we set out for Pensacola and are now within fifteen miles of that place. The General and the Spanish governor are negotiating the business. We are at a Spanish gentlemen's waiting the exchange of flags and then we go into that city of contention. Oh, how they dislike the idea! They are going to Havana—don't like the Americans nor the government. Oh, how shall I make you sensible

of what a heathen land I am in? Never but once have I heard a gospel ser-
mons nor heard the song of Zion sounded in my ear. Often I think of the
Babylonish captivity when they tauntingly called on them to sing the song of
Zion. The answer was, 'Oh how shall I sing the lord's song here in a foreign
land?' One replied, 'When I forget thee, O Jerusalem let my right hand forget
its craft or cunning; let my tongue cleave to the roof of my mouth when I
esteem not Jerusalem above my chief joy.' Oh, I can, with all my heart and
soul, say with truth, I, above all things, prefer the prosperity of the Church.
Oh, I feel as if I was in a vast howling wilderness, far from my friends in the
Lord, my home and country. The Sabbath is entirely neglected and profaned.
The regiment in Montpelier, where we stayed for five weeks, were no better
than the Spanish at this place. I was twice at the memorable Fort Mims, Fort
Montgomery near the Alabama [line]. Stayed two nights with Mrs. Mims she
is an intelligent woman in worldly affairs. Every step I have traveled on land
is a bed of white sand; no other timber other than long-leaf pine on the rivers
and live oak and magnolia. The most odoriferous flowers grow on them I ever
saw. Believe me, this country has been greatly overrated. The land produces
nothing but sweet potatoes and yams. One acre of our fine Tennessee land is
worth a thousand."[64]

Rachel told Eliza that Jackson wanted to go home as much as she did.
"We have the best house in town, I am told, and furnished."[65] Rachel oversaw
repairs to the residence and supervised the furnishings.[66]

Pensacola itself did not meet with Rachel's standards. She said houses
were in ruins, fine flower gardens neglected, the inhabitants spoke Spanish
and French and there were only a few white people there. "I am living on
Main Street which gives me an opportunity of seeing a great degree from
the upper galleries." She did find the ocean view to her liking with its vivid
colors but apparently found nothing to like in the people. "Seamen strolled
with knives in their belts and coin burning their pockets; absurd little Spanish soldiers; yellow women with well-turned limbs and insinuating glances;
Jamaican blacks bearing prodigious burdens on their heads; a fish peddler
filling the streets with incomprehensible cries; a Seminole Indian with an expression of unfriendliness in his carriage, and I must say the worst people are
the cast off Americans."[67]

"The General," Rachel told her friend, "I believe wants to get home
again as much as I do. He says to Captain Kingsley he will write to him as
soon as he reaches Pensacola. So much detention, I think the General wishes
he had taken my advice. His health is not as good as when he left home."
Rachel begged Eliza to write her often. "Remember me in prayer for I can't
find one in all my travels to help me on to God. The scripture says, 'as iron
sharpeneth iron so doth the face of friend his follow.' No, not one in this
wilderness. Oh, how I wept when I read your letter. Oh, be thankful for your

privilege. I have never seen Major Nicholas yet, but you would be surprised to see how many of our Tennesseans I have seen come to try to mend or better their situation."[68]

Rachel was not one to recoil from using whatever power was at her disposal to tamper down Pensacola's proclivity for disregarding the Sabbath. After three weeks of the city ignoring the Sabbath, Rachel was no longer an idle spectator. With Jackson's approval, she sent a major to announce new city ordinances for Sundays in Pensacola. The following Sabbath order was observed, doors were kept shut, gambling houses were closed, and cursing was not heard in the streets.[69]

Rachel's maid Betty was so carried away with her new environment that she apparently neglected her duties. While Rachel demanded a Sabbath ordinance be imposed, she appeared unable to deal with their slaves in a timely manner. She told Jackson about Betty's action and he threatened to order fifty lashes for her if the slave did not behave herself.[70]

On July 23, Rachel wrote Eliza Kingsley a long, rambling letter often repeating subjects she related in earlier correspondence.

> I have been here in this place for four weeks. The reason I have denied myself the pleasure of writing you is that I was waiting for the great events which have taken place in this our day. Oh, that I had the pen of a ready writer that I might give you a correct detail of the great transaction but it is as follows. We having a house prepared and furnished, the General advised me to move down and remain until he could propriety march in with the fourth regiment.[71]
>
> Three weeks the transports were bringing the Spanish troops from St. Mark's in order that they should all sail to Cuba at the same time. At length they arrived but during all this time the [Spanish] Governor of this place and the General had daily communications, yet his lordship never waited on the General in person. After the vessels returned from St. Mark's, the General came within two miles of Pensacola. They were then one week finishing the preliminaries and ceremonies to be observed on the day of his entrance into the city. At length, last Tuesday was the day. At seven o'clock, at the precise moment, they have in view under the American flag and a full band of music. The whole town was in motion. Never did I ever see so many pale faces. I am living on Main Street which gave me opportunity of seeing a great deal from the upper galleries. They marched by to the government house, where the two Generals met, in the manner prescribed then his Catholic majesty's flag was lowered and the American hoisted high in the air—not less than one hundred feet.[72]
>
> Oh, how they wept to see the last hope departed of their devoted city and country—delivering up the keys of the archives, the vessels lying at anchor, in full view, to waft them to their distant port. Next morning they set sail under convoy of the Hornet, a sloop of war, Anna Maria and the Tom Shields. How did the city sit solitary and mourn. Never did my heart feel more for any people. Being present, I entered immediately into their feelings. Their manners, laws and customs all changed and really a change was necessary. My pen almost drops from my hand, the effort is so far short so limited to what it might be.[73]
>
> Three Sabbaths I spent in this house before the country was in possession under

American government. In all that time, I was not an idle spectator. The Sabbath profanely kept; a great deal of noise and swearing in the streets; trade going on I think more than on any other day. They were so boisterous on that day, I sent Major Stanton to say to them that the approaching Sunday would be differently kept. I must say the worst people here are the cast out Americans and Negroes. Yesterday, I had the happiness of witnessing the truth of what I had said. Great order was observed; the doors kept shut; the gambling houses demolished; fiddling and dancing not heard any more on the Lord's Day; curses not to be heard.[74]

What, what has been done in one week? A province delivered to the American people; the laws of the land we live in they are now under. You can't conceive what an important, arduous, laborious work it has been and is. I had no idea of it until daily it unfolded the mystery to view. I am convinced that no mortal man could do this and suffer so many privations unless the God of our salvation was his help in every time of trouble. While the General was in camp fourteen miles from Pensacola, he was very sick. I went to see him and to try and persuade him to come to his house. But, no. All his friends tried. He said that when he came in it should be under his own standard and that would be the third time he had planted the flag on that wall. And, he has done so. Oh, how solemn was his pale countenance when he dismounted from his horse. Recollections of the perils and scene of war not to be discovered presented themselves to view.[75]

There were no shouts of joy or exultation heard but on the contrary we sympathized for these people. Still I think the Lord had a controversy with them. They were living far from God. If they would have the gospel of Jesus and his apostles it would have been otherwise but they did not. The field is white for harvest but where are the laborers? Not one. Oh, for one of our faithful ministers to come and impart the word to them. I have heard but one gospel sermon since we left home. But I know my Redeemer liveth. He is my shield. I shall not want. He will not leave me nor forsake me in all my trials through this wilderness. Oh, pray for me. I have need of their aid from my dear Christian friends.[76]

Rachel was an expert on wildernesses, having survived the 1,100-mile river trip in 1780 with her family. Harrodsburg, where she began her married life with Lewis Robards in 1785, was in the middle of a vast wilderness. Bayou Pierre, where she lived with Jackson in 1790, was only a bit more civilized.

"I will give you a faint description of the country and his place," Rachel wrote Eliza, "knowing that my dear friend will throw a veil over my errors and imperfections. Pensacola is a perfect plain, the land nearly as white as flour, yet productive of peach trees, oranges in abundance, grapes, figs, pomegranates, etc. etc."[77] In one of her earlier letters to Eliza, Rachel wrote that only sweet potatoes and yams grew in the Florida panhandle.

Fine flowers growing spontaneously for they have been neglected in gardens expecting a change of government. The town is immediately on the bay. The most beautiful water prospect I ever saw and from ten o'clock in the morning until ten at night we have the finest sea breeze. There is something in it so exhilarating, so pure, and so wholesome it enlivens the whole system. All the houses look in ruins, old as time. Many squares of the town appear grown over with the thicket shrubs, weeping willows and the Pride of China. All look neglected. The inhabitants all speak Spanish and French. Some speak four or five languages. Such a mixture you, nor any of us, ever had an idea of. There are fewer white people far than any other mixed with all nations under the canopy of heaven, almost in nature's darkness. But, thanks to the Lord that has put grace in this His servant to issue His proclamation in a language they all understand. I think the sanctuary is about to be purged for a minister of the Gospel to come over to the help of the Lord in this dark region.[78]

There is a Catholic church in this place and the priest seems a divine looking man. He comes to see us. He dined with us yesterday, the governor and secretary, French, Spanish, American ladies and all. I have as pleasant a house as any in town. We have a handsome view of the bay on Main Street. You will scarcely believe me but it is a fact the vessels are daily coming in loaded with people. The place is nearly full. A great many come for their health. It is very healthy—so pure and wholesome. No fields of corn or wheat in all my travels except one place near Montpelier. The growth entirely pine, some live-oak, magnolia, bay which are all evergreens. The weather is oppressively warm to me and raining every day. Sometimes the streets are two feet deep in water. But for the sand, we could not live. It has rained three months, almost every day since we left New Orleans. I have the society of Amanda Grage, the mother of Mr. Grage and two more Christian ladies. I fear I shall put your patience to the test. I pray you bear with me a little. I have so many things to write you and it may be the last opportunity I shall have and I know I have not half done justice to the picture. My dear husband is, I think, not any better as to his health. He has indeed performed a great work in his day. Had I heard by the hearing of the ear I could not have believed.[79]

Have we all gone from you so far that no intelligences can reach our place of destination? There is no mail; no post office here. All these inconveniences will be remedied shortly. Miss Grage received a letter from Mrs. Berryhill wherein she states the illness of Mr. Campbell and several others in Nashville but some pleasant news of the church. Oh, for Zion! I am not at rest nor can I be in such a heathen land. Say to Captain Kingsley the General sends his best wishes to you both. He will write when he can have a moment. Remember me with much love to all my friends. Say to Mrs. Foster not to forget me, Mrs. Judge Campbell, Miss P. Lewis, Miss Nancy Ayers, Mrs. Somerville and all and every one. How happy and thankful you should be in a land of gospel, light and liberty. Oh, rejoice and be glad far more it is to be desired than all the honor and riches in this vain world. Farwell, my dear friend and should the great Arbiter of fate order His servant not to see her kindred and friends again, I hope to meet you in the realms of everlasting bliss. Then I shall weep no more at parting. Do not be uneasy for me.[80]

Rachel ended the long letter saying, "Although the vine yield no fruit and the olive no oil, Yet, I serve the Lord." Could this have been a reference to Rachel's barren state? Little was known of her feelings about being unable to have children. She only mentioned young Andrew in the July letter to Eliza Kingsley once in a post script saying he was learning Spanish. Conditions in Pensacola, whatever they were, led Rachel and Jackson to decide to send young Andrew back to Tennessee. Col. Robert Butler was placed in charge of taking the young boy back to Rachel's brother, John Donelson, in Nashville.[81]

On August 25, Rachel wrote her brother about Jackson's disappointments in appointments he was unable to make as Florida's territorial governor. "In the first place, he has not the power to appoint one of his friends; which I thought was in part the reason for his coming. But far has it exceeded every calculation; it has almost taken his life. Captain Call says it is equal to the Seminole campaign. Well, I knew it would be a ruining concern. I shall not pretend to describe the toils, fatigue and trouble. Those Spaniards had as leave die as give up their country. He has terrible scenes. The governor has been put in the calaboose which is a terrible thing really. I was afraid there would be a rebellion but the Spanish troops were all gone to Havana. Several officers remaining here yet. We have little hope of setting out on the first of October for home. Little Andrew and Colonel Butler have started for Tennessee. He was the most anxious creature I ever saw in my life. They all begin to think with me that Tennessee is the best country yet. Tell our friends I hope to see them again in our country and to know it is the best I ever saw. What a pity that some do not know when they are well of in this world. They not only hurt themselves but those that are innocent."[82]

Rachel must have told Eliza Kingsley that she went to the theater in New Orleans and her friend questioned her actions. In a September letter to her, Rachel wrote, "You named, my dear friend, my going to the theater. I went once and then with much reluctance. I felt so little interest in it, however, I shall not take up much time in apologizing. My situation is a peculiar one at this time. I think you all must feel a great deal for me knowing how my heart recoiled at the idea of what I had to encounter." Rachel elaborated on the prayer meetings every Sunday. "The house is crowded so there is not room for them. Sincere prayers are constantly sent up to the Hearer of Prayer for a faithful minister. Oh, what a reviving, refreshing scene it would be to the Christians through few in numbers. The non-professors desired it. Blessed be God, He has a few even here that are bold in declaring their faith in Christ."[83]

Rachel's surviving correspondence from her time in Pensacola made no mention of her health although she often commented about Jackson aliments. In a September 24 letter to Rachel's brother John Donelson, Jackson said he expected to leave Pensacola by the first of October. "Mrs. Jackson's health is not good and I am determined to travel her as early as my business and her health will permit, even if I should be compelled to come back to settle my business and turn the government over to my successor. I am determined to resign my office the moment Congress meets and live near you the balance of my life."[84]

Jackson missed his departure deadline by a week. The Jacksons left Pensacola on October 7, following the Natchez Trace to Nashville. On November 4, Rachel's carriage and four arrived at The Hermitage.[85]

Rachel was concerned with furnishing their new home and, aside from the furniture purchased in New Orleans, the couple bought additional pieces.

Moving into a spacious eight-room home from basically a three-room dwelling required additional furnishings. Jackson claimed their plantation looked like it had been abandoned for a season when they returned from Florida. Jackson himself was in no better shape. "He had come perilously near a complete break down on their return from Florida," Brady wrote. "She believed he needed rest and relaxation to recover."[86]

Rachel, for the next two years, had her husband home most of the time except for trips to Alabama to supervise their plantation and that of Andrew Jackson Hutchings. There were ceremonial dinners honoring her husband. An English gardener, William Frost, designed a formal garden for Rachel behind the new house. She delighted in ordering flower seeds and bulbs from Cincinnati and watching their growth.[87]

She was also watching something else grow at The Hermitage—the increasing number of national newspapers arriving in her husband's office. Jackson's friends were pushing him to run for president and he was not turning them away.

Rachel was happy with those months of comparative quiet, Burke wrote. "She clung to her all too popular husband with apprehensions lest his friends would come take him away from her again." Burke pointed to a letter Rachel wrote her niece Emily Donelson, "I do hope they will leave Mr. Jackson alone. He is not a well man and never will be unless they allow him to rest. He has done his share for his country. How little time has he had to himself or his own interests in the thirty years of our married life? In all that time he has not spent one fourth of his days under his own roof."[88]

During those thirty years of their marriage Rachel wrote about, she was certainly aware of Jackson's engagement in the world of politics.

Her husband, however, was a careful creature of politics. Both the Jacksons enjoyed the recuperative waters of mineral springs. In April 1821, Jackson advised John Coffee on the benefits of visiting Harrodsburg Springs Spa in Mercer County, Kentucky. In April 1822, Jackson wrote James Gadsden he planned to spend a few weeks at the spa known as the Saratoga of the West. "It is probable I shall visit the Harrodsburg Springs this summer," he wrote Andrew Jackson Donelson when he was at Transylvania College in Lexington studying law. "Should I, I will send for you or see you in Lexington." On June 28, Jackson wrote Donelson that he had changed his mind and took a trip to Alabama. "The fatigue of the journey would counterbalance any prospect of benefit to be received from the water."[89]

More than likely Jackson knew the Tennessee legislature planned to nominate him for president the following month.[90] Traveling to Harrodsburg, Kentucky, would do nothing more than open up old wounds about Rachel and her first husband Lewis Robards. Their divorce trial, which branded Rachel an adulteress, had not been forgotten by members of the Robards family who were still living in Harrodsburg and Mercer County at that time.[91]Jackson was wise not to reopen old wounds.

Jackson discussed plans to run for president, Brady theorized, with his wife and she was opposed as it was not what she had envisioned for their retirement at The Hermitage. "I saw from the first," Rachel wrote, "it was wrong for him to fatigue Himself with such an important office. Even if he obtains it, in the end it will profit him nothing. Mr. Monroe is going out poor and much dissatisfied."[92]

The Jacksons' finances were not much better than Monroe's. The Tennessee legislature elected Jackson to the United States Senate in October 1823. When he left for Washington the next month he had to borrow money from John Overton to make the trip.

Jackson had previously been elected to the Senate in 1797 and served until April 1798 when he resigned to become a Tennessee Superior Court judge. The 1823 appointment had little to do with representing Tennessee in Senate business and everything to do with Jackson making himself available for the 1824 presidential election.

12

Rachel Goes
to Washington

Rachel was once again left at home to keep the plantation running, look after their business affairs and raise three boys. Their finances were at a low ebb. Jackson charged George Elliott $65 to breed his mares to Pacolet.[1] Rachel was slowly furnishing The Hermitage. On October 8, chairs costing $24 were purchased.[2] Four months later, it was discovered that the shipment of furniture they purchased in New Orleans from Joseph and Robert Woods was one package short.[3]

Rachel and Jackson had a number of furnishings with Tennessee origins. One unusual piece was a large walnut sugar chest, with a lower drawer. The sugar chest, circa 1815, had various wood inlays. Another was a cherry card table, circa 1810, crafted in Nashville by Thomas Houston, a brother of Sam Houston. A walnut chest of drawers, with brass hardware, circa 1810, was attributed to Nashville furniture maker Joseph McBride.[4]

Again, her husband was off to Washington in pursuit of the ultimate political goal and, as usual, he continued to promise they would never again be separated.

"Mrs. J. is more disconsolate than I ever knew her before," Jackson wrote John Overton on November 11, 1823. "I do assure you I leave home with more reluctances that I ever did in my life. It was so unlooked for, unwished for and so inconsistent with my feelings."[5]

En route to Washington, he wrote her from Staunton, Virginia, detailing his travel plans with John Eaton and Richard Call. "I have been greeted by the people wherever I have halted. To avoid much of this was one reason why I took the stage and even then in many places, on the way side, were collections who hailed and stopped the stage to shake me by the hand. This through Virginia, I did not calculate on. Although tiresome and troublesome still it is gratifying the find that I have triumphed over the machinations of my enemies and still possess the confidence of the people. Were you only with me,

I could be satisfied. But, should providence once more permit us to meet again, I am solemnly resolved, with the permission of heaven, never to separate or be separated from you in this world."[6]

Jackson asked her to tell Andrew Jackson Donelson, who was just beginning his law practice and courting his first cousin Emily Tennessee Donelson, that he would write him later. Donelson was also assisting his aunt in managing the plantation and their business affairs. "Say to my son and my little ward Hutchings that I expect them to be obedient and attentive to you. Bless them for me and accept my prayers for your health and happiness until I return and believe me to be your affectionate husband."[7]

Jackson and Eaton, as Senators from Tennessee, arrived in Washington on December 3. The two men joined Richard Keith Call, a territorial representative from Florida who served under Jackson from the Creek Wars through the First

Sugar was a scarce commodity in the late 1700s and early 1800s and was kept under lock and key. The Jacksons' sugar chest, circa 1815, was large even for the number of people it served. Made of walnut with various wood inlays, it is an elegant piece of furniture (Andrew Jackson's Hermitage, Nashville, TN).

Rachel and Andrew Jackson enjoyed fine furnishings when they were able to afford them. Often it was Jackson, during his extensive travels, who purchased them. The mahogany candle stand, shown above, is circa 1820 and its maker is unknown (Andrew Jackson's Hermitage, Nashville, TN).

Seminole War, as boarders in the home of William and Rhoda O'Neal and their daughters. Soon thereafter, Eleanor Parke Custis Lewis, Martha Washington's granddaughter known as Nelly, presented Jackson with a china plate used by George Washington at his birthday galas. Her brother George Washington Parke Custis gave Jackson the pocket spyglass General Washington used during the Revolutionary War.[8]

Four days later Jackson found time to write Rachel, saying he went to church and heard a young Presbyterian minister. "I had a hope by this days' mail to have received a letter from you or Capt. A.J. Donelson. In this I have been disappointed; still hope I shall receive one soon. This separation has been more severe to me than any other, it being one that my mind was not prepared for nor can I see any necessity for. Still, my country did and no alternative was left for me but to obey. If providence permits us again to

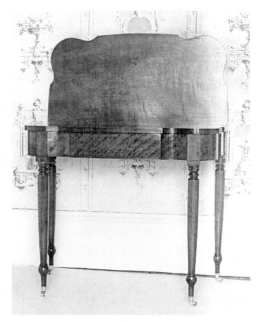

The beautiful cherry wood card table, shown above, was crafted in Nashville, circa 1810, by James Houston, a brother of General Sam Houston, a close military and political friend of Jackson's. Card tables, when not in use for games, were utilized as pier, console and end tables (Andrew Jackson, Hermitage, Nashville, TN).

The Jacksons' four-drawer chest, in walnut with tulip poplar with brass pulls, is attributed to Nashville furniture maker Joseph McBride. In 1801 and 1803, McBride had enough business to take in two apprentices (Andrew Jackson's Hermitage, Nashville, TN).

unite, we must travel together and live together whilst permitted to remain tenants here below. Before I leave this, I shall engage rooms for your reception next fall. I shall expect you to write me as often as you can."[9]

He asked for a statement of his crops from Parsons (another overseer) as soon as they were housed and expected Donelson to write him often. "I shall be delighted to receive a letter from our son, little Hutchings and even Lyno-cya. The latter I would like to exhibit to Mr. Monroe and the Secretary of War as I mean to try and have him received at the military school [West Point] as early as I can. I shall examine the college here with a view, if I like it, and its moral government to bring the two Andrews here next fall and leave them here." Jackson was referring to Columbia College, later George Washington University.[10]

In replying to Rachel's November 23 letter, Jackson said he was glad to know she was well and said he was enjoying good health. "When we trust in providence, it is well placed and under every circumstance in life as you will observe, in Him alone we ought to trust, He is the fountain of all good, He giveth life and health and at pleasure taketh it away and we ought to conduct in all things that we ought always to be prepared to say His will be done. Therefore, I am sure in this variable climate if it is His will I shall enjoy as much health here as at home provided I can bring my mind to be calm under our separation. This, being informed of your health, I shall endeavor to do."[11]

Jackson's reply about their crops getting out indicated Rachel wrote him about plantation business. "I hope," he continued, "Mr. Parsons will in all things do what you desire. I have confidence in him and I am sure he will obey you in all things you require. I do not wish my hands labored too hard and if you think they are, I know you will name it to him and he will moderate. I wish them well fed and warmly clothed and they will be then content and happy. This is my wish. I do not want them in any way oppressed and if they behave well I am sure Mr. Parsons, knowing my wishes, will treat them well."[12]

Jackson asked Rachel to tell Colonel Robert Butler he would write him soon. "I shall either get him into the army again or a civil appointment," he wrote.[13]

A week later, Eaton wrote Rachel, "The general is in very fine health and in just as good spirits. He has so many visits however to make as well amongst the ladies and the gentlemen that it is quite probably he is not a punctual correspondent and therefore it is that I write to you. He is constantly in motion to some dinner party or other and tonight stands engaged at a large dancing party at Gen. Brown's; but whether or not he will become one of the dancers shall become the subject of some future letter. I assure you he is in most excellent health, much better than he has been in a long time. The journey was of great service to him and since arriving here is in just as comfortable quarters as he could have."[14]

Eaton closed his letter by telling Rachel that all his old quarrels had been settled. "The general is at peace and in friendship with Gen. Scott, Gen. Cocke and Mr. Clay and what you would never have expected Col. [Thomas H.] Benton. He is in harmony and good understanding with everybody, a thing I know you will be happy to hear."[15]

Eaton's letter to Rachel further reinforced her knowledge of Jackson's actions during the First Seminole War with his mention of her husband's opponents. Eaton, however, was politically naïve if he ever considered Jackson and Henry Clay to be in good harmony. They both wanted the same position and would spare no quarter to achieve their goal.

Jackson wrote a postscript to Eaton's letter. "The enclosed information is all true but highly colored as it respects the dining and visits. Too much of that is true and as yet I cannot free myself from them. It is a pleasing subject to me that I am now at peace with all the world. The kindness and attention of my friend, Major Eaton, has added much to my comfort and health. I shall write you soon. Hope to hear that your health is good."[16]

In a December 21 letter Jackson took great pains to assure Rachel he was living and behaving in Washington in the same manner as if she were there with him. "The kind attention of my friend Eaton has been great and to him I feel truly indebted for the comfortable quarters we occupy. We are in the family of Mr. O'Neal whose amiable pious wife and two daughters, one married the other single, take every pains in their power to make us comfortable and agreeable. Mr. O'Neal himself is an agreeable man. This family has been wealthy, but by misfortune and endorsements for others, has been reduced to the necessity of keeping a boarding house. I can with truth say I never was in a more agreeable and worthy family."[17]

Jackson, however, was not finished spouting the worthiness of the O'Neal family. Rachel must have been wondering just what was happening. "When we have a leisure hour in the evening," he continued, "we spend it with the family. Mrs. Timberlake, the married daughter whose husband belongs to our navy, plays on the piano delightfully and every Sunday evening entertains her pious mother with sacred music to which we are invited and the single daughter, who is also pious, and sings well unites with the music. I am thus particular in giving you a narrative of our situation with which I know you will be pleased. Every Sunday we spend at church. This family belongs to the Methodist society. On last Sunday, as I named to you I went with Mrs. Watson to her church. She belongs to the Presbyterians. Today I went to hear a Baptist whose church in near us and was edified by a good concise discourse. So, my dear, you see that, not withstanding, I am in the midst of intrigue, gaiety and bustle, I spend my Sundays and leisure hours agreeable and I hope profitably. As to leisure, I have but little and could I get clear of the dining parties, I think with care, I can maintain my health. But under existing circumstances, I cannot yet (until I go the rounds) refuse; the president is very kind to me; indeed amidst the intrigue for the next presidency here. I get on pretty well as I touch not, handle not that of unclean procedures. I keep myself entirely aloof from the intriguers and caucus mongers with a determination that if I am brought into that office it shall be by the free unsolicited voice of the people. I trust that the God of Isaac and of Jacob will protect you and give you health in my absence. In Him alone we ought to trust. He alone can preserve and guide us through this troublesome world and I am sure He will hear your prayers. We are told that the prayers of the righteous prevail much and I add mine for your health and preservation until we meet again."[18]

It is unfortunate that few, if any, of Rachel's letters from this period have survived. Would she have shared Jackson's opinion of the O'Neal family if she had been with him in Washington? Would she have detected the social intimacy between Margaret O'Neal Timberlake and Eaton? At that time, Eaton was already deeply involved in the O'Neal's fiscal affairs which Jackson failed to mention especially since a big part of William O'Neal's financial problems came from endorsing notes for Benjamin G. Orr, a former Washington mayor who held a government contract to supply the army with rations during the Creek War.[19]

Harold D. Moser, David R. Hoth and George H. Hoemann, editors of *The Papers of Andrew Jackson Volume V*, wrote, "Among others, O'Neal had endorsed notes for Benjamin G. Orr, who had suffered financial collapse. John H. Eaton had helped the O'Neals through financial difficulties, assuming their debts in exchange for their property, then deeding the property back to the family and building a house for Mrs. O'Neal on land owned by her husband."[20]

Orr contracted with Secretary of War John C. Calhoun to furnish rations for troops fighting the Creek War in Georgia from June 1, 1818 to May 31, 1819. Orr was advanced $80,000 by the federal government, failed to honor his commitment and asked friends and associates, including O'Neal, to sign notes for him. Orr died before everything was settled and the federal government sued his estate for the $45,000 owed them.[21]

Eaton was no stranger to the ways of Washington, having served as a United States Senator from Tennessee since 1818.[22] Consequently, Eaton knew the O'Neal family quite well, which included their older daughter Margaret O'Neal Timberlake, destined to be his second wife. It is doubtful if Eaton undertook to assist another Washington family in financial straits in the manner he extended to the O'Neals. Jackson mentioned Mrs. Timberlake in his next letter to Rachel.

"Major [William] Davenport is now with us with his young and amiable wife that he has lately married in Philadelphia. He has given this family your character and Mrs. Timberlake (from what she has heard from Major Eaton and Major Davenport) has requested me to present you with her respects. When you come here I am convinced you will be much pleased with this family. The only consolation to friends who are separated is the pleasure of communicating with each other by writing. How grateful this converse between husband and wife. I will therefore, as you have requested me, endeavor to content myself through this winters' absence, endeavoring by occasionally writing you, to console myself and expecting often to hear from you. I have received the letter from my son. I have read it with great pleasure and have answered it which I enclose. I hope in the next to see his handwriting improve."[23]

Jackson told Rachel he was so glad that her niece Milberry Donelson, the daughter of William and Charity Dickinson Donelson, was staying with her and that other ladies were visiting her. "I hope their cheerful dispositions will keep your spirits up," he wrote before turning his attention to their plantation. "I am much pleased with the information of my crop and the forwardness with which Mr. Parsons has got it. I hope before the cold weather sets in he will have it housed and ready for market. The weather here has been very fine this season although variable. Capt. A. J. Donelson writes me often. Present me to him affectionaly and to the Andrews and Miss Milberry." He also mentioned writing Parson William Hume and asking him to visit Rachel and inquired about the church building being constructed at The Hermitage.[24]

There was something else building on the national political scene. People in Pennsylvania and Ohio in late December 1823 were talking about an issue which would have a profound meaning for both Jacksons. "Like most rumors," Brady wrote, "they were lurid and exaggerated. Evoking Andrew's reputation for violence, gossips claimed that he had driven Rachel's husband away and then lived with her for several years before she was divorced. Still imagining the general to be an outside choice [for the presidency] his political enemies didn't yet bother to go into print with those charges."[25]

In February 1824, Eleanor Custis Lewis began questioning the rumors about the Jacksons' marriage and asked Congressman George Tucker, a fellow Virginian, to conduct an investigation. Lewis and her brother George Washington Parke Custis were informally adopted by their paternal grandmother, Martha Custis, and stepgrandfather George Washington after the death of their father, John Parke Custis, in 1781. Two older sisters remained with their mother, Eleanor Calvert Custis, and stepfather, David Stuart.[26]

Who Tucker asked about the Jacksons' background was not clear but the report he sent Lewis was riddled with inaccuracies but satisfied her curiosity. After Lewis received Tucker's narrative she wrote her friend, Elizabeth Bordley Gibson, "I am happy to assure you, my friend, that Gen. Jackson is

In 1823, Andrew Jackson and several neighbors donated money to build a local church. Jackson provided the land. Completed in January 1824, the brick building measured 50 by 30 feet. Benches were arranged in a semi-circle around the pulpit. Originally called the Ephesus Church, the congregation soon became affiliated with the Presbyterian Church (Andrew Jackson's Hermitage, Nashville, TN).

not the wretch he is represented. Tucker has conversed with several persons of great respectability and well acquainted with every circumstance within the last week. He left us this morning and this is declared to be the real state of the case. Miss Donelson ran away with and married her first husband at fourteen-years-old. Gen. Jackson had lived a long time with her parents and was under obligation to them. He did not see the daughter for two years after her marriage during which time she endured the most cruel treatment from her husband. He frequently beat her severely, forced her to fly for refuge to a neighbor's house. She was persuaded to return several times and was obliged to leave him as often. At last Gen. Jackson happened to witness this conduct and was called upon, as her parents' friend, for protection. He interfered and threatened to chastise the husband if he was ever guilty again. He still persisted and she was obliged to sue for divorce."[27]

Lewis wrote that a considerable time elapsed before the Jacksons were married. "Her first husband was never a soldier under Jackson and has been dead many years. Mr. Tucker adds that the circumstances and the case gained Jackson the esteem and approbation of the whole neighborhood in which they occurred. Col. [James] Gadsden always speaks of Mrs. Jackson as an excellent woman and he is devoted to Gen. Jackson. [Sen. Robert] Hayne assured me that no man was ever more vilely calumniated than Jackson and these are the most honorable and very correct evidences."[28] Lewis expressed her preference for president being either Jackson or Calhoun. "I think them the most honest and pure patriots."[29]

Lewis, however, was hardly an uninterested observer. She pushed Jackson to find a position in the Marines for Elizabeth Gibson's nephew. Lewis' daughter Parke, who she described as twenty-three and on the shelf, was being courted by a former ward of Jackson's, Edward George Washington Butler. They later married.[30]

Lewis' older sister Elizabeth (Eliza) Parke Custis was in many respects similar to Rachel—she was headstrong, her education was limited because of her gender and she was fond of music and horses. A relative later commented Eliza's tastes and pastimes were more those of a man than a woman and she regretted being unable to wear pants. Unlike Rachel, she had someone, her stepgrandfather George Washington, to warn her about the pitfalls of love and marriage but she did not listen. John Donelson hastily approved of Rachel's marriage to Lewis Robards but was too busy acquiring land to stay around for the wedding. It was almost as if Donelson could not wait to get his youngest daughter off his hands. Then, after the wedding, the Donelson family moved back to Nashville. Consequently, the eighteen-year-old Rachel had no one in Harrodsburg to turn to when her marriage became rocky; no one to advise her and no one to listen to her side of the story.

In 1796, Eliza married wealthy Englishman Thomas Law, twenty years her senior, whose fortune was derived from the East India Company. He arrived in America two years earlier with at least one of his three half-Indian sons. The couple separated in 1804—she received $1,500 a year and he got custody of their only child, a daughter. Law obtained a divorce in Vermont in 1811.[31] Eliza's annual stipend represented $32,100 in 2017.[32]

Rachel, however, had only the clothes on her back when Robards told her mother to send someone to take her off his hands—he was through with her. Where Eliza Custis had a caring stepgrandfather, Rachel's male Donelson relatives (her father had been murdered) appeared to be disinterested in her plight except for her brother Samuel, who came to her rescue from the abusive Robards in Harrodsburg.

Rachel knew exactly what happened in her relationship with Jackson before Robards divorced her and what the information would do to her husband's presidential ambitions. Her brother John Donelson wrote John Coffee, "Sister Rachel is making a great fuss about him [Jackson] for whenever she is alone she goes to crying tho he writes to her almost every week. She thinks he is in a bad state of health which keeps her constantly uneasy."[33]

"Why did Rachel weep?" Burke asked. "Not so much for the absence of her beloved; she had become accustomed to that after more than thirty years of married life. Did she have a woman's intuition of the torrents of criticism even then forming along the general's enemies that were about to break upon?"[34]

In his reply to her December 28 letter on January 15, 1824, Jackson made an effort to assure Rachel about the state of his health. "I am rejoiced to hear of your health and spirits and pray that they may continue until I return. I have been kept too busy since my arrival to adopt your advice of retiring early; you know my habits when at home, when I am without company, I retire at nine; when I have company, at ten to eleven as the company desires. But, here when the early part of the evening is spent with my friends who visit me; the latter must be spent in attention to duty and to business. One thing I can assure you [is] that I take as much care of my health as I can and am happy to say to you it has improved and is a good as I have any right to expect. I thank you for your prayers. Mine is offered up for a continuation of your health; may they be heard."[35]

Rachel had many things to consider that occurred before and during her marriage to Jackson but darker thoughts included her being legally designated as an adulteress in Robards divorce case. The trip to Natchez with Jackson and the time they spent living together on Bayou Pierre all transpired before Robards divorced her and before she married Jackson in 1794.

Burke hinted at that when she wrote that Rachel certainly did not court the public attention being conferred on Jackson:

> She thought of her impetuous marriage, of the Dickinson duel and of other incidents in the stormy life of the man she had married and worshiped. No, she did not invite the scrutiny of his enemies. It was all right between her soul and her God; she had a clear conscience and always felt that no matter what her husband did it was with the best of intentions. But, some things are difficult to explain. Hence she wept and prayed—for what she herself hardly knew—but there was gloom in her heart which was reflected in Jackson's own [letters] who wrote; "Still my love, there has been a gloom unusual over my spirits this winter that I cannot account for. I still try to arouse my former energy and fortitude to banish it but will obtrude itself on me at times."[36]

Rachel did not attempt to hide her misery—she had injured an eye—and other problems according to her January 4 letter to Jackson in Washington. Jackson replied on January 21, saying he sincerely regretted that she was indisposed. "I trust that kind providence will soon relieve you from the pain that the inflammation of your eye must inflict—with what pleasure would I apply the *cooling wash* was I with you. How painful it is to me to hear the least affliction in my absence." His next sentence did nothing to eliminate her misery. "I trust and hope that we will meet again when we will here below travel together while life lasts."[37]

Jackson assured Rachel his health was good although he was pressed with business and company. "The attentions I have received lose all their relish I assure you whilst you are absent. Still it is gratifying that, after all the shafts of envy and malice that has been leveled at me by my enemies, my country approves of my public conduct and that too amidst the combined intrigue and efforts of those who would by falsehood the most vile deprive me of public confidence if they could. But that providence who will always protect those who take virtue as their guide, has protected me and will shield me from the efforts of my enemies. In Him I always have put my trust and He has and will protect me."[38]

Jackson knew very well what Rachel's problem was when he referred to her health. "My love, remember you have promised me that you would bear up under my absence—recollect that your health much depend upon you keeping your mind calm and at ease and I pray you do so." He told her how much he appreciated her nieces staying with her. Jackson said he saw Edward G. W. Butler in Washington. Daniel S. Donelson and Samuel J. Hays were doing well at West Point but he was concerned that young Andrew and Hutchings were not paying proper attention to their studies.[39]

"Present me to Col. Butler and family. Say to him I will write him as soon as a bill that is now on its passage directing the lands in Florida to be surveyed is passed into law. Finding all things uncertain here, I will not write him until I can do so with more certainly."[40]

Rachel returned the greetings of Mrs. O'Neal and her daughters in her January 12 letter to Jackson who told her they reciprocated. Even before asking about Rachel's health, Jackson wanted to clear up any questions she might have about his leisure time in Washington. "It is true when I have leisure, my time passes with this family, but of leisure I have but little. Every mail brings me at least one dozen letters which are on business and requires answering. This occasions me much labor, which added to my congressional duties, is really oppressive. However, I am blessed with better health than when I left you and learning from your letter that you are blessed with health will add greatly to mine."[41]

He assumed Rachel had read in the newspapers about the comet(s) seen in Washington on January 23 and was sure they were responsible for the extraordinary winter. "I believe this is a phenomena, not before recorded in history. I have no recollection of hearing of two comets being seen at once in any country before the present."[42]

The comet Jackson wrote about was a single comet with two tails, one pointed toward the sun and the other away from the sun.[43]

Jackson expressed his appreciation that the church at The Hermitage was finished and hoped it would be a blessing to their neighborhood. Once again, he told Rachel,

> It was my desire to retire to private life and live free from the bustle of public life and the scenes of intrigue and corruption that appear to be the order of the day as practiced in this great city. There is one consolation left for me and that is, that I mingle not in it. I pursue my old course of doing that which my judgment dictates and fearing no consequences thus my conscience is left free from remorse, which is better than all earthly things can bestow.[44]
>
> I am pleased that everything appertaining to my farm goes well and that you have resolved to be contented in my absence. This is truly a consolation to me and I trust in that kind and overruling providence that He will bless you with health and that He will permit us once more to have a happy meeting." Jackson asked Rachel to have their son write him more often as he needed the exercise in improving his handwriting and diction.[45]

Jackson's February 6 letter to Rachel was redundant with a discussion of The Hermitage church, Eaton's letter to her three weeks earlier and the O'Neal family. "Our friends Call, Eaton and myself are the only occupants of one-half of the house of our worthy and amiable hostess Mrs. O'Neal and her charming family. I say hostess because the house is kept under her name, from the pecuniary losses of her husband Mr. O'Neal who is a good and worth man. We are as comfortable as we could be under my separation from you."[46]

Rachel was probably glad to hear her husband was abstaining from activities of the Washington social circle except for events he felt compelled to attend. Those included Mrs. Louisa Adams, wife of Secretary of State John Q. Adams, Mrs. Floride Calhoun, who was married to Secretary of War John C. Calhoun and Mrs. Elizabeth Wirt, wife of Attorney General William Wirt. "I have not yet visited Mrs. Monroe's drawing room. This I intend once and that the first good evening on which it happens." Jackson told Rachel about being presented the pistols given by the Marquis de Lafayette to George Washington.[47]

The pistols, he told Rachel, was the most acceptable gift he could receive—precious relics worthy of preservation. "I know you will think me vain but I assure vanity has no seat in my bosom but to be thought worthy of this deposit has confirmed me, that the independent course I have pursued, following the dictates of that judgment that the wise creator has endured me with has been right when approved by those whose approbation I ought most to esteem and is the greatest gratification I could enjoy by any expression or any portion of my country. It is, under the influence and intrigues of this city, a triumph over my enemies, of honest worth over corruption and will save the nation from the rule of demagogues who by intrigue are and have been attempting to cheat the people out of their constitutional rights by a caucus of congressional members."[48]

Two days later, Eaton replied to a letter he received from Rachel. He apologized for not having replied sooner:

> But, then my head is as full just not of politics, bills, laws and such like trash as to be wholly unable to work my fancy up to any point that can give interest to a letter. Well, this makes no difference … for inasmuch as there is a very strong probability that ere long you may be required to come into our political corps and join with us in the great affairs of the nation. It would not be a misplaced attempt even were I to tell you all about the little workings, management and intrigues that passes on here amidst our learned band of Congressmen. Would you believe it, we are so depraved as scarcely even to go to church unless to the Capitol where visits are made rather for the purpose of showing one's self than any pious feeling prompts and then it has such an air of fashion and show to go there more like going to the theatre than to a house of worship. Oh, we are truly a wondrous set; not much inferior to the good people of Sodom and Gomorrah spoken of in olden time who perished not on account of their virtues. In this list the general is not included for every Sunday he takes himself to some one of the churches and returns again about one o'clock. Now, while writing you, he is off attending to the admonitory voice of some good divine.[49]

The reference Eaton made to Rachel joining them in their Washington endeavors again indicated she was privy to their political plans for Jackson to win the presidency.

Eaton's letter reassured Rachel that her husband was not gallivanting around in the evenings any more than was absolutely necessary, that he had the most comfortable quarters, attended church every Sunday, suffered no exposure to weather as he traveled to and from the Capitol in a warm comfortable carriage and was in excellent health. "If the general had remained at home, I am satisfied he would not have enjoyed such good health. His farm would have annoyed him, business would have soon called him to Alabama or Nashville, exposure and wet would have been met with but here nothing of that is found. Going and returning from the Capitol is ample exercise and when at home reading and replying to letters and sitting with a round of pleasant company that is perpetually calling to see him keeps his mind employed and his spirits cheerful."[50]

Rachel asked Jackson when the congressional session would end. "I would to God answer that question; we have done little and there is so much to do" he replied on February 20. "I have a hope we will adjourn by the middle of April; some say not before the middle of May and others the middle of June. Believe me, I shall not stay a moment longer than I can leave it with propriety. The moment I can determine when this time will be, I shall advise you. I shall return the most expeditious route and that I expect will be by Pittsburgh and take the steamboat to Louisville. But, in due time you shall be advised of the time I leave here and my route. Be assured, my love, I shall not detain a moment longer than I can help. I am and will be as anxious to reach you as you can be to see me." He again advised that the two Andrews learn to behave well and be comfortable with company. Jackson asked about their friends and said he was glad Milberry was staying with Rachel.[51]

On March 16, Jackson wrote Rachel about his fifty-eighth birthday celebration in Washington:

> I had a few friends to dine with me among whom were our friend Gov. [David] Holmes of Mississippi, Mr. [Nathaniel] Macon of the Senate and Major [William] Bradford of the army who presented our son with "Coosa" and whom you recollect. There were heads of departments with the Honorable Speaker Mr. [Henry] Clay with many others from Boston, New York, etc., etc., and etc. Our friends Eaton and Call presided and the evening was pleasantly spent. I had like to have forgot to tell you our friend Edward Livingston was among the number. This morning at 11, I was requested to attend Mr. Monroe to receive the medal voted me by Congress on the 27th of February 1815. I attended accompanied with Eaton and Call and in the presence of Mrs. Monroe, Mrs. Hay, others and the heads of the departments and navy board with many members of Congress and my voluntary aide Edward Livingston. It was delivered in due form.[52]

Jackson's gold medal had a profile of him with the words, "Major General Andrew Jackson," on one side and figures on the other with the wording, "Resolution of Congress February 27, 1818, Battle of New Orleans January 8, 1815."[53] Jackson furnished the medal's design.[54]

"You are aware how disagreeable to me these shows of pomp and parade are and how irksome it is for me to speak of myself. Still it was necessary and I with reluctance performed it—not without a tremor which always seizes me on such occasions. I trust however when you read the sentiments expressed by me, some of them will be pleasing to you. I therefore have named it as I know everything that concerns me is interesting to you."[55]

Education of the two Andrews was apparently more important to Jackson than Rachel. He constantly asked her in his letters to make sure the two boys, especially Andrew Jr., spent time on not only their lessons but learn social interaction. "Tell my son how anxious I am that he may read and learn his book that he may become the possessor of those things that a grateful country has bestowed upon his papa. Tell him that it is his good conduct, happiness thro life that depends upon his procuring an education now, and with it, to imbibe proper moral habits that can entitle him to the possessions of them. To acquire those proper habits, he must be aware religiously on all occasions to adhere to truth and on no occasion to depart from it. Never to make a promise unless on due consideration and when made, to be sure to comply with it. This rule observed, with a proper attention now to his learning, will make him a great, good and useful man, which his papa wishes him and his little cousin Hutchings to become. Having experienced so much inconvenience from the want of a perfect education myself makes me so solicitous that his may be perfect. My dear wife, urge this upon him."[56]

Andrew Jackson, Jr., was fifteen years old and Jackson was still concerned about his reading!

There were more pressing concerns in Jackson's presidential campaign. His winning in a near landslide in Pennsylvania made him a leading contender by early March. As a result, Eaton wrote John Overton on March 12, suggesting they assemble information for a possible defense of the Jackson marriage. "Heretofore," Eaton wrote, "the radicals have not dreaded him. But now seemingly a most prominent rival, they are bringing all their batteries to bear against him."[57]

Overton responded to Eaton's request around April 22 when Overton sent Eaton his signed broadside dealing with the Jacksons' marriage. According to *The Papers of Andrew Jackson, Volume V,* the date on the signed broadside was May 4, 1827.[58]

Opposition research and documentation dealing with the Jacksons' marriage was not used in the 1824 presidential campaign. Moser, Hoth and Hoemann, editors of *The Papers of Andrew Jackson, Volume V,* opined that opposition newspapers in the 1824 campaign focused on his military temperament and authoritarian personality not his marriage.[59]

The March and April 1824 correspondence between Eaton and Overton regarding the Jackson marriage in *The Papers of Andrew Jackson, Volume V* partially refuted Parton's statements in Volume I of his *Life of Andrew Jackson.* "In fairness," Parton wrote, "it should be mentioned that Overton's statement was prepared and published in 1827, when Jackson was a candidate for the presidency. In fairness, too, it should be added that a gentleman [William B. Lewis] of high consideration in Tennessee spent months in investigating this single affair, and accumulated a mass of evidence in support of this version of it, which demonstrates the truth."[60] Eaton's correspondence clearly stated Overton prepared the letter three years earlier.

Jackson, Eaton, Call, Overton and probably Rachel were aware of the possibility that the adultery charge could surface at any time. Brady speculated whether Jackson warned Rachel. "Perhaps he told her when he arrived back at The Hermitage. Or perhaps he kept silent to avoid worrying her."[61]

Jackson's April and May letters to Rachel dealt mainly with his travel arrangements back home, the tariff bill, Colonel Butler being appointed surveyor general in Florida and getting payment for John Donelson's commission work at the Big Bend. "My love," he wrote on April 12, "I hope to leave here in the early part of May. I am truly wearied with lounging here doing nothing but feeding on public funds. We have really done nothing yet beneficial and for nine weeks the House of Representatives has engaged debating the Tariff that could have been as well decided in two. The moment I can say with certainty, the day I can leave here, I will inform you." He added that Mrs. O'Neal and her daughters sent their kind compliments and good wishes.[62]

Rachel had suggested the she start out to meet her husband in Louisville. In his May 19 letter, Jackson said it was uncertain when he would get to Louisville. "I think it will be best for you not to set out to meet me. If I get a steamship at Wheeling when I arrive there, I shall. I hope to reach you shortly after you receive this letter."[63]

Jackson finally arrived at The Hermitage on June 4. Burke described the couple's reunion. "By the time Rachel heard the uproar there were blacks, young and old, gathered to meet him. Then came his wife 'on wings of purest affection' to welcome him. The warmth of a June sun was no greater than the embrace to these two, husband and wife, still lovers after thirty-one years of married life."[64]

The summer and fall of 1824 were busy months for Rachel. On June 10, Jackson was honored at a public dinner in Nashville. Twelve days later, the Jacksons hosted a dinner at The Hermitage for their friends and neighbors and attended Independence Day celebrations. On July 15, the Jacksons' friends, Richard Keith Call and Mary Letitia Kirkman, were married at The Hermitage.[65]

In her entertaining, Rachel probably used the silver they owned, some of which was created by Joseph Thrope Elliston, Nashville's first silversmith. The Hermitage has some of those silver pieces—coin silver teaspoons, circa 1815, and silver sugar tongs, circa 1810.

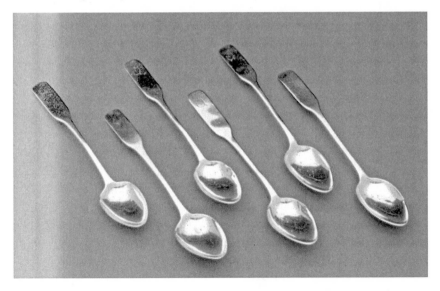

Silver teaspoons used at The Hermitage are attributed to Nashville silversmith Joseph Thorpe Elliston, circa 1815. Elliston, aside from being a silversmith, was a planter, politician, and Nashville's fourth mayor (Andrew Jackson's Hermitage, Nashville, TN).

A pair of coin silver cups, circa 1826, owned by the Jacksons were made by Pelletreau, Bennet & Cook, New York silversmiths. Mathey Pelletreau, son of famous Long Island silversmith Elias Pelletreau, had advanced ideas of marketing and opened a shop in Charleston, South Carolina (Andrew Jackson's Hermitage, Nashville, TN).

Gradually, the Jacksons were completing the furnishing of The Hermitage. On July 20, Thomas Weston was paid $100 for painting, papering the house and furniture.[66] This was the only known wallpaper receipt during the time Rachel lived in the house and was assumed to be for the pictorial wallpaper in the foyer depicting the travels of Telemachus in search of his father Ulysses and his landing on the island of Calypso with Mentor.[67]

Catherine Lynn, in her book, *Wallpaper in America: From the Seventeenth Century to World War I*, wrote that Andrew Jackson chose the wallpaper for the grand entrance stair hall of The Hermitage. "The scenic wallpaper was de-

Rachel Jackson was an avid tea drinker and would have used the coin silver sugar tongs daily and for entertaining. The tongs were crafted by Nashville silversmith Joseph Thorpe Elliston in 1810 (Andrew Jackson's Hermitage, Nashville, TN).

Rachel Jackson's silver teapot was made by Abraham Dubois in Philadelphia, circa 1815. Dubois had been crafting fine silver in that city since 1797 (Andrew Jackson's Hermitage, Nashville, TN).

signed between 1815 and 1820 for Dufour by Xavier Mader—2,027 blocks and eighty-five colors were required to execute Mader's interpretation of the adventures of the son of Ulysses (Telemachus in English) on the Island of the nymph Calypso. Dufour's wallpaper was based on the *Telemaque*, a prose work by Francois Fenelon (1651–1715)."[68]

Another marriage was planned for September 16, between Andrew Jackson Donelson, the son of Rachel's brother Samuel, and Emily Tennessee Donelson, the daughter of Rachel's brother John.[69]

Rachel found time on August 12 to reply to a letter from her friend Latitia Dalzell Chambers in Florence, Alabama. "I thank you, my dear friend, for your kind congratulations on the return of my dear husband. Yes, I was so rejoiced to see him in his own house after an absence of nearly seven months. Oh, the time was long but in this world we shall have tribulations. Says the Blessed Savior, in me ye shall have peace. Oh, glorious hope."[70]

Both Rachel and Jackson expected him to be elected president but she was not looking forward to accompanying him to Washington as she wrote her friend. She was also aware of the rupture of his long friendship and business association with James Jackson. Rachel knew what was happening in her husband's campaign and business life. She was the archivist of both his business and personal papers. It was unlikely that she was kept in the dark about

A section of the French wallpaper from the front hall of The Hermitage. The scenic wallpaper depicted the travels of Telemachus in search of his father Ulysses
and his landing on the Island of Calypso with Mentor. The wallpaper came in
2,027 blocks and used eighty-five colors when it was produced between 1815 and
1820 by Dufour, a Paris firm (Andrew Jackson's Hermitage, Nashville, TN).

the possibility their marriage history could become an issue in the election.
After all, she and Jackson knew all about what transpired.

"Shortly," she continued, "I have to experience another trial. I must
go with him or be as unhappy as I was last winter and how could I bear it.
I shall have to go with him. At my time of life, it is disagreeable but if the
Almighty wills it with humble submission I can say Amen to the decree.
The General sets out next Thursday to Florence then I trust you will see him
to talk with him about all the things you named—the General losing some
friends on account of the vote of the tariff bill. James Jackson he is guilty
of black ingratitude to one of the best friends he ever had. It would take
two sheets of paper but I shall not attempt to describe what he has proved
himself to be.[71]

"We have had another camp meeting at the camp you and I went to last
summer. Sally Knox never went near. She frolics and dances. She lives with
her cousin Rachel [the daughter of Rachel's brother, Severn, who married
William Donelson, son of Rachel's brother John]." She wrote about their acquaintances who were sick and the weather before discussing religion

The neighborhood is as when you left us. We have no minister to take charge of this little flock. It grieves me from day to day but the Lord knows what we are and what is best for us. I pray to be fed with that bread that perishes not but hath life everlasting. Although you have journeyed from us, I often think of you and yours. How glad I would have been could you have lived near me. We often converse on heavenly things. I know I love a Christian. Oh, that God may smile on you in temporal, bless you in life and when His gracious will to call and give you an inheritance in the churches of the first borne assembles of the just made perfect in the Redeemers righteousness there I hope to meet you. No more shall we meet and sigh for parting or absent friends. There no more shall I dread the wintry blasts. Those tears that now flow will be washed away by the hand of my blessed savior.[72]

The young Donelsons were married on September 16, and their cousin Rachel Donelson, daughter of Rachel's brother William died on the same day. "In the heavily intertwined Donelson family, any death reverberated beyond simple sorrow," Brady wrote.[73]

Emily Tennessee Donelson, the daughter of Rachel's brother John, and Andrew Jackson Donelson, the son of Rachel's brother Samuel, were married in The Hermitage garden in 1824. Emily's portrait was painted by The Hermitage's resident artist Ralph E. W. Earl circa 1832. She was Jackson's official hostess for much of his two presidential terms (Andrew Jackson's Hermitage, Nashville, TN).

Rachel prepared for the trip to Washington between social events. There was a dinner in Nashville on October 15 honoring Eaton. Harriett Temple delivered a dress she made for Rachel on October 20. Rachel made other purchases: two dresses ordered from Rachel Williams, shoes from Jared Whitney and fabric and accessories from Clogett and Norris.[74]

Rachel Williams' charge for assembling the material, nine yards of silk, and notions making one of the dresses was $21.77, and the bill was paid on December 13, 1824. The $21.77 would today be equivalent to well over $600.[75]

While disdaining Washington society to her Presbyterian friends, Rachel had no intentions of being caught is the same

Washington dressmaker Rachel Williams' bill to Rachel Jackson for materials, notions and labor for making a dress (Library of Congress, Prints and Photographs Division).

situation—inappropriate clothes for social events—she experienced on her first trip to New Orleans.

Andrew Jackson Donelson was designated to be his uncle's secretary if Jackson was elected president and his wife, Emily, would be a companion/ assistant to Rachel in their official entertaining in the President's House. On November 8, the Jacksons, with the young couple and slaves, departed for Washington. "Rachel," Burke wrote, "settled herself comfortably in her carriage, which for those days was a most luxurious turnout, so much so that there was criticism from some of Jackson's democratic supporters, whereas Jackson had thought only of his wife's comfort."[76]

There was a stop in Lexington, Kentucky, for a ball on November 16. During their journey, presidential electors cast their votes which would be opened after Congress convened in January. When they arrived in Washington on December 7, Jackson took his seat in the Senate and awaited the political machinations required for running for president. The Jacksons and Donelsons were lodged at Gadsby's, formerly the O'Neals' Franklin House, where they were joined by Richard K. Call and his bride and the Marquis de Lafayette, with whom Rachel was delighted.[77]

"We are boarding in the same house as the nation's guest, Lafayette," Rachel wrote Elizabeth Kingsley on December 23.

I am delighted with him. All the attention, all the parties he goes to never appear to have any effect on him. In fact, he is an extraordinary man. He has the happy talent of knowing those he has once seen. For instance, when we first came to this house, the general said he would go and pay the Marquis the first visit. Both having the same desire at the same time, met on the entry of the stairs. It was truly interesting. The emotion of revolutionary feeling was aroused in them both. At Charleston, General Jackson saw him on the field of battle, one a boy of twelve, the Marquis twenty-three. He wears a wig and is a little inclined to corpulence. He is very healthy, eats hearty, goes to every party and this is every night."[78] To tell you of this city, I would not do justice to the subject. The extravagance is in dressing and running to parties. But, I must say they regard the Sabbath and attend preaching for there are churches of every denomination and able ministers of the gospel. We have been here two Sabbaths. The General and I were both days at church. Mr. Daniel Baker is the pastor of the church we go to. His is a fine man, a plain good preacher. We were waited on by two of Mr. Stephen Bloomer Balche's elders [who] invited us to take a pew in his church in Georgetown but previous to that I had an invitation to the other. General Call, Mary, Emily and Andrew went to the Episcopal Church."[79]

Rachel Jackson's lavender moire taffeta dress, circa 1825, was indicative of more than just her sense of fashion. She apparently favored dresses with an empire waist. The bodice's high collar lent itself to being accessorized with a fancy collar. The length of the dress gave the impression that she was not an extremely tall nor a short woman in stature (Andrew Jackson's Hermitage, Nashville, TN).

Oh, my dear friend, how shall I get through this bustle? There are not less than fifty to one hundred persons calling in a day. My dear husband was unwell nearly the whole of our journey but, thanks to our Heavenly Father, his health is improving. Still his appetite is delicate and company and business are oppressive. But, I look unto the Lord, from hence comes all my comforts. I have the precious promise and I know my Redeemer lives."[80]

Rachel hastened to assure her friend the Washington parties held no interest to her.

"Don't be afraid of my giving to these vain things," she continued. "The apostle says I can do all things in Christ who strengthened me. The play actors sent me a letter requesting my countenance to them. No. A ticket to ball and parties. No, not one. Two dinnings and several times to drink tea. Indeed, Mr. Jackson encourages me in my course. He recommends it to me to be steadfast."[81]

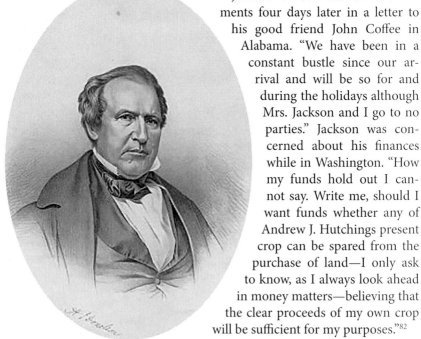

Jackson echoed his wife's sentiments four days later in a letter to his good friend John Coffee in Alabama. "We have been in a constant bustle since our arrival and will be so for and during the holidays although Mrs. Jackson and I go to no parties." Jackson was concerned about his finances while in Washington. "How my funds hold out I cannot say. Write me, should I want funds whether any of Andrew J. Hutchings present crop can be spared from the purchase of land—I only ask to know, as I always look ahead in money matters—believing that the clear proceeds of my own crop will be sufficient for my purposes."[82]

The son of Rachel's brother Samuel, Andrew Jackson Donelson was educated by the Jacksons at West Point and Transylvania College of Law in Lexington, Kentucky. He became an aide to his uncle and was Jackson's secretary after he was elected president (Library of Congress, Prints and Photographs Division).

On August 1, 1821, $10,000 had been credited to Jackson's account as governor of Florida.[83] That $10,000 would today be equivalent to around a quarter of a million dollars.[84]

On December 27, 1824, Jackson wrote William Berkley Lewis in Nashville, asking how the two Andrews were doing and that he was anxious to hear from them. "We are all well, the young at parties—Mrs. J. and myself at home chatting, smoking our pipes and thinking of our Tennessee friends."[85]

Rachel and Jackson returned to their Tennessee friends sooner than expected. Pending events determined the path of the rest of their lives.

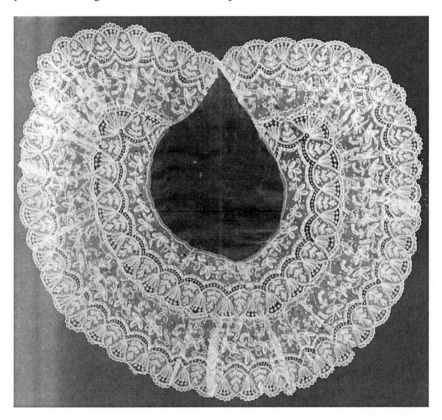

Rachel Jackson's lace collar, made of embroidered net, was a fashion accessory she would have worn with different dresses (Andrew Jackson's Hermitage, Nashville, TN).

13

The 1828
Campaign Begins

In addition to the clothes Rachel assembled in Tennessee, she did some shopping in early January 1825 in Washington. On January 4, she purchased fabrics and notions for dressmaking from E. Albert. The next day she purchases shoes from Thomas B. Griffin. On January 6, she purchased articles from John Petit, a hat maker.[1]

Her purchase of fabrics and notions indicated that she found a seamstress in Washington or one of the slaves accompanying the Jacksons had a talent for dressmaking.

There were exceptions to Rachel's refusals to attend Washington parties during Jackson's second Senate term while they awaited the electoral vote count. Rachel and Jackson were invited to a ball in Lafayette's honor given by General Jacob Jennings Brown, Retired, at the Indian Queen Hotel. Brown was Jackson's counterpart commanding the Northern division of the Army fighting the British in the War of 1812. He became the commanding General of the Army in 1821.[2]

For two years there had been whisperings about Rachel's marriages but they had not yet risen to the level of publication. In a letter to her sister-in-law Mary Purnell Donelson, who was Emily Donelson's mother, Rachel talked about how Jackson yearned for retirement at his own fireside. Those were Rachel's yearnings, more than Jackson's. "I knew from the first how wrong it was but my advice was nothing," she wrote. "I leave the *Event* to the Almighty whom I know will do all things well." Rachel made an unusual admission about being in Washington. "I feel more enjoyment [here] than I had expected."

Then she immediately referred back to her church activities. "I have the privilege of going to church twice every Sunday and prayer meetings twice a week. If it were not for Mrs. [Elizabeth] Watson, dear woman, I should have no one to go with me. While I am at meetings, they [Andrew and Emily,

Keith and Mary Call] are at the theatre or parties. The church I mostly attend is Presbyterian. The parson, an excellent man, puts me in mind of Mr. Hume but more condensed in his preaching."[3]

Rachel found the pious in Washington quite different from those in Tennessee. "They [the pious] are too much divided with the world that is not according to the Scripture. You may depend I have taken a strong ground. I have resisted all those invitations except the eighth of January [General Brown's party]. We get two and three invitations a day sometimes. I think some of our friends might write to us now and then while in this terrible place. It is enough to ruin any man's fortune. Every week our board is nearly one hundred [dollars]. Mr. Jackson set out with two thousand dollars, all spent and gone. He pays the board every week. How much better at home he would be. His health is not good but a continual uneasy mind keeps him unwell." Rachel did not elaborate on the cause of Jackson's uneasy mind. "I saw from the first it was wrong for him to fatigue himself with such an important office. Even if he obtains it in the end it will profit him nothing." She complained that her brother John has not written them nor his son William. "I received two letters from my dear Andrew. I pray to God almighty to permit us to meet again. I feel requited by his love."[4]

On January 9, Jackson answered the letter of Charles Pendleton Tutt, a Loudoun, Virginia, planter and supporter, alerting him to rumors circulating about Rachel's first marriage. Jackson, of course, had long been aware of the rumors and that Overton's reply had been prepared. "I never had a doubt of the honor of some of my political enemies but that they would attempt to disturb the repose of an innocent female in her declining years is a species of wickedness that I did not suppose would be attempted." Jackson was convinced such rumors were being used to provoke his temper as they had in the past. "One thing I can assure you whenever my enemies shall think it worthwhile to investigate my or the character of Mrs. J., I fear not the result. I as well know how to defend my and her character as I have done the rights of my country. Whenever it can be traced to a source worthy of notice, I am aware of the plan of my enemies to endeavor to excite and provoke me. This cannot be done until calm reflection convinces my judge that justice requires atonement of the invaders of female character."[5]

Undoubtedly, Jackson took Rachel and their entourage to Washington expecting to be elected president but he underestimated the cost of their expedition. Room—a bedroom and large parlor—and board for the Jacksons, three servants and stabling four horses at the Franklin House Hotel was $61per week or $244 per month. Add to that sum, $288 per month for whiskey, wine, beer and cigars and their total monthly expenses, aside from any incidentals or charges for entertaining that Jackson did, were around $532.00 per month. In 2017, that amount was $13,600.[6]

Jackson wrote John Coffee on January 23 to send him $500 out of funds belonging to his ward, A. J. Hutchings, and he would pay it back, with interest, as soon as his cotton sold at market. Jackson added that Rachel, who was in good health, spent her time on Sundays at church, on Thursdays at prayer meetings and the balance of the week in receiving and paying visits.[7]

Certainly Jackson, despite Rachel's objections, wanted to be president but few ever lusted after the office with such determination and persistence as Henry Clay did for a quarter of a century. He ran for the office in 1824, 1832 and 1844 but was never elected. He unsuccessfully sought his party's nomination in 1840 and 1848.[8]

Prior to the 1824 presidential election, the office of secretary of state had been a springboard to the presidency—an occurrence not overlooked by Clay. Thomas Jefferson had been secretary of state for President George Washington. James Madison, James Monroe and John Quincy Adams served in that position under Presidents John Adams, James Madison and James Monroe respectively.[9] Clay, in 1824, was speaker of the house. Since neither Jackson with ninety-nine electoral votes; nor Adams with eighty-four; nor William H. Crawford with forty-one or Clay with thirty-seven received a majority of votes, the election went into the House of Representatives to be decided on February 9, 1825.[10]

"In two days our troubles begin, if in fact they have not already begun," Eaton wrote John Overton on February 7, "what may and will be the issue a higher intelligence than mine alone can decide."[11]

Eaton was right. Clay announced on January 24 he would support Adams which the Jackson camp assumed, correctly it turned out, and there was a reward for Clay. On February 9, the House voted: thirteen for Adams, seven for Jackson and four for Crawford. The next day, Jackson wrote John Overton the disturbing news. "Thus you see here, the voices of the people of the west have been disregarded and demagogues barter them as sheep in the shambles for their own views and personal aggrandizement. Mrs. J. has not been well for some days [and] is now better. We will be on our return home in March and hope to reach the Hermitage in April."[12]

Of course, Rachel was feeling better—it was the outcome she wanted.

Jackson's description of the "corrupt bargain" between Adams and Clay where the Kentuckian became secretary of state, forever attached itself to the presidential election of 1824.[13]

Burke wrote that Rachel "thanked the almighty for the deliverance of her husband from the presidential chair." A friend called on Rachel to express his condolences. "Condole with me, sir! Condole with the people—their loss in my gain," she replied self-righteously.[14]

"On this day in February [9], 1825, the campaign of 1828 began," Burke wrote,

Happily the gentle soul of Rachel Donelson Jackson did not know it but even then the cruel daggers that later pierced her heart were being sharpened. The circumstances of the all too hasty marriage of Andrew Jackson and Rachel Donelson Robards had already become undercover gossip. Some of the women even debated whether they should pay her the customary first call but curiosity regarding her carried the day and they came in far too great numbers to suit Rachel. And when they came they found a gentlewoman whose serenity of soul shone from the depths of her dark eyes—a woman singularly detached from the world and interested only in the things of God. One who called on her in January 1825, has left this pen picture. "The visit of Mrs. Jackson to this place has given a damper to those who have used her in an argument against him [Jackson]. She had proven the falsity of the thousand slanders which have been industriously circulated of her awkwardness, ignorance and indecorum. I have been made acquainted with her and find her striking characteristics to be an unaffected simplicity of manners with great goodness of heart. So far from being denied the attentions usually extended to strangers, as was predicted, she has been over powered by the civilities of all parties."[15]

The evening after the House vote, President and Mrs. Monroe held their usual Wednesday levee and everyone, Burke said, anticipated the meeting between Jackson and Adams. "As General Jackson approached," Burke wrote, "with a large handsome lady on his arm and saw Mr. Adams. Seeing Adams standing alone, he reached out his left hand to his successful rival and said, 'How do you do, Mr. Adams? I give you my left hand for my right as you see is devoted to the fair. I hope you are well, sir.'" Adams took Jackson's hand and replied, "Very well, sir. I hope General Jackson is well." Burke added that it was probably the last time the two men ever spoke to each other.[16]

On February 17, Jackson invited Willie Blount and twenty-one others to dinner at the Franklin House Hotel. A hotel bill, dated February 18, 1825, indicated the dinners cost $46 and the adult beverages, including apple toddy, punch, wine, brandy, whiskey, cider and champagne, $40.25.[17]

In modern terms the cost would have been be several thousand dollars.[18]

The next day, Jackson wrote John Coffee saying he had received a $1,000 from the sale of his cotton and would be returning the $500 borrowed from young Hutching's plantation earnings. "My situation here was one of great expense. I had anticipated this and brought on with me $2,300. This with my pay [$1,344 for the Second and Special Sessions of the Eighteenth Congress] I did suppose would be sufficient. In this I was mistaken." Jackson said Rachel had a bad cold and as soon as Congress adjourned they would start for home by way of Baltimore and Philadelphia.[19]

Rachel, on March 8, wrote Benjamin Bakewell to thank him for two celery glass vases and said she would like to stop in Pittsburgh on their way home to thank him in person. "But having been seriously indisposed for some weeks and being still so. Mr. Jackson is on this account compelled to relinquish the pleasures we had promised ourselves with this visit. You will, therefore, be pleased to receive this feeble expression of my thanks for so flattering a token of your esteem. Besides its value and a beautiful example of domestic industry, it is doubly dear to me as an evidence of the friendly feelings entertained toward me by your daughter Mrs. Campbell."[20]

Bakewell, who came to America from England in 1808, was the father of flint glass manufacturing. Until 1819, Bakewell's factory was the only one making cut and engraved tableware. Among their important early commissions was a service of engraved glassware for President Monroe to use in the President' House.[21]

The Bakewell daughter Rachel referred to was married to Allan Campbell, Nashville's first Presbyterian minister. "Be assured sir," Rachel's letter continued, "that the little attentions which I have been enabled to bestow upon her and her excellent husband are far short of their merits and are more than requited by their kind opinion which you have always authorized me— regard these glasses together with your own as a token. Accept, with my own, the best wishes of my dear husband for your prosperity and happiness and be pleased to present us respectfully to all your family."[22]

There was little or no respect shared by Jackson and Clay for each other. "The poor devil Henry Clay," Jackson told John Coffee, "has come out with an address to his constituents, in a begging cringing tone, to clear himself from the corrupt intrigue and management to procure for himself the office of secretary of state but he steers entirely clear of denying this charge. The various papers are commenting upon and will bring to his recollections before they are done the adage, 'O that my enemy would write a book.' How little common sense this man displays in his course. A man who dwells, as he does, in a glass house, ought never to cast stones."[23]

That thought was somewhat shared by Charles Francis Adams, Jr., a son of President John Q. and Louisa Adams.

Benjamin Bakewell, known as the father of the America's flint-glass industry, presented Rachel with a pair of celery glass vases made in the Pittsburgh factory of Bakewell and Page in 1824. One of the vases, shown above, is on loan to The Hermitage (Andrew Jackson's Hermitage, Nashville, TN).

After attending a party given by Mrs. Henry Clay on December 12, 1826, the nineteen-year-old Adams wrote in his diary that the entertainment went off very well. "He [Clay] has in all his situations kept her much in the background and rumor says he has not been altogether an example of fidelity during his long absences. I have not much opinion of his morals myself but a very high estimation of his talents. The last to me are of the most important as the former require a little mending in my own case before I criticize others."[24] Young Adams at that time was single.

"Unfortunately, Clay's ability to wield his authority [as speaker] effectively gave him delusions of power that were unrealistic," Robert V. Remini wrote in his biography of Clay. "He presumed to act as though his will constituted the final decision of any dispute. His arrogance, his overbearing conceit, his presumptuousness eventually turned men against him. They recoiled from his brazen audacity and they branded him with the nick-name, The Dictator. Indeed, it was later gossiped that on leaving a party at sunrise—not an unusual occurrence—Clay was asked how he could expect to preside over the House that day. 'Come up,' he bragged, 'and you shall see how I will throw the reins over their necks.'"[25]

Rachel's lost letters could have provided a most interesting insight on Clay. She was, however, in his debt for the "corrupt bargain" that sent her husband back to The Hermitage.

Jackson remained in Washington long enough to vote against Clay's confirmation as secretary of state on March 7. The vote was twenty-four for Clay and fourteen opposed. The Senate adjourned two days later and the Jacksons left Washington on March 10, but it would a long winding trip back to The Hermitage.[26]

They paid Nelson Davidson $85.50 for painting and repairing their carriage. John M. Scott provided distances and recommended inns between Baltimore and Wheeling, Virginia. They arrived in Baltimore on March 11, where supporters met them several miles out of town and escorted them to their hotel. The Jacksons were feted with a dinner and a ball that night. On March 12, they were honored with another dinner and a visit to the theater. Two days later they arrived in Elkton, Maryland, where a dinner was held to celebrate Jackson's birthday on March 15.[27] There was no indication that Rachel failed to attend the dinners, balls and theater.

On March 25, the Jackson entourage reached Wheeling, where they boarded a steamboat. The fare for their party of four, three servants, four horses and carriage, was $133. After lengthy stays in Cincinnati and Louisville for dinners, militia reviews and Rachel's shopping for plants, the Jacksons arrived at The Hermitage on April 13. Three days later, a public dinner honoring Jackson was held at the Nashville Inn. Two companies of soldiers, the Nashville Guard and the Lafayette Rifle Corps escorted Jackson's party to the courthouse where John Overton formally welcomed them home, praising Jackson's accomplishments, private virtues and his conduct during the recent presidential campaign. Jackson replied to the lively welcome saying he did not seek the presidency but would serve if elected.[28]

Rachel probably cringed at those words but she was busy with preparations for Lafayette's visit and entertaining him at The Hermitage. The general arrived by steamboat and was greeted by, among others, forty Revolutionary War veterans from across Tennessee. Jackson introduced Lafayette to each of the veterans, whose travel expenses had been paid by Nashville's municipal government. Thousands gathered in Nashville's public square to honor the Frenchman. He was feted by a dinner that evening, presided over by Jackson, before a large reception was held in the Masonic Lodge. After touring the Nashville Female Academy, Cumberland College and a militia encampment, Lafayette and his party made their way to The Hermitage where Rachel planned a large dinner with not only local dignitaries but their friends and neighbors to meet Lafayette. After a tour of the plantation, everybody returned to Nashville for a grand ball.[29]

Rachel and Jackson were exhausted after Lafayette departed. He told Richard Keith Call he was in dry dock for repairs and that Rachel had regained her health.[30]

"Lafayette's visit to The Hermitage was one of the happiest memories of Rachel Jackson's life," Burke wrote. "Hostess in her own home, a role she loved, it gave her opportunity to extend pleasure to many others—men in public life, friends and innumerable relatives."[31]

Rachel apologized to Katherine Daune Morgan whose husband, Thomas, a lawyer and former state legislator, edited the pro-Jackson *Democratic Eagle* in Washington, Pennsylvania, in a May 18 letter for being tardy in replying to her correspondence. "Were I, like you, in the possession of that power by which the heart engraves its features upon the letters that guide the distant friend to its feelings, I might attempt the expression of those pleasures which the humble and peaceful Hermitage present to me and I might offer them as a feeble testimony of my gratitude for the kindnesses you paid us while within the reach of your hospitality and subsequently for the favorable recollection with which you are pleased to associate my name with that of my dear husband."[32]

Rachel's words here were enhanced by Andrew J. Donelson's careful editing. Had she not been writing to a woman from such a prominent family—her father William Duane edited a Philadelphia newspaper—would Donelson have been involved? "Here, however, as I feel not less assured of my own inadequacy than of the safety with which I may rely upon your indulgence, I must be silent and leave to you the picture of the rural scenery now surrounding us, in contrast with the substitute you have so eloquently

On April 15, 1825, Andrew Jackson purchased two large sofas created by Irish furniture maker Robert West of Philadelphia for The Hermitage. He paid $140 for the two sofas. One of the sofas, shown above, is of carved mahogany with black horsecloth upholstery (Andrew Jackson's Hermitage, Nashville, TN).

described. I mean the duties which would have fallen to me had the presidential election terminated differently. I need only assure you that referred to my own wishes that question would no longer disturb Mr. Adams so far as the general is concerned. To me the *presidential charms* by the side of a *happy retirement from public life* are as the tale of the candle and the substantial fire. The first of which it is said is soon blown out by the wind but the latter is only increased by it."[33]

Rachel mentioned their journey home had been interrupted by Emily Donelson's illness but she had entirely recovered. "With this exception, our time was delightfully occupied on the road with the various objects presented by a country through which I had never passed before. It would take more space than is allotted for a letter to give you the details of our journey. One remark, however, I will not omit in justice to the citizens with whom we had the pleasure of an acquaintance, this is, and from Baltimore to our farm we were honored by the most friendly and hospitable attentions for which I shall ever feel grateful. I assure you at your pleasant town, instead of being reminded of the privations at Fort Strother, my husband was penetrated with the warmest feeling of gratitude for the generous testimonials of confidence and esteem which were exhibited by all your citizens for both his public and private character."[34]

The letter closed with Rachel speaking of her mother-in-law. "Mr. J's mother was called Elizabeth. She encountered many hardships while on this earth but is now at rest I trust with the spirits of the good and the just. It is probably that from this cause my husband obtained the fortitude which has enabled him to triumph with so much success over the many obstacles which have diversified his life. May their history benefit your little Jackson and contribute to perfect your own hopes of him, with which permit me to mingle mine. Tender to Mr. Morgan, with Mr. Jackson's assurances of my best wishes for your mutual prosperity and happiness, as a token of which and my esteem for you receive a lock of my hair enclosed."[35]

A postscript was added saying, "Mr. and Mrs. Donelson also unite with us in a tender of their thanks for your attentions while at Washington. They have not forgotten the supply of medicines and cakes which were received from you and of which they often speak in terms of the warmest gratitude."[36]

Rachel's health was of concern to two of Jackson's supporters in May and June 1825. "When I parted from Mrs. Jackson," James Buchanan wrote from Lancaster, Pennsylvania, on May 29, "I felt some apprehensions concerning her disease. I hope ere this she has been completely restored to health." Less than a week later, Charles Pendleton Tutt wrote from Locust Hill, near Leesburg, Virginia, "I have felt great anxiety to hear of Mrs. Jackson's restoration to health. Be pleased, my dear sir, to remember me most kindly to her."[37]

It would have been impossible for Rachel to be unaware of the preparation of Jackson's team of politicians running his 1828 presidential campaign from The Hermitage. They were constantly in and out of The Hermitage. Eaton raised funds to purchase a Washington, DC, newspaper, to have a media outlet in the nation's capital free of Adams' influence. That newspaper, later edited by Duff Green, was the *United States' Telegraph*. A number of newspapers were bought or buttressed by Jackson's supporters.[38]

Rachel actually participated in some of the political appearances with her husband. On September 13, Rachel, Jackson, John Overton and Eaton left Nashville for Jackson, in Madison County, to attend a celebration in the general's honor. While in West Tennessee they visited a number of Rachel's Donelson relatives, attended events in Winchester and Paris and returned to The Hermitage on October 7.[39]

Two months later, Rachel became seriously ill. Jackson wrote John Coffee on December 1 that he had planned a trip to Alabama but was unable to leave due to his wife's deteriorating condition. "She is much debilitated, her mind much affected and spirits remarkable depressed with want of appetite and cannot sleep. I have had Dr. Samuel Hogg with her and have this day sent for him." Jackson said Rachel was unable to sleep the previous night.[40]

Hogg received his medical training, according to the *North Carolina Encyclopedia*, in Sumner County, Tennessee, an indication, since there was no mention of a medical teaching institution, he was trained by another physician. He was Jackson's surgeon during the Creek War. After a term in the Tennessee legislature, he returned to private medical practice.[41]

"Mrs. J., although mended, is still in very bad health," Jackson wrote Coffee on December 28. "If I could keep up her spirits, I think she would soon get well."[42] Rachel was certainly a frontier woman whose formal education was lacking but she was no fool. Part of her successful business acumen was the ability to read people and events. Her future held two certainties—Jackson was again running for president and his enemies intended to make her marriages the focal point of their campaign against him expecting him to lose his well-known temper and commit an act which would destroy his campaign. Instead Jackson's enemies attempted to destroy Rachel.

Depending on the closeness of the relationship, Jackson's answers to questions about Rachel's health varied. In a letter to George Winchester, a Baltimore supporter, on January 15, 1826, Jackson wrote that Rachel had recovered from a severe illness which lasted six months. In a January 30 letter to his close confidant Edward Livingston, Jackson wrote that Rachel "has had a severe illness from which she is slowly recovering."[43] His February 24 letter to Coffee might have been too optimistic. "I hope she will shortly be restored to perfect health."[44]

"Mrs. J., has had a severe illness," he told Richard Keith Call in a March 9 letter. "Her health is measurably restored and her spirits regained although her complexion remains somewhat sallow." On September 30, in another letter to Call, Jackson announces Rachel was in good health.[45]

Jackson's letters on Rachel's health covered a period from December 1, 1825 to March 9, 1826. That was three months of her dealing with either emotional or physical issues; maybe both.

It is possible that Andrew Jackson's greatest victory was not surviving the Revolutionary War, the Creek War, the War of 1812, and the First Seminole War, winning two presidential elections but convincing his wife to regain her grit, courage and determination to stand beside him during the vicious attacks both knew would be aimed at them during the 1828 presidential campaign. Those impending attacks were probably the underlying cause of Rachel's lengthy illness.

Cincinnati newspaperman and Henry Clay aficionado Charles Hammond hired an Englishman, Edward Day, to gather material on Rachel, Robards and Jackson, in 1825.[46] That undertaking may have well prompted Rachel's lengthy illness—from December 1825 to March 1826—that Jackson described as her mind being much affected, her spirits remarkably depressed and her inability to eat or sleep.[47] On March 10, 1826, William B. Lewis learned from a source in Cincinnati that a public discussion of the Jackson's marriage was about to begin. Six days later the *Richmond Whig* picked up portions of a pamphlet which discussed the Jacksons' marriage. Hammond's *Cincinnati*

Gazette, on March 23, accused Jackson of convincing Rachel, then the wife of Lewis Robards, to live with him in the character of a wife. Three days later, the *National Journal,* an Adams administration newspaper in Washington, reprinted the *Richmond Whig* article on the Jacksons' marriage.[48]

Jackson went about obtaining depositions from three women who had known Rachel from the time of her marriage to Lewis Robards. In a December 12 letter to William B. Lewis, Jackson enclosed the deposition of Mrs. Sarah Michie Smith for Lewis to copy. He emphasized that the original document must be returned to him. Mrs. Smith, the widow of former U.S. Senator Daniel Smith and the maternal grandmother of Samuel Donelson's sons—John, Samuel, Andrew Jackson and Daniel Smith Donelson—was a longtime neighbor of both the Widow Donelson and the Jacksons. In her December 10 deposition, Mrs. Smith detailed Lewis Robards' cruel treatment of Rachel, their final separation and the Jacksons' marriage when they learned of Robards' divorce action. She called Rachel "a most prudent and virtuous female."[49]

Mary Henley Russell Bowen's deposition, dated December 12, 1826, stated that she had personal knowledge of the cruel treatment Rachel received from Robards. Mrs. Russell also attested to the character of Rachel and Andrew Jackson. A niece of Patrick Henry and the widow of Sumner County pioneer William Bowen, her statement repeated much that was in Mrs. Smith's deposition.[50]

The third deposition, of Mrs. Elizabeth Brown Craighead, widow of the Reverend Thomas B. Craighead, Nashville's Presbyterian first minister, was the most troubling. On December 2, she attested to Rachel's good character, becoming manners, actions deriving from her first marriage and the Jacksons' marriage. Mrs. Craighead came from a prominent Frankfort, Kentucky, family. Her brothers were all well educated and conspicuously successful in their fields. James Brown was a U.S. senator from Louisiana, who was elected a second time in 1819, as an Adams-Clay Republican. Mason Brown, a Yale-educated lawyer, was Kentucky secretary of state under Governor Charles S. Morehead (1855–59). Samuel Brown, Lexington, Kentucky, was an Edinburgh University–trained physician who was an early advocate of the use of the cowpox virus for smallpox vaccinations. It was her brothers John Brown, a U.S. senator from Kentucky, and James Brown, the Louisiana senator, who raised questions about using her deposition.[51] John Brown was Lewis Robards' attorney in his divorce action against Rachel in 1793, and James Brown was an Adams-Clay supporter.

Jackson surely knew that Mrs. Craighead's brother, John Brown, had been the architect of the divorce action that branded Rachel an adulteress. To use her deposition indicated Jackson was desperately to defend his wife.

"The high character of these ladies and their numerous respectable connections will carry credence with their statement wherever it is seen," he told Lewis. "I am more anxious on this subject than perhaps I ought to be but the rascality of the attempt to blacken the character of an ancient and virtuous female who has through life maintained a good reputation and has associated with the best circles of society in which she has been placed. This for the basest purpose, by a coalition at the head of which I am sure is Mr. Clay—raises in my mind such feelings of indignation that I can scarcely control—but a day of retribution as it respects Mr. Clay and his tool Colonel Hammond must arrive should I be spared."[52]

Jackson could have produced hundreds of depositions in Rachel's defense and the facts would not have changed. They lived as man and wife while she was still married to another man. The claim of a Natchez marriage, made by some Jackson biographers, was never proved because, unless Rachel received a divorce in Mississippi (and there is no evidence of that), she was still married to Lewis Robards. Their divorce became final when the decree was issued on September 27, 1793, in Danville, Kentucky.[53]

Consequently, the three women's depositions, presenting flattering descriptions of Rachel, changed few minds but gave the Jacksons some comfort in displaying the approval of their peers.

On February 12, 1827, Thomas Arnold, a congressional candidate from east Tennessee published a handbill titled *To the Freemen of the Counties of Cocke, Sevier, Blount, Jefferson, Grainger, Claiborne and Knox,* saying that Jackson spent the prime of his life in gambling, in cock-fighting, in horse racing and to cap it off tore from a husband the wife of his bosom. "A vote for Jackson," the handbill declared, "meant a vote for a man who thinks that if he takes a fancy to his neighbor's pretty wife he has nothing to do but take a pistol in one hand and a horse whip in the other and possess her."[54]

Arnold's handbill said that Rachel's first husband Lewis Robards caught her and Jackson exchanging kisses and shortly thereafter they slept under the same blanket. In his book, *Presidential Wives,* Paul F. Boller, Jr., wrote that the Arnold handbill and its republication in the *National Journal,* a Washington newspaper supporting Adams, created an emergency meeting of Jackson's campaign managers. Hammond's *Cincinnati Gazette* joined the fray and announced that "General Jackson prevailed on the wife of Lewis Robards to desert her husband and live with himself."[55]

The Richmond Whig on March 16 printed quotes from Arnold's pamphlet and discussed the circumstances of the Jacksons' marriage. The next day the Nashville Committee was organized as a vehicle to refute such charges. John Overton was the chairman. These accusations were only the beginning of a year of abusive and vicious charges to fall upon Rachel. On March 23, Hammond's *Cincinnati Gazette* accused Jackson of convincing "the wife of

Lewis Robards of Mercer County, Kentucky, to desert her husband and live with himself in the character of a wife." Three days later, the *National Journal* reprinted the *Richmond Whig's* article on the Jacksons' marriage. On April 7, the *Nashville Republican* printed their account of Rachel's first marriage, separation, divorce and her marriage to Jackson. *The Frankfort Commentator*, on April 14, printed an illustration comparing Rachel to "a dirty black wench." Four days later, the *Frankfort Argus* responded with the three women's affidavits on the Jacksons' marriage.[56]

When a newspaper supporting Adams attacked Rachel, a Jacksonian publication responded in her defense. Consequently, she was humiliated twice as her husband's political enemies continued incessantly in their efforts to provoke his temper, using Rachel to force him into a fatal campaign blunder. Using an elderly woman as their battering ram bothered them none at all. That Rachel survived such viperous and constant attacks was a testament to her determination, her faith and the steadfastness of the relationship of her marriage to Jackson.

Rachel certainly had her defenders such as Edward George Washington Butler, who was then stationed in Cincinnati. Jackson had written Butler asking him to find a copy of Hammond's newspaper and send it to him. Butler was unable to locate a copy but said he read the article when it appeared. "They were sufficiently rude and indelicate towards Mrs. Jackson to have justified the punishment which he would have received but for the remonstrance of your most estimable friend Colonel William Piatt. I am now convinced that the colonel advised the prudent and proper course as he assured me on learning your wishes, which I communicated to him alone that Hammond and his instigators are deterred from the promised publications and the good colonel begged me to entreat you, by the friendship which he cherishes for you and by the solicitude which he feels for the welfare of his country, to allow no consideration to induce you to notice anything which may flow from the *Sources* or *Tributaries* of corruption. To this, my Dearest General, allow me to add my humble—my affectionate entreaties. The character of my Dear Mrs. Jackson has ever been above the suspicion of friends and honest men and if the baseness of desperate and unprincipled wretches make it necessary at this late period in her long, pious and exemplary life to vindicate the actions of its earliest period, and to blast, by contemporaneous evidence, their villainous assailants, let the painful yet proud task be assigned, as I have reason to believe it is, to the historian."[57]

Historians' views were an after fact for the Jacksons in the 1828 presidential campaign. The voters, all male at that time, were the focal point of the election. By June 1827, the Nashville Committee decided it was time to present the Jacksons' side of the marriage issue and printed John Overton's narrative with some questionable dates.[58]

In the fall of 1787, I was a boarder in the family of Mrs. [William] Robards, the mother of Lewis Robards in Mercer County, Kentucky. Captain Robards and his wife [Rachel] lived with Mrs. Robards. I had not lived there many weeks before I understood that Captain Robards and his wife lived very unhappily on account of his being jealous of Mr. [Peyton] Short. My brother, who was also a boarder, informed me that great uneasiness had existed in the family for some time before my arrival. As he had the confidences and good will of all parties, a portion of his confidence fell to my share, particularly the old lady's, than whom, perhaps a more amiable woman never lived. This uneasiness between Captain Robards and said lady continued to increase, and with it a great distress to the mother and considerably with the family generally. Until early in the year 1789, as well as now recollected, I understood from the old lady, and perhaps others of the family, that her son Lewis had written to Mrs. Robards' mother, the widow Donelson, requesting that she would take her home as he did not intend to live with her any longer. Certain it is, that Mrs. Robards' brother, Samuel Donelson, came up to carry her down to her mother's and my impression is in the fall or summer of 1789. I was present when Mr. Samuel Donelson arrived at Mrs. Robards' and when he started away with his sister; and my clear and distinct recollection is, that it was said to be a final separation at the instance of Captain Robards. For I well recollect the distress of old Mrs. Robards, on account of her daughter-in-law, Rachel, going away and on account of the separation the old lady's embracing her affectionately. In unreserved conversations with me, the old lady always blamed her son Lewis and took the part of her daughter-in-law.[59]

During my residence in Mrs. Robards' family, I do not recollect to have heard of any of the family censure young Mrs. Robards on account of the differences between her husband and herself. If they thought otherwise, it was unknown to me but rec-ollect frequently to have heard the old lady and Captain [John] Jouett, who was married to the eldest daughter of the family at that time, express the most favorable sentiments of her.[60]

Having finished my studies in the winter of '88–'89, it was determined to fix my residence in the country now called West Tennessee. Previous to my departure from Mrs. Robards', the old lady earnestly entreated me to use my exertions to get her son Lewis and daughter-in-law to live happily together. Their separation for a consider-able time had occasioned her uneasiness as she appeared to be much attached to her daughter-in-law and her [Rachel] to her. Captain Robards appeared to be unhappy and the old lady told me he regretted what had taken place and wished to be recon-ciled to his wife. Before I would agree to concern myself in the matter, I determined to ascertain Captain Robards' disposition from himself and took occasion to converse with him on the subject. When he assured me of his regret respecting what had passed; that he was convinced his suspicious were unfounded; that he wished to live with his wife, and requested that I would use my exertions to restore harmony.[61]

I told him I would undertake it, provided he would throw aside all nonsensical notions about jealousy for which I was convinced there were no grounds and treat his wife kindly as other men. He assured me it should be so; and it is my impression now, that I received a message from old Mrs. Robards to Mrs. Lewis Robards which I delivered to her on my arrival at her mother's where I found her sometime in the month of February 1789. The situation of the country induced me to solicit Mrs. Donelson to board me, good accommodations and boarding being rarely to be met with, to which she readily assented.[62]

Mr. A. Jackson had studied law at Salisbury, North Carolina, as I understood, and had arrived in this country in company with Judge [John] McNairy, Bennett Searcy and perhaps David Allison, all lawyers seeking their fortunes more than a month or two before my arrival. Whether Mr. Jackson was at Mrs. Donelson's when I got there in March 1789, I cannot say; if he was living there, it must have been but a little time. My impression now is that he was not living there, and having just arrived, I introduced him into the family as a boarder after becoming acquainted with him. So it was we commenced boarding there about the same time. Jackson and myself, our friends and clients, occupying one cabin and the family another, a few steps from it.[63]

Soon after my arrival, I had frequent conversations with Mrs. Lewis Robards on the subject of living happily with her husband. She, with much sensibility, assured me that no effort to do so should be wanting on her part; and I communicated the results to Captain Robards and his mother, from both of whom I received congratulations and thanks.[64]

Captain Robards had previously purchased a preemption in this country on the south side of the Cumberland River, in Davidson County, about five miles from where Mrs. Donelson then lived. In the arrangement for a reunion between Captain Robards and his wife, I understood it was agreed that Captain Robards was to live in this country instead of Kentucky; that until it was safe to go on his own land, which was yearly expected, he and his wife would live at Mrs. Donelson's. Captain Robards became united with his wife sometime in the year 1788 or 1789. Both Mr. Jackson and myself boarded in the family of Mrs. Donelson—lived in the cabin room and slept in the same bed. As young men of the same pursuits and profession, with but few others in the country and with whom to associate, besides sharing, as we frequently did, common dangers, such an intimacy ensued as might reasonably be expected.[65]

No many months lapsed before Robards became jealous of Jackson, which I felt confident, was without the least ground. Some of his irritating conversation on this subject, with his wife, I heard amidst the tears of herself and her mother, who were greatly distressed. I urged to Robards the unmanliness of his conduct after the pains I had taken to produce harmony as a mutual friend of both families and my honest conviction that his suspicious were groundless. These remonstrances seemed not to have the desired effect. As much commotion and unhappiness prevailed in the family as in that of Mrs. Robards in Kentucky. At length I communicated with Jackson the unpleasant situation of living in a family where there was so much disturbance and concluded by telling him that we would endeavor to get some other place. To this he readily assented; but where to go we did not know. Being conscious of his innocence, he said he would talk to Robards.[66]

What passed between Captain Robards and Jackson, I do not know, as I was absent somewhere not now recollected when the conversation and results took place but returned soon afterwards. The whole affair was related to me by Mrs. Donelson, the mother of Mrs. Robards. And as well as I recollect by Jackson himself. The substance of their account was that Mr. Jackson met Captain Robards near the orchard fence and began mildly to remonstrate with him respecting the injustice he had done his wife as well as himself. In a little time, Robards became violently angry and abusive and threatened to whip Jackson; made a show of doing so, etc. Jackson told him he had not bodily strength to fight him nor would he do so feeling conscious of his innocence and retired to his cabin telling him at the same time that, if he insisted on fighting, he would give him gentlemanly satisfaction, or words to that effect. Upon Jackson's return out of the house, Captain Robards said he did not care for him nor his wife—abusing them both—that he was determined not to live with Mrs. Robards.

Jackson retired from the family and went to live at Mansker's Station. Captain Robards remained several months with his wife and then went back to Kentucky in the company of Mr. Thomas Cruthers and probably some other persons.[67]

Soon after this affair, Mrs. Robards went to live at Colonel [Robert] Hays's who married her sister [Jane]. After a short absence, I returned to live at Mrs. Donelson's at her earnest entreaty—every family then desiring the association of male friends as a protection against the Indians. This took place, to the best of my recollections, in the spring of 1790."[68]

Overton's recollection at this point began to shade the timeline. Perhaps he was unaware that Jackson's account with Melling Woolley, on July 1, 1790, in Natchez, indicated a feminine presence at his Bayou Pierre cabin.[69]

Some time in the fall the following, there was a report afloat that Captain Robards intended to come down and take his wife [back] to Kentucky. Whence the report originated I do not now recollect but it created great uneasiness with Mrs. Donelson and her daughter, Mrs. Robards; and of this opinion was I, with all those conversed with who were acquainted with the circumstances. Sometime afterwards, during the winter of 1791, Mrs. Donelson told me of her daughter's intentions to go down the river to Natchez, to visit some of their friends in order of keep out of the way of Captain Robards as she said he had threatened to "*haunt her*." Knowing, as I did, Captain Robards' unhappy jealous disposition and his temper growing out of it, I thought she was right to keep out of the way though I do not believe that I so expressed myself to the old lady or to any other person.[70]

The whole affair gave Jackson great uneasiness and this will not appear strange to one as well acquainted with his character as I was. Continually together during our attendance on the wilderness courts, whilst other young men were indulging in familiarities with females of relaxed morals, no suspicion of this kind of the world's censure ever fell to Jackson's share. In this—in his singularly dedicated sense of honor, and in what I thought his chivalrous conception of the female sex, it occurred to me that he was distinguishable from every other person with whom I was acquainted.[71]

About the time of Mrs. Donelson's communication to me respecting her daughter's intention of going to Natchez, I perceived in Jackson symptoms of more than usual concern. I determined to ascertain the cause when he frankly told me that he was the unhappy of men in having innocently and unintentionally been the cause of the loss of peace and happiness of Mrs. Robards whom he believed to be a fine woman. In this I concurred with him but remonstrated on the propriety of his not giving himself any uneasiness about it. It was not long after this before he communicated to me his intentions of going to Natchez with Colonel [Robert] Stark, with whom Mrs. Robards was to descend the river, saying she had no friend or relation that would go with her or assist in preventing Stark and his family and Mrs. Robards from being massacred by the Indians then in a state of war and exceedingly troublesome. Accordingly, Jackson in company with Mrs. Robards and Colonel Stark, a venerable and highly esteemed old man and friend of Mrs. Robards, went down the river from Nashville to Natchez sometime in the winter or spring of 1791. It was not, however, without the urgent entreaties of Colonel Stark, who wanted protection from the Indians that Jackson consented to accompany them; of which I had heard before Jackson's conversation with me previously alluded to."[72]

Correspondence, letters and court documents confirmed Jackson was in Nashville from January to April 1791.[73] In October 1791, a letter from George Cochran indicated both Jackson and Rachel had left Natchez.[74]

> Previously to Jackson's starting, he committed all his law business to me, at the same time assuring me that as soon as he should see Colonel Stark and family and Mrs. Robards situated with their friends in the neighborhood of Natchez, he would return and resume his practice. He descended the river, returned from Natchez to Nashville and was at the Superior Court in the latter place in May 1791, attending to his business as a lawyer and solicitor general for the government. About or shortly after this time, we were informed that a divorce had been granted by the legislature of Virginia, through the influence principally of Captain Robards' brother-in-law, Major John Jouett, who was probably in the legislature at that time."[75]

In May 1790, Jackson was in Nashville where he drew up an indictment against Henry Lane.[76] In April 1791, Jackson was also in Nashville, where in participated in an arbitration.[77] Further throwing Overton's time line askew was the settlement of Colonel John Donelson's personal estate between January and April 15, 1791, where Rachel was referred to as Mrs. Rachel Jackson.[78]

> The application had been anticipated by me. The divorce was understood by the people of this country to have been granted by the legislature of Virginia in the winter of 1790–1791. I went in Kentucky in the summer of 1791, remained at old Mrs. Robards', my former place of residence part of that time and never understood otherwise than that Captain Robards' divorce was final until the latter part of the year 1793. In the summer of 1791, General Jackson went to Natchez and, I understand, married Mrs. Robards, believed to be free from Captain Robards by the divorce in the fall of 1790. They returned to Nashville, settled in the neighborhood of it, where they have lived ever since much beloved and esteemed by all classes.[79]
>
> About the month of December, 1792, after General Jackson and myself had started to Jonesborough, in East Tennessee, where we practiced law, I learned for the first time that Captain Robards had applied to Mercer [County] Court, in Kentucky, for a divorce which had recently been granted and that the legislature had not absolutely granted a divorce but left it for the court to do."[80]

Both Jackson and Overton were lawyers. John Overton was considered among the better lawyers in Tennessee. That neither of them were familiar with the legal procedure for divorce in Kentucky, where they both had clients, stretched credulity.[81]

Overton continued,

> I need not express my surprise on learning that the act of the Virginia Legislature had not divorced Captain Robards. I informed General Jackson of it, who was equally surprised; and during our conversation I suggested the propriety of his procuring a license on his return home and having the marriage ceremony again performed so as to prevent all future caviling on the subject.[82]
>
> To this suggestion, he replied, that he had long since been married on the belief that a divorce had been obtained which was the understanding of every person in

the country; nor was it without difficulty he could be induced to believe otherwise. On our return home from Jonesborough in January 1794, to Nashville, a license was obtained and the marriage ceremony was performed.[83]

The slowness and inaccuracy with which information was received in West Tennessee at that time will not be surprising when we consider its insulated and dangerous situation surrounded on every side by the wilderness and by hostile Indians and that there was no mail established till about 1797, as well as I recollect.[84]

Since the year 1791, General Jackson and myself have never been apart except when he was in the army. I have been intimate in his family and from the mutual and uninterrupted happiness of the General and Mrs. Jackson, which I have at all time witnessed with pleasure as well as those delicate and polite attentions which have ever been reciprocated between them. I have been long confirmed in the opinion that there never existed than what was believed to be the most honorable and virtuous intercourse between them. Before going to Natchez, I had daily opportunities of being convinced that there was no other; before being married in Natchez country, after it was understood that a divorce had been granted by the Legislature of Virginia, it is believed there was none.[85]

14

Political Briars

In February 1827, Charles Hammond, in his *Cincinnati Gazette* wrote, "in the summer of 1790, Gen. Jackson prevailed upon the wife of Lewis Robards of Mercer County, Kentucky, to desert her husband and live with himself in the character of a wife."[1]

"I have no doubt through the newspapers, you have seen the base attempts by Clay & his partners to harrow up the feeling of Mrs. Jackson and myself," Jackson wrote Richard Keith Call on May 3, 1827. "This unheard of procedure in any civilized community was well calculated to harrow up my feelings but situated as I am for the present, my hands are pinioned as it is evident that it is the last effort of the combined coalition to save themselves & destroy me. They calculated that it would arouse me to some desperate act by which I would fall prostrate before the people. In this they shall be disappointed but the day of retribution & vengeance must come when the guilty will meet with their just reward."[2]

On May 14, Overton wrote Jackson concerned about Hammond having identified Hugh McGary, the divorce witness in Robards trial who testified that Rachel and Jackson slept under the same blanket on their return trip from Natchez, in his March 23 issue of the *Cincinnati Gazette's* pamphlet, *Truth's Advocate and Monthly Anti-Jackson Expositor.* "In the defense," Overton wrote, "now in progress by the Jackson Committee it may be necessary to state explicitly that Hugh McGary *never saw you and Mrs. Jackson together before or since he came in company with you both in September 1791 in company with nearly 100 assembled for protection in the trip from Natchez to Nashville.* Such I believe to be the fact and if so, please to communicate it. This letter, not your answer is intended for publication, but your answer may be necessary to satisfy some of the Committee."[3]

Overton's previous paragraph indicated that some on the Nashville Committee might have been having second thoughts about the validity of continuing to defend the Jacksons on the issue of Rachel's marriages.

Jackson's reply to Overton was that McGary, "Never saw Mrs. J and myself

194

together only in the wilderness with Capt. Caffery [Rachel's brother-in-law] and a hundred or more [others]." The Committee used Jackson's statement saying that McGary only saw them in September 1791, when they believed themselves to be married.[4] That was another example of Jackson, Overton and the Nashville Committee unnecessarily hanging Rachel out for more abuse. Nobody disputed that Rachel, Jackson and McGary were among the travelers on the Natchez Trace. What was pinching the Nashville Committee's toes was that McGary was the only person on that trip who knew she was still married to Robards and he later provided that material in Robards' divorce trial in Danville, Kentucky. Since McGary died in 1808, the committee began searching through court records of the divorce.[5]

"Major Moore of Harrodsburg," Overton continued, "has been addresses on the subject of this same Col. H. McGary and requested to examine the clerk's office of Mercer County, Kentucky, to know if there is any deposition of his on file there, and if so to send us a copy."[6]

Major Moore apparently did what was required of him, perhaps more. In her biography of Hugh McGary, Mary P. Hammersmith wrote, "Worthy of noting, incidentally, is the frequency with which records crucial to this whole matter [Robards' divorce] have vanished since 1827–1828."[7]

The larger question was why Jackson, Overton and the committee even called attention to Hugh McGary in the first place when his two days of testimony was the focus of Robards' divorce trial against Rachel. At that point in Jackson's presidential campaign, such actions were a signal of some anxiety for his success.

"This base attack," Jackson told Call, "was first issued from the press of the scoundrel Hammond and reiterated through all administration prints. It has recoiled upon them by a united indignation of every just man in society and in Ky. I am told will prostrate Clay for all believe that he is the author of this base and cowardly procedure. He keeps himself under the cloak of Hammond who he knows in beneath any other notice than cowhide."[8]

Without a doubt, all those accusations, revelations and rumors reach Rachel's ears. In an effort to divert her mind from the vicious presidential campaign rhetoric as well as her mourning the death of the Indian boy, Lyncoya, they raised, Jackson asked John Decker and Isham Dyer, who owned a Nashville confectionary firm, to purchase a parrot. Jackson paid them twenty-five dollars for a parrot name Poll, who became a favorite of Rachel's. Not only did Poll out live both the Jacksons but acquired a rather colorful vocabulary.[9]

Rachel managed the household at The Hermitage, entertained an endless array of guests, and supervised her weavers and possibly other domestic industries she created. However, she made time to keep up her correspondence. In March, Rebecca Matte Alston Hayne wrote Rachel, renewing their friendship, and sent her card racks and a watch case. On April 15, she wrote Mrs. L. A. W. Douglas and thanked her for a recent letter and some seeds that were enclosed. She wrote George W. Martin, stepson of her brother Stockley and thanked him for a gift he sent her. She also invited him to bring his mother, Elizabeth Glasgow Martin Donelson Anderson, to visit them at The Hermitage. Rachel wrote Henry Lee in July thanking him for his letter and sent him a lock of Jackson's hair.[10]

Duff Green, editor of the *United States Telegraph*, wrote Jackson on June 9, expressing his being excised by those closer to Jackson. "You will appreciate the embarrassments which surround me unaided as I am by that advice and necessary counsel which could guide me from committing many errors. I have endeavored to make my paper an organ of correct principles and have carefully avoided the falsehood which characterize our opponents. In truth, I have endeavored to prove myself opposed to them."[11]

Green forwarded a June 10 letter to Rachel from "A Female Friend." It was not clear whether or not the letter was published in his newspaper:

> Madam, pardon a lady for addressing you on a subject of a delicate nature but believing that every illiberal attack upon the female character ought not to be viewed with indifference by any, I view it as a duty to apprize you of a fact that perhaps few besides myself has come to the knowledge of. You no doubt have seen the brutish attach upon your reputation with the real intention of thereby injuring the standing of the General with the public and although the attack and the *real authors* will ultimately fall to the ground. You may then Madam rest assured that the real instigators, managers and directors of this attack, made through the Cincinnati newspapers, is John McClean, Postmaster General, and Mr. Clay—the first active agent. Previous to the last election, he suggested and urged that mode of attack on your husband but the coalition then thought it unnecessary. It was kept back for a forlorn hope and the present trip of the Postmaster General to Ohio is but an excuse to see how far this project is likely to succeed and to direct its application. He [assuming it is Clay] is constantly detailing his stories of your illiterate chats as he calls your remarks and it is the constant theme with others about him who obtain their observations from his stream of scandals—on its being suggested to him that the General might be elected by a confidential friend he replied that he will soon throw dust in his eyes sufficient to do any impression away. That the General had his vanity and, of course, his weak side.[12]

In a June 16 letter to William B. Keene, a Georgetown, Kentucky, physician, Jackson wrote that Rachel was not well. "Mrs. J's physician [Miles B. McCorkle] has advised her to visit the Harrodsburg Springs this season for her health and we were preparing for the journey when an act of providence interposed, which will postpone if not prevent it, this season. By a stroke of lightening she is left without a carriage horse and myself without a riding horse."[13]

Harrodsburg Springs, with its flowing mineral waters, was a popular resort with a four-story hotel known as the "Saratoga of the West."[14] Harrodsburg was also the location of Rachel's unpleasant life with Lewis Robards who still had relatives living there. For Jackson to even consider taking Rachel there could have tanked his entire campaign and worsened whatever ailment she was suffering from. They did not make the trip.

Jackson allowed that attacks on Rachel to get the best of him but only momentarily. In June 1827, Jackson wrote a note to Peter Force, editor of the *Washington National Journal*, which supported Adams. The note in Jackson's handwriting and spelling read, "When the midnight assassins plunges his dagger to the heart and rifles your goods the turpitude of this scene loses all its horrors when compared with the act of the secrete assassins poniard levelled against female character by the hired minions of power." The newspaper printed a reply from an anonymous columnist calling himself HONESTUS. "To be serious, it is impossible to decide which is the most wounded at the audacity which endeavors to palm on public credulity the answers at New Orleans as the productions of Gen. Jackson; the meanness of the general in an attempting the imposture; or the insensibility to the honor of the country, which would elevate to the presidency a man so ignorant that he is the mere mouthpiece of others."[15]

Again, Rachel was whiplashed when Green's newspaper, the *United States' Telegraph,* printed the Nashville Committee's letter on her marriage to Jackson. Duff Green, the editor, was jubilant believing she was completely vindicated. In a July 8 letter to Jackson, he wrote, "Permit me, through you, to tender to Mrs. Jackson the congratulations of a sincere friend on the satisfaction and conclusive vindication of her innocence which has been presented to the public by the Nashville Committee. To a lady of her great sensibility the knowledge of her own innocence would bring much consolation but that sensibility must have been the more acute when she saw that the envenomed shafts of malice were aimed at her on your account. Let her rejoice—her vindication is complete—the voice of slander is hushed and she must be gratified to know that your magnanimity to her is rightly appreciated by an intelligent public. That so far from impairing the confidence of the people in you this attack has made you many friends."[16]

She may not have seen that newspaper but she was probably aware of the *Knoxville Register's* resurrection of the Dickinson duel and their branding Jackson a murderer. However, Rachel did have an extended spa visit when she and Jackson left The Hermitage on July 24 for Robertson Springs, in Robertson County, and returned in early August. The resort's springs of surging waters, containing salts of iron, flowed at 120 gallons per hour.[17]

Before Rachel left for the spa, she wrote Elizabeth Courts Love Watson a long letter on July 18, indicating that she was indeed aware of the abominable print campaign about her marriages to Robards and Jackson.

It is a long time since you wrote me a line but having so favorable an opportunity by Major [Benjamin Fort] Smith I could not deny myself that pleasure. For rest assured my dear friend you are as dear to me as a sister. I am denied many pleasures and comforts in this life and that is one and sister Hays and her family, your family with hers, would have been my joy in this world but alas you are all far from me. Well, the Apostle says I can do all things in Christ who strengthened me. I can say my soul can be a testimony to the truth of that Gospel for who has been as cruelly tried as I have. My trials have been severe. The enemies of the General have dipped their arrows in wormwood and gall and sped them at me. Almighty God, was there ever anything to equal it. My old acquaintances were as much hurt as if it was themselves or their daughters. To think that thirty years had passed in happy social friendship with society knowing or thinking no ill to no one—as my judge will know—how many prayers have I offered up for their repentance. But, woe unto them if offenses come they have disquieted one that they had no right to do. They have offended God and man—in as much as you have offended one of the least of my little ones you offend me. Now, I leave them to their selves. I fear then not; I fear Him that can kill the body and cast the soul into hell fire. O, eternity, awful is the _____. This has been a subject, my dear friend, that I fear has pained your sympathizing friendly disposition toward your friends. Let not your heart be troubled—I am the rock of ages—in the world I have tribulation—Jesus says in me you shall have peace. My peace I gave unto you not as the world gives etc., etc. Your brother and family are all well; are living in style [in] a fine fertile plantation, fine brick house with every comfort.[18]

Rachel found Nashville of that day not to her liking.

Nashville has gone beyond description in point of improving in good fashion. Dress is finer than anywhere I ever was. The theatre and parties have become the church. The pastor of the Presbyterian Church has been dismissed [and] is now in Pittsburgh. Religion has got a wound but I thank God He has promised that the deep waters shall not overflow us nor the flames shall not hurt. He will be with us in all our afflictions. How is my dear friend, Mrs. Jane Love Forrest and family, Dr. Thomas and Mrs. Harriet Love Sim, Colonel Graham and family and Colonel Towson and Mrs. Towson? Dr. Marrible told me what a true friend she was to me in this time of persecution. I pray God to bless her days on earth that they may be happy. Can I forget you all? No.[19]

Mrs. Call has paid us a visit and returned. She had her daughter with her. She had twins but lost them [and] will be confined in September again. Her mother never saw her. We stayed a week in Nashville. She had nearly as much attention paid to her as was to Gen. Lafayette. A committee of gentlemen of the first respectability waited on her with an address. She answered them appropriately. The ball was splendid attended by at least one-hundred ladies. The party spirit her mother aided in getting an opposition party but failed. The mother against the daughter. The matrons wept for it when they saw so fine a woman abandoned by her mother. She is happy with husband and daughter. I have seen sister Hays once since I saw you. How is my dear Mary Ellen [Watson]? Tell her W D [one of Rachel's nephews] is married. She would not come out to Tennessee. I wish she would come and see me."[20]

The nephew Rachel referred to was William Donelson, the son of John and Mary Purnell Donelson and the widower of Rachel Donelson. He married

Elizabeth Anderson, the daughter of Stockley Donelson's widow, Elizabeth Glasgow Martin Donelson, and John Anderson, her third husband.[21]

"Poor dear John [Mrs. Watson's son], how is he? Grown, I suppose. I had a hope, when I last saw you, of having the happiness of having you beside me [as] a neighbor but in that I am disappointed. Well, I remember you always and should I not see you here I hope to see you with Jesus in the New Jerusalem [where] we shall have no more sorrow, no malevolent enemies to harm us. Farewell my much loved friend and sister."[22]

Rachel added a postscript with gossip about Ann McCarty Lee and her husband Harry who was writing a biography of Jackson while boarding at the Fountain of Health Spa. "She will not see any company," Rachel wrote, "and appears somewhat deranged. She is invisible to all but myself and is fond of me. I got and see her occasionally. Oh, that I could pour the wine and the oil to her wounded spirit."[23]

In the second paragraph of the postscript, she mentioned that Jackson was not well, "but surrounded with crowds from one week's end to the other as one carriage full goes another comes. Well, I am fond of society. Many friends but will they bear the test in times of trial? A volume I have to write you. My son is one of the sweetest youths in the world." Andrew Jackson, Jr., at that time was eighteen years old.[24]

Toward the end of 1827, there was a flurry of activities to occupy Rachel's time: the inauguration of Governor Sam Houston, a dinner for newly re-elected Senator Hugh L. White and graduation activities at the University of Nashville. Jackson made a week-long trip to Florence, Alabama, at the end of October. Rachel prepared for an extended absence from The Hermitage.[25] In May, she had purchased a silk dress, shoes and other clothing from Kirkman and Livingston. In September, she paid Matilda Adams twelve dollars for a bobbinet cape.[26]

It appeared she was preparing for another trip to Washington. In the meantime, the political plummeting and persecution of both Rachel and Jackson continued and the worst was yet to come.

The Jacksonians had an advantage the Adams-Clay party lacked—a presidential candidate who had been a national hero in the Battle of New Orleans on January 8, 1815, but they appeared reluctant to use it to their advantage.

Not everybody, however, considered Jackson a hero. In a July 1827 column in the *Angus*, New Orleans journalist John Gibson suggested the next January 8, 1828, celebration in New Orleans should have a great parade with banners portraying the Constitution being pierced by Jackson's sword; Judge D. N. Hall in prison, Louis Louaillier about to be shot; the Louisiana legislature being driven from its building, flames consuming New Orleans and the six Tennessee militiamen led before a firing squad.[27]

Jackson's opponents decided they had been handed an enormous political plum and printed Gibson's column in pro–Adams publications across the nation. William B. Lewis was apparently the first to see the advantage of turning a bitter lemon into sweet political lemonade. That led to what Joseph G. Tregle, Jr., professor emeritus of history at the University of New Orleans, called the first presidential electioneering junket in American history.[28] In 1828, and for some years thereafter, presidential candidates refrained from campaigning, leaving it to subordinates.

Lewis' grand plan for Jackson's return to New Orleans, according to Tregle, was approved by the Louisiana legislature but they forgot to ask the lawmakers for funds to pay for the event. Money for travel and lodging had to come from somewhere. A plan was hatched to raise the funds by popular subscription. The Adams campaign thought it was a lark they contributed. When Jackson said only the intervention of divine providence could keep him from making the trip, raising money became no problem.[29]

The steamboat *Pocahontas* left New Orleans on December 13, and arrived in Nashville two weeks later to pick up Rachel, Jackson, a batch of Donelsons, Governor Sam Houston, John Overton, William Carroll, William B. Lewis, Colonel James Hamilton (son of Alexander Hamilton) and other supporters. Jackson, ill and sickly, gave orders for the *Pocahontas* to proceed directly to Natchez. They arrived in Natchez on January 4, 1828, met by the New Orleans welcoming committee and boats filled with veterans of the War of 1812. After Natchez citizens hosted a dinner and ball for the Jacksons, they proceeded downriver, escorted by a flotilla of boats carrying veterans of the War of 1812 to New Orleans, arriving on January 8. A three-gun salute announced their arrival, answered by a 24-gun blast from cannons in the Palace d'Armes.[30]

The Jacksons were the guests of influential New Orleans businessman and politician Bernard de Marigny, whom they knew from previous trips. The wealthy Frenchman and Jackson grew up on opposite ends of the economic spectrum, but they shared a number of personal foibles. Both were land speculators, gamblers and fought duels in connection with comments about their wives. Jackson's duel with John Sevier began with his disparaging remarks about Rachel but their marriage continued, for the most part, to be successful. Bernard de Marigny was said to have fought seven duels in seven days over the fair Mathilde but in the last six years of the de Marigny's marriage, Mathilde lived on the first floor of their plantation mansion and he lived on the second floor. However Jackson's dueling activities certainly faded in comparison to de Marigny, who was said to have fought nineteen duels beneath the Allard Oaks Dueling Grounds. In 1817, he challenged James Humble, who was six feet, ten inches tall. Humble, who had never used a sword or fired a gun, chose blacksmith's hammers in six feet of water in Lake

Pontchartrain. Bernard de Marigny made his apologies and took Humble out to dinner.[31]

Bernard and Anna Mathilde Morales de Marigny, according to their account, gave the Jacksons exceptional and expensive entertainment during their visit.[32]

Rachel agreed as she wrote her friend Hannah Davenport on February 25, after they returned to The Hermitage. "I was delighted," she said of the honor paid her husband, the entertainment and visit, "and never enjoyed myself more."[33]

"I received your kind letter," Rachel continued, "December 9, and am happy to hear you and Major Davenport's good health and your safe arrival in Cincinnati. I wanted to have answered your letter immediately on receiving it but for our trip to New Orleans of which you have received various accounts in the papers long since. Therefore, it would be useless for me to attempt a discussion as I observed as we approached the city escorted by twenty-four steamboats and the firing of artillery and acclamation of the people. The printer may employ his pencil, the poet and historian therefore but none could do justice to the scene."[34]

Rachel wrote that she saw a number of my old friends and acquaintances that she never expected to see again. "Yet, there was a great many I should have been happy to see those who were not there. For instance, the major and yourself, Mr. and Mrs. [Richard Keith] Call and several others. Had the pleasure of seeing Colonel [Robert] and Mrs. Butler. She appeared to be in delicate health. The general stood the trip better than I expected. He was very much gratified, excited to see the children that had strewn his path with flowers." Rachel added a tongue-in-cheek remark about the women who showered Jackson with attentions and remarked that some of them were married.[35]

"We also met with a great many of his old friends and fellow soldiers. The general and I would be happy indeed to see you and the major at The Hermitage again. I hope the next time you will give yourself more time. I shall always be extremely grateful to hear from you. I am a poor correspondent myself but am always happy to keep up a correspondence with my absent friends. The general joins me in fond remembrance to Major and Mrs. [words not readable] also to all the Gaines and to Mr. and Mrs. Butler if they have returned. Mr. and Mrs. [Andrew Jackson] Donelson. Little Jackson [the Donelson's son] grows finally. Cousin Mary Eastin is here and requests to be kindly remembered to you and others. Accept from the general and me our every most and best wishes for your prosperity and happiness."[36]

Pere Antoine greeted Jackson at the Cathedral Saint Louis, where banners were wrapped around the altar with signage, VICTORY TO GOD AND TO JACKSON. Jackson strode, erect and bareheaded, on to the Plains of Chalmette where he affirmed decisions he made there thirteen years earlier. More than

35,000 people crowded into New Orleans for the four-day celebration—cantatas, receptions, theatrical galas, balls and banquets—which generated more media coverage for Jackson than anything the Adams campaign could imagined.[37]

Rachel and Jackson's January 1828 trip to New Orleans was a groundbreaking political event for a number of reasons. It occurred in a period when presidential candidates did not campaign—that was left to associates, committees and party newspapers. Jackson had a special bond with the thousands of his former soldiers who attended the event. Rachel could have been the first presidential candidate's wife to accompany her husband on what many called the first electioneering junket. While New Orleans' finest wined and dined the Jacksons, Rachel, who hated leaving her beloved Hermitage, said she really enjoyed herself in the city. That was a missing element when she accompanied Jackson on other trips to Washington and Florida.

"Receptions by uniformed veterans, respect shown Rachel by the great ladies of the city, speeches, banquets adoring crowds—their four days in New Orleans were a constant festival. And, every day's events were covered by newspapers in every state," wrote Brady. "The majority of voters simply did not care if he [Jackson] had a bad temper, wrote poorly or had eloped with a married women."[38]

Back in Washington, President John Quincy Adams fussed and fumed about the Jacksons' New Orleans trip. He called it "pompous pageantry" and referred to Jackson's speeches as being "tawdry elegance."[39]

Another critic of the event was none other than Vincent Nolte, known for his scathing criticism of Rachel on her first visit to New Orleans. Nolte wrote of Rachel in 1815 as being "an emigrant of the lower classes whom he [Jackson] had from a Georgia planter and whose enormous corpulence was explained by the French saying, 'she shows how far the skin can be stretched.'"[40]

Thirteen years later, Nolte set his sights on the New Orleans businessmen who arranged the Jacksons' visit, calling them cabinet makers by trade, low cart men, dirty wood sawyers and contemptible bricklayers. Jackson's allies pointed out that most people earned their living by the sweat of their brows. John Slidell, a maritime lawyer and later a U.S. senator from Louisiana, demanded Nolte apologize. He refused. F. B. Ogden, a mapmaker and businessman, attempted to kill Nolte and failed. When Nolte finally left New Orleans in 1829, his friends hired guards to protect him en route to boarding his ship.[41]

Jackson was so exhausted after the celebration that they stayed at the Ormond plantation of Samuel McCutchon for two days prior to their departure back to Nashville.[42]

Rachel and Jackson hardly had time to settle back into a routine at The Hermitage before Charles Hammond printed 5,000 copies of a twelve-chapter, 190-page pamphlet about the Jacksons' married life.

15

Rachel Becomes
a Political Battering Ram

The cost of printing, assembling and distributing 5,000 copies of Charles Hammond's verbal and venal indictment of Rachel and Andrew Jackson in *Truth's Advocate* in March 1828 was a massive undertaking for which the Adams campaign paid dearly both in money spent and in the political marketplace.

An ardent supporter of Henry Clay in the 1824 presidential campaign, Hamilton toyed with the idea of acting as Clay's agent in negotiating with supporters of William H. Crawford, who was in ill health and leaving the race. He was much closer to Clay than he ever admitted in his publications about the Jacksons' domestic life. At the same time he declared his absolute hatred of Andrew Jackson. In one of his letters to Clay, Hammond said if Jackson was classed as an animal he would be a monkey-tiger cross. "I dislike him for cause," his letter to Clay continued, "I hate him peremptorily and I wish all his supporters for the presidency, one and all, were snugly by themselves in some island of Barrataria and he being their king, provided they constituted the entire population. They would make a glorious terrestrial pandemonium as fast as they cut each other's throats. The world would be rid of very troublesome politicians and in general worthless citizens."[1]

What better way to express the hatred Hammond felt for Jackson than attempt to make him lose his famous temper by ridiculing Rachel? If Jackson retaliated and went on some sort of insane rant, Hammond could crow about his success in denying the Tennessean the presidency. If Jackson refused the bait, which he did, Hammond then skewered Rachel with more merciless vengeance than that heaped on Catherine de Medici, Lucrezia Borgia and Elizabeth Bathory, all pilloried one way or another by pamphleteers.[2]

William Henry Smith, in his 1884 address about Hammond and Clay to the Chicago Historical Society, called attention of a November 1827 letter from the Cincinnati lawyer and newspaper editor to the Speaker of the

House from Kentucky. "I sent you the prospectus of a new work," Smith read, "intended spirits and calculated to travel all the byways of politics. It will be adapted to the meridian of Ohio, Indiana, and Ohio and not unsuited to Pennsylvania. If the press can effect anything we are determined to do what we can in that very way." Smith went on to say Hammond was referring to *Truth's Advocate* and his own newspaper, *The Cincinnati Gazette*.[3]

Hammond's carefully orchestrated plans to destroy Jackson's presidential campaign began with the first issue of *Truth's Advocate* in January 1828 coinciding with the Jacksons' trip to New Orleans and built up to a crescendo with the massive March printing.[4]

Chapter nine in Hammond's March 1828 issue of *Truth's Advocate* was titled, "View of Gen. Jackson's Domestic Relations in Reference to His fitness For the Presidency," but was focused foremost on Rachel. Hammond maintained that when national interests, national character and national morals were at stake she was a proper subject of investigation. He attempted to take responsibility alone for the exposé, saying the time had come and denied he had consulted with a single individual. It was his solemn duty, he said.[5]

"Whatever may be thought or said of other offices, every candid man must agree that the office of president necessarily brings the immediate family of the officer into direct connection with the public," Hammond wrote. "It is impossible to separate them from public observation. If the president be a married man, his wife at least must share the distinction of the station he occupies. If she does not, the reason will be sought after. If she does, her qualifications for the station, her character and standing, her personal defects, or excellences, must be drawn out and made subject of remark and will be commended, caricatured or ridiculed as they may furnish occasion."[6]

Hammond dealt Rachel a most vile, licentious public thrashing—most of which was untrue—of any American presidential candidate's wife. "It has so happened, in other countries, as well as our own," he wrote, "that highly gifted men have associated themselves in the connubial relation with ignorant and vulgar women."[7]

That must have been a real shock for an evangelical Presbyterian woman like Rachel who knew she made mistakes early in her life and, from all indications, attempted to do restitution for them. Hammond continued to describe Rachel in that manner as he described such men as her husband. "This association never fails to lessen our respect for the individual. We feel that it impeaches his taste, his judgment or his moral conceptions. Whilst, however, it would not operate to deter us from employing him as a lawyer or a mechanic or confiding in his judgment as a merchant, it would assuredly indispose us to engage him as our clergyman or to select him as the guardian for our daughters."[8] Hammond carefully ignored the fact that no scandals appeared to be associated with the numerous wards Rachel and Andrew Jackson raised or sheltered in their home.

> Every prudent and discreet person, entrusted with the charge of a family holds it a duty to examine well the female character where they cultivate an acquaintance. If the female family head be destitute of the characteristics and accomplishments which adorns the station she moves in, it never fails to produce an unfavorable effect upon her connections. A talented husband or great wealth may assure her a cold endurance but they can do no more. The law of society is more irrevocable than any law of the Medes and Persians. It is founded in the pure morals, exquisite sensibility and pervading influence of the female sex in every Christian country. An attempt to subvert it, an effort to inculcate the doctrine that an enquiry into the character of a man's wife for the purpose of regulating intercourse with his family in an unhallowed invasion of the domestic sanctuary can never be successful. This enquiry must and will be made in all cases where the station or the employments of the husband necessarily places his wife in connexion [connection] with society.[9]
>
> Such being the relation in which the wife of a president is placed. The character and the interest of the nation must be more or less affected by her capacity, or incapacity, to acquit herself with credit in the elevation to which she is called. If she be weak and vulgar, she cannot escape becoming a theme for ridicule a portion of which must attach to her husband and to the people that have selected him for their chief ruler. If she be intelligent and accomplished, the influence of her talents, her virtue and manners must inevitably reflect a mild and benignant luster upon all around her and all connected with her.[10]

Certainly Rachel was overweight and tanned from years in the outdoors. She smoked a pipe; so did Dolley Madison. With the exception of Martha Washington, no presidential candidate's wife had successfully managed a plantation and other business affairs while her husband was absent.

Jackson, when advising Andrew Jackson Hutchings on taking a wife, said, "Recollect the industry of your dear aunt [Rachel] and with what economy she watched over what I made and how we waded thro the vast expenses of the mass of company we had. Nothing but her care and industry with good economy could have saved me from ruin. If she had been extravagant the property would have vanished and poverty and want would have been our doom."[11]

Rachel's signature sin was leaving an abusive marriage the only possibly way she could at that time. By living with another man, who happened to be the love of her life, she gave her abusive husband an excellent reason to divorce her. Most women of the 1780s and 1790s had no choice but to remain in such atrocious relationships and often paid the price with their lives. But, they were not married to men with the political aspirations Jackson had.

"When, then, in our country," Hammond continued, "a man is suggested as a candidate for the presidency, the matrons and the maidens of the land have a deep stake in knowing the character of his wife and if she be a weak and vulgar woman, for that reason alone, his pretensions should be passed by.

But if a stain be cast on her, which in general cases, exclude the unfortunate subject from society altogether then the investigation and enquiry becomes double indispensable. It applies not only to the propriety of permitting her to occupy the station proposed but it touches also the character and qualifications of her husband."[12]

While Hammond insisted that insinuation and suspicions, which he was guilty of making, were insufficient reasons for such an investigation. He also admitted that "present correct conduct and the possession of countenance and respect from reputable persons should be received to silence all these.[13]

"But, when the stigma is affixed by legislative acts and judicial records, the case is widely different. It then calls for an enquiry and there is no escape from the conclusion. We must see a degraded female placed at the head of the female society of the nation or we must proclaim and urge the fact as grounds for excluding her husband."[14]

Hammond, Edward Day and whomever else his collaborators were, carefully avoided concrete facts as to when and where events occurred. They leave the reader with the impression the Robards divorce was granted in Virginia, when it was not. Another application for divorce was applied for and granted in Kentucky, after statehood. Hammond made no mention of the strong allegations of Rachel's marital abuse by Robards, who apparently bragged of committing adultery with his family's slave women while still living with Rachel. Hammond also managed to overlook the fact that Robards was a bigamist before their divorce was final and that Rachel did not contest the divorce. Hammond's aim, aided by the clever use of innuendo, was solely concentrated on destroying a woman's reputation— over a youthful indiscretion committed thirty years earlier—to defeat her husband in a presidential campaign. Americans had never seen anything in past political campaigns to match Adams, Clay and Hammond's efforts to totally destroy one woman who took the only avenue available to her to escape an abusive husband.

Hammond admitted the case of Rachel and Andrew Jackson was unusual and used that idea to fuel the fire of his rhetoric. "Wherever he was known," Hammond wrote, "public rumor circulated suspicions as to the correctness of his matrimonial alliance long before he was dreamed of as a man in whose connubial connections the nation could have any possible interest. It was no case of mere surmise against an unmarried female arising out of possible indiscretions and resting upon a peculiar freedom of manners too little regardful of the restraints of society. On the contrary, it involved an accusation of the most exceptionable character, extending to the gentleman as well as the lady, and resting for proof upon a legislative act and a record of a court of justice. It was an accusation of gross adultery, in which outrage upon the right of the husband was urged upon Gen. Jackson and desertion from her husband to the arms of a paramour was charged against the wife. Such were the charges; upon which they rested."[15]

Did Hammond really expect his readers to believe the United Stated had a two-tiered executive branch of government headed by a president and a first lady? "Whether true or false necessarily became a matter of public concern," he continued, "from the fact that the parties accused were presented as candidates for the most conspicuous stations in our country in which the accused female must be placed at the head of the female society of the land. Were she innocent of the crimes alleged against her, their long circulation, the strong evidence to sustain them and the serious manner in which they affected the present claims of her husband, coincided to call for an investigation. Any upright and an honorable man, confident of the purity of his wife and sensible that he occupied a station which connected that purity with the character of his country, would have rejoiced at an opportunity to repel a long endued calumny. He would have seen, in a call for inquiry and investigation, no spirit but that of manly patriotism. He would have regarded the man who moved it as the friend of himself and of the country rejoicing as one who has found a pearl of great price. It had not been so received; it has not been so met. Why has it not, there can be but one opinion."[16]

In Hammond's version of the Robards divorce, he failed to explain Robards' initial filing against Rachel in Virginia in 1790, and the reason the actual divorce trial in Kentucky occurred three years later, in 1793. Hammond also failed to note that the Virginia legislature did not grant divorces but only approved a petition to proceed in obtaining one. Nor does Hammond explain the timeframe from the initial filing in Virginia to the divorce granted in Kentucky.

"Mrs. Jackson was the wife of Lewis Robards," Hammond commented, "of Mercer County, Kentucky, than a component of the Commonwealth of Virginia. In December 1790, Lewis Robards applied to the legislature of Virginia, charging his wife with adultery and for that cause praying for a divorce. Such proof was offered as induced the legislature to act upon that charge. A law was passed directing a judicial investigation and, providing that if it were found true, Lewis Robards would stand divorced from his wife. These proceedings were instituted and prosecuted to final trial. In September 1793, twelve men, constituting a jury, after hearing proof, declared on their oaths that Mrs. Robards was guilty of adultery charged upon her and Lewis Robards obtained the divorce prayed for."[17]

It was most convenient for Hammond to ignore the makeup of the jury, their relationships to Robards and his principal witness, Hugh McGary. The editor had other things to do in setting himself up as an arbitrator of Christianity.

Hammond asserted,

This fact being thus established, the question fairly presents itself to a Christian and moral people, ought a convicted adulteress and her paramour husband to be placed in the highest offices of this free and Christian land? It is useless to answer with ranting vituperation. It is a plain and a fair question; one which no citizen should be denounced for asking. Was the offense committed? Can lapse of time eradicate its contamination? Party prejudice, party passions may answer as they please. Those who value good character and the institutions and moral sentiment that preserve it can give but one answer.[18]

An answer has been attempted, not by denying the fact of the adultery, but by admitting and attempting to excuse it. This vindication is the work of able men; it has been skillfully adapted to the sympathies and passions of the multitude totally disregarding all moral feeling and just intelligence. It shall be reviewed and expressed, not by appeals to passion and vulgar prejudice, but by submitting such a commentary as is applicable to ever case similarly circumstanced.[19]

The Nashville Committee commenced their vindication by noticing an allegation against the chastity of Mrs. Jackson, which none had before objected against her, in any tangled form. A number of witnesses were brought forward who testified her husband was jealous of her before she was acquainted with Gen. Jackson. Judge Overton is made to name the individual of whom her husband was jealous and to state that some of facts transpired under his own observations. I am unable to perceive how these facts can be determined elucidatory of Mrs. Jackson's good conduct. But I rely on nothing upon them as proof against her. I would be the last man to impeach a lady's chastity upon the single circumstance of her husband's jealousy. Yet, every man must admit that jealousy is a very old evidence to bring forward in support of her character. And when a second fit of jealousy turns out to be well founded it is singular enough to allege the first to excuse it. Such, however, is the case before us.[20]

Judge Overton lived in the family of Robards' mother, with Robards and his wife, in 1787 and in 1788. They lived unhappily in consequence of his jealousy. In the fall or summer of 1787, Mrs. Robards' brother, at the request of Robards, who had said he did not intend to live with her any longer, removed her to her mother's in Tennessee, leaving Robards in Kentucky. [21]

This removal "was said to be a final separation at the instance of Robards." The whole family held Mrs. Robards blameless.[22]

After her departure, the elder Mrs. Robards spoke to Judge Overton, who was about to settle in Tennessee, to interest himself to "get her son Lewis and daughter-in-law Rachel to live happily together." He conversed with Robards who expressed regret, acquitted his wife of all impropriety and joined in requesting the judge's good offices to restore harmony and this the judge undertook. In consequence of Robards' assurances that he would give up all nonsensical notions about jealousy.[23]

In March 1889, Judge Overton was at Mrs. Donelson's, mother of Mrs. Robards, in Tennessee where he and Gen. Jackson about that time became boarders [with Rachel's mother]. The judge "frequently conversed with Mrs. Robards on the subject of living happily with her husband." He communicated this to Robards and his mother and received their thanks and Robards and his wife became reunited in 1788 or 1789. In the arrangement for reunion, Robards agreed to reside in Tennessee and, for a time, at Mrs. Donelson's. "Not many months lapsed before Robards became jealous of Jackson," and his upbraiding's reached the ear of the judge who remonstrated with him but to no effect. The judge then informed Jackson who determined to remonstrate with Robards. This resulted in a quarrel and Jackson left the house to board elsewhere. [24]

Hammond again was wrong. Both Jackson and Overton moved away from Mrs. Donelson's.[25]

"Robards remained several months with his wife and then went to Kentucky in company with Mr. Thomas Crutcher." There came a report that "Robards intended to come and take his wife to Kentucky." After this, again, Mrs. Donelson told the judge "her daughter intended to go down the river to Natchez to some of their friends, IN ORDER TO KEEP OUT OF THE WAY OF ROBARDS, as she said he had threatened to haunt her." Jackson became greatly distressed and made the judge his confident communications [of] his intention of going to Natchez with Col. [Robert] Stark, with whom Mrs. Robards was to descend the river saying that she had no friends or relations to go with her and assist in preventing Mr. Stark, his family and Mrs. Robards from being massacred by Indians. He went accordingly and returned in May, 1791. About or shortly after this time, information was received that a divorce had been granted upon the application of Robards. The judge remarked, "THIS APPLICATION HAD BEEN ANTICIPATED BY ME." Jackson returned to Natchez in the summer of 1791, and in the fall brought Mrs. Robards back as his wife. The general never knew there was no divorce until after the decree was pronounced, when the judge informed him of it, and advised a second marriage, which was solemnized in January 1793. [26]

Hammond made a major error, saying the Jacksons were married in January 1793. Had that occurred, Hammond would have been loudly screaming that Rachel was a bigamist since Robards' divorce decree was not issued until September 27, 1793. The actual date of the Jacksons' marriage was January 18, 1794.[27]

Such is the palliatory narration of a partial friend. It is an insult to common sense to say that it does so to place the seduction and adultery in as prominent and reprehensible light as it is placed by the legislative and judicial proceedings themselves. Jackson avows his attachment to a married woman and his determination to travel with her as her protector in a journey undertaken avowedly to "keep out of the way of her husband." The apology for this journey is that her husband threatened to take her to Kentucky. Jackson united himself as a husband to this same married woman upon the mere report of a divorce and lived with her between two and three years in open adultery. For this, the plea of ignorance is advanced; as if the perpetrator of an acknowledged enormity, which nothing but the knowledge of facts could palliate, might be permitted to justify himself upon the plea of ignorance. [28]

In the whole course of my life, I have never witnessed a defense, even of the lowest criminal by the meanest pettifogger, of such a demoralizing and profligate tendency as the one here attempted. It is maintained that a convicted and avowed adulteress shall be permitted to say, that the unfounded and unjust accusations of her husband were the occasion of her crime and constituted her apology. Assuming an innocence, negative by every part of the transaction, as the very ground of the defense making strong and almost irresistible presumptions of guilt an excuse for its undisguised consummation.[29]

The affection of Robards for his wife and his anxiety to enjoy her company is evident from all the statements furnished. Judge Overton confirms this, in terms, and he states clearly that after Jackson left the house of Mrs. Donelson, "Robards remained several months with his wife and then went to Kentucky in the company of Mr. Thomas Crutcher."[30]

Hammond conveniently omitted Overton's firsthand account of living with the Robards family in Mercer County. "I had not lived there many weeks before I understood that Captain Robards and his wife lived very unhappily on account of his being jealous of Mr. Short. My brother, who was a boarder, informed me that great uneasiness had existed in the family for some time before my arrival."[31]

"Mr. Crutcher," Hammond continued, "relates the parting of Robards and his wife when this journey was taken and he also relates their conduct after Jackson left Mrs. Donelson's. He says, 'Captain Robards continued to live with Mrs. Donelson without interruption as long as he remained in the country. I have seen Mr. and Mrs. Robards together in Nashville and have seen them together at Col. Hay's, where they have staid days and night.' On their parting, he says, 'When I was ready to set out on my journey, I went by Mrs. Donelson's for Captain Robards. On my arrival I found Mrs. Robards and her mother busily engaged in packing his clothes and provisions. I suppose it was about an hour before Capt. Robards was ready to start. When we were ready to start, Capt. Robards, with much apparent friendship, took his leave of Mrs. Donelson and his wife, walking to the gate with him, in a very tender and affectionate manner took her leave of him.'"[32]

Crutcher, a bachelor, was surely an expert on married life. He served as Tennessee treasurer under the first five governors.[33] He and Jackson, along with Alfred Balch, were executors of the estate of William Terrell Lewis.[34] A Jackson sycophant and apparent gossip, it was odd that Crutcher was as supportive of Robards as Hammond purported him to be. According to Harriet C. Owsley in her *Tennessee Historical Quarterly* article, Crutcher was one of about twenty people who were asked by the Nashville Committee to make statements about the situation concerning Rachel's first marriage.[35]

"Thus the parties lived," Hammond wrote, "and thus they separated after Jackson left Mrs. Donelson's, which Overton says was several months. Robards' jealousy subsided when the object was no longer in association with his wife. Let us enquire what he was subsequently guilty of that should justify a wife to abjuring his authority and society. On this journey, he [Robards] said to Mr. Crutcher that, 'The friends of Mrs. Robards would not like, and perhaps would not consent, for her to go back to Kentucky to live. He said he did not care what they liked or disliked, she should do what he thought proper.'"[36]

Finally, Hammond brought up the abuse question in the Robards' marriage by attempting to refute John Breckinridge's statement in defense of Rachel. "He is absurd enough to say, 'I was a young man at the time and the deep impression made on my mind was the severity and importance of the case combined with the interest which I felt in behalf of the female concerned remain with great distress. Mr. Robards was represented to be a man of vile, wild habits and harsh temper and his wife lovely and blameless in her disposition and deportment and so cruelly treated by her husband as to make a separation necessary to her happiness. It was under impressions produced by a state of facts like these that I voted for a judicial enquiry into the subject, which I have understood eventuated in a divorce.'"[37]

Hammond went berserk over Breckinridge's statement. "When a man of sense utters such absurdities as these we know he does not speak the truth. His assertions are in direct contradiction with our common sense. They prove his readiness to stultify himself to support Gen. Jackson and they prove nothing further."[38]

The man Hammond called a liar was elected the Virginia House of Delegates when he was still at student at the College of William and Mary in 1780, and served until 1784. After moving to Kentucky, Breckinridge served as attorney general of the commonwealth; wrote most of Kentucky's second constitution in 1799; was elected U.S. Senator in 1801; became a spokesman for President Thomas Jefferson on the Judiciary Act and the Louisiana Purchase, and later was the U.S. attorney general.[39]

Hammond apparently agreed with Robards' dictatorial opinions about women, especially his wife, in late 1700s. Mary Boykin Chestnut, a Charleston, South Carolina, intellectual, later described men like Robards as "a magnate who run a hideous black harem with its consequences under the same roof with his lovely white wife and accomplished daughters. He holds his head high and poses as a model of all human virtues to these poor women whom God and laws have given him. From the height of his awful majesty, he scolds and thunders at them as if he never did a wrong in his life."[40]

Hammond agreed with Robards decades later for, if nothing else, political expediency. "Most men I believe, act pretty much upon this principle [dictating his wife's actions] certainly deem it necessary to consult 'the likes and the dislikes' of their wives' friends as to their place of residence. And surely, no man who values our institutions, and social intercourse founded upon them, can contend that a jealous temper in a husband and an unwillingness to reside where he may prefer can justify a wife placing herself 'beyond his reach' in a society of a person toward whom he has once expressed a feeling of jealousy. Yet, these are the only reasons adduced in the vindication of the conduct of Mrs. Robards."[41]

At that point, according to Hammond, Crutcher again entered the picture. "Mr. Crutcher tells us, 'it was reported, however, that he 'threatened to come and take his wife to Kentucky and compel her to live there.' She, as well as all her friends, was much opposed to this and 'in order to place herself beyond his reach,' as I understood at that time, determined to descend the river [Mississippi] in company with Col. Stark's family and under his protection in Natchez."[42]

Again, Hammond erred. Rachel had no need for Stark's protection in Natchez. Her protectors there were Thomas Marston Green's family and other friends of the Donelson family.

Hammond said he had the same information from Overton as Crutcher provided. "Both concur in stating that Mrs. Robards made her journey to Natchez to avoid her husband and in disregard of the duty which required her to accompany him to Kentucky. There is no essential difference in the case whether she left her husband's own house or that of her mother, where he left her in kindness and in contemplation of meeting her again in the same spirit. The facts of the case, so exhibited by Overton, in connection with Crutcher, when divested to the strong opinion which the gentlemen themselves give, present a case of very gross misconduct in both parties; and such as the record evidence would naturally lead us to expect."[43]

Hammond, using Overton and Crutcher's statements, called the allegations of abuse curious anomalies. "At the time when Mr. Robards separated from his wife, applied for a divorce, obtained it and Gen. Jackson married her, when all the facts were fresh and distinct, public opinion was formed and the contemporaneous judgments of the society in which those persons resided, came to a clear and decisive result in their favor."[44]

Hammond then excoriated Overton, whose statements he previously used to his advantage, for his "anticipation" that Robards would apply for a divorce.

Whatever he may say now, it is very clear he did not THEN ANTICIPATE that Robards would apply for a divorce, without a supposition that he had one cause for it. The idea would be absurd. Robards had confessed the injustice of his first suspicions and he has become reconciled to his wife after his second fit of jealousy, had parted from her in tenderness and wished her to come and reside with him in Kentucky.[45]

It is useless to insist, in a case where a single man has avowed his affections for another man's wife (for the admission to Judge Overton "that he was the most unhappy of men in having been innocently and unintentionally the cause of the loss of peace to Mrs. Robards whom he believed to be a fine woman" amounts to neither more or less) and who accompanies that wife in a long journey to "keep her out of her husband's way" and "place her beyond his reach" and where the unhappy swain and the "fine woman" live in union as man and wife and their conduct is made the subject of legislation and judicial investigation resulting in a conviction of adultery. It is useless, I say, to assert in such a case that the contemporaneous and judgment of society was in their favor and there "did not exist an injurious suspicion as to their previous conduct." The assertion is a libel upon all society, where female chastity is valued or connubial fidelity regarded, as well as an idle contradiction of the recorded evidence in the cause.[46]

Hammond had no forgiveness for Rachel's youthful indiscretions regardless of how she lived her life in the interim. She could have been canonized and he would not have been satisfied. The woman was simply grist for his political mill and he had no intention of being diverted.

It is alleged as an apology that "thirty-seven years of domestic peace and useful virtue have given a sanction which must operate upon every candid and generous mind with irresistible power." This is a persuasive and plausible appeal. It addresses itself to our kindest sympathies and were it a cause for the indulgence of sympathy would be almost incontrovertible. In most cases of female aberration, there are very many extenuating circumstances by which the sympathy in one sex and both sympathy and gallantry in the other would be almost persuaded to forgive the offender. It is because of this that a stern uncompromising judgment of censure is universally past. The unfortunate is resolved to have fallen never to rise again unless all memory of her fall can be obliterated. So great are the temptations, so numerous and so seducing the approaches to the commission of the offense in question nothing short of utter and irremediable disgrace is sufficient to hold it in proper check.[47]

Hammond could not contain himself and compared Rachel to Elise D. Whipple, an Albany, New York, woman famous as an accused accomplice in the 1827 murder of her husband, John Whipple, by Jesse Strange, her alleged paramour. Elsie was arrested and indicted as an accessory but there was no proof, other than Strange's word, of her involvement in the murder of her husband. She was acquitted and two years later remarried.[48]

"Can forty years of exemplary virtue restore the wretched Elsie D. Whipple to the station she has lost in Society?" Hammond asked. Then, he doubled down writing, "Would not we be startled at the bare suggestion that forty year hence she might be placed as the wife of our president at the head of the females of our country? There is no recorded proof of her adultery and no evidence to charge her with further crime but the assertions of a most abandoned villain. The cases are not analogous but the principle is the same and however painful it may be felt the more recent one is a decisive illustration of the unsoundness of the apology in question."[49]

The case comparisons of Rachel and Elsie were not analogous. Elsie's deceased husband had not been campaigning for president nor had Rachel ever been arrested. Hammond attempted a lame denial that his repetitive recital of the life of Rachel Jackson had nothing do with her husband running for president and endeavored to make the case that details of their marriage were well known.

"That oblivion had not cast her shade upon the offenses of Mrs. Jackson is most notorious nor has it in the canvass for the presidency been raked up from a comparative forgetfulness to be used for the purpose of prejudicing her husband. From the period of the transaction themselves, the subject has never ceased to circulate and supply a theme of conversation wherever Gen. Jackson was known."[50]

Robards' unfaithfulness to Rachel, his pathological jealous rages, his decision to send her back to her mother in Nashville because he no longer wanted to live with her were of little consequence to Hammond, whose actions were not acceptable in his driven motivations to keep Andrew Jackson out of the President's House at any cost.

"In the view here presented of the case," Hammond continued, "upon facts stated by the vindicating committee themselves, no intelligent mind is permitted to doubt that Mrs. Jackson was unfaithful to her marriage vows with Robards. No man of the world can believe that she would have been guilty of the great indiscretion of flying beyond the reach of her husband, with a man charged to be her paramour, were she innocent of the charge. Her conduct, his conduct in the flight, in the alleged marriage, in the illegal union, in the subsequent legal marriage furnish presumptions of guilt which of no explanation consistent with correctness and duty."[51]

Hammond, who had long since abandoned any semblance of journalistic ethics in his opus, scraped the bottom of the rotten political barrel. "It would be as rational to give credit to asseverations of innocence had they been found at midnight undressed in the same bed. In that case, there would be proof of a single indiscretion, whilst in the real case there is a succession of corroborative facts, which could not in any probability take place were the parties innocent."[52]

Imagine Rachel's distress and embarrassment in having herself publicly portrayed as being naked in bed with Jackson! It was the year 1828, when women still wore skirts covering their ankles, were still considered chattel of their husbands as she had been in her marriage to Robards, were severely criticized if they attempted to participate in public discourse and were allowed no financial assets in their names. Without a doubt, Rachel knew about the pamphlet even if she did not read all of Hammond's assertions as noted in her correspondence with Moses Dawson, editor of the *Cincinnati Advertiser*, who defended her against Hammond's abominable screeches.[53]

Hammond was on a roll and nothing was going to stop him.

It has been urged that the effect of the record is invalidated by the fact that the proceedings were *ex parte*. But, with what propriety can General Jackson or any one of his advocates advance this argument? The transcript does not show when the judicial proceedings were first instituted. But, Judge Overton places the first union of Gen. Jackson and Mrs. Robards in the summer of 1791. When they assumed the open relation of husband and wife, it was an illegal and criminal act. They were upon their own assumptions greatly mistaken. How was it practicable to effect such a state of things for them to continue in the relation of husband and wife? The answer admits no dispute. It is nowhere pretended that Mrs. Robards could apply for a divorce with any hope of success.[54]

Again, Hammond failed to do his homework. Rachel could have applied for a Spanish divorce in Natchez as numerous women did. The Thomas Marston Green family was prominent enough to assist her in establishing residency and there were attorneys, such as Cato West, in the family. In 1789, Green, a friend of the Donelson family, had given Jackson his power of attorney.[55] Rachel was said to have divided her extended visit in Natchez between the Springfield plantation of Thomas Marston Green, Jr., and the Second Creek plantation of his brother Abner. It was a mystery why Rachel did not apply for a Spanish divorce. There was another avenue to consider. Did the Jacksons declare themselves as having a common law marriage? Granted, Rachel was still married to Robards but may have been convinced he had divorced her. Common law marriages were legal in Mississippi until 1956.[56]

Hammond was correct in saying Robards' only avenue to divorce was proving Rachel had deserted him and committed adultery with Jackson, which they voluntarily did. Hammond, however, went a bit farther—as he was prone to do—saying, "To this conviction they must submit, or separate or continue to live in open defiance of law and decency."[57] As of 1794, Rachel and Jackson were certainly free to marry but once Hammond started down a road he seldom turned back. Rachel did not appear nor did she contest the divorce, which was the only way she could legally marry Jackson.

It is absurd to suppose, that in such a predicament, they could either of them desire that the application of Robards should be defeated. It is obvious to the meanest understanding that they could scarcely do otherwise than pander to their own disgrace or remain quiescent and hope for it. We are told the marriage took place in confidence that the legislature of Virginia had granted a divorce upon the application of Robards. He could not apply upon an allegation of his own misconduct. He must have charged some dereliction of duty, some crime upon his wife, as the foundation of granting him a divorce. He must have adduced some proof in support of his charge. The parties both knew this and they married in 1791, if indeed, they then did marry at all, of which there is no proof, with a full knowledge that the capacity to do so arose against Mrs. Robards and none other than adultery could be supposed.[58]

Those, then, who believe that an adulteress, who has become after a time the legal wife of her paramour, is not a suitable person to be placed at the head of the female society of the United States cannot with propriety vote for General Jackson. Those who are of opinion that all enquiry as to the character of a president's wife is improper and are therefore indifferent what her character may be and those who conceive that a fallen female may be restored by subsequent good conduct may conscientiously give General Jackson their support. But to ground themselves upon an affected belief that the allegation of un-chastity is not true is to defy the lights of truth and to close the understanding against conviction. [59]

Hammond then went for the jugular.

The state of facts, as the exposition I have made shows them to have existed, vitally affects General Jackson's pretensions to the presidency in many views that relate principally to himself. They affect him as a man, as a husband, as a patriot in each character evidencing his unfitness for the station to which he aspires. They affect him as a man. His acquaintance with Mrs. Robards commenced in March 1789. He was then a veritable stripling to cast the eyes of affection on another man's wife and less than two years secured her for himself. A gallant, gay lothario, according to Mrs. Smith, who assures us that "his character and standing (twenty-two years old and a few months in the country!!) added to his engaging and sprightly manners were enough to inflame the mind of poor Robards." They certainly did inflame the mind of Mrs. Robards and a perception of this would very naturally inflame that of her husband.[60]

We learn from Judge Overton, the Pandarus of the play, that after Gen. Jackson and Mrs. Robards became acquainted "not many months lapsed before Robards became jealous of Jackson but without the least grounds." This unfounded jealousy broke out in reproaches against Mrs. Robards and violent altercations with Jackson who in consequences changed his residence to keep out of the way of giving offense. After this, Robards remained several months with his wife and parted from her in apparent confidence and kindness in the month of June 1790. From the time of the altercation with Jackson, which must have taken place in the summer of 1789, we hear of difficulties between Robards and his wife until the fall of 1790, when his determination to remove his wife to Kentucky was known. Then new troubles arose; then "the whole affair gave Gen. Jackson great uneasiness"; then he informed Judge Overton "he was the unhappy of men in having innocently and unintentionally been the cause of the loss of peace and happiness of Mrs. Robards, whom he believed to be a fine woman."[61]

This disclosure is utterly irreconcilable with the whole case set up by the Nashville Committee, of which Judge Overton is the main effective witness. It is an additional instance, to the thousands, that have occurred, how very difficult it is to give a gloss to matters of fact, different from that which they naturally import. How, in the fall of 1790, was General Jackson "innocently and unintentionally the cause of the loss of the peace and happiness of Mrs. Robards?" I think it will puzzle Judge Overton and the Nashville Committee to boot, to make a satisfactory explanation upon the facts they have adduced.[62]

The jealousy of Robards in 1789, they say, was unfounded. At that time, then, Mrs. Robards had conceived no affection for Gen. Jackson. It could not be the eroding canker of unhallowed attachment that destroyed her peace and happiness, of which attachment, Gen. Jackson was the innocent object. Robards had become reconciled to his wife and there is no pretense that he either deserted her or was in the habit of unbraiding her upon the account of Jackson. He could not be the corroding canker of unhallowed attachment that destroyed her peace and happiness, of which attachment, Gen. Jackson was the innocent object. Robards had become reconciled to his wife and there is no pretense that he had either deserted her or was upbraiding her upon account of Jackson.[63]

Actually, there was an account of Robards' treatment of Rachel when they lived with Mrs. Donelson and it came from Overton, "Not many months had elapsed," Overton wrote the Nashville Committee, "before Robards became jealous of Jackson, which I felt confident was without the least grounds. Some of his irritating conversations on this subject with his wife, I heard amidst the tears of herself and her mother who were greatly distressed. I urged to Robards of the unmanliness of his conduct after the pains I had taken to produce harmony, as a mutual friend to both families, and my honest conviction that his suspicions were groundless. These remonstrations seemed not to have the desired effect. As much

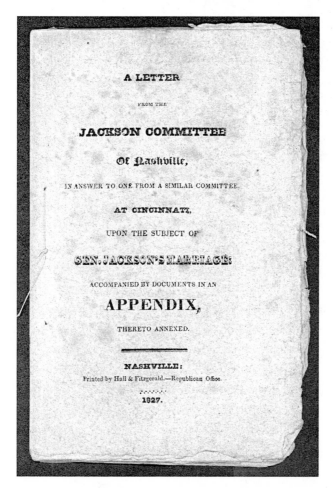

John Overton, Andrew Jackson's longtime friend, advisor and business partner, was selected to write "A Letter from the Jackson Committee of Nashville in an Answer to one from a Similar Committee at Cincinnati upon the Subject of Gen. Jackson's Marriage." Overton and Jackson's relationship began when both were young Nashville lawyers in 1790, and they shared lodgings, and often, clients. It was deemed Overton had known both Jackson and Rachel the longest and was the person best suited to write a defense of their marriage in reply to the charges they lived together prior to Rachel being divorced by Lewis Robards, her first husband (Andrew Jackson's Hermitage, Nashville, TN).

commotions and unhappiness prevailed in the family as in that of Mrs. Robards in Kentucky."[64]

Hammond, however, was on a subject he refused to leave. "Why, then, was she unhappy and Jackson the cause of that unhappiness?" he asked. "Was it a continuance of the unfounded jealousy of Jackson that induced Robards to wish the removal of his wife?"[65]

The Cincinnati newspaperman failed to mention this was not the first time Robards had thrown Rachel out but that fact did not fit his narrative.

This does not appear. If it did, upon what common principle of action would it make Jackson "the unhappy of men?" Or wherefore should it cause "the loss of the peace and happiness of Mrs. Robards?" She, conscious of innocence and devoted to the performance of conjugal duties, had no cause for a total loss of peace. In fact, her husband wished to remove her from the occasional society of a man against whom he had entertained suspicions. On the contrary, such removal was pursuing the plain path of prudence and of duty and was exactly that, which should have given confidence and comfort to the mind of an affectionate wife. Jackson having felt no attachment himself, conscious that the lady felt none and double conscious no act of his had given cause for the jealousy of Robards, could have no reason to feel unhappy or indulge regrets. If there was no intercourse between Mrs. Robards and himself, but that of common politeness, he could have no knowledge of her "loss of peace and happiness" much less were it possible for him to know that he was the occasion of it. After the ebullition of jealousy which had escaped Robards, every principle of prudence, of duty, of decent respect for themselves and for the society in which they moved, forbade any intercourse but that of distant civility between Gen. Jackson and Mrs. Robards. Had such been the feelings and the conduct of the parties, there could have been no "loss of peace" on one side; no "most unhappy of men" on the other.[66]

The avowal made that Jackson was most unhappy because he was innocently the cause of the "loss of peace" of Mrs. Robards, inevitably asserts a state of facts totally different from that which the vindication attempts to make out, is includes the admission that Mrs. Robards was attached to Jackson, that he reciprocated this attachment; that this mutual attachment had been mutually disclosed and had deeply affected the peace and happiness of both. In such circumstances, it is possible that the grossest indulgence of this criminal attachment had not taken place? But, when the parties so far forget what is due to themselves and to the world, as to become partners in a journey avowedly to place the wife "beyond the reach" of her husband. It is an insult to our common sense to talk of their virtue or to tell us that the man is incapable of seducing his neighbor's wife.[67]

Here we find Gen. Jackson, in the first stages of his manhood, conceiving an attachment for his neighbor's wife while a resident in the bosom of her family and indulging that attachment so as to secure a reciprocation from its object. We find him accompanying her in a flight to get beyond her husband's reach, finally giving occasion for a divorce upon the board grounds of the wife's adultery and afterwards making her the partner of his life and probable mother of his children. Were an occurrence like this now to take place, no matter what was the conduct of the husband, how should we estimate the youthful hero of such an adventure? Let us exclude Gen. Jackson's case from our recollections until we reflect upon the proper answer to the inquiry here made.[68]

To indulge an affection for a married woman, even in a man's own secret heart, is a great aberration from correctness; it is permitting unhallowed passion to obtain mastery over reason and duty. To approach a married woman with such a declaration of affection is an indecent outrage. If she does not so feel and receive it, she is already more than half a participant. The outrage against society and the husband is not the less and he who has the hardihood to make such an approach would at once be regarded as a youth prepared to sacrifice his own duties and the rights and happiness of others to the gratification of his own appetites. When the rein is so given to indulgence that it runs the whole race and ends in divorce and marriage the most favorable estimate we can make of the parties is that they are the mere creatures of passion and the victims of ungoverned predominance. We should draw the conclusion that he whose career appetite was not restrained by a regard of his obligations to society nor by a dread of reproach nor by an apprehension of vindictive or retributive justice could never be a safe depository of power over others. Such would be the natural inference in the case stated and, in Gen Jackson's case, would be a correct one. Thus does this transaction vitally affect Gen. Jackson's pretensions to the presidency? It does not stand an isolated act of self-willed gratification regardless of duty and of right but it stands the first in a series of similar acts extending over his whole life and assimilated in principle, though not always in degree with much of his conduct. It touches him too, in the relation of husband.[69]

Notwithstanding the criminality attending their courtship and marriage, the evidence is full and clear that as Mrs. Jackson the lady's conduct has been exemplary and irreproachable. There is no situation that imposes on a man higher and more responsible duties than the relations of a husband to a woman once known to have fallen from the virtue of chastity. If he were the original occasion of her fall and cognizant of all the circumstances, united his character with hers he owes her the most scrupulous delicacy of deportment as well as the tenderest affections. She is a bruised and broken flower which he alone can properly appreciate and cherish. To raise her to respectability, to obliterate the remembrance of her offenses, to reconcile her to herself, to restore her peace of mind should be the great effort of his life to which his whole conduct should be directed. Unobtrusive retirement from the world and respectful deference for those with whom he associated would be the plain course of a man who felt as he ought to feel in such a predicament. He should do nothing, say nothing, and place himself in no position which would bring his wife before the public. To act otherwise, is to be as regardless of her feelings as he had formerly been of the feelings of others and to expose her, in the wayward indulgence of his own temper, to the remarks and sarcasms of those whom he encounters. It is no evidence of a good or of a great man to attempt by a high hand to force a suspected wife into society or to imagine that the tongues of men are to be paralyzed by terror. Were Gen. Jackson possessed of the enlarged, the subdued and the correct intelligence, essential to the proper discharge of the presidential functions, affections for his wife and the tenderness for her feelings would have decided him never to be a candidate. And more especially, were he a true patriot who esteemed the honor, the fame and the interest of his country as deserving all consideration, he would feel that his matrimonial relation ought to exclude him from the office of president."[70]

After Hammond was finished with Rachel and Jackson, he turned his sights on their defenders.

Since this affair was brought before the public, we have had a goodly portion of sickly and mawkish sentiments from Mr. [Robert] Walsh, from Duff Green and Amos Holton about gallantry and the respect due to the female character and the cowardice and baseless of dragging a lady before the public in matters of electioneering concern. These things sound very finely and would always apply when female crime called for investigation and exposure as well as in the present case. But what would constitute female excellence, if no difference were made between her who subjected all her actions to the restraints and regulations of propriety and her who gave a loose to her feelings, inclinations and passions regardless of the decorum which alone renders the sex estimable.[71]

I have already noticed the imperious necessity for imposing severe penalties upon certain female aberrations if she who has offended in this particular so rankly that her offense has become matter of legislative and judicial record may aspire to high places and may claim to silence all censure and all inquiry who does not see the dangerous consequences that may be produced in society? What father, who descants earnestly upon the duty of throwing a mantle over the domestic relations of Gen. Jackson, shall be at liberty to reproach a fallen daughter? No true patriot would seek distinction, when to obtain it, would be to inflict a stab upon the morals and upon the female morals too of his country. The wife of a distinguished public man should not only be pure but unsuspected. If her character be stained with suspicion, it affects all around her the whole of the community of which she is the head.[72]

Obviously, Hammond did not believe in second chances for women to redeem themselves from difficult circumstances. "Gen. Jackson cannot be insensible to the true state of his own case. He cannot be deceived by the glossing's of his vindicators; though possibly enough he may be mistaken as to public opinion. But, where he a lofty patriot, such as he is represented to be, his love of country would compel him to decline being a candidate for the presidency. He would never consent that the wife of his bosom should be exposed to the ribald taunts and dark surmises of the profligate or to the cold civility or just remarks of the wise and good."[73]

Give Hammond credit for here he scored some points. Jackson, astute politician that he was, knew after the 1824 campaign that the next presidential contest, if he was a candidate, was bound to be as down and dirty as his opponents could make it. There is no doubt that he loved Rachel but he loved attaining the presidency more. Otherwise, he would have withdrawn from the campaign as Hammond suggested. Rachel was nobody's fool and she was aware that she would probably be pushed to second place in Jackson's determination to be president. Her letter to Jackson on February 8, 1813, was clear. "Do not, my beloved husband let love of country, fame and honor make you forget you have me. Without you, I would think them all empty shadows. You will say this is not the language of a patriot but it is the language of a faithful wife, one I know you esteem and love sincerely."[74]

"He would never consented that his name should be associated with sneers at his country or with the suggestions of evil and dangerous examples to her daughters," Hammond continued.

The truth of what I have asserted must be felt by every candid man. It presents an obstacle to the election of Gen. Jackson which can only be surmounted by the lead-long devotion of party.[75]

The denunciations which have been uttered against those who consider Gen. Jackson's domestic relations a proper subject of investigation have not been confined to the writers of newspapers essays or to the disclaimers in booths and taverns nor have these denunciations have been levelled only at those who were concerned in perpetrating the alleged offense. The legislature of Tennessee have made them the matter of solemn legislative resolve and have included "some of the members of the present administration" in their charges. The following is their language. "But the retreats of private life are no longer sacred." This beloved citizens, this genuine republican venerable for his age, illustrious for his services and still more illustrious for his inflexible patriotism, has seen not only his conduct distorted by slander and his glory tarnished by calumny but the partner of his bosom traduced and exposed for the sport of the idle and malice of the infamous. That couch which has so often been forsaken that other might sleep in peace, that breast that has so often braved danger that others might not even feel its alarms; which felt a stain on the honor of the country, like a stab into its own vitals, have been invaded and cruelly outraged.[76]

That some of the members of the present administration, of the general government are accountable for the slander and persecution of General Jackson's wife is reluctantly though solemnly asserted. No moral distinction can be drawn between the act of hiring a man to commit a crime and that of rewarding him after he has committed it and it is notorious that the prostituted miscreants who invent and circulated are the continued objects of ministerial favor patronage and pay. Hired with the money of the very people whose willing gratitude and just admiration are the real causes of this of this defamation and rancor this foul injustice not only aggravates the demerit of it procurers but should endear to his country the hero who sustains it.[77]

Hammond attempted to defend his friend, Secretary of State Henry Clay, from being implicated in gathering materials on Mrs. Jackson marriages. Somebody funded Edward Day's multi-state research efforts, gave him money for travel, food and lodging and paid for the massive printing and mailing project. Hammond was unlikely to have the funds to pay those large bills but the Adams campaign, which included Clay, certainly did.

"I make no remark upon the principles avowed or the language employed in this extract," Hammond wrote, "God help us when such morals and such taste prevail in the legislatives assemblies. But it is an act of duty to repel the insinuation that Mr. Clay is accountable for anything published with respect to Mrs. Jackson for it would be affections not to understand the allusion of some of the members of the cabinet as being aimed at him." Hammond used Clay's reply to John Eaton's letter asking about the material gathered on Rachel as evidence of the secretary of state's innocence.[78]

"I had a curious call the day before yesterday," Clay wrote Hammond on December 26, 1826. "He [Eaton] came at the instance of Gen. Jackson to inform me that the general had received a letter from someone in Kentucky (whose name was not given) communicating to him that you had, during your visit to Kentucky last summer, obtained from me papers which I had collected for the purpose of an attack on Mrs. Jackson which you were preparing and to enquire if I had furnished any such papers. As there was not a particle of truth in the communication which had been made to the general, I of course contradicted it adding what is perfectly true I have never seen the papers relating to the transaction referred to nor did I know that you had, on your above mentioned visit, any such papers. I have now no recollection that the case of Mrs. Jackson formed any topic of conversation between us when you were in Lexington."[79]

Surely Hammond's pen wobbled a bit when the wrote, "These papers [the correspondence between Eaton and Clay] show conclusively that Mr. Clay is in no respect 'accountable' for the investigations that have taken place through my agency and they warrant the inference that he has in no way interfered to aid or countenance the course pursued. It is just that he should be exonerated from an imputation so wholly unfounded in fact."[80]

The pen wobbling became more prolific as Hammond attempted to defend his attacks on Rachel. "Gen. Jackson's application to Mr. Clay was certainly a curious one. Whilst Gen. Jackson made his domestic hearth and social circle the theatre for uttering various imputations against the character of Mr. Clay what just cause of offense could be taken had Mrs. Clay furnished papers bearing upon the general himself through his wife or other relations? Suppose Mr. Clay had collected copies of the different papers in existence touching the divorce of Mrs. Robards and had put those papers in my hands, what right had Gen. Jackson to question him about it? I can conceive none. General Jackson had put an end to all relations of amity with Mr. Clay by his Swartout [Swartwout] letter and other slanders. As an avowed antagonist, Gen. Jackson could have no just pretension to prescribe to Mr. Clay the weapons he should use or the manner in which he should employ them. It is therefore (a) matter of 'curious' speculation what could be the object of the call and upon what ground the general assumed the right to make it. The most obvious conclusion is that it was made with the intention of operating as an engine of intimidation. As much as to say the standing of my wife shall not be impugned by any man I hold my equal but at the risk of direct responsibility. If a more apposite explanation be given, I shall be glad to hear it."[81]

Hammond made his final exclamation for dragging Rachel's through the mud and mire because he hated her husband. "Those who have perused this article are now apprised of the ground on which I have deemed this investigation a proper and necessary one. They are possessed of what I think a just view of the case. It is for all who have pretensions to intelligence and candor to say whether the subject is not one which it is the right and duty of a free and moral people to investigate? And, whether the facts are such as to justify the charge of slander and calumny against all who have dared to speak plainly the clear convictions of their judgment upon it? I am prepared to abide the sentence of the just and reflecting men; of men who do not judge of the fitness and propriety in reference to a particular case but who make the broad principles of general right the foundation of their judgments. The censure or the applause of those who accommodate their opinions to the circumstances that surround them is of but little consideration. The one inflicts no pain, the other gives very personal satisfaction."[82]

Hammond managed to inflict personal and political pain on Rachel and Jackson from January to October 1828, but without success.

16

Rachel Survived
and Departed

There was a lot of iron in Rachel Donelson Robards Jackson's spine and she needed every ounce to withstand the ten-month siege of attacks from her husband's political enemies. She had advocates outside of their close friends and supporters but none were more consistent in defending her than Moses Dawson, a transplanted Irishman in Cincinnati.

Charles Hammond was consumed with smugness for the political damage he thought he did Jackson by his unctuous attacks on Rachel. Moses Dawson used his newspaper to counter those attacks. A member of the United Irishmen who fought British domination in Ireland, Dawson feared no man. He was arrested twice and barely escaped hanging before leaving the linen draper business he shared with his father to come to America. Dawson arrived in Philadelphia in 1817 and taught school there before moving to Cincinnati. In 1821, he became the associate editor of the *Cincinnati Advertiser*, the forerunner of the present day *Cincinnati Enquirer*. Within two years he was the editor and proprietor of the newspaper and became the most prominent Jacksonian supporter in the area.[1]

"It is proper to state," Xavier University archivist Anne Ryckbost wrote, "that the prominent trait of Mr. Dawson's life was his conduct as a partisan editor (using the term in its best sense) during the heated contests preceding General Jackson's election and the warm discussions during Jackson's and [Martin] van Buren administrations. Mr. Dawson did more to elect Jackson and to make Van Buren his successor than any other of their contemporaries and he did it with the purest motives."[2]

His defense of Rachel through *The Friend of Reform and Corruption's Adversary*, printed by his newspaper, Ryckbost said, was one of his proudest accomplishments.[3]

"Dawson, from 1825 to 1828, shared with Charles Hammond supremacy in the city's newspaper field," Charles T. Greve wrote in *Centennial History of Cincinnati and Representative Citizens.* "Dawson and Hammond kept up a running fight which resembled a literary Donney-Brook fair. Despite their contests they were boon companions and often met to wrangle over their toddy."[4]

Both newspapers had circulations of around 5,000. When Hammond attacked Rachel and Jackson with his *Truth's Advocate,* Dawson responded with his *Friends of Reform and Corruption's Adversary.* "These papers," Greve wrote, "were edited with great ability but with very little regard to the decent properties of journalism."[5]

However, Thomas L. Koberna, in his Xavier University thesis about the Irishman, maintained that Dawson outstripped Hammond in skill and in his sense of ordinary decency.[6] "Dawson defended the Jacksons against what he called Hammond's primacy attacks as soon as he could set up type to provide a defense of the general's wife," Koberna wrote. "Dawson told his readers even if Hammond had been speaking about a strumpet instead of Rachel Jackson, he should be chastised. Better it should be so than he be protected in disturbing the peace and harmony of social intercourse by raking up long since forgotten by those whom it concerned."[7]

Dawson, Koberna pointed out, had a long memory and reminded Hammond of a speech he gave, while a member of the Ohio state senate, defending women against public criticism. Hammond lamely replied in print that the current Republican code was to look into no woman's character whether she was chaste or not. The private life of the Jacksons became a ping-pong game between Hammond's *Truth's Advocate* and Dawson's *Friends of Reform and Corruption's Adversary.*[8] Rachel was, again, left swinging in the wind.

"During the attack on Mrs. Jackson," Koberna wrote, "Moses Dawson outstripped his adversary in skill and in his sense of ordinary common decency. While engaged in this battle, it is the impression of this writer that Dawson defended Mrs. Jackson not because it was politic but because it was right."[9]

Koberna noted that Dawson changed the rules of the game somewhat when he reached back to 1824, presidential election and attacked Adams and Clay for their "corrupt bargain." However, Dawson did not let up in his defense of Rachel, Koberna wrote, as he continued to brand Hammond with the same sword he used to shame Rachel.[10] "If the responsibility for this scandalous episode can be attributed to anyone, it should be Henry Clay," he wrote. "The popular politician knew Hammond well enough and was close enough to him to put an end to the muck-raking."[11]

Here again was another instance indicative that Rachel knew about Hammond's rants and rages about her. Koberna wrote that Rachel was so grateful of Dawson's defenses of her and Jackson that she sent him a suit made of fabric woven at The Hermitage. "Dawson was not only appreciative of Rachel's thoughtfulness but the fact that the suit was a product of her household industry," he wrote.[12] On November 11, 1828, Dawson thanked Rachel for the gift and assured her the task of defending her was no effort and that the privilege had its own reward.[13] The suit was not only indicative of how Rachel expanded home industries at The Hermitage but had special meaning for Dawson since he and his father had been linen drapers in Ireland.

Two years earlier, Rachel sent fabric from The Hermitage to William Douglass, a Louisville, Kentucky, businessman who was a friend and supporter of Jackson. Douglass thanked her in a letter dated May 27, 1826. "I postponed my [word not visible] till I can have the satisfaction of letting you know that I had put the material into the process of being manufactured," he wrote. "I am happy to acquaint you that no time shall elapse before I shall be dressed in a full suit of Hermitage domestic and I would entreat you to believe that if I ever felt pride in my life it will be when I wear that suit."[14]

Another Irishman, Colonel Robert Patterson from Philadelphia, who emigrated from County Downs, Ireland, was an admirer of Rachel and her innovations of home industries. Patterson, after serving in the Revolutionary War as a brigade major, was a professor of mathematics and provost at the University of Pennsylvania for more than four decades. He was asked by President Thomas Jefferson to assist Meriwether Lewis and William Clark in preparation for their expedition to the Pacific Northwest.[15]

In March 1823, Patterson invited the Jackson to visit him in Philadelphia. Jackson replied that Rachel's health prevented them from making the trip. Later that spring, Patterson sent Rachel a straw hat and said he hoped it would be worn as an encouragement of domestic manufacture. Rachel appreciated Patterson's recognition of the domestic industry and wrote of her "admiration of this industry and the talents which are displayed in that specimen of American manufacture."[16]

When Jackson wrote John Coffee on June 20, 1828, he sounded resigned to enduring, along with Rachel, four more months of the slings and arrow of the Adams campaign. "How hard it is to keep the cowhide from some of the villains," he wrote. "I have made many sacrifices for the good of my country but the present, being placed in a situation that I cannot act and punish those slanderers not only of me but Mrs. J. is a sacrifice too great to be well endured yet a little I must bear with it." Jackson went on to excoriate Andrew Erwin for accusing him of being in the "negro trade." "He [Erwin] knows my hands are bound. He does this to vex me and being detected in a lie, shifts his ground and gives his own assertions for proof."[17]

The work of the Jacksons' villains and slanderers came to an end with the November 1828 election. Jackson and his running mate, John C. Calhoun, received 642,553 popular votes. Adams and his vice-president candidate Richard Rush had 500,879 popular votes. The Electoral College vote was even more lopsided with 178 for Jackson-Calhoun and 83 for Adams-Rush.[18]

"The news of General Jackson's overwhelming victory brought rejoicing to the family circle even greater than among his political supporters," Burke wrote. "In the heart of the chastened Rachel, however, there was little joy in the thought of becoming First Lady of the land—a position any woman in the country would be proud to occupy. Rachel simply said, 'Well for Mr. Jackson's sake, I am glad but for myself I had rather be a doorkeeper in the house of my Lord than to live in that palace in Washington.'"[19]

Burke said Rachel did not wish to go to Washington. "The terrible campaign of 1828 had so crushed her that it is doubtful if she even cared to live." Burke recounts the story told by Emily Donelson's daughter Mary Emily about Rachel's Nashville shopping trip where she overheard a conversation by several women at the Nashville Inn discussing the charges made against her. "My mother, alarmed at her unusual excitement advised her to dismiss it all as malicious gossip. 'No Emily, I'll never forget it! Listening to them it seemed as if a veil was lifted and I saw myself, whom you all have all guarded from outside criticism and surrounded with such flattering delusions, as other see me a poor old woman. I will not go to Washington but stay here as often before in Mr. Jackson's absences.'"[20]

Burke wrote about the 1828 presidential campaign crushing Rachel but then presented a statement that she was unaware of what happened in the campaign which contradicts that.

Ann Toplovich, in her 2005 article in *Ohio Valley Historical Journal,* had another version of Mary Emily Donelson's account. "Now in December," Toplovich wrote, "she sat sheltered in the newspaper office owned by a kinsman while she waiting for servants to bring the carriage round. At her elbow lay a pamphlet and idly she picked it up to pass the time. To her shock, she found descriptions of herself as a Jezebel, an adulteress a bigamist rehashing all the horror of her marriage to Lewis Robards and her flight with Andrew Jackson. Why had these attacks been kept from her? Rachel Donelson Robards Jackson felt her chest tightening from the blow. Fleeing Nashville in her carriage, she had her driver stop at a creek to wash away her tears. This effort to keep her grief from her husband triggered a severe cold on top of the trouble within her breast."[21]

Toplovich cited as her source Spencer Bassett's *Life of Andrew Jackson* printed in 1916. Bassett claimed Jackson kept all knowledge of the attacks on Rachel from her. "About a month after the election," Bassett wrote, "she drove to Nashville to purchase clothes for use in her own station. She was quite happy in the occasion and went from shop to shop till her strength was gone. Then she retired to the private office of a newspaper editor, one of her kin, to rest until her carriage was ready for the return. Here she came upon a copy of a pamphlet issued by her husband's friends in her defense. It came as a surprise and she was overwhelmed. When companions came an hour later they found her crouching in a corner, weeping and hysterical. On her way home she made every effort to resume her composure so as to avoid giving pain to her husband but she was not successful. The forced gaiety which she assumed attracted his attention at once and he had the story of the day's happening."[22]

Bassett, a history professor at Smith College, cited his source as Elizabeth Blair Lee, daughter of Francis F. Blair, a Jackson advisor. She remembered hearing the story from Major William B. Lewis when she was a young girl.[23] Bassett place the event at about a month after the election. The popular voting period for the 1828 president election began on October 31 and closed on November 13, with electors casting their votes on December 3.[24]

Conversations such as those of Mary Emily Donelson and Elizabeth Blair Lee may have taken place but there was too much firsthand evidence—much of it from her own letters—to refute Rachel being oblivious to what newspapers and periodicals had written about her during the campaign. Much of Jackson's campaign was run out of The Hermitage and Rachel was always there. His office was littered with newspapers and to say that she never read any of them nor the anti–Jackson publications in Nashville would be misleading. The fact that she sent Moses Dawson a suit of clothes from fabric woven at The Hermitage clearly indicated she was not only aware of his defense of her against Charles Hammond's lengthy rants and rages but was most appreciative. Rachel was the archivist of her husband's professional documents and she was aware of his political activities. In May 1827, Jackson subscribed to the *Philadelphian* for her, to keep up with campaign news.[25]

To subscribe to Bassett's theory, one would have to assume Rachel never read any of the letters to Jackson from their good friends such as John Coffee, Edward G. W. Butler, Keith Call or John Eaton.

On December 1, 1828, it was obvious from a letter she wrote Louise Livingston, that Rachel intended to accompany her husband to Washington to live in the President's House.

> My dear friend, we had the pleasure of the colonel's company for a day or two as he passed southward. He was in good health and fine spirits. It is at his suggestion that I now write you and, although it may be imposing upon you too much trouble, I find I am compelled to avail myself of your kind offer through him to assist in the selection of such articles of dress as might be considered necessary for the circles of the city. This voluntary tender on your part, madam, to serve me is viewed as an additional proof of that distinguished friendship which has always characterized the conduct of your family toward myself and the General whether surrounded by the plaudits of the virtuous and the upright or by the dark mists of slander and detraction.[26]
> I could have spent at The Hermitage the remains of my days in peace and were it not that I should be unhappy by being so far from the general. No consideration

could induce me again to abandon this delightful spot but since it has pleased a grateful people once more to call him to their service since by the permission of providence he will obey that call I have resolved, indeed it is a duty I owe to myself and my husband to try to forget, at least for a time, all the endearments of home and prepare to live where it has pleased heaven to fix our destiny.[27]

Rachel's letter to Livingston expressed sense of duty, not only to her husband but her country as well and certainly contradicted images of a hysterical woman said to be found weeping in the corner of a public place. "I shall want two dresses, the measure for the waist and skirt you will find enclosed respectively marked. The color and quality I leave entirely up to your better judgment. When completed have them carefully put up and consigned to my address in the city care of Mrs. Watson and should I ever meet with you and Miss Cora it will afford me great pleasure to have it in my power to show how sensible we are of your civility and goodness. For the future health and happiness of yourself and family be pleased to accept the best wishes of the general accompanied by those of your friend and most obedient servant."[28]

The next day, December 3, Rachel replied to a letter from Mrs. L. A. W. Douglas from Chillicothe, Ohio.

It was with great pleasure I received you truly interesting letter a few weeks since and I assure you nothing has given me more heartfelt satisfaction than the perusal of it. I had hoped long ere this to have the pleasure of seeing you in Tennessee. I sincerely regret that your husband's business compels you to reside such a distance from so many warm friends as you have in Nashville. You are frequently the subject of conversation here, particularly with Harriet Berryhill, and myself who I believes loves you sincerely and regrets your removal from Nashville almost as much as she would a sister.[29]

You mention your expectations of seeing the general and myself on our way to Washington; I suppose from the accounts we have received there is no doubt of the general's being elected. I shall be much pleased to see you on my way but believe me when I tell you dear Mrs. Douglas were it not for the many base attempts that have been made to defame the characters of my husband and myself and the ungrateful exertions that were used to prevent his election, I could hardly be induced to leave this peaceful and delightful spot. But, as a grateful people have elected my husband to the highest office in the Union it is my duty to follow him without a murmur and to rejoice at not being separated from him who is dearer to me that all other earthly considerations. Hitherto, my Savior has been my guide and support thru all my afflictions (which I must confess for the last four years have been many and unprovoked) and now I have no doubt but He will still aid and instruct me in my duties which I fear will be many and arduous.[30]

Rachel again made it obvious that she had every intention of traveling to Washington with her husband and fulfilling her duties as first lady in the President's House. She considered those duties a challenge but certainly was not turning away from them. In her letter to Mrs. Douglas, Rachel pointedly spoke of the many political attempts to denigrate their reputations—another clear signal, from her own pen, that she was acutely aware of the attacks on her character in anti–Jackson publications.

> I was so sorry to hear of Mr. Douglas' indisposition. It must have been a great trial to you. I hope ere this he is entirely recovered. Miss Harriet Berryhill is here and desires to be affectionately remembered to you and says she would have written you long since but has never received an answer to the letter which we wrote you after our return from Orleans. Her mother's health is not very good this winter. She expects to spend a few months in Orleans. If Mrs. [Hannah] Davenport has not left, be so good as to present my love to her and say to her I should be happy to receive a letter from her. Be so kind as to present the general's and my most respectful compliments to Mr. Douglas and accept the sincere prayers for your health and happiness of your friend. [31]

Rachel had made her plans and required no convincing from Eaton, who wrote her from Washington on December 10 encouraging her to make the trip with Jackson. It was doubtful if she ever read the letter given the time frame. "My dear friend," Eaton wrote, "for so I feel I may style you, the friends you have here, firm and numerous both male and female, have constantly inquired of me since my arrival to know if you would arrive with the general. They regret that it can be even considered doubtful what your determination may be. Their reasons are very satisfactory and therefore have I undertaken to speak to you about it."[32]

Eaton's letter also made it clear that Rachel was well aware of the slings

John Henry Eaton, a Nashville attorney, was a major player in both Jackson's 1924 and 1828 presidential campaigns. While they were in Washington before the 1824 election, Eaton often wrote Rachel assuring her that Jackson was doing well. It was Eaton who suggested John Overton write the pamphlet on the defense of the Jacksons' marriage. After Jackson won the 1828 presidential election, Eaton was concerned that Rachel would remain at The Hermitage and wrote her, underscoring the importance of accompanying her husband to the inauguration (Andrew Jackson's Hermitage, Nashville, TN).

and arrows aimed at her by Jackson's political enemies. His correspondence, from someone who had been alongside the couple in the midst of the political briars, was further evidence that Rachel was aware of the content of newspapers and pamphlets about her past. "The past I need not repeat, for you know it well. To prejudice your husband, you well know what envenomed slander has been aimed at both of you. Not you alone but others too have felt its keen edge and, although this is slender atonement to your own aggrieved feelings, it affords this consolation that the assaults made proceeded exclusively from motives. The storm has now abated. The angry tempest has ceased to howl. The verdict by the American people has been pronounced of that high and grateful character. That for the honor of your husband, you cannot look back on the past as an idle fading vision carrying in it nothing substantial—nothing that should produce to you one moments feeling of a moments pain. No man has ever met such a triumph before. The voice of his country has placed him at a sightless distance above his little tribe of little assailants and in this high and gratifying consideration should both of you repose pleased and rejoiced."[33]

Eaton said his remarks could have been omitted but he wanted to let Rachel know he was in accord with all of her friends in Washington. "The attentions intended to be meted out to the general, and to you, are such as will evince to both of you a continuance of the same high and glowing feeling which has produced his unequalled and triumphant vote from the people. The ladies from a distance—from remote parts of the Union will be here—brought essentially and altogether on your account and to manifest to you their feelings and high regard. They will be present to welcome and to congratulate you. If you shall be absent how great will be the disappointment. Your persecutors then may chuckle and say that they have driven you from the field of your husband's honors. By all means then, come on and as you have had to bear with him the reproaches of foes, participate with him in the greeting of his friends."[34]

Eaton said he originally thought it might be best for Rachel to wait until May to come to Washington but had changed his mind. "That opinion is changed since that I have arrived here and heard the reasoning of your friends. I am especially invited to write to you on this subject and in the name of those who are your warm and sincere friends to desire that you will be here at all events by the first of March, ready and rested for the 4th."[35]

Eaton left no doubt that her absence at Jackson's inauguration would be a disappointment. "Such is my confidence that you will be along with the general, under the suggestions I have made, that I shall no longer speak of it as at all doubtful but say that you intended to proceed with the general and will certainly be here. A failure on your part will create disappointment and prove to your friends exceedingly trying."[36]

Rachel's failure to arrive in Washington with Jackson had nothing to do with her commitment to her husband, her country and her friends. Jackson wrote in the postscript of his December 18 letter to Francis Preston, former congressman, War of 1812 veteran and supporter, "Whist writing, Mrs. J. from good health has been taken suddenly ill, with excruciating pain in the left shoulder, arm and breast. What may be the result of this violent attack God only knows. I hope for her recovery and in haste close this letter. You will pardon any inaccuracies."[37]

Rachel was going over household chores with Hannah, the slave who ran The Hermitage mansion and who was very close to Rachel, when the president-elect's wife clutched her chest, screamed in agony and fell back into a chair. Rachel had suffered a severe heart attack. Physicians were summoned but at that time medical science had no real solutions for dealing with heart attacks. Jackson suggested they bleed her. Rachel was dosed with castor oil and mercury but her irregular heartbeat continued.[38]

Jackson's world came to a halt. Gloom descended on The Hermitage. He remained by Rachel's bedside as Rachel's relatives came. The enormous Nashville gala celebrating Jackson's election planned for John Edmonson's City Hotel on December 23 was cancelled.[39]

On December 22, Jackson wrote Richard Keith Call about Rachel's illness. "Mrs. J. was a few days past suddenly and violently attacked with pains in her left shoulder and breast and such the contractions of the heart that suffocation was apprehended before the necessary aid could be afforded. Dr. Hogg has relieved her and although worse today than yesterday, I trust in a kind providence that He will restore her to her usual health in due time to set out for Washington so that I may reach there by the middle of February. We have been waiting to hear from you in hopes you may reach us before we set out which will be between the 10th and 15th of January. Should the Ohio keep open, we will go by water to Wheeling or Pittsburgh. Mrs. J. will make this route necessary as I am fearful that her strength would not be able to undergo the journey overland and I cannot bear to leave her, believing as I do, that my separating from her would destroy her. And, the persecution she has suffered has endeared her more if possible than ever to me."[40]

Jackson told Call he and Rachel would be pleased to meet he and his wife in Washington if they did not arrive at The Hermitage before they departed.[41]

That evening changed Jackson's life forever. After bending over Rachel's bedside for days, she finally convinced her husband to get some rest in the adjoining bedroom. Hannah helped Rachel to a chair beside the bed so the servants could refresh the bed linens. Rachel cried out, fell into Hannah's arms and died. Jackson rushed into the room. Rachel was lifted into her bed. He insisted the physicians bleed her but they had no success. Jackson refused to believe she was dead and remained beside her during the night. "Only when her body grew cold and stiff," Brady wrote, "did he accept the truth." Some of Rachel's nieces prepared her for burial and dressed her in one of the gowns she had purchased to take to Washington.[42]

Henry Wise, a Tennessee congressman and stalwart Jackson supporter, attended Rachel's funeral according to a book, *Seven Decades of the Union*, he wrote forty-four years after her death and after he and Jackson parted company politically over banking matters. "The day of burial [December 24] came and we witnessed the solemn scene," Wise wrote in his nineteenth-century prose style. "This we can confidently testify that more sincere homage was done to her dead than was ever done to any woman in our day and country living."[43]

Wise said thousands flocked to her funeral. Other estimates placed the crowd at 10,000, but that was extreme unlikely as the Nashville population in 1830 was 5,566, making it the fiftieth largest city in the nation.[44] Communication was conducted strictly by letters or special messengers; there was no telegraph. Consequently, the crowd of mourners was restricted to Nashville and environs.

Nashville Mayor Felix Robertson, whose father settled Nashville with Rachel's father, ordered all businesses closed for her funeral. Church bells rang out at the time of her services.[45] Robertson, a physician and a Jackson friend, later led a party to Texas to survey along the Brazos River.[46]

"The poor white people, the slaves and adjoining plantations and the neighbors crowded off the gentry of town and country," Wise wrote, "and filled the large garden in which internment took place. She had been a Hannah and Dorcas to every needy household. She had been more than a mistress, a mother to her servants and dependents and the richest and best were proud of the privilege of her sincere and simply friendship. She was without question loved and honored by high and low, white and black, bond and free, rich and poor and that love was so unaffectedly expressed by a wail so loud and long there was no mistaking its grief for the loss, not of the departed one but of the living left behind her."[47]

Jackson, Wise wrote, assisted by General William Carroll, followed the pallbearers as they carried Rachel's coffin from their home and lowered it into the burial site in her garden. Burke, however, wrote, "The strong arm of towering John Coffee supported his [Jackson's] bent form."[48] Coffee, residing in Alabama, would not have had time to received notice of Rachel's death and make the trip to Nashville.

"Weeping and mourning were heard on every side," Wise continued, "but at the moment of his coming up to that clod portal of clay, a favorite old servant of Mrs. Jackson's burst through the group around the pit and tried to get into the grave with the coffin. She was about sixty years of age but robust and strong and, falling near the brink, got both feet over the edge of the grave when the sexton and others took hold of her and prevented her descending and were trying to raise her up and remove her. Her cries were agonizing, 'my mistress, my best friend, my love, my life is gone! I will go with her.'"[49]

Wise said he watched Jackson intently and not a muscle in his face moved. "Steady as a rock, without a teardrop in his eyes nor a quaver in his voice, he quickly raised the point of his cane and said, 'let that faithful servant weep for her best friend and mistress. She has the right and cause to mourn for her loss and her grief is sweet to me.' The persons who had hold of her immediately released her and left her sitting over the fresh clods weeping and there she remained hindering the burial until after a while some of her friends persuaded her to leave the side of the grave and let the ceremony go on."[50]

Rachel's minister, the Reverend William Hume, conducted her last rites. "The righteous shall be in everlasting remembrance," he intoned. "The death of this worthy lady in much deplored by a majority of the people of the United States. In acts of piety, as adoration, thanksgiving and praise, she took delight. Her seat was seldom empty in the House of God. Her love for God was displayed by an unusual obedience to His commands and by a humble submission to His providence. She put on righteousness and it clothed her. Her judgment was a robe and diadem. She was the eye to the blind and feet to the lame and a mother to the poor."[51]

Jackson, Wise wrote, addressed the mourners after Rachel's body was interred. "Friends and neighbors, I thank you for the honor you have done to the sainted one whose remains now repose in yonder grave," he quoted the president-elect as saying. "She is now in the bliss of heaven and I know that she can suffer here no more on earth. That is enough for my consolation; my loss is her gain. But, I am left without her to encounter the trials of life alone. I am now the president-elect of the United States and in a short time must take up my duties in the metropolis of my country and, if it had been God's will, I would have been grateful for the privilege of taking her to my post of honor and seating her by my side but providence knew what was best for her. For myself, I bow to God's will and go alone to the place of new and arduous duties and I shall not go without friends to reward and I pray God that I may not be allowed to have enemies to punish. I can forgive all who have wronged me but will have fervently to pray that I may have grace to enable me to forget or forgive any enemy who has ever maligned that blessed one, who is now safe from all suffering and sorrow whom they tried to put to shame for my sake."[52]

"We were called this morning to announce an event of the most awful and melancholy nature," the December 24 issue of the *Nashville Banner* reported.

In the midst of preparations for festivity and mirth, the knell of death and on this very day when it was arranged and expected that our town should be the scene of general rejoicing we are suddenly checked in our career and are called on to array ourselves in garments of solemnity and woe. Mrs. Rachel Jackson, wife of General Andrew Jackson, president-elect of the United States, died last night at the Hermitage in this vicinity.[53]

The intelligence of this awful and unlooked for event has created a shock in our community almost unparalleled. It was known a few days ago that Mrs. Jackson was violently attacked by disease, which however, was supposed to have been checked so as to afford a prospect of immediate restoration to health. This day being the anniversary of an interesting and important event in the last war was appropriately selected to testify the respect and affection his fellow citizens and neighbors to the man who was to soon leave his sweet domestic retirement to assume the responsibilities and discharge the important duties of the Chief Magistrate of the nation.[54]

December 23, 1814, was when Jackson was informed that the British had landed on American soil nine miles below New Orleans during the War of 1812.[55] That was the reason December 23 was selected for a grand ball honoring Jackson and Rachel at John Edmondson's City Hotel in Nashville. Invitations were sent out on December 12.[56]

"The preparation were already made," the *Banner's* obituary for Rachel continued. "The table was well-nigh spread and our citizens had sallied forth on that happy morning with spirits high and buoyant and countances glowing with animation and hope—when suddenly the scene changed. Congratulations are converted into expressions of sympathy, tears are submitted for smiles and sincere and general mourning pervades a community where but a moment before universal happiness and rejoicing prevailed. But we have neither time nor room at present to indulge in further reflections on this melancholy occurrence. Let us submit, with resignation and fortitude, to the degree however affecting, of a just and merciful though mysterious and inscrutable Province."[57]

Where the *Banner* mentioned Rachel's name, *The Washington Telegraph* did not. Their headline read, "A Nation Mourns in Sympathy with Her Favorite Son." She was simply referred to as Andrew Jackson's wife and consort. "Society has lost one of its brightest ornaments," the obituary continued. "The friend of the widow and orphan, the pious Christian, the amiable wife and consort of Andrew Jackson is no more. She departed this life at the Hermitage about 9 o'clock on the evening of December 22nd. A letter dated the 26th, at Cincinnati gave the first notice of this melancholy intelligence on Sunday last. Since then, a deep anxiety has pervaded the city. Unwilling to believe it, we were held in sad suspense until yesterday when several letters from Nashville disputed all doubts. As of yet, we have not heard the particulars. It is understood that her illness was of short duration and her death sudden and unexpected."[58]

The *Boston Statesman*, which had previously attacked Rachel, outlined its pages in black out of respect to her passing.[59] Other eastern newspapers such as the *New Hampshire and Statesman* and the *Concord Register*, which supported John Q. Adams in both the 1824 and 1828 presidential elections, were unable to pass up one last opportunity to skewer Rachel. The publications were critical of the Boston newspaper's decision to trim its pages in mourning black but their own comments were a failed attempt to straddle a journalistic fence.[60]

"We would tread lightly on the ashes of the lady whose decease is announced above and would gladly erase from our memory," the *New Hampshire Statesman* and *Concord Register* stated, "and from the records we may have been instrumental of giving to the world any and every reflection upon the frailties and foibles of her early existence. Of these we have said less than some others but we probably have said something."[61]

The newspapers, however, were unable to contain themselves. "We are content that newspaper editors should say nothing of the dead if they cannot speak well—but that they should task their vocabulary as on the demise of Mrs. Jackson they seem to have done to furnish out the most high-sounding and superlative epithets to proclaim her exemplary virtues—and should, as the *Boston Statesman* and some other papers have done, dress their sheets in the habiliments of mourning—is at once derogatory to the fearless independence of a free press and a wanton reflection upon real living worth and excellence. The standard of female character in our country can hardly be thought sufficiently elevated if Mrs. Jackson, under the known circumstances of the case, is to be spoken of as exhibiting the most 'exemplary virtues and exalted character.' Or, if the inflated panegyric of the *Washington Telegraph,* contrasted with the unpretending notice that thousands who in truth live and die are Mrs. Jackson's superiors in every accomplishment, is to go forth to the world as the test of comparative merit.[62]

"A nation, says the *Telegraph,* 'mourns in sympathy with her favorite son. Society has lost one of its brightest ornaments. The friend of widows and orphans, the pious Christian, the amiable wife, the consort of Andrew Jackson is no more.' But enough of such flummery. In plain truth, Mrs. Rachel Jackson is dead."[63]

Nobody was more aware of that fact than President-elect Andrew Jackson.

After her death, Jackson wrote in the memoranda section of Rachel's Bible, "My dear wife, Rachel Jackson, departed this life Decbr. 22nd 1828, between the hour of 10 & 11 o'clock P.M. In the strong hope that she sleeps in the bosom of her savior, I will prepare to unite with her in the realms of bliss. A. Jackson."[64]

Jackson's grief was palpable in his December 27 letter to Jean Baptiste

Plauche in New Orleans. "I had the satisfaction," Jackson wrote, "to receive several weeks since you friendly letter of the [November] 15. But, have been prevented from answering it by that afflicting dispensation of Providence which has deprived me of the partner of my life. A loss so great, so sudden and so unexpected, I need not say to you can be compensated by no earthly gift." Despite his burden of grief, Jackson saw something else in Rachel's passing. "Could it be," he continued in his letter to Plauche, "it might be found in reflection that she lived long enough to see the countless assaults of our enemies disarmed by the voice of our beloved country."[65]

Plauche served under Jackson and organized the Louisiana Legion, made up of planters, businessmen and lawyers, in the Battle of New Orleans.[66]

Even Charles Hammond was said to have lamented Rachel's death, claimed Francis P. Weisenberger in his journal article, "Charles Hammond, The First Great Journalist of the Old Northwest." Weisenberger quoted from a letter Hammond was said to have written to J. C. Wright of Steubenville, Ohio, on January 10, 1829. "In his private correspondence," Weisenberger wrote, "Hammond expressed regret at the death of Mrs. Jackson since he would

Andrew Jackson, soon after his wife's death, wrote the following words in the memoranda section of Rachel's Bible. "My dear wife Rachel Jackson departed this life Decbr. 22nd 1828 between 10 & 11 o'clock p.m. In the strong hope that she sleeps in the bosom of her savior, I will prepare to unite with her in the realms of bliss. A. Jackson." (Andrew Jackson's Hermitage, Nashville, TN).

have been pleased to have seen her preside at the White House [President's House] over the mighty *shes of the South*."⁶⁷

Two years after Rachel's death, her clothes and jewelry remained where she left them at The Hermitage.

John Coffee and his family visited The Hermitage in April 1831. Coffee wrote Jackson about the fine condition of his crops and informed him that his horse, Bolivar, was in grand shape and that Dinwiddie had done him full justice. After lunch, Coffee said they visited Rachel's tomb in the garden and the ladies asked Steel, the overseer, if he would open her wardrobe. "They looked at the robes they had so often seen their dear Aunt clothed in [and] it revived gone by times and feelings, and filled us all with mingled grief and joy—grief to know that she who was beloved and idolized by all who knew her and more particularly her relatives, was no more—and joy to see the robes and jewelry which she usually wore when mixing with us in social life in the world but, above all, that she is now enjoying that bliss which is provided for the just and righteous and which will have no end and where we all one day hope to join her in immortality. My dear general, this was a visit of great interest to us all and we left with mingled feelings."⁶⁸

The book of poems of William Cowper was published in New York in 1814. Cowper, an Englishman, wrote not only of the sorrows of the everyday world but about those who lived in the country. For her time, Rachel Jackson read a wide variety of material. She also enjoyed accessorizing her clothes. The photograph also shows her earrings, a bracelet and necklace (Andrew Jackson's Hermitage, Nashville, TN).

Jackson instructed architect David Morrison, while he was expanding the mansion in 1831, to design a tomb over Rachel's grave. Morrison's design resembled the Greek temple in the Telemachus wallpaper in The Hermitage foyer. Eight limestone Doric columns support a cooper roof over her epitaph.[69]

Andrew Jackson's bedroom at The Hermitage, shown after his death, had one of the Earl portraits of Rachel hanging over the mantel, where her image would be the first thing he saw every morning and the last thing at night (Library of Congress, Prints and Photographs Division).

"Here lie the remains of Mrs. Rachel Jackson, wife of President [Andrew] Jackson, who died December 22nd 1828, age 61. Her face was fair, her person pleasing, her temper amiable and her heart kind. She delighted in relieving the wants of her fellow creatures and cultivated that divine pleasure by the most liberal and unpretending methods. To the poor she was a benefactress; to the rich she was an example; to the wretched a comforter; to the prosperous an ornament. Her pity went hand in hand with her benevolence; and she thanked her Creator for being able to do well. A being so gentle and so virtuous, slander might wound could but could not dishonor. Even death, when he tore her from the arms of her husband, could but transplant her to the bosom of her God."[70]

Jackson wrote Emily Donelson that he appreciated her visit to Rachel's grave. "She *still* and must *ever* live fresh in my memory and affections. *She often hovers around me in my nightly visions.*"[71]

Chapter Notes

Chapter 1

1. Harold D. Moser, J. Clint Cliff, and Wyatt C. Wells, editors. *The Papers of Andrew Jackson, Volume VI, 1825–1828* (Knoxville, Tennessee: University of Tennessee Press, 2002), 355.

2. Kathleen Kennedy and Sharon R. Ullman, *Sexual Borderlands: Constructing America's Sexual Past* (Columbus, Ohio: Ohio State University Press, 2003), 106.

3. www.thehermitage.com/potus7-ladies-hermitage-association. Accessed 18 February 2019.

4. *Ibid.*

5. Sarah Jeanine Hornsby, "The Protection of an Icon: Nashville, the Ladies' Hermitage Association and the Image of Rachel Jackson, 1925–1945," thesis, Vanderbilt University, April 1994, 12.

6. *Ibid.*, 12–13.

7. *Ibid.*, 14.

8. *Ibid.*, 16.

9. Meade Minnigerode, *Some American Ladies: Seven Informal Biographies* (New York: G. P. Putnam's Sons, 1926), 185.

10. *Ibid.*, 186.

11. *Ibid.*, 187.

12. Hornsby, 19.

13. James W. Campbell, "Gaines, John Wesley & Edmond Pendleton Gaines Papers, 1793–1926." Accession Number 235, Archives and Manuscript Unit, Tennessee State Library and Archives. Minnigerode, 188.

14. Minnigerode, 188.

15. *Ibid.*, 189.

16. *Ibid.*, 189–190.

17. *Ibid.*, 190.

18. *Ibid.*, 191.

19. *Ibid.*, 191–192.

20. *Ibid.*, 195.

21. www.thehermitage.com/the-jacksons-go-to-washington. Accessed 3 March 2019.

22. Minnigerode, 195–196.

23. *Ibid.*, 227–228.

24. *Ibid.*, 199.

25. *Ibid.*, 204.

26. *Ibid.*, 308.

27. *Ibid.*, 214–215.

28. Hornsby, 17–18.

29. Minnigerode, 218.

30. Horsnby, 19.

31. Minnigerode, 222.

32. Hornsby, 21.

33. www.imdb.com/title/tt0027690/fallcredits/?=tt_on_st_sm. Accessed 10 March 2019.

34. *Ibid.*

35. Hornsby 22, 25.

36. *Ibid.*, 25.

37. *Ibid.*, 27

38. Minnigerode, 220.

39. Hornsby, 27.

40. Nellie Treanor Stokes, *Rachel Jackson* (Nashville, Tennessee, Ladies' Hermitage Association, 1942), 16.

41. Hornsby, 29.

42. www.imdb.com/title/tt0046204. Accessed 15 March 2019.

43. Rachel E. Stephens, "America's Portraitist: Ralph E. W. Earl and the Imaging of the Jacksonian Era," PhD, dissertation, University of Iowa, 2010, 144.

44. Stephens, 144, 181. Earl's portrait of John Reid had to be a copy of another painting of the Jackson aide who traveled to Washington with him in 1815 and died in January 1816 on the return trip to Nashville. Earl did not arrive in Nashville until January 1, 1817. Joseph G. Tregle, Jr., in

a review of *The Life of Andrew Jackson* by Reid, John H. Eaton and Frank L Owsley, Jr., in *Louisiana History* (New Orleans, Louisiana, the Journal of the Louisiana Historical Association, 1976), Vol. 77, No. 3, Summer 1976, 352.

45. www.tennesseeencyclopedia.net/entries/ralph-e-w-earl. Accessed December 18, 2018.

46. www.tennesseeencyclopedia.net/entries/ralph-e-w-earl. Accessed 22 February 2019. Tulip Grove was the home of Andrew Jackson and Emily Donelson.

47. Stephens, 147.

48. Minnigerode, 233–234.

49. Stephens, 147.

50. Sam B. Smith and Harriet C. Owsley, editors, *The Papers of Andrew Jackson Vol. I, 1770–1803* (Knoxville, Tennessee: University of Tennessee Press, 1987), 427–428.

51. Stephens, 181–182.

52. Portraits painted by Earl or attributed to him included Mrs. Thomas Clairbourne, Carolina M. Lawrence, Catherine Donelson Martin and Eleanor R. Nichol. www.tnportraits.org/site-index-artist. Accessed 15 March 2019. Mary Wells Davenport, Mrs. Elijah Boardman, Mrs. Richard Alsop and Sarah Lewis King Clairbourne, www.google.comsearch?q=ralph-e.-w-earl+paintings. Accessed 15 March 2019. Mrs. Williams. www.metmuseum.org/art/collection. Accessed 15 March 2019. Martha Ruggles and her husband Nathaniel Ruggles. www.christies.com/lot/ralph-e-w-earl. Accessed 15 March 2019. Emily Tennessee Donelson, www.thehermitage.com. Accessed 15 March 2019.

53. www.catholicismpure&simple.worldpress.com/2014/01/15/why-women-wear-mantillas-in-church. Accessed 15 March 2019.

54. Stephens, 148, 182–183.

55. Hornsby, 47–48.

56. Ann Harwell Wells, "Lafayette in Nashville, 1825," *Tennessee Historical Quarterly*, V-34, N-1, Spring 1975, 23–30.

57. www.library.virginia.edu. Melissa Gismondi, "Rachel Jackson and the Search for Zion, 1760s-1830s," PhD, University of Virginia, 2012.

58. *Ibid.* www.britannica.com/topic/worcester-v-georgia. Accessed 28 April 2019. www.loc.gov/collections/andrew-jackson-papers/articles-essays/andrew-jackson-timeline-1767-1845. Accessed 28 April 2019.

Chapter 2

1. Pauline Wilcox Burke, *Emily Donelson of Tennessee* (Knoxville, Tennessee: Tennessee, University of Tennessee Press, 2001), 19.

2. Wilma A. Dunaway, *The First American Frontier: Transition to Capitalism in Southern Appalachia* (Chapel Hill, North Carolina: University of North Carolina Press, 2000), 73. www.bioguide.congress.gov. Accessed 3 January 2017.

3. George W. Knepper, *The Official Ohio Lands Book* (Columbus, Ohio: State Auditor Jim Petro, 2002), 30.

4. Boynton Merrill, Jr. *Jefferson's Nephews* (Lincoln, Nebraska: University of Nebraska Press, 2008), 170–171. www.whitehouse.org/1600/first-ladies/annaharrison. Accessed 6 January 2017.

5. Leona T. Aiken, *Donelson, Tennessee, Its History and Landmarks* (Nashville, Tennessee: Leona T. Aiken, 1968), 310.

6. "Mrs. Rachel Donelson Jackson," *Lineage Book, Daughters of the American Revolution Magazine* (Washington, DC, Judd and Dotweiler, 1895) Vol. 6, No. 58.

7. Burke, 3.

8. *Ibid.*

9. Richard D. Spence, "John Donelson and the Opening of the Old Southwest," *Tennessee Historical Quarterly*, Vol. 50, No. 3, Fall 1991, 157–172. "Washington Iron Furnace," Department of the Interior, National Park Service, National Register of Historic Places Inventory/Nomination Form, 20 March 1973.

10. Natalie Inman, *Networks in Negotiations of Family and Kinship in Intercultural Diplomacy on Trans-Appalachian Frontier, 1680-1840*, Ph.D. dissertation, Vanderbilt University, December 2010, 48–49.

11. Irene M. Griffey, *Earliest Tennessee Land Records & Earliest Tennessee Land History)* Baltimore, Maryland: Clearfield Company, 2000), 165.

12. Stokes, 4–5.

13. www.oldhalifax.com/county/Dan RiverCharts. Accessed 8 June 2017.

14. Stokes, 5, 8.

15. Burke, 3–4. Anne-Leslie Owens, "John Donelson," *Tennessee Encyclopedia of History and Culture*. www.tennesseeencyclopedia.net/entry.php?rec=390. Accessed 11 June 2017.

16. Owens.

17. *Journal of the House of Burgesses of*

Virginia 1773–1776. (Richmond, Virginia: E. Waddey Company, 1905), 26, 68.

18. *Ibid.*

19. Spence, 157–172.

20. *Ibid.* Donelson's last son, Leven, was not yet born.

21. *Ibid.*

22. William H. Masterton, editor, *The Papers of John Gray Blount Vol. III* (Raleigh, North Carolina: North Carolina State Department of Archives and History, 1965), 368.

23. www.virginia.gov/public/guides/m8_varev. Accessed 18 July 2017.

24. "Revolutionary War Allotments Paid by Virginia," Kentucky Secretary of State's Office, Frankfort, Kentucky.

25. Maud C. Clement, *The History of Pittsylvania County, Virginia* (Baltimore, Maryland: Genealogical Publishing Company, 1929), 154. Spence. "Fort Patrick Henry," *Tennessee Encyclopedia of History and Culture.*

26. Stokes, 5.

27. Spence, 162. "Washington Iron Furnace," National Register of Historic Places Inventory/Nomination Form. Early's great-grandson was Confederate General Jubal B. Early.

28. Milnor Ljungstedt, "The Ancestry of John Donelson of Tennessee, Explorer and Pioneer," *The County Court Note-Book*, Vol. 6, No. 6, December 1927. www.measuringworth.com. Accessed 18 July 2017. Marshall Wingfield, *An Old Virginia Court* (Baltimore, Maryland: Genealogical Publishing Company, 1996), 217. Clement, 94. Hugh Innis was one of the sheriffs of Franklin County.

29. John E. Kleber, editor, "Richard Henderson," *The Kentucky Encyclopedia* (Lexington: University Press of Kentucky, 1992), 422–423.

30. *Ibid.*, "Daniel Boone, 96–98; "Boonesborough," 100–101.

31. *Ibid.*, 100.

32. Walter Lowrie,*Documents, Legislative and Executive of the Congress of the United States in Relation to Public Lands* (Washington, DC, Duff Green, 1834), 18.

Chapter 3

1. Griffey, 164–165. Griffey, on the same pages John Donelson, Jr., entered for 55,485 acres in Davidson and Sumner counties.

2. Vicki Rozema, *The Footsteps of the Cherokee* (Winston-Salem, North Carolina: John F. Blair Publishers, 2007), 160.

3. www.americanrivers.org. Accessed 17 October 2017.

4. *Annual Reports of the War Department for the Fiscal Year Ended June 30, 1900, Report of the Chief of Engineers Part 5.* (Washington: Government Printing Office, 1900), 3060.

5. Ann Toplovich, "Tennessee River System." www.tennesseeenncyclopedia.net/entries/Tennessee-river-system. Accessed 20 July 2017.

6. Spence, 152–172.

7. *Ibid.*

8. Bill Curry, "Adventures on the Cumberland," *The Tennessee Magazine*, November 2006, 23–25.

9. "Broadhorn or Kentucky Boats on Ohio—circa 1788." www.steamboattimes.com/flatboats. Accessed 20 July 2017.

10. *Ibid.*

11. Dunbar Rowland, editor, *Encyclopedia of Mississippi History Vol. 1*, (Madison, Wisconsin: Selwyn Brant, 1907), 796–798.

12. Griffey, 166.

13. www.emergingrevolutionarywar.org/2016/01/23/the-winter-of-1779-1780. Accessed 20 July 2017.

14. Spence, 157–172.

15. John Donelson's Journal, which was only partially written by Colonel Donelson; it was later completed by his son, Captain John Donelson.

16. Donelson's Journal. Pages unnumbered.

17. John R. Finger, *Tennessee Frontier: Three Regions in Transition* (Bloomington, Indiana: Indiana University Press, 2001), 73

18. Paul H. Bergerson, Paths *of the Past: Tennessee 1770-1970* (Knoxville, Tennessee: University of Tennessee Press, 1979), 12.

19. *Ibid.*

20. *Ibid.*

21. *Ibid. House Executive Documents,* Vol. 15, (Washington: Government Printing Office, 1875), 3.

22. Donelson's Journal.

23. *Ibid.*

24. *Ibid.*

25. *Ibid.*

26. *Ibid.*

27. Finger, 73. William R. Garrett, *History of Tennessee: Its People and the Institutions From the Earliest Times to the Year 1903* (Nashville, Tennessee: Brandon Print-

ing Company, 1903), 70. Alfred F. Young, Gary B. Nash and Ray Raphael, *Revolutionary Founders: Rebels, Radicals and Reformers* (New York: Knopf, 2012), 193.

28. Young, Nash and Raphael, 193.
29. Donelson's Journal.
30. *Ibid.*
31. *Ibid.*
32. William B. Stevens, *A History of Georgia* (New York: D. Appleton and Company, 1859), 418.
33. Donelson's Journal.
34. John Trotwood Moore, "Andrew Jackson and His Beloved Rachel," *Saturday Evening Post,* July 25, 1925.
35. Edward Albright, *Early History of Middle Tennessee* (Nashville, Tennessee: Brandon Printing Company, 1909), 61–62.
36. Donelson's Journal.
37. *Ibid.*
38. *Ibid.*
39. *Ibid.*
40. *Ibid.*
41. *Ibid.*
42. *Ibid.*
43. www.gopher.com/web/results. Accessed 2 April 2019.
44. www.earthquakes.usga.gov/earthquakes/events/1811-1812newmadrid. Accessed 20 July 2017.
45. *Report to the Secretary of War To The Two Houses of Congress, Second Session, Fifty-Third Congress* (Washington, DC: U.S. Government Printing Office, 1881), 273–274. Paul Schneider, *Old Man River: The Mississippi River in North America* (New York, Macmillan, 2013), 224.
46. Donelson's Journal.
47. *Ibid.*
48. *Ibid.*
49. *Ibid.*
50. *Ibid.*
51. *Ibid.*
52. *Ibid.* Spence, 157–172.
53. Albright, 65.
54. Donelson's Journal.
55. *Ibid.*
56. *Ibid.*
57. *Ibid.*
58. Burke, 11–13.
59. Ramsey, 204.
60. *The Papers of Andrew Jackson Vol. I,* 419.
61. Griffey, 164.
62. Burke, 13.
63. "Stations," *The Kentucky Encyclopedia,* 851–852.

64. W. Woodford Clayton, *History of Davidson County, Tennessee* (Nashville, Tennessee: J. W. Lewis & Company, 1880), 135.
65. Francis Baily, *Journal of a Tour in the Unsettled Parts of North America in 1796 & 1797* (London: Baily Brothers, 1856), 384–385, 417.
66. Josephine L. Harper, *Guide to the Draper Manuscripts* (Madison, Wisconsin: Wisconsin Historical Society, 2015), lxix.

Chapter 4

1. Burke, 13.
2. Willard R. Jillson, "Old Kentucky Entries and Deeds," *Filson Club Publication No. 34* (Louisville, Kentucky: Standard Printing Company, 1926), 29, 199. *Index for Virginia Surveys and Grants* (Frankfort, Kentucky: Kentucky Historical Society, digital publisher), 87.
3. Harper, xxxix, xlii.
4. Charles G. Talbert, "A Roof for Kentucky," *A Kentucky Sampler: Essays from the Filson Club Historical Quarterly, 1926–1976* (Lexington, Kentucky: University Press of Kentucky, 2015), 71.
5. *Ibid.* Robert Morgan, *Boone: A Biography* (Chapel Hill, North Carolina: Algonquin Press, 2008), 328,
6. Talbert, 72.
7. Morgan, 328.
8. *Executive Papers of Gov. Benjamin Harrison, 1781–1784* (Richmond, Virginia, The Library of Virginia), Boxes 1–19. Burke, 13.
9. Burke, 13.
10. A. P. Whitaker, "The Muscle Shoals Speculation 1783–1789," *Mississippi Valley Historical Review,* Vol. 13, No. 3, December 1926, 365–386.
11. Munsell's 1818 map of Mercer County, Science and Engineering Library Map Collection, University of Kentucky.
12. William H. Whitwill, *The Life and Times of Judge Caleb Wallace* (Louisville, Kentucky: J. P. Morton Printers, 1888), 110.
13. Southern Campaign American Revolution Pension Statements & Rosters, Pension Application of Lewis Robards W581, Hannah, f76VA. www.revwarapps.org.Accessed 2 August 2017.
14. Brandi M. Hatfield, *Two Become One,* master's thesis, Liberty University, spring 2010).
15. James H. Robards, *History and Gene-*

alogy of the Robards Family (Whiteland, Indiana: James H. Robards, 1910), 14.

16. *The Papers of Andrew Jackson Vol. I,* 421.

17. Alice B. Keith and William H. Masters, editors, *The John Gray Blount Papers* (Durham, North Carolina: Christian Publishing Company, 1959), Vol. 1, 101. Hereinafter referred to as Keith and Masters.

18. Keith and Masters, Vol. 2, 660. Griffey, 164–175.

19. Robards, 25.

20. Robards, 12.

21. *Southern Campaign American Revolution Pension Statements & Rosters,* Pension Applications of Lewis Robards W581, Hannah (Robards), f76VA, www.revwarapps. org/W8563. Accessed 2 August 2017.

22. "Nelson, Thomas, Jr., 1739–1789," National Park Service, Colonial National Historical Park—Yorktown Battlefield, Yorktown, Virginia. Nelson so firmly believed in the pledge taken by those who signed of the Declaration of Independence—"We mutually pledge our lives, our fortunes and our sacred honor," which he signed, that he never recouped the $2 million of his own money given to finance Virginia's war costs. He died in 1789 a near pauper with eleven children.

23. *Ibid. Southern Campaign American Revolution Pension Statements & Rosters,* Pension Application of Jesse Robards W8563. www.drevwarapps.org. measuringworth. com. Accessed 4 August 2017.

24. Pension Application of Jesse Robards, W8563.

25. Robards, 12–18.

26. *Ibid.*

27. Hatfield, 22.

28. "Three Greek Revival Houses of Mercer County, Kentucky," U.S. Department of the Interior, National Register of Historic Places Inventory, Nomination Form, 4.

29. *Ibid.* "Early Virginia Marriage Records," Research Notes Number 26, Library of Virginia, Archive Research Services, 1.

30. *The Papers of Andrew Jackson, Vol. I,* 423.

31. *Ibid.*

32. Burke, 16.

33. Keith and Masters, Vol. 1, 522.

34. *Ibid.*

35. Keith and Masters, Vol. 2, 417.

36. Keith and Masters, Vol. 1, 534.

37. Griffey, 164.

38. Burke, 13–14.

39. Clayton, 136.

40. Griffey, 165.

41. Clayton, 136.

42. Spence, 157–172. *American State Papers: Documents, Legislative and Executive of the Congresses of the United States in Relations to Public Lands* (Washington, DC: Duff Green, 1832), Vol. III, 352.

43. *Ibid.,* 334.

44. *American State Papers,* Vol. III, 330–339.

45. *American State Papers: Documents Legislative and Executive of the Congresses of the United States in Relations to Public Lands* (Washington, DC: Gales & Seaton, 1859), Vol. II, 866–867.

46. Spence, 157–172.

47. *American State Papers* Vol. III, 330–338.

48. *Ibid.*

49. www.measuringworth.com. Accessed 7 March 2019.

Chapter 5

1. Benton R. Patterson, *The Generals: Andrew Jackson and Sir. Edward Pakenham and the Race to the Battle of New Orleans* (New York: New York University Press, 2005), 19.

2. Spence, 169. Benjamin Logan to Gov. Patrick Henry, *Virginia State Papers* (Richmond, Virginia: R. C. Derr, 1884) Vol. 4, 120.

3. Spence, 169.

4. Spence, 170.

5. William Blackstone, Commentaries *on the Laws of England* (Oxford, England: Oxford Clarendon Press, 1768), Vol. 1, 442–445.

6. Thomas M. Green, *Historic Families of Kentucky* (Cincinnati, Ohio: Robert Clark & Company, 1889), 269.

7. *The Papers of Andrew Jackson, Vol. VI,* 322. Harriet C. Owsley, "The Marriages of Rachel Donelson," *Tennessee Historical Quarterly,* Vol. 36, No. 4, Winter 1977, 480–481.

8. Ann Toplovich, "Marriage, Mayhem and Presidential Politics," *Ohio Valley Historical Quarterly* (Cincinnati, Ohio: Cincinnati Museum Center, 2005), Vol. 5, No. 4, Winter 2005, 3–77.

9. S. G. Heiskell, *Andrew Jackson and Early Tennessee History* (Nashville, Ten-

nessee: Ambrose Printing Company, 1921), 276.

10. Toplovich, 7.

11. *Ibid.*

12. George G. Shackelford, editor, "To Practice Law: Aspects of The Era of Good Feelings Reflected in the Short-Ridgley Correspondence, 1816–1821," *Maryland Historical Magazine* (Baltimore, Maryland: Maryland Historical Society, 1969), Vol. 64, No. 4, Winter 1969, 344. Mary W. M. Hargreaves and James Hopkins, *The Papers of Henry Clay, Vol. I* (Lexington, Kentucky: University Press of Kentucky, 1881), 227.

13. Archer B. Hulbert, "Boone's Wilderness Road," *Historic Highways of America, Vol. Six* (Cleveland, Ohio: the Arthur Clark Company, 1903), 130–131.

14. Toplovich, 7.

15. *Ibid.*

16. Hulbert, 130. "As the Crow Flies," tjpeiffer.com. Accessed 17 August 2017.

17. Burke, 16.

18. Griffey, 345. Andrew Jackson Papers, Library of Congress, www.loc.gov/mass/maj/000006. Accessed 20 August 2017.

19. *Tennessee Encyclopedia of History and Culture* (Nashville, Tennessee: Tennessee Historical Society, 1998), online edition, "Land Grants," Irene M. Griffey.

20. Stokes, 8.

21. Harriet C. Owsley, "The Marriages of Rachel Donelson," *The Tennessee Historical Quarterly* (Nashville, Tennessee:Tennessee Historic Society, 1977), Vol. 38, No. 4, Winter 1977, 481.

22. Thomas A. Foster, *Sex and the Eighteenth-Century Man* (Boston, Massachusetts: Beacon Press, 2007), 215.

23. *The Papers of Andrew Jackson, Vol. I,* 416–421.

24. "Rachel Jackson," *Encyclopedia Britannica.* www.britannica.com/biography/rachel.jackson. Accessed 21 August 2017. "Rachel Donelson Robards Jackson (1767–1828), National Women's History Museum, www.nwhm.org/resources/rachel-donelson-robards-jackson. Accessed 17 August 2017. Patricia Brady, *A Being so Gentle: The Frontier Love Story of Rachel and Andrew* Jackson (New York: Palgrave Macmillan, 2011), 35–36. Toplovich, 16.

25. Owsley, 481–482. Toplovich, 7–8.

26. *Ibid.*

27. Patterson, 20–21.

28. Owlsey, 482.

29. Toplovich, 8.

30. Patterson, 20–21.

31. *Ibid.*

32. *Ibid.* Owsley, 482.

33. H. W. Brands, *Andrew Jackson: His Life and Times* (New York: Doubleday, 2005), 62–63.

34. Owsley, 483. Dennis J. Mitchell, *A New History of Mississippi* (Jackson, Mississippi: University Press of Mississippi, 2014), John C. Hammond, *Slavery, Freedom and Expansion in the Early American West* (Charlottesville, Virginia: University of Virginia Press, 2007), 17.

35. *The Papers of Andrew Jackson, Vol. I,* 17. Hammond, 17. www.fws.gov/Mississippi. Accessed 20 August 2017.

36. "John Jouett," *The Kentucky Encyclopedia,* 480–481.

37. *The Papers of Andrew Jackson, Vol. I,* 424.

38. *Ibid.*

39. Owsley, 484.

40. www.womenhistoryblog.com 2011/11/rachel-jackson. Accessed 20 August 2017.

41. Stokes, 11–12.

42. Andrew Burstein, *The Passions of Andrew Jackson* (New York: Knopf, 2002) 244.

43. *The Papers of Andrew Jackson, Vol. I,* 424.

44. *Ibid.,* 425. www.measuringworth.com. Accessed 20 August 2017.

45. *The Papers of Andrew Jackson, Vol. I,* 432.

46. *Ibid.,* 427.

47. *Ibid.,* 425–427. Davidson County Wills, Inventories and Settlements, Will Book I, 109.

48. Davidson County Wills, Inventories and Settlements, Will Book, I, 109.

49. *Ibid.*

50. *The Papers of Andrew Jackson, Vol. I,* 426–427.

51. Davidson County Wills, Inventories and Settlements, Will Book I, 109. Email to author from Kelley Sirko, librarian at the Metropolitan Government Archives of Nashville and Davidson County, April 18, 2018. Harold D. Moser, Daniel R Hoth, Sharon Macpherson, and John H. Reinbold, editors, *The Papers of Andrew Jackson, Vol. III, 1814-1815* (Knoxville, Tennessee: University of Tennessee Press, 1991), 533.

52. *The Papers of Andrew Jackson, Vol. III,* 533.

53. Griffey, 164–165, 165–174. Jillson, 29, 199. Index to Virginia Surveys and Grants,

Kentucky Historical Society, Frankfort, Kentucky. *American State Papers, Vol. III*, 330–339.

54. *American State Papers, Vol. III*, 330–353.

55. *Ibid.*

56. *Ibid.*

57. *Ibid.*

58. Email from The Hermitage curator Marsha Mullin to author, June 20, 2018.

59. *Ibid. The Papers of Andrew Jackson, Vol. I*, 417.

60. *American State Papers, Vol. III*, 368–369.

61. *American State Papers, Vol. III*, 330–339.

62. *The Papers of Andrew Jackson, Vol. I*, 425–427.

63. *Ibid.* www.measuringworth.com. Accessed 20 August 2017.

Chapter 6

1. *The Flora of the Catahoula Sandstone: Shorter Contributions to General Geology, 1916.* www.pubs.usgs.gov/179946416/report. Accessed 24 August 2017.

2. "Bayou Pierre," Mississippi Department of Fish and Wildlife Services. *Mississippi Sportsman,* 24 March 2008.

3. James, 63. "Bruinsberg," Mississippi Historical Marker.

4. Dunbar Rowland, editor, *Mississippi: Comprising Sketches of Towns, Events, Institutions and Persons* (Atlanta, Georgia: Southern Historic Publishing Association, 1909), Vol. 1, 319–320. www.britannica.com/events/irish/rebellion-irish-history. Accessed 24 August 2017.

5. D. Clayton James, 40–46. *The Concordia Sentinel,* 2 April 2014.

6. Jonathan Daniels, *The Devil's Backbone* (New York: McGraw-Hill Book Company, 1971), 44. D. Clayton James, 40–46.

7. *The Papers of Andrew Jackson, Vol I*, 22.

8. *Ibid.*

9. Daniels, 44–45.

10. *The Papers of Andrew Jackson, Vol. I*, 29–33.

11. *Ibid.*, 129–130.

12. *Ibid.*

13. www.adams.msghn.org/census.1792. naychez-9620district. Accessed 24 August 2017.

14. Mary P. Hammersmith, *Hugh McGary, Senior, Pioneer of Virginia, North Carolina, Kentucky and Indiana* (Wheaton, Illinois: Nodus Press, 2000), 154–171.

15. Daniels, 71, 75.

16. Daniels, 71.

17. *Edinburgh Gazetteer* (Edinburgh, Scotland: Archibald Constable and Company, 1822), Vol. 6, 28.

18. "Hugh McGary," *The Kentucky Encyclopedia*, 597.

19. Hammersmith, 171.

20. Daniels, 72–73.

21. Daniels, 74.

22. Daniels, 75.

23. Daniels, 78.

24. *The Papers of Andrew Jackson, Vol. I*, 29.

25. *The Papers of Andrew Jackson, Vol. I*, 427. "John Brown," *The Kentucky Encyclopedia*, 128–129.

26. "John Brown, *The Kentucky Encyclopedia*, 128–129.

27. "Spanish Conspiracy," *The Kentucky Encyclopedia*, 839. "James Wilkinson," *The Kentucky Encyclopedia*, 955–956. "Morning Edition," *National Public Radio*, 28 April 2010.

28. *The Papers of Andrew Jackson, Vol. I*, 427.

29. "Christopher Greenup," *The Kentucky Encyclopedia*, 388–389. *The Papers of Andrew Jackson Vol. I*, 427.

30. *Ibid.*

31. www.britannica.com/westward-movement. Accessed 3March 2018.

32. *The Papers of* Andrew *Jackson Vol. I*, 28.

33. *Transactions of the Indiana Horticultural Society* (Indianapolis, Indiana: The Society, 1872), Vol. 11, 122. R. D. Prall, *The McPherson and Miller Families* (Albuquerque, New Mexico: Geno's Copy Center, 2010), 520. *Prairie Farmer* (Chicago, Illinois: Prairie Farmer Publishing Company, 1886), 764. Hammersmith, 167.

34. Lyon G. Tyler, "Lightfoot Family," *William and Mary Quarterly* (Williamsburg, Virginia: Omohundro Institute of Early American History and Culture, 1893–1894), Vol. 2, No. 2 (October 1893), 91–97; Vol. 2, No. 3 (January 1894), 204–207; Vol. 3, No. 2 (October 1894), 104–111; Vol. 3, No. 4 (April 1894), 259–262. www.mtaunton@mindspring.com Accessed 20 August 2017. "Descendants of John Minor." John M. McAllister, editor, *Genealogies of the Lewis and Kindred Families* (Columbia, Missouri: E. W. Stephens Publishing Company, 1906).

Lawrence Babits, *A Devil of a Whipping: The Battle of Cowpens* (Chapel Hill, North Carolina: University of North Carolina Press), 2000.

35. Dunbar Rowland, "Mississippi Territory in the War of 1812," *Centenary Series, Vol. IV* (Jackson, Mississippi: Mississippi Historical Society, 1921), 162.

36. "Gabriel Slaughter," *The Kentucky Encyclopedia*, 828–829.

37. Chester County, South Carolina, Deed Book C, 323.

38. Kandie Adkinson, Land Office Division, Kentucky Secretary of State, for the Harrodsburg-Mercer County Oral History Committee.

39. *Weekly Messenger*, 5 July 1827.

40. Washington County, Kentucky, Deed Book C, 28. "A Bill for the Benefit of Benjamin Lawless," *Journal of the House of the General Assembly of Kentucky* (Frankfort, Kentucky: State Journal Company, 1822), November 2, 1822, 107.

41. W. W. Stephenson, "The Old Courthouse and the Courts and Bar of Mercer County, Ky.," *Register of the Kentucky State Historical Society* (Frankfort, Kentucky: The Frankfort Printing Company, 1909), Vol. 7, 31–35.

42. Lewis Collins, *History of Kentucky* (Covington, Kentucky: Collins & Company, 1884), Vol. 1, 514. Daniels, 78.

43. Morgan, 328. "Battle of Blue Licks," *The Kentucky Encyclopedia*, 92–93; "Hugh McGary," 597.

44. Morgan, 325.

45. Charles McKnight, *Our Western Borders in Early Pioneer Days* (Chicago, Illinois: Education Company of Chicago, 1902), 360. "Moluntha," Ohio Historical Marker, Logan County, Ohio, erected in 1951. "Hugh McGary," *The Kentucky Encyclopedia*, 597.

46. Jacob Stevens interview by John Shane, Draper Manuscripts located at Wisconsin Historical Society, Madison, Wisconsin, CC12, 133–138.

47. Walter Durham, "Kasper Mansker, Cumberland Frontiersman," *Tennessee Historical Quarterly* (Nashville, Tennessee: Tennessee Historic Society, 1971), Vol. 30, No. 2, 155–171.

48. Daniels, 78.

49. Toplovich, 14.

50. Hammersmith, 171.

51. Daniels, 78.

52. *The Papers of Andrew Jackson, Vol. I*, 424.

53. Hammersmith, 167.

54. Toplovich, 14–15. "Marriages," *Register of the Kentucky State Historical Society* (Frankfort, Kentucky:The Society, 1922), Vol. 20, No. 13.

55. Pension Application of Lewis Robards, W581, *Southern Campaign American Revolutionary Pension Statements and Rosters*. Hannah Winn Robards made her mark (x) on the pension application and received $120 per annum. *History and Genealogy of the Robards Family* (Whitland, Indiana: James Harvey Robards, 1910), 24.

56. Robards, 24–28.

57. *The Papers of Andrew Jackson, Vol. I*, 428.

58. Daniels, 78–79. *The Papers of Andrew Jackson, Vol. I*, 44.

59. *The Papers of Andrew Jackson, Vol. I*, 44.

60. Owsley, 486–487.

61. Betty Malesky, "Divorce: Dilemma for Early Americans," June 21, 2012, www.archives.com. Accessed 21 August 2017.

62. Daniels, 68.

63. *The Papers of Andrew Jackson, Vol. I, 17–18*.

64. *The Papers of Andrew Jackson, Vol. I, 245–246*.

65. "Springfield Plantation," Department of the Interior, National Park Service, National Register of Historic Places Inventory-Nomination 71–11–28–2013, November 23, 1971.

66. *Ibid.*

67. *Ibid.*

68. Robert Lowery and William H. McCardle, *A History of Mississippi* (Jackson, Mississippi: R. H. Henry & Co., 1891), 140–141.

69. *Ibid.* www.vaiden.net/mississippi_county_formation. Accessed 4 April 2018.

70. Lowery and McCardle, 141. W. H. Sparks, *The Memory of Fifty Years* (Macon, Georgia: J. W. Burke & Co., 1870), 150–151.

71. Rowland, *Encyclopedia of Mississippi History, Vol. 1*, 954.

72. Marquis James, *Andrew Jackson: The Border Captain* (New York: Grosset & Dunlap, 1933), 382.

73.), Joyce L. Broussard, "Naked Before the Law: Married Women and the Servant Ideal in Antebellum Natchez" in *Mississippi Women: Their Histories, Their Lives Vol. II* edited by Martha H. Swain, Elizabeth A. Payne, and Marjorie J. Spruill (Athens,

Georgia: University of Georgia Press, 2010), 65.

74. Broussard, 75.

75. Rowland, *Encyclopedia of Mississippi History, Vol. I*, 796–798, *Vol II*, 950–953. Burke, 16.

76. May Wilson McBee, *The Natchez Court Records 1767–1805* (Baltimore, Maryland: Genealogical Publishing Company, 1929), 94, 104, 110, 113, 120, 128–129, 157,190, 212, 225, 228, 257, 296, 328, 271, 410.

77. Rowland, *Mississippi Comprising Sketches of Towns, Events, Institutions and Persons*, 319–320.

78. www.britannica.com/topic/alcade. Accessed 11 February 2017.

79. www.refdesk@mdah.ms.gov.us, 13 February 2017, email to author.

80. Franklin L. Riley, *School History of Mississippi: for Use in Public and Private Schools* (Richmond, Virginia: B. F. Johnson Publishing Company, 1915), 77–79.

81. Riley, 79–81. www.vaiden.net/mississippi_county_formation. Accessed 13 February 2017.

82. Z. T. Leavell and T. J. Bailey, *A Complete History of Mississippi Baptist from the Earliest Times* (Jackson, Mississippi: Mississippi Baptist Publishing Company, 1904), 17–28. Rowland, *Encyclopedia of Mississippi History*, 319–320.

Chapter 7

1. *The Papers of Andrew Jackson, Vol. I*, 432–435. George and Molly were slaves Rachel inherited from her father along with livestock and personal estate items.

2. Mary C. Dorris, *The Hermitage, Home of General Andrew Jackson* (Nashville, Tennessee: Ladies' Hermitage Association, 1941), 17. *The Papers of Andrew Jackson, Vol I*, xxxviii.

3. *The Papers of Andrew Jackson, Vol I*, xxxviii.

4. www.encyclopediavirginia.org/gentry-in-colonial-virginia. Accessed 28 August 2017.

5. *Ibid.*

6. Natalie Inman, *Brothers & Friends: Kinship in Early America* (Athens, Georgia: University of Georgia Press, 2017), 80.

7. Griffey, 184.

8. Jillson, 29, 199. "John Donelson, "Index for Virginia Surveys and Grants,"

The Kentucky Historical Society, Frankfort, Kentucky. www.kyhistory.com/edm/compoundobject/collection/LIB/id/1144/rec/1. Accessed 28 August 2017.

9. Griffey, 164–165.

10. Griffey, 165–174.

11. Inman, *Brothers & Friends*, 81, 84–87.

12. Natalie Inman, "Networks in Negotiations: The Role of Family and Kinship in Intercultural Diplomacy on the Trans-Appalachian Frontier 1680–1840," Ph.D. dissertation, Vanderbilt University, 2010, 128.

13. Ibid, 45.

14. Burke, 17.

15. Burke, 18.

16. Joyce L. Broussard, *Stepping Lively in Place, The Not-Married Free Women of Civil War-Era Natchez, Mississippi* (Athens, Georgia: University of Georgia Press, 2016), 60.

17. Elizabeth Fries Ellet, *Pioneer Women of the West* (New York: Charles Scribner, 1859), 60.

18. Ellet, 33–34.

19. Ellet, 67, 73–75.

20. Burke, 17–18.

21. *Ibid.*, 30.

22. *Ibid.*

23. *The Papers of Andrew Jackson, Vol. I*, 455–476.

24. Anita A. Stamper, *Clothing Through American History* (Santa Barbara, California: ABC-CLIO, 2011), 206. *The Lady's Monthly Museum*(London, England: Vernon and Hood, 1825), 348. Lorraine Olson, *Little Lone Star Quilts* (Lafayette, California: C & T Publishing, Inc., 2010), 6. Emanuel A. Possett, *The Structure of Fibers, Yarn and Fabrics* (Philadelphia, Pennsylvania: E. A. Possett, 1900), 129.

25. *The Papers of Andrew Jackson, Vol. I*, xxxvii, 46.

26. *Ibid.*, xxxvii.

27. Flora Fraser, *The Washingtons: George and Martha* (New York: Alfred A. Knopf, 2015), 13, 25–27.

28. Maxine L. Margolis, *Mothers and Such: Views of American Women and Why They Changed* (Berkeley, California: University of California Press, 1985), 191.

29. John S. Bassett, *The Correspondence of Andrew Jackson*, www.loc.gov/resource/maj.06158_0103_0105. Accessed 8 September 2017.

30. Harold D. Moser and Sharon Macpherson, editors. *The Papers of Andrew Jackson, Volume II, 1804-1813* (Knoxville,

Tennessee: University of Tennessee Press, 1984), 494.

31. *The Papers of Andrew Jackson, Volume III*, 432.

32. *The Papers of Andrew Jackson, Vol. I*, 54. Eugene M. Wait, *The Second Jackson Administration* (Hauppauge, New York, Nova Publishers, 2002), 42

33. Wait, 42. *The Papers of Andrew Jackson, Vol I*, 58.

34. www.measuringworth.com. Accessed 15 October 2017.

35. Email from The Hermitage curator Marsha Mullin to author, October 19, 2017.

36. James, 105.

37. *The Papers of Andrew Jackson, Vol I*, 64, 79.

38. *Ibid.*

39. www.measuringworth.org. Accessed 15 October 2017.

40. *The Papers of Andrew Jackson Vol. I*, xxxvii–xxxviii; V-3, 316–317.

41. James, 90.

42. *The Papers of Andrew Jackson Vol. I*, xxxvii–xxxviii.

43. Neva Goodwin, *Encyclopedia of Women in American History* (London, Routledge Press, 2015), 94.

44. *The Papers of Andrew Jackson, Vol. I*, 91–92.

45. *Ibid.*

46. Thomas K. McGraw, *The Founders and Finance: How Hamilton, Gallatin and Other Immigrants Forged a New Economy* (Cambridge, Massachusetts, Harvard University Press, 2012), 197.

47. James, 90–91.

48. Griffey, 165.

49. Jason E. Farr, "The Glasgow Land Fraud and the Emergence of Andrew Jackson, 1783–1804" master thesis, University of Virginia, 2010, 22.

50. Farr, 20–21.

51. Charles R. Holloman, "James Glasgow," *North Carolina Encyclopedia*. wwwncpedia.org/biography/glasgow-james. Accessed 18 March 2018.

52. *Ibid.*

53. Russell S. Koonts, "An Angel Has Fallen" master thesis, University of Virginia, 2010, 9, 20, 23, 34, 40.

54. Farr, 30–31, 33–34, 47.

55. *The Papers of Andrew Jackson, Vol. I*, 157–158.

56. Farr, 20–21.

57. *Ibid.* Farr, 5.

58. Finger, 214.

59. *The Papers of Andrew Jackson, Vol. I*, 174.

60. Kay Baker Gaston, "Tennessee Distilleries: Their Rise, Fall and Reemergence," *Journal of the Kentucky-Tennessee American Studies Association* (Murfreesboro, Tennessee: Middle Tennessee State University, 1999), No. 12, 1999, Online Edition.

61. Philip S. Klein and A. A. Hoogenboom, *History of Pennsylvania* (University Park, Pennsylvania: Pennsylvania State University Press, 2010), 116.

62. Theodore Brown, Jr., "John Overton," *Tennessee Encyclopedia of History and Culture*, www.tennesseeencyclopedia.net/entries/john-overton. Accessed 1 April 2019.

63. *The Papers of Andrew Jackson, Vol. I*, 220–221.

64. *Ibid.*

65. *The Papers of Andrew Jackson, Vol. I*, 174–175.

66. *Ibid.*, 323–324.

67. *Ibid.*, xxxviii.

68. *Ibid.*, 326–327.

69. *Ibid.*

70. *Ibid.*, 233. www.omnihotels.com/homestead-virginia. Accessed 15 October 2017.

71. *The Papers of Andrew Jackson, Vol. I*, 233.

72. *Virginia Minerals* (Richmond, Virginia: Department of Mines, Minerals and Energy, May 1997), Vol. 43, No. 2, 1.

73. *The Papers of Andrew Jackson, Vol. I*, 214.

74. *The Papers of Andrew Jackson, Vol. I*, 239–240.

75. Brady, 90.

76. *The Papers of Andrew Jackson, Vol. I*, 274–275.

77. Hollonman, "James Glasgow." Farr, 34.

78. Griffey, 200–201.

79. www.thenashvillecemetery.org/50017.whyte. Accessed 18 October 2017. *The Papers of Andrew Jackson, Vol. I*, 419.

80. Margaret I. Phillips, *The Governors of Tennessee* (Gretna, Louisiana: Pelican Publishing, 1978), 24–25. *Washington Post*, 1 August 2010. www.nga.org/governors/postgovernors-bio. Accessed 15 October 2017.

81. James, 91–93. See Jeanette Hussey, *Code Duello in America* (Washington, D.C.: Smithsonian, 1980).

82. Cheatham, 48.

83. James, 91–93. A. C. Quisenberry, *The*

Life and Times of Hon. Humphrey Marshall (Winchester, Kentucky: The Sun Publishing Company, 1892), 100–103

84. *The Papers of Andrew Jackson, Vol. II*, 211.

85. James, 94.

86. Brady, 83–85. *The Papers of Andrew Jackson, Vol. II*, 11–13.

87. *Ibid.*, 447–454.

Chapter 8

1. Email to author from The Hermitage curator Marsha Mullin, February 16, 2018. *The Papers of Andrew Jackson Vol. I*, xxxviii, 84.

2. "The Hermitage," www.npr.gov. www. thehermitage.com. www.claiborne.msghn. org/plantations. All accessed 16 October 2017. Chris Makowski, Kristopher D. White, and Daniel D. Davis, *Don't Give an Inch: The Second Day at Gettysburg, July 2, 1863* (El Dorado Hills, California: Savas Beatie LLC, 2016), 102. www.mshistorynow.mdah. gov/articles/265/index-php?s=extraid=129. Accessed 16 October 2017. Benjamin Humphreys, governor of Mississippi from 1865 to 1868, was dismissed from West Point, along with forty other cadets, in December 1826 for Christmas Eve riots. Some called it the Eggnog Rebellion.

3. www.thehermitage.com. Accessed 16 October 2017.

4. Brady, 88.

5. www.thehermitage.com/learn/andrew-jackson/orphan. Accessed 19 October 2017. *The Papers of Andrew Jackson, Vol. I*, 415.

6. *The Papers of Andrew Jackson Vol. I*, 153, 435. Meredith, 71–72.

7. *The Papers of Andrew Jackson V-l*, 350–351.

8. Burke, 30. Email from The Hermitage curator Marsha Mullin to author, August 13, 2018.

9. Rachel Meredith, "Somebody Always Dying and Leaving Andrew Jackson Guardian," thesis, Middle Tennessee State University, 2013, 84–85. www.measuringworth. com/uscompare. Accessed 19 October 2017.

10. Meredith, 84–85.

11. Gay-Butler Family Papers, Louisiana and Lower Mississippi Valley Collections, Special Collections, Hill Memorial Library, Louisiana State University, Mss. 4872

12. www.hnoc.org/13no/pdf/mss102,

Folders 26, 89, 96,190–192. Accessed 19 October 2017.

13. Burke, 29–30.

14. *Ibid.* Email from The Hermitage curator Marsha Mullin to author, 19 October 2019. www.tennesseeencyclopedia.net/entry/.php?rec=391. Accessed 19 October 2017. Burke, 92–93.

15. Meredith, 48–49.

16. Mark Cheathem, *Old Hickory's Nephew: The Political Struggles of Andrew Jackson Donelson* (Baton Rouge, Louisiana: Louisiana State University Press, 2007), 41–43.

17. Meredith, 49–51. www.tennesseeencyclopedia.net/entries-andrew-jackson-donelson. Accessed 129 October 2017.

18. Cheathem, 2.

19. Meredith, 56–57. www.ncpedia.org/governors/branch. www.bioguide.congress. gov/john-branch. Accessed 20 October 2017.

20. Meredith, 66.

21. *The Papers of Andrew Jackson Vol. I*, 244–245.

22. *The Papers of Andrew Jackson Vol. I*, 350–351.

23. Meredith, 28–30.

24. Burke, 30. Meredith, 77.

25. Meredith, 100.

26. *Ibid.*

27. Meredith, 97–100. www.tennesseeencyclopedia.net/john-henry-eaton. www. ncpedia.org/biography/eaton-john-henry. Accessed 20 October 2017.

28. Meredith, 98–99.

29. Hutchings Family papers 1804–1970, Department of State, Tennessee State Library and Archives, Accession Number: 1971:124. Meredith, 62.

30. Meredith, 63, 67.

31. Daniel Feller, Harold D. Moser, Laura-Eve Moss, and Thomas Coens, editors, *The Papers of Andrew Jackson Vol. VII, 1829* (Knoxville, Tennessee: University of Tennessee Press, 2007), 104–105.

32. Meredith, 62

33. Meredith, 72–73.

34. *Ibid.*

35. *The Papers of Andrew Jackson Vol. VII*, 398–399. Meredith, 72–75.

36. Meredith, 33. www.thehermitage. com/andrew-jackson-junior. Accessed 20 October 2017.

37. Kate S. Robeson, *An Historical and Genealogical Account of Andrew Robeson of Scotland* (Philadelphia, Pennsylvania: J.

B. Lippincott, 1916), 151. John W. Jordan, *Colonial Families of Philadelphia* (Philadelphia, Pennsylvania: Lewis Publishing Company, 1911), Vol. 2, 1611–161

38. Daniel Feller, Thomas Coens, and Laura-Eve Moss, editors, *The Papers of Andrew Jackson, Vol. X, 1832* (Knoxville, Tennessee: University of Tennessee Press, 2016), 505. Jordan, 1611–1612.

39. Andrew Jackson Papers, Library of Congress, Manuscript Division, MSS27532. Vol. 102

40. University of Delaware, Special Collections Department, Alfred Gratz Family Papers, Manuscript Collection Number 320.

41. Parton, *Life of Andrew Jackson in Three Volumes, Vol. III* (New York: Mason Brothers, 1860), 649–652.

Chapter 9

1. Theodore A, Cook, *A History of the English Turf* (London, England: Virtue and Company, 1901), Vol. III, Title Page. Lady Ashbury, a grand dame of the court, was Mistress of the Wardrobe to Queen Victoria.

2. www.britannica.com/sports/horseracing. Accessed 22 November 2017.

3. *Ibid.*

4. *Ibid.*

5. www.history.org/history/teaching/newsletter. Accessed 9 March 2019.

6. *Ibid.* www.pedigreequery.com/bulle+rock. Accessed 15 March 2019. www.horseracingbusiness.com/the-old-dominion-where-american-thoroughbred-racing-began. www.racingmuseum.org/hall-of-fame/sir-archy. Accessed 15 March 2019. www.historyofparlimentonline.org/volume1750-1790/member/burbury-thomas-charles/1740-1821. Accessed 18 March 2019.

7. "William Whitney," *The Kentucky Encyclopedia* (Lexington, Kentucky: University Press of Kentucky 1992), 949.

8. Frederich M. Burlew, "Silks and Satins" (no city, no publisher, no date), A typescript, not numbered, prepared for the Keeneland Association Library. Part II, Chapter X, Brought to the Colonies. Part II, Chapter XIII, Lacking Enforcement.

9. Gayle C. Herbert, *A History of Racing Silks* (Lexington, Kentucky: The House of Corrington, 1993), 25.

10. *The Gateway* (Detroit, Michigan:

John F. Hagan, 1904), Vol. II, No. I, February 1904, 29.

11. Augustus C. Buell, *History of Andrew Jackson: Pioneer, Patriot, Soldier, Politician, President* (New York, Charles Scribners' Sons, 1904), 246–248.

12. James, *Andrew Jackson: The Border Captain, 35*

13. *National Freemason* (New York, The National Freemason Company, 1867), Vol. VLLL, No. 3, January 19, 1867, 1. www.loc.gov/collections/andrew-jackson-papers/articles-and-essays. Accessed 30 October 2017.

14. James D. Anderson, *Making the American Thoroughbred, Especially in Tennessee 1800–1805* (Norwood, Massachusetts: The Plimpton Press, 1916), 239–240.

15. According to Thoroughbred records there were two fillies named Indian Queen foaled in 1795, making it difficult to trace Indian Queen's pedigree. www.allbreedpedigree.com/index.php?querytype=check&search/pars=horse=indianqueen. Accessed 19 March 2019. Patrick N. Edgar in his *American Race-Turf Register, Sportsman Herald and General Stud Book* (New York: Press of Henry Mason, 1833), 264–265, listed twelve Thoroughbred horses named Indian Queen.

16. Anderson, 239–240.

17. *Ibid.*

18. *Ibid.*

19. Anderson, 240–241. William H. P. Robertson, *The History of Thoroughbred Racing in America* (New York: Bonanza Books, 1964), 41.

20. www.allbreedpedigree.com/truxton. Accessed 4 November 2018.

21. *The Papers of Andrew Jackson, Vol. III*, 56–57. Truxton's stud fees in 1807 were $20 or $30 with longer credit. In 1809, while standing at John W,. Clay's farm his stud fee was $50. In 1816, his fee was $20. Anderson, 48.

22. Mark R. Cheatham, *Andrew Jackson, Southerner* (Baton Rouge, Louisiana: Louisiana University Press, 2013), 50.

23. www.allbreedpedigree.com/Greyhound. Accessed 19 March 2019.

24. John Durant, "Tennessee Turfman," *Sports Illustrated*, 16 July1956.

25. *Trotwood's Monthly Devoted to Farm, Horse and Home*, Vol. 1, No. 5, February 1906. (Nashville, Tennessee: Trotwood Publishing Company, 1906), 253.

26. Robertson, 41.

27. Anderson, 240–242.

28. Anderson, 242.

29. www.fpcnashville.org/home/history. Accessed 20 March 2019.

30. *The Papers of Andrew Jackson Vol. II*, 77–78. "Peach Blossom," Special Collections, Nashville Public Library. www. allbreedpedigree.com/ploughboy. Accessed 4 November 2017.

31. *The Papers of Andrew Jackson Vol. II*, 77–78. www.blog.loc.gov/law/2015/04/frontier-racing-injured-pride-the-duel-between-andrew-jackson-and-charles-dickinson. Accessed 20 March 2019.

32. *The Papers of Andrew Jackson Vol. II*, 89. Parton, *Life of Andrew Jackson, Vol. I*, 268–269.

33. www.samhoustonmemorialmuseum.com/history. www.tennesseeencyclopedia.net/entry.pphp?rec=663. Accessed 4 November 2018.

34. *The Papers of Andrew Jackson, Vol. II*, 77, 83–84, 90.

35. Anderson, 54. Robertson, 42, 89–90.

36. Robertson, 89–90, 96.

37. *The Papers of Andrew Jackson, Vol. II*, 98–99.

38. James, 122.

39. Burke, 36.

40. Parton, 299. Brands, 137–138.

41. Parton, 300–301.

42. Burke, 38.

43. Brands, 139–141.

44. www.io.com/gibbons/pos/codeduello. Accessed 28 July 2018.

45. *The Papers of Andrew Jackson, Vol. II*, 104–105.

46. William E. Clement, *Plantation Life on the Mississippi* (Gretna, Louisiana: Pelican Publishing Company, 2000), 32, 39–40.

47. *Ibid.* Nathan A. Burman, "Two Histories, One Future: Louisiana Sugar Plantations, Their Slaves and The Anglo-Creole Schism," Ph.D. dissertation, Louisiana State University, 2013, 15. After Erwin's death, his widow, Lavinia Erwin, then in her sixties, enlisted the assistance of her son-in-law and attorney, John Craighead, in Nashville, and they took the plantation from the edge of bankruptcy to a solvent basis. When Mrs. Erwin died on February 13, 1832, her share in the estate was valued at $262,105. Adjusting for inflation, that would be well over $8 million today. Clement, 42–43. www.measuringworth.com. Accessed 20 March 2019.

48. *The Papers of Andrew Jackson, Vol. II*, 189.

49. Anderson, 248–250.

50. *Ibid.*, 253–254. Robert Holladay, "Raging Moderates: Second Party Politics and the Coalition of Willing Aristocracy in Williamson, County, Tennessee, 1812–1846," thesis, Florida State University, May 2007, 16.

51. James, 374–375.

52. Robert E. Corlew, Stanley J. Follmsbee, and Enoch L. Mitchell, *Tennessee: A Short History* (Knoxville, Tennessee: University of Tennessee Press, 1990), 116.

53. *Ibid.*

54. Roderick Heller, *Democracy's Lawyer: Felix Grundy of the Old Southwest* (Baton Rouge, Louisiana: Louisiana State University Press, 2010), 86. Tennessee historians have been arguing ever since whether or not Cannon, Tennessee governor (1835–39), sat on the Magness jury. Will T. Hale and Dixon L Merritt, in *A History of Tennessee and Tennesseans* (Chicago, Illinois: Lewis Publishing Company, 1913), 838, stated Cannon was on the Magness jury. Nancy Capace, in *Encyclopedia of Tennessee* (Syracuse, New York: Somerset Publishers, 2000), 205, agreed with Hale and Merritt. John H. Dewitt, William A. Province and St. George L. Sioussat contended Cannon did not sit on the Magness jury in their article in *Tennessee Historical Magazine* (Nashville, Tennessee: Tennessee Historical Commission and Tennessee Historical Society, 1971), 94.

55. Burke, 34.

56. *The Papers of Andrew Jackson, Vol. I*, 421.

57. *The Papers of Andrew Jackson, Vol. II*, 218.

58. *Hartsville Vidette*, 9 July 2018. *American Turf Register and Sporting Magazine* (St. Louis, Missouri: J. S. Skinner, 1879), Vol. 8, No. 5 January 1907, 180. Robertson, 41.

59. Josephus C. Guild, *Old Times in Tennessee With Historical, Personal and Political Scraps and Sketches* (Nashville, Tennessee: Travel, Eastman and Howell, 1878), 246–247, 250–253, 269–270.

60. Anderson, 259. Bradley, a Revolutionary War Veteran, served under Jackson in the War of 1812 and built one of Nashville's first racetracks. He and Jackson owned horses in partnerships. Bradley County in Tennessee was named in his honor. www.chattanoogan.com/2001/4/17/8223/hoe-were-cleveland-and-bradley-county-named. Accessed 21 March 2019.

61. Anderson, 249.

62. *Ibid.*, 259.
63. Jesse Holland, *The Invisibilities: The Untold Story of African American Slaves in the White House* (Guilford, Connecticut: Rowman & Littlefield, 2016), 139.
64. Robertson, 43.
65. *Ibid.* www.racingmuseum.org/hall-of-fame/william-ransom-johnson. Accessed 9 November 2018.
66. Elbert B. Smith, "Now Defend Yourself, You Dammed Rascal," *American Heritage* (Rockville, Maryland: American Heritage Publishing Company, 1958), Vol. 9, Issue 2, February 1958. www.loc.gov/resource/maj.01012_0061_0064. Accessed 9 November 2018.
67. *The Papers of Andrew Jackson, Vol. II,* 273.
68. *The Papers of Andrew Jackson, Vol. II,* 354.
69. *Ibid.*
70. *Ibid.*
71. *Ibid.*, 364.
72. *Ibid.*, 371–372.
73. *Ibid.* George W. Martin married Rachel's niece, Lucinda, the daughter of Severn Donelson.
74. *Ibid.*, 378, 400.
75. *Ibid.*, 400. Gregory M. Thomas, "The Battle of New Orleans," master's thesis, Louisiana State University, December 6, 2005. 6.
76. *The Papers of Andrew Jackson, Vol. II,* 400.
77. Smith, "Now Defend Yourself, You Dammed Rascal."
78. *Ibid.* www.loc.gov/resources/maj.019 12_0061_0064/?sp=1&st=text. Accessed 23 March 2019. Jesse Benton and William Carroll died with a year of each other in 1843 and 1844. Benton, a colonel in the Second Division of the Texas Rangers, had a simple but elegant marker. Carroll, twelve-year governor of Tennessee, had an elaborate monument. They were buried in the Nashville City Cemetery across from each other. www.thenashvillecitycemetery.org/110245_benton; www.thenashvillecitycemetery.org/120016_carroll. Accessed 23 March 2019.
79. Julie Nelson, *American Presidents Year by Year* (London, England: Routeledge, 2015), 124–125. www.loc.gov/andrew-jackson-papers/articles-and-essays/andrew-jackson-timeline. Accessed 10 November 2018.
80. *The Papers of Andrew Jackson Vol. II,* 437.
81. *Ibid.*, 416–417, 444.
82. *Ibid.*, 459.

83. *Ibid.*, 353–355.
84. *Ibid.*, 486–487.
85. *Ibid.*, 515.
86. Burke, 48.
87. *The Papers of Andrew Jackson, Vol. III,* 28–29. Brady, 130.
88. Thomas, 27–29. www.sharetngov. tnsosfiles.com/tula/sxhitibs/veterans/1812. Accessed 14 November 20018.
89. Brady, 133.
90. www.loc.gov/collections/andrew-jackson-papers/articles-and-essays/andrew-jackson-timelene. Accessed 15 November 2018. www.measuringworth.com. Accessed 15 November 2018.
91. Frank Phelps, *The Thorough Record,* V-153, N-12, March 10, 1951, 12.
92. Robertson, 41.
93. Burke, 56–57.
94. Phelps, 13–24.
95. *The Papers of Andrew Jackson, Vol. X,* 272.
96. Robertson, 42. www.whitehouse history.org/the-executive-stable. Accessed 23 March 2019.

Chapter 10

1. Burke, 52–53.
2. *The Papers of Andrew Jackson, Vol. III,* 186–189
3. *The Papers of Andrew Jackson, Vol. III,* 34–35.
4. *Ibid.*
5. *The Papers of Andrew Jackson Vol. III,* 101–102, 104–105.
6. Brian Kilmeade and Don Yeager, *Andrew Jackson and the Miracle of New Orleans* (New York: Penguin Random House, 2017), 91–201.
7. *Ibid.*, 145.
8. *Ibid.*, 114–115.
9. *Ibid.*, 186–189, 190–181, 194–195.
10. Burke, 57. Brady, 141.
11. Burke, 61.
12. Burke, 58, Brady, 145.
13. Brand, 293.
14. Burke, 58.
15. Burke, 59.
16. James, 279–281.
17. Minnigerode, 214–215.
18. *Ibid.*
19. Burke, 59.
20. Brady, 143.
21. Brand, 293.
22. www.Shannonselin.com/2014/05/

vincent-nolte-reminscenses-extraordinary-businessman. Accessed 4 November 2017.

23. www.andrewjackson.org/p/jackson-rachel-born-1767. Accessed 4 November 2017.

24. Burke, 59.

25. *Ibid.*, 59–60.

26. *Ibid.*, 61.

27. Brand, 289.

28. *Ibid.*, 293.

29. *Ibid.*, 298.

30. Brady 148. Parton, 291.

31. Brady, 148.

32. John McDonough, "Andrew Jackson Papers: Provenance," Manuscript Division, Library of Congress.

33. *Ibid.*

34. *Ibid.*

35. Brady, 148.

36. *Ibid.*, 149–50.

37. *Ibid.*

38. Anthony S. Pitch, "The Burning of Washington," *White House History* (Washington, DC: White House Historical Association, 1998), Vol. 4, Fall 1998. N.p.

39. www.smithsonianmag.com/sciencernatural-the-tornado-that-saved-washington. Accessed 5 November 2017.

40. Pitch.

41. *Ibid.* Congress established a new library by purchasing 6,487 volumes for $23,950 from former President Thomas Jefferson in 1815. www.loc.gov/exhibits/jefferson/jefflib. It would take nearly five years to rebuild the House chambers, four years to replace the Senate building and a decade before the Capitol was completed. www.house.gov/historical-highlights/1800-1850/the-burning-of-the-capitol-in-1814. www.senate.gov/about-history-minute/a-capitol-in-ruins. Accessed 5 November 2017.

42. Pitch.

43. *Ibid.*

44. *The Papers of Andrew Jackson Vol. III*, 392.

45. www.nps.gov/octagonhouse. Accessed 16 November 2017.

46. Parton, Vol. II, 335.

47. Brady, 152–153.

48. Harold D. Moser, David R., Hoth, and George Hoemann, editors, *The Papers of Andrew Jackson, Vol. IV, 1816-1820* (Knoxville, Tennessee: University of Tennessee Press, 1994), xxix. www.lib.unc.edu/collection-number-01092-z. Accessed 6 November 2017.

49. Samuel G. Heiskell, *Andrew Jackson and Early Tennessee History* (Nashville, Tennessee: Ambrose Printing Company, 1920), 77–79.

50. *The Papers of Andrew Jackson, Vol. IV*, 27.

51. *Ibid.*

52. www.loc.gov/resources/Maj.06159_0341_0348/?&st=text. Accessed 6 November 2017.

53. Jill Lepore, "Bound for Glory," *The New Yorker*, October 20, 2008.

Chapter 11

1. *The Papers of Andrew Jackson, Vol. IV*, xxix–xl.

2. Brady, 154–155.

3. *The Papers of Andrew Jackson, Vol. IV*, 14.

4. Harold D. Moser,l David R. Hoth, and George H. Hoemann, editors, *The Papers of Andrew Jackson Vol. V, 1821-1824* (Knoxville, Tennessee: University of Tennessee Press, 1996), 378.

5. *Ibid.*, 391.

6. *The Papers of Andrew Jackson, Vol. IV*, 62.

7. *Ibid.*

8. *The Papers of Andrew Jackson Vol. IV*, xxx.

9. www.tennesseeencyclopedia.net/entries/chickasaws. Accessed 6 May 2018.

10. Melton's Bluff Receipts, University Libraries, Special Collections, The University of Alabama.

11. Loretta Gillespie, "Melton's Bluff," *Moulton Advertiser*, 23 April 2015.

12. *The Papers of Andrew Jackson, Vol. IV*, xxxii. Hutchings Family Papers, 1804–1970, Accession Number, 1971.124, Tennessee State Library and Archives, Nashville, Tennessee.

13. *The Papers of Andrew Jackson, Vol. IV*, xxxiii. www.britannica.com/event/first-seminole-war. Accessed 12 May 2018.

14. "Transfer of Florida," Florida Center of Instructional Technology, College of Education, University of South Florida, 2002. Fred Cubberly, "John Quincy Adams and Florida," *The Florida Historical Quarterly*, Vol. 5, No. 2, October 1926, 88–93.

15. Daniel Preston, "James Monroe: Foreign Affairs," University of Virginia, Miller Center.

16. *Ibid.*

17. Samuel T. Morison, "History and Tra-

dition in American Military Justice," *University of Pennsylvania Law Journal*, Vol. 35, No. 33, October 30, 2011, 121–171.

18. *Ibid.*
19. *Ibid.*
20. *The Papers of Andrew Jackson, Vol. IV*, xxxiii.
21. *Ibid.*, 191–192.
22. Morison, 153.
23. *Ibid.*, 155–156.
24. *The Papers of Andrew Jackson, Vol. IV*, 212–213.
25. *Ibid.*, 244.
26. *Ibid.*
27. Brady, 161.
28. *The Papers of Andrew Jackson, Vol. IV*, 244.
29. Morison, 159.
30. *Ibid.*, 167.
31. *Ibid.*, 140.
32. *Ibid.*, 140–141.
33. *American State Papers: Documents Legislative and Executive of the Congress of the United States* (Washington, DC: Gales and Seaton, 1832), Part 5, Volume 1, 743. Congress also had some questions about Jackson's land dealings. His adjutant general, Robert Butler, testified that in the summer of 1819 Rachel's nephew John Donelson went to Pensacola and bought land. Butler said that James Jackson was involved in the purchase but Jackson was not. It was his understanding that Donelson went to Florida for his health. Senator Eaton said he, James Jackson and six others sent Donelson, carrying $16,000, to Pensacola and he purchased sixty-acres adjoining Pensacola and 2,000 acres on the bay. Part 5, Volume 1, 750–751. However, Andrew Jackson and John Coffee, on January 26, 1822, gave Peter Richardson and Patrick Maguire a promissory note for $200 for one share of stock in the Cypress land Company for Andrew Jackson Hutchings. *The Papers of Andrew Jackson Vol. V*, 520.
34. *The Papers of Andrew Jackson, Vol. IV*, xxxvi, 271–172.
35. *Ibid.*, 272. Rachel E. Stephens, "America's Portraitist: Ralph E. W. Earl and the Imaging of the Jacksonian Era." PhD dissertation, University of Iowa, 2010.
36. *The Papers of Andrew Jackson, V–IV*, 272.
37. *Ibid.*
38. *Ibid.*, xxxvi–xxxvii, 277.
39. Parton, Vol. II, 277–280.
40. *Ibid.*, xxxvii–xxxviii.

41. *Ibid. The Nashville Whig*, 10 and 12 June 1819. *The Nashville City and Business Directory* (Nashville, Tennessee: Campbell and Eastman, 1859), 245–246.
42. James, 643–644.
43. James, *The Border Captain*, 338–340. www.thehermitage.com. Accessed 24 June 2018.
44. *The Papers of Andrew Jackson, Vol. IV*, xxxvii.
45. www.britannica.com/places/united-states-from-1816-to-1850. Accessed 24 June 2018.
46. James, *The Border Captain*, 332.
47. *The Papers of Andrew Jackson, Vol. IV*, xxxix.
48. www.loc.gov/collections/andrew-jackson-papers/articles-and-essays/andrew-jackson-timeline. Accessed 26 June. 2018. Morison, 163.
49. Morison, 163.
50. *The Papers of Andrew Jackson, Vol. IV*, 270–271.
51. Burke, 70.
52. Parton, Vol. II, 595–596. James, *The Border Captain*, 334. www.measuringworth.com. Accessed 27 June 2018.
53. Parton, Vol. II, 595–596.
54. *The Republican Compiler*, 5 May 1821.
55. Parton, Vol. II, 595.
56. James, *The Border Captain*, 356. www.measruingworth.com. Accessed 28 June 2018.
57. *Ibid.*
58. Parton, Vol. II, 595.
59. *Ibid.*
60. *Ibid.*
61. *Ibid.* Burke, 71.
62. Parton, Vol. II, 597.
63. *Ibid.*
64. *Ibid.*
65. *Ibid.*
66. *Ibid.*
67. *Ibid.*, 598.
68. *Ibid.*
69. *Ibid.*, 599–601.
70. *Ibid.*, 603.
71. *Ibid.*, 604.
72. *Ibid.*
73. *Ibid.*
74. *Ibid.*
75. *Ibid.*, 605.
76. *Ibid.*
77. *Ibid.*
78. *Ibid.*, 605–606.
79. *Ibid.*, 606.
80. *Ibid.*

81. *Ibid.*, 610.
82. *Ibid.*
83. *Ibid.*, 610–611.
84. Burke, 74.
85. Brady, 168.
86. *Ibid.*
87. Burke, 78.
88. *The Papers of Andrew Jackson, Vol. V,* 28, 177, 180, 195. "Harrodsburg Springs," *The Kentucky Encyclopedia,* 414.
89. *The Papers of Andrew Jackson, Vol. V,* xxix.
90. George M. Chinn, *The History of Harrodsburg and the Great Settlement Area of Kentucky, 1774–1800* (Harrodsburg, Kentucky: George M. Chinn, 1985), 145.
91. Brady, 174.
92. Brady, 178.

Chapter 12

1. *The Papers of Andrew Jackson Vol. V,* 522.
2. *Ibid.*, 511.
3. *Ibid.*, 520.
4. Email from The Hermitage Curator Marsha Mullin to author, April 29, 2019.
5. Brady, 176.
6. *The Papers of Andrew Jackson, Vol. V,* 320.
7. *Ibid.*
8. www.thegrovemuseum.com. Accessed 30 June 2018. Burke, 176–177.
9. *The Papers of Andrew Jackson Vol. V,* 322–323.
10. *Ibid.*
11. *Ibid.*, 324–325.
12. *Ibid.*
13. *Ibid.*
14. *Ibid.*, 327–328.
15. *Ibid.*, 327.
16. *Ibid.* 327–328.
17. *Ibid.*, 330–332.
18. *Ibid.*
19. *Ibid.*
20. *Ibid.*
21. *The United States v Walter Jones, Administrator of Benjamin G. Orr, United States Supreme Court Reports,* Vol. 8 (Rochester, New York: Lawyers Co-operative Publishing Company, 1918), 399–418.
22. www.bioguide.congress.gov. Accessed 1 July 2018.
23. *The Papers of Andrew Jackson, Vol. V,* 330–333.
24. *Ibid.*
25. Brady, 178.
26. www.encyclopediavirginia.org/custis_eleanor_nelly_parke_1779-1852. Accessed 1 July 2018.
27. Toplovich, 16.
28. *Ibid.*, 17.
29. Brady, 179.
30. www.archives.mountvernon.org/agents/people. Accessed 1 July 2018.
31. www.encyclopediavirginia.org/custis-elizabeth-parke-1776-1831. Accessed 1 July 2018. A portion of Washington's letter to his stepgranddaughter reveals a seldom seen side of the first president:

Do not then in your contemplation of the marriage state look for perfect felicity before you consent to wed. Nor conceive that heaven has taken its adobe on earth. Nor conceive, from the fine tales of poets and lovers of old have told us of the transports of mutual love, that heaven has taken its adobe on earth. Nor do not deceive yourself in supposing that the only means by which these are to be obtained is to drink deep of the cup and revel in an ocean of love. Love is a mighty pretty thing, but like all other delicious things, it is cloying; and when the first transports of the passion begins to subside it serves to evince that love is too dainty a food to live upon *alone* and ought not to be considered farther than as a necessary ingredient for that matrimonial happiness which results from a combination of causes; none of which are of greater importance than that the object on whom it is placed, should possess good sense—good disposition and the means of supporting you in the way you have been brought up. Such qualifications cannot fail to attract (after marriage) your esteem and regard into which or into disgust, sooner or later, love naturally resolves itself and who at the same time has a claim to the respect and esteem of the circle he moves in. Without these, whatever may be your first impression of the man, they will end in disappointment. For be assured, and experience will convince you, that there is no truth more certain, that that all our enjoyments fall short of our expectations and to none does it apply with more force that to the gratification of the passions.

Would Rachel have taken such paternal advice if John Donelson had been alive during the later years of her marriage to Lewis Robards?

32. www.measuringworth.com. Accessed 1 July 2018.

33. Burke, 84

34. *Ibid.*, 85.

35. *The Papers of Andrew Jackson, Vol. V,* 337–338.

36. Burke, 85.

37. *The Papers of Andrew Jackson, Vol. V,* 345–346.

38. *Ibid.*

39. *Ibid.*

40. *Ibid.*

41. *Ibid.*, 348.

42. *Ibid.*

43. Amedee Guillemin, *The World of Comets* (London, England: Sampson, Low, Marston, Searle and Rivington, 1877), 209–210.

44. *The Papers of Andrew Jackson, Vol. V, 349.*

45. *Ibid.*

46. *Ibid.*, 351.

47. *Ibid.*, 341–342, 352.

48. *Ibid.*, 352.

49. *Ibid.*

50. *Ibid.*

51. *Ibid.*, 360–361.

52. *Ibid.*, 375–376.

53. Library of Congress, Prints and Photographs Division, Digital Id cph3b15566// hdl.loc.gov/loc.pnp/cph3b15566. Accessed 22 February 2018. Major General Jacob Brown and Major General Winfield Scott were approved for the Congressional Gold Medal on November 3, 1815.

54. *The Papers of Andrew Jackson Vol. V, 511.*

55. *Ibid.*, 376.

56. *Ibid.*

57. *Ibid.*, 361.

58. *Ibid.*, 562.

59. *Ibid.*, 371.

60. Parton, Vol I, 147.

61. Brady, 179.

62. *Ibid.*, 393.

63. *Ibid.*, 410–411.

64. Burke, 88.

65. *The Papers of Andrew Jackson, Vol. V,* xxxii.

66. Dorris, 41.

67. Email from The Hermitage curator Marsha Mullin to author, November 20, 2018.

68. Catherine Lynn, *Wallpaper in America: From the Seventeenth Century to World War I* (New York: W. W. Norton & Company, 1980), 201, 219. Joseph Dufour entered the wallpaper business in the 1790s with his brother Pierre, in Macon. In 1808, they moved to Paris. In the early years of the nineteenth century, Dufour papers won prizes at all the French industrial exhibitions in which they were entered.

69. Burke, 92.

70. *The Papers of Andrew Jackson, Vol. V,* 432–433.

71. *Ibid.*

72. *Ibid.*

73. Brady, 183.

74. *The Papers of Andrew Jackson, Vol. V,* 574.

75. Library of Congress, Andrew Jackson Papers, 1775–1874, Series 1, General correspondence, MSS 27532, Vol. 65. A copy of the dressmaker's bill was furnished by Marsha Mullin, The Hermitage curator. www. measuringworth.com. Accessed 27 April 2019.

76. Burke, 93.

77. *The Papers of Andrew Jackson, Vol. V,* xxxii, 456.

78. *Ibid.*, 456.

79. *Ibid.*

80. *Ibid.*

81. *Ibid.*

82. *Ibid.*, 457–458.

83. *Ibid.*, 499

84. www.measuringworth.com. Accessed 6 July 2018.

85. *The Papers of Andrew Jackson, Vol. V,* 459.

Chapter 13

1. *The Papers of Andrew Jackson, Vol. VI,* 549–550.

2. *The Papers of Andrew Jackson, Vol. VI,* xxvii. Burke, 100. The five-story Indian Queen Hotel was located on the north side of Pennsylvania Avenue halfway between the President's House and the Capitol.

3. Burke, 101–102.

4. *The Papers of Andrew Jackson, Vol. VI,* 20–21.

5. *Ibid.*, 12.

6. *Ibid.*, 16. www.measuringworth.com. Accessed 6 July 2018.

7. *The Papers of Andrew Jackson, Vol. VI,* 18–19.

8. www.britannica.com/biography/ henry-clay. Accessed 6 July 2018.

9. Luman H. Long, editor. *The 1971 World Almanac and Book of Facts* (Chicago: Newspaper Enterprise Association, 1970), 735.

10. Burke, 103.

11. *The Papers of Andrew Jackson, Vol. VI*, 23.

12. *Ibid.*, 28.

13. *Ibid.*, 20.

14. Burke, 103

15. *Ibid.*

16. *Ibid.*, 104.

17. *The Papers of Andrew Jackson, Vol. VI*, 33.

18. www.measuringworth.com. Accessed 6 July 2018.

19. *The Papers of Andrew Jackson, Vol. VI*, 35–36.

20. *Western Pennsylvania Historical Magazine* (State College, Pennsylvania: Penn State University, 1923), Vol. VI, 191–192.

21. www.britannica.com/art/bakewell-glass. Accessed 7 July 2018.

22. *Western Pennsylvania Historical Magazine*, 192.

23. *The Papers of Andrew Jackson, Vol. VI*, 63.

24. www.masshist.org/apdez. Accessed 8 July 2018.

25. Robert V. Remini, *Henry Clay: Statesman for the Union* (New York: W. W. Norton, 1993), 84.

26. James F. Hopkins, editor, *The Papers of Henry Clay, Vol. I* (Lexington, Kentucky: University Press of Kentucky, 2015), 80. *The Papers of Andrew Jackson, Vol. VI*, 62.

27. *The Papers of Andrew Jackson, Vol. VI*, xxx. Parton, 80.

28. *The Papers of Andrew Jackson, Vol. VI, xxxi*, 62.

29. www.thehermitage.com/marquis-de-lafayette. Accessed 8 July 2018. Wells, 23–24.

30. *The Papers of Andrew Jackson, Vol. VI*, 68.

31. Burke, 107.

32. *The Papers of Andrew Jackson, Vol. VI*, 72–73.

33. *Ibid.*

34. *Ibid.*

35. *Ibid.*

36. *Ibid.*

37. *Ibid.*, 77–79.

38. *Ibid.*, 92.

39. *Ibid.*, 101.

40. *Ibid.*, 124.

41. www.ncpedia.org/biography/hogg-samuel-e. Accessed 20 February 2018.

42. *The Papers of Andrew Jackson, Vol. VI*, 128.

43. *Ibid.*, 132, 134.

44. *Ibid.*, 136.

45. *Ibid.*, 130, 219.

46. *Ibid.*, 236–237.

47. *Ibid.*, 124.

48. *Ibid.*, xxxvi, xxxvii.

49. *Ibid.*, 240. *The Papers of Andrew Jackson Vol. I*, 420.

50. *Ibid.*, *The Papers of Andrew Jackson, Vol. VI*, 240.

51. "James Brown," wwwbioguide.congress.gov. Accessed 25 February 2018. "John Brown," "Mason Brown," "Samuel Brown," *The Kentucky Encyclopedia*, 128, 130, 131.

52. *The Papers of Andrew Jackson, Vol. VI*, 240.

53. *Ibid.*, *The Papers of Andrew Jackson, Vol. I*, 428.

54. Paul F. Boller, Jr., *Presidential Wives* (New York: Oxford University Press, 1988), 65–66.

55. *Ibid.*, 66.

56. *The Papers of Andrew Jackson, Vol. VI*, xxxvi, xxxvii.

57. *Ibid.*, 258–260.

58. *Ibid.*, xxxvii.

59. John Overton, *A Letter from the Jackson Committee of Nashville in Answer to One from a Similar Committee at Cincinnati upon the Subject of Gen, Jackson's Marriage* (Nashville, Tennessee: Hall & Fitzgerald, 1827).

60. *Ibid.* John and Sallie Robards Jouett were the parents of Matthew Harris Jouett, called the most significant portraitist of the Antebellum South. "John Jouett," *The Kentucky Encyclopedia*, 480–481.

61. Overton letter.

62. *Ibid.*

63. *Ibid.*

64. *Ibid.*

65. *Ibid.*

66. *Ibid.*

67. *Ibid.*

68. *Ibid.*

69. *The Papers of Andrew Jackson, Vol.I*, 433.

70. Overton letter.

71. *Ibid.*

72. *Ibid.*

73. *The Papers of Andrew Jackson, Vol. I*, 25–27.

74. *Ibid.*, 29–33.

75. Overton letter.
76. *The Papers of Andrew Jackson, Vol. I*, 23.
77. *Ibid.*, 27.
78. *The Papers of Andrew Jackson, Vol. I*, 425–427.
79. *Ibid.*
80. *Ibid.*
81. *The Papers of Andrew Jackson, Vol. I*, 48, 92.
82. Overton letter.
83. *Ibid.*
84. *Ibid.*
85. *Ibid.*

Chapter 14

1. *The Papers of Andrew Jackson, Vol. VI*, 314–315.
2. *Ibid.*, 316.
3. *Ibid.*, 319.
4. *Ibid.*
5. "Hugh McGary," *The Kentucky Encyclopedia*, 597.
6. *The Papers of Andrew Jackson, Vol. VI*, 319. The Major Moore whom Overton referred to was probably Major Thomas P. Moore from Harrodsburg, who led the 18th Infantry in the War of 1812 under Jackson. He was elected to Congress, serving from 1823 to 1829. Jackson appointed him minister to New Grenada where he served from 1829 to 1833. www.stampcommentary.org. Accessed 3 January 2019.
7. Hammersmith, 171.
8. *The Papers of Andrew Jackson, Vol. VI*, 316.
9. *Ibid.*, 336. Brady, 210.
10. *The Papers of Andrew Jackson, Vol. VI*, 580, 583, 591, 593, 607.
11. *Ibid.*, 338–339.
12. *Ibid.*, 340.
13. *Ibid.*, 344.
14. "Harrodsburg Springs," *The Kentucky Encyclopedia*, 414–415.
15. *The Papers of Andrew Jackson, Vol. VI*, 351–352. Allen W. Read, "Could Andrew Jackson Spell?" *American Speech* (Durham, North Carolina: Duke University Press, 1963), Vol. 38, No. 3, October 1963, 188.
16. *The Papers of Andrew Jackson, Vol. VI*, 354–355.
17. *The Papers of Andrew Jackson, Vol. VI*, xxxviii. *Bulletin of the United States Geological Survey, Department of the Interior, No.*

32 (Washington, DC: Government Printing Office, 1886), 101
18. *The Papers of Andrew Jackson, Vol. VI*, 367.
19. *Ibid.*
20. *Ibid.*, 368.
21. *The Papers of Andrew Jackson, Vol. VI*, 419. When Elizabeth Anderson Donelson died in 1841, William Donelson married her sister Martha.
22. *The Papers of Andrew Jackson, Vol. VI*, 368.
23. *Ibid.*
24. *Ibid. The Papers of Andrew Jackson, Vol. I*, 421.
25. *Ibid., The Papers of Andrew Jackson, Vol. VI*, xxxix.
26. *Ibid.*, 556, 594. Bobbinet was a net fabric, usually silk, originally made by hand until Englishman John Heathcoat invented a machine to produce the cloth in 1806. www.vintagegashionguild.org.
27. John G. Tregle, Jr., "Andrew Jackson and the Continuing Battle of New Orleans," *Journal of the Early Republic* (Philadelphia, Pennsylvania: University of Pennsylvania Press, 1981), Vol. I, No. 4, Winter 1981, 373–393.
28. *Ibid.*
29. *Ibid.*
30. *Ibid.*
31. *New Orleans Times-Picayune*, 28 February 2018. *American Annual Cyclopedia and Register of Important Events of the Year 1868* (New York: D. Appleton and Company, 1869), Vol. VIII, 560. www.neworleansbar.org/uploads/file/duel/%20personality-12-3pdf. Accessed 14 February 2019. William de Marigny Hyland's speech to Mandeville Horizons, Inc., May 26, 1984.
32. Minnigerode, 233.
33. Rachel Jackson to Hannah Israel Davenport, February 25, 1828, Historical Society of Philadelphia.
34. *Ibid.*
35. *Ibid.*
36. *Ibid.*
37. Lisa M. Brown, *Jockeying Into the American Presidency: The Political Opportunism of Aspirants* (Amherst, New York: Cambria Press, 2010), 136. Parton, Vol. III, 316.
38. Brady, 213.
39. John Quincy Adams, *Memoirs of John Quincy Adams* (New York, AMS Press, 1970), V–VII, 479.
40. www.Shannonselin.com/201405/

vincent-nolte-reminscenses-extraordinary-businessman. Accessed 2 July 2018.

41. Tregle, 373–393.

42. *The Papers of Andrew Jackson, Vol. VI*, 407. McCutcheon, a former ship's captain who served with Jackson in the War of 1812, had married into the Butler family.

Chapter 15

1. William Henry Smith, *Charles Hammond and His Relations to Henry Clay and John Quincy Adams* (Chicago: Chicago Historical Society, 1885), 33–37, 35–36. The pamphlet contained the speech Smith delivered before the Chicago Historical Society on May 20, 1884. It was not clear whether Hammond's reference to Barrataria was to the fictional territory governed by Sancho Panza or the patch of land—fifteen miles long and twelve miles wide—in Jefferson and Plaquemines parishes said to be the home of the pirate Jean Lafitte. The area is now the Jean Lafitte National Park and Preserve. www.npr.gov/jela/barrataria-preserve. Accessed 3 March 2018.

2. Catherine de Medici was blamed by pamphleteers for the St. Bartholomew's Day Massacre where thousands of Huguenots were killed. www.britannica.com/biography/catherine-de-medici. Accessed 3 March 2018. Lucreza Borgia, the illegitimate daughter of Pope Alexander VI, was accused of bearing him a son. www.britannica.com/biography/lucrezia-borgia. Accessed 3 March 2018. Countess Elizabeth Bathory was accused of torturing and murdering approximately 650 girls in what is now Slovenia, and slander pamphlets by her enemies motivated her arrest. www.britannica.com/biography/elizabeth-bathory. Accessed 3 March 2018.

3. Smith, 36–47.

4. Smith, 35.

5. Charles Hammond, *Truth's Advocate and Monthly Anti-Jackson Expositor* (Cincinnati, Ohio, March 1828), 5.

6. *Ibid.*

7. *Ibid.*

8. *Ibid.*

9. *Ibid.*

10. *Ibid.*

11. Boller, Jr., 65–66

12. Hammond, 5.

13. *Ibid.*

14. *Ibid.*

15. *Ibid.*, 6.

16. *Ibid.*

17. *Ibid.*

18. *Ibid.*

19. *Ibid.*

20. *Ibid.*

21. *Ibid.*

22. *Ibid.*

23. *Ibid.*

24. *Ibid.*, 6–7.

25. Overton letter.

26. Hammond, 8.

27. *The Papers of Andrew Jackson Vol. I*, 427–428.

28. Hammond, 8.

29. *Ibid.*

30. *Ibid.*

31. Overton letter.

32. *Ibid.*

33. www.thenashvillecitycemetery.org/280201-crutcher. Accessed 23 February 2019.

34. *The Papers of Andrew Jackson, Vol. VI*, 553.

35. Owsley, 480.

36. Hammond, 8.

37. *Ibid.*, 10.

38. *Ibid.*

39. "John Breckinridge," *The Kentucky Encyclopedia*, 116–117.

40. Broussard, 4.

41. Hammond, 9.

42. *Ibid.*

43. *Ibid.*

44. *Ibid.*

45. *Ibid.*

46. *Ibid.*

47. *Ibid.*

48. Catharina V. R. Bonney, *A Legacy of Historical Gleanings* (Albany, New York: J. Munsell, 1875), Vol. II, 423–435.

49. Hammond, 10.

50. *Ibid.*, 10–11.

51. *Ibid.*, 11.

52. *Ibid.*

53. *The Papers of Andrew Jackson, Vol. VI*, 525.

54. Hammond, 11.

55. *The Papers of Andrew Jackson, Vol. I*, 17.

56. *The Clarion-Ledger*, 27 September 2017.

57. Hammond, 11.

58. *Ibid.*

59. Hammond, 11–12.

60. Hammond, 12.

61. *Ibid.* Hammond's use of the word

Pandarus probably came from Chaucer's *Troilus and Criseyde,* where a character named Pandarus is a go-between for the lovers, hence the word *pander.* Or, the reference could have been to Homer's Iliad where Pandarus broke the truce between the Trojans and the Greeks and committed treachery against Menelaus. www.britannica.com/topics/pandarus/greek/mythology. Accessed 27 September 2017.

62. Hammond, 12.
63. *Ibid.*
64. Overton letter.
65. Hammond, 12.
66. Hammond, 12–13.
67. Hammond, 13.
68. *Ibid.*
69. *Ibid.*, 14.
70. *Ibid.*
71. *Ibid.*
72. *Ibid.*, 14–15.
73. *Ibid.*, 15.
74. *The Papers of Andrew Jackson, Vol. II,* 361–362.
75. Hammond, 15.
76. *Ibid.*
77. *Ibid.*
78. *Ibid.*
79. *Ibid.*, 15–16.
80. *Ibid.* 16.
81. *Ibid.*, 16–17. Samuel Swartwout, from Poughkeepsie, New York, was one of Jackson's more unsavory friends. They first met during the Aaron Burr controversy and Swartwout was one of Jackson's early supporters and he rewarded him with an appointment as Collector of the Customs for the Port of New York. Jackson's successor, Martin Van Buren, refused to reappoint him. Swartwout embezzled $1,225,705.95—one-fourth of the federal government's annual income—from his job and fled to England. In a plea agreement, the federal court reduced the amount to $792,654.74, confiscated his property and allowed him to return to America. *Orlando Sentinel,* 20 July 2017. www.law.lsu.edu/maritimeart/jackson1834. Accessed 5 March 2018.
82. Hammond, 17.

Chapter 16

1. Anne Ryckbost, "Biographic Information About Moses Dawson," Moses Dawson Papers, Archives and Special Collections, Xavier University.

2. *Ibid.*
3. *Ibid.*
4. Charles T. Greve, *Centennial History of Cincinnati and Representative Citizens* (Cincinnati, Ohio: Biographic Printing Company, 1904), Vol. I, 792.
5. *Ibid.*
6. Thomas L. Koberna, "Moses Dawson: Jacksonian Spokesman of the West," thesis, Xavier University, August 5, 1957, 64-93.
7. *Ibid.*, 49.
8. *Ibid.*, 50.
9. *Ibid.*, 48.
10. *Ibid.*, 50.
11. *Ibid.*, 51.
12. *Ibid.*
13. *The Papers of Andrew Jackson, Vol. VI,* 525. Koberna, 53.
14. www.loc.gov/resources/maj.01066_0426_0427/?st=single. Accessed 2 January 2019. *The Papers of Andrew Jackson, Vol. VI,* 521.
15. www.archives.upenn.edu/exhibits/pem-people/birgraphy/robert-patterson. Accessed 2 January 2019.
16. Koberna, 37. *The Papers of Andrew Jackson, Vol. VI,* 554.
17. *The Papers of Andrew Jackson Vol. VI,* 469. Erwin and his large family, with close alliances to Clay, were intent of the election of Adams with plans for Clay to succeed him. *Ibid.*, 217.
18. www.loc.gov/program/bib/elections/election1828. Accessed 3 January 2019.
19. Burke, 119.
20. Burke, 120–121.
21. Toplovich, 3.
22. Spencer Bassett, *The Life of Andrew Jackson, Volume II* (New York: Macmillan Company, 1916), 405–406.
23. *Ibid.*
24. *Ibid.* www.presidentialcampaignselectionsreference.wordpress.com. Accessed 2 January 2019.
25. *The Papers of Andrew Jackson, Vol. VI,* 587.
26. *Ibid.*, 536.
27. *Ibid.*, 537.
28. *Ibid.*
29. *Ibid.*, 537–538. Harriet Berryhill, the daughter of Nashville merchant William M. Berryhill and his wife, the former Mary Craig, was a companion to Rachel and accompanied the Jacksons to New Orleans earlier in the year.
30. *The Papers of Andrew Jackson, Vol. VI,* 537.

31. *Ibid.*
32. *Ibid.*, 543.
33. *Ibid.*
34. *Ibid.*
35. *Ibid.*
36. *Ibid.*
37. *Ibid.*, 546. www.bioguide.congress. gov/scripts/biodisplay/P?index=P000514. Accessed 3 January 2019.
38. Brady, 219–220.
39. www.loc.gov/resources/rbpe. 1742000/?St=text. Accessed 3 January 2019.
40. *The Papers of Andrew Jackson, Vol. VI*, 546.
41. *Ibid.*
42. Brady, 221.
43. Henry A. Wise, *Seven Decades of The Union* (Philadelphia, Pennsylvania: J. B. Lippincott, 1872), 277–278.
44. Katherine W. Cruze, *An Amiable Woman: Rachel Jackson* (Nashville, Tennessee: The Hermitage and the Ladies' Hermitage Association, 1994), 26. www.census. gov/population/www/documentation/ twps0027/tab06.txt. Accessed 3 January 2019.
45. Brady, 221.
46. www.tshaonline.org/handbook/ online/articles/fro25. Accessed 4 January 2019.
47. Wise, 278.
48. *Ibid.* Burke, 122.
49. Wise, 278.
50. *Ibid.*
51. Burke, 131–132.
52. Wise, 278–279.
53. *Nashville Banner*, 24 December 1828.
54. *Ibid.*
55. Kilmeade, 144.
56. www.loc.gov/resource/rbpe. 174202000/?St=text. Accessed 8 January

2019. The City Hotel, a three-story edifice, was located on the east side of Nashville's public square and the back of the building overlooked the Cumberland River. www. nashvillehistoryblogspot.com/2013/02/the-city-hotel. Accessed 4 January 2019.
57. *Nashville Banner*, 24 December 1828.
58. *Ibid.*
59. www.firstladies.org/biographies/ firstladies/asopx?biography=7. Accessed 12 January 2019.
60. *Convention of New Hampshire Publishers, Editors and Printers Held at Wolfeborough* July 24 and 25, 1868 (Concord, New Hampshire: McFarland and Jenks, 1868), 39.
61. *New Hampshire Statesman and Concord Register*, 17 January 1829.
62. *Ibid.*
63. *Ibid.*
64. Email from The Hermitage curator Marsha Mullin to author, April 29, 2019.
65. *The Papers of Andrew Jackson, Vol. VI*, 547.
66. Kilmeade, 127.
67. Francis P. Weisenburger, "Charles Hammond, The First Great Journalist of the Old Northwest," *Ohio Archeological and Historical Quarterly* (Columbus, Ohio: F. J. Neer Printing Company, 1934), Vol. XLIII, No. 4, October 1934, 390–391.
68. David Feller, Laura-Eve Moss, Thomas Coens, and Erik B. Alexander, editors, *The Papers of Andrew Jackson, Vol. IX, 1831* (Knoxville: University Press of Tennessee, 2013), 218.
69. www.thehermitage.com/learn/ mansion-grounds/jacksons-tomb. Accessed 12 January 2019.
70. *Ibid.*
71. *The Papers of Andrew Jackson, Vol. IX*, 34.

Bibliography

Books

Adams, John Quincy. *Memoirs of John Quincy Adams.* New York: AMS Press, 1970.

Aiken, Leona T. *Donelson, Tennessee: Its History and Landmarks.* Nashville: Leona T. Aiken, 1968.

Albright, Edward. *Early History of Middle Tennessee.* Nashville: Brandon Printing Company, 1909.

Anderson, James D. *Making the American Thoroughbred: Especially in Tennessee 1800–1805.* Norwood, Massachusetts: The Plimpton Press, 1916.

Appleby, Joyce, Eileen K. Cheng, and Joanne L. Goodwin, editors. *Encyclopedia of Women in American History.* New York: Routledge Press, 2015.

Babits, Lawrence E. *A Devil of a Whipping: The Battle of Cowpens.* Chapel Hill: University of North Carolina Press, 2000.

Baily, Francis. *Journey of a Tour in the Unsettled Parts of North America.* London: Baily Brothers, 1856.

Bassett, Spencer. *The Life of Andrew Jackson, Volume 2.* New York: The Macmillan Company, 1916.

Bergerson, Paul H. *Paths of the Past: Tennessee 1770–1970.* Knoxville: University of Tennessee Press, 1979.

Blackstone, William. *Commentaries on the Laws of England.* Oxford: Oxford Clarendon Press, 1769.

Boller, Paul F., Jr. *Presidential Wives.* New York: Oxford University Press, 1988.

Bonney, Catherina V. R. *A Legacy of Historical Gleanings.* Albany, New York: J. Munsell, 1875.

Brady, Patricia. *A Being so Gentle: The Frontier Love Story of Rachel and Andrew Jackson.* New York: Palgrave Macmillan, 2011.

Brands, H. W. *Andrew Jackson: His Life and Times.* New York: Doubleday, 2005.

Broussard, Joyce L. *Stepping Lively in Place: The Not-Married Freewomen of Civil War-Era Natchez, Mississippi.* Athens: University of Georgia Press, 2016.

Brown, Lisa M. *Jockeying for the American Presidency: The Political Opportunism of Aspirants.* Amherst, New York: Cambria Press, 2010.

Buell, Augustus C. *History of Andrew Jackson; Pioneer, Patriot, Soldier, Politician, President.* New York: C. Scribner's Sons, 1904.

Burke, Pauline W. *Emily Donelson of Tennessee.* Knoxville: University of Tennessee Press, 2001.

Burlew, Frederich M. *Silks and Satins.* no city, no publisher, no date. A typescript (pages unnumbered) prepared for the Keeneland Association Library.

Burstein, Andrew. *The Passions of Andrew Jackson.* New York: Knopf, 2002.

Cheathem, Mark. *Andrew Jackson: Southerner.* Baton Rouge: Louisiana State University Press, 2013.

_____. *Old Hickory's Nephew: The Political Struggles of Andrew Jackson Donelson.* Baton Rouge: Louisiana State University Press, 2007.

Chinn, George M. *The History of Harrodsburg and the Great Settlement Area of Kentucky, 1774–1900.* Harrodsburg: George M. Chinn, 1985.

Clayton, W. Woodford. *History of Davidson County, Tennessee.* Nashville: J. W. Lewis & Company, 1880.

Clement, Maud C. *The History of Pittsylvania County, Virginia.* Baltimore: Genealogical Publishing Company, 1929.

Clement, William E. *Plantation Life on the Mississippi.* Gretna, Louisiana: Pelican Publishing, 2000.

Collins, Lewis. *History of Kentucky.* Covington: Collins and Company, 1884.

Cook, Theodore A. *A History of the English Turf.* London: Virtue and Company, 1901.

Corlew, Robert E., Stanley J. Follmsbee, and Enoch L. Mitchell. *Tennessee: A Short History.* Knoxville: University of Tennessee Press, 1990.

Cruse, Katherine W. *An Amiable Woman.* Nashville: Ladies' Hermitage Association, 1994.

Daniels, Jonathan. *The Devil's Backbone: The Story of the Natchez Trace.* New York: McGraw-Hill Book Company, 1971.

Dorris, Mary C. *The Hermitage: Home of General Andrew Jackson.* Nashville: Ladies' Hermitage Association, 1941.

Dunaway, Wilma A. *First American Frontier: Transition to Capitalism in Southern Appalachia.* Chapel Hill: University of North Carolina Press, 2000.

Edgar, Patrick N. *American Race-Turf Register, Sportsman Herald and General Stud Book.* New York; Press of Henry Mason, 1883.

Ellet, Elizabeth F. *Pioneer Women of the West.* New York: Charles Scribner, 1859.

Feller, Daniel, Harold D. Moser, Laura-Eve Moss, Thomas Coens, editors. *The Papers of Andrew Jackson, Volume VII.* Knoxville: University of Tennessee Press, 2007.

Feller, Daniel, Laura-Eve Moss, Thomas Coens, and Erik B. Alexander, editors. *The Papers of Andrew Jackson, Volume IX.* Knoxville: University of Tennessee Press, 2013.

Feller, Daniel, Thomas Coens, and Laura-Eve Moss, editors. *The Papers of Andrew Jackson, Volume VIII.* Knoxville: University of Tennessee Press, 2010.

_____, _____, and _____. *The Papers of Andrew Jackson, Volume X.* Knoxville: University of Tennessee Press, 2016.

Finger, John R. *Tennessee Frontier: Three Regions in Transition.* Bloomington, Indiana: Indiana University Press, 2001.

Foster, Thomas A. *Sex and the Eighteenth-Century Man.* Boston: Beacon Press, 2007.

Fraser, Flora. *The Washingtons: George and Martha.* New York: Alfred A. Knopf, 2016.

Garrett, William R. *History of Tennessee: Its People and the Institutions from the Earliest Times to the Year 1903.* Nashville: Brandon Printing Company, 1903.

Green, Thomas M. *Historic Families of Kentucky.* Cincinnati: Robert Clarke & Company, 1889.

Greve, Charles T. *Centennial History of Cincinnati and Representatives Citizens.* Cincinnati: Biographic Printing Company, 1904.

Griffey, Irene M. *Earliest Tennessee Land Records and Earliest Tennessee Land History.* Baltimore: Clearfield Company, 2001.

Guild, Josephus C. *Old Times in Tennessee with Historical, Personal and Political Scraps and Sketches.* Nashville: Travel Eastman and Howell, 1878.

Guillemin, Amedee. *The World of Comets.* London: Sampson, Low, Marston Searle & Rivington, 1877.

Hale, Will T., and Dixon I. Merritt. *A History of Tennessee and Tennesseans.* Chicago: Lewis Publishing Company, 1913.

Hammersmith, Mary P. *Hugh McGary, Senior: Pioneer of Virginia, North Carolina, Kentucky and Indiana.* Wheaton, Illinois: Nodus Press, 2000.

Hammond, John C. *Slavery, Freedom and Exploration in the Early American Press.* Charlottesville: University of Virginia Press, 2007.

Hargreaves, Mary W.M., and James F. Hopkins. *The Papers of Henry Clay, Volume I.* Lexington: University Press of Kentucky, 1959.

Harper, Josephine L. *Guide to the Draper Collection.* Madison: Wisconsin Historical Society, 2015.

Harrison, Lowell H., and Nelson L. Dawson, editors. *A Kentucky Sampler: Essays from the Filson Club Historical Quarterly 1926–1976.* Lexington: University Press of Kentucky, 2015.

Heiskell, S. G. *Andrew Jackson and Early Tennessee History.* Nashville: Ambrose Printing Company, 1921.

Heller, Roderick. *Democracy's Lawyer: Felix Grundy of the Old Southwest.* Baton Rouge: Louisiana State University Press, 2010.

Herbert, Gayle C. *A History of Racing Silks.* Lexington: House of Corrington, 1993.

Holland, Jesse. *The Invisibilities: The Untold Story of African American Slaves in the White House.* Guilford, Connecticut: Rowman & Littlefield, 2016.

Hopkins, James F., and Mary W. M. Hargreaves, editors, *The Papers of Henry Clay, Volume IX.* Lexington: University Press of Kentucky, 1963.

Inman, Natalie. *Brothers & Friends: Kinship in Early America.* Athens: University of Georgia Press, 2017.

Jackson, Ronald, Altha Polson, and Shirley Pearl Jackson. *Andrew Jackson and Rachel Donelson Ancestors.* Bountiful, Utah: Acceleration Indexing Systems, 1980.

James, Marquis. *Andrew Jackson: The Border Captain.* New York: Grosset & Dunlap, 1938.

_____. *The Life of Andrew Jackson.* New York, Garden City Publishing, 1940.

Jillson, Willard R. Filson Club Publication No. 34. Frankfort: Kentucky Historical Society, 1926.

Jordan, John W. *Colonial Families of Philadelphia.* Philadelphia: Lewis Publishing Company, 1922.

Keith, Alice B., and William H. Masters, editors. *The John Gray Blount Papers.* Durham, North Carolina: Christian Publishing Company, 1959.

Kennedy, Kathleen, and Sharon R. Ullman. *Sexual Borderlands: Constructing America's Past.* Columbus: Ohio State University Press, 2003.

Kilmeade, Brian, and Don Yeager, *Andrew Jackson and the Miracle of New Orleans.* New York: Penguin Random House, 2017.

Kleber, John, editor. *The Kentucky Encyclopedia.* Lexington: University Press of Kentucky, 1992.

Klein, Philip S., and A.A. Hoogenboom. *History of Pennsylvania.* University Park: Pennsylvania State University Press, 2010.

Knepper, George W. *The Official Ohio Lands Book.* Columbus: State Auditor Tom Petro, 2002.

Leavell, Z.T., and T.J. Bailey. *A Complete History of Mississippi Baptist from the Earliest Times.* Jackson: Mississippi Baptist Publishing Company, 1904.

Lourie, Walter. *Documents, Legislation and Executive of the Congresses of the United States in Relation to Public Lands.* Washington: Duff Green, 1834.

Long, Luman H., editor. *The 1971 World Almanac and Book of Facts.* Chicago: Newspaper Enterprise Association, 1970.

Lowery, Robert, and William H. McCardle. *A History of Mississippi.* Jackson: R.H. Henry & Company, 1891.

Lynn, Catherine. *Wallpaper in American: From the Seventeenth Century to World War I.* New York: W. W. Norton, 1980.

Makowski, Chris, Kristopher D. White, and Daniel D. Davis. *Don't Give an Inch: The Second Day at Gettysburg.* El Dorado Hills, California: Savas Beatie, 2006.

Margolis, Maxine L. *Mothers and Such: Views of American Women and Why They Changed.* Berkeley: University of California Press, 1985.

McAllister, John M., editor. *Genealogies of the Lewis and Kinder Families.* Columbus: E.W. Stephens Publishing Company, 1906.

McBee, May Wilson. *The Natchez Court Records 1767–1865.* Baltimore: Genealogical Publishing Company, 1929.

McGraw, Thomas K. *The Founders and Finance: How Hamilton, Gallatin and Other Immigrants Forged A New Economy.* Cambridge: Harvard University Press, 2012.

McKnight, Charles. *Our Western Borders in Early Pioneer Days.* Chicago: Illinois Education Company of Chicago, 1902.

Merrill, Boynton, Jr. *Jefferson's Nephews.* Lincoln: University of Nebraska Press, 2005.

Minnigerode, Meade. *Some American Ladies: Seven Informal Biographies.* New York: G. P. Putnam's Sons, 1926.

Mitchell, Dennis, Jr. *A New History of Mississippi.* Jackson: University of Mississippi Press, 2014.

Morgan, Robert. *Boone: A Biography.* Chapel Hill: Algonquin Press, 2008.

Moser, Harold D. and Sharon Macpherson, editors. *The Papers of Andrew Jackson, Volume II.* Knoxville: University of Tennessee Press, 1984.

Moser, Harold D., David R. Hoth, Sharon Macpherson, and John H. Reinbold, editors. *The Papers of Andrew Jackson, Volume III*. Knoxville: University of Tennessee Press, 1991.

Moser, Harold D., David R. Hoth, and George H. Hoemann, editors. *The Papers of Andrew Jackson, Volume IV*. Knoxville: University of Tennessee Press, 1994.

_____, _____, and _____. *The Papers of Andrew Jackson, Volume V*. Knoxville: University of Tennessee Press, 1996.

Moser, Harold D., J. Clint Cliff, and Wyatt C. Wells, editors. *The Papers of Andrew Jackson, Volume VI*. Knoxville: University of Tennessee Press, 2002.

Nelson, Julie, *American Presidents Year by Year*. London: Routledge, 2015.

Olson, Lorraine. *Little Lone Star Quilts*. Lafayette, California: C & T Publishing Company, 2010.

Overton, John. *A Letter from the Jackson Committee of Nashville in Answer to One from a Similar Committee at Cincinnati: Upon the Subject of Gen. Jackson's Marriage*. Nashville: Hall & Fitzgerald, 1927.

Parton, James, *Life of Andrew Jackson in Three Volumes*. New York: Mason Brothers, 1860.

Patterson, Benton R. *The Generals: Andrew Jackson and Sir. Edward Pakenham and the Battle of New Orleans*. New York: New York University Press, 2005.

Phillips, Margaret I. *The Governors of Tennessee*. Gretna, Louisiana: Pelican Publishing, 1978.

Possett, Emanuel A. *The Structure of Fibers, Yarn and Fabrics*. Philadelphia: E.A. Possett, 1900.

Quisenberry, A. C. *The Life and Times of Hon. Humphrey Marshall*. Winchester, Kentucky: The Sun Publishing Company, 1892.

Remini, Robert V. *Andrew Jackson: The Course of American Democracy 1933–1845*. Baltimore: John Hopkins University Press, 1998.

_____. *Andrew Jackson: The Course of American Empire 1767–1821*. Baltimore: John Hopkins University Press, 1998.

_____. *Andrew Jackson: The Course of American Freedom 1822–1833*. Baltimore: John Hopkins University Press, 1998.

_____. *Henry Clay: Statesman for the Union*. New York: W.W. Norton, 1993.

Riley, Franklin L. *School History of Mississippi for Use in Public and Private Schools*. Richmond: B.F. Johnson, 1915.

Robards, James H. *History and Genealogy of the Robards Family*. Whiteland, Indiana: James H. Robards, 1910.

Robertson, William H. P. *The History of Thoroughbred Racing in American*. New York: Bonanza Books, 1964.

Robeson, Kate S. *An Historical and Genealogical Account of Andrew Robeson of Scotland*. Philadelphia: J. B. Lippincott Company, 1916.

Rowland, Dunbar. *Encyclopedia of Mississippi History*. Madison, Wisconsin: Selwyn Brant, 1907.

_____. *Mississippi: Comprising Sketches of Towns, Events, Institutions and Persons*. Atlanta: Southern Historical Publishing Company, 1909.

Rozema, Vicki. *The Footsteps of the Cherokees*. Winston-Salem: John F. Blair, 2007.

Schneider, Paul. *Old Man River: The Mississippi River in North America*. New York: Macmillan, 2013.

Smith, Sam B., and Harriet C. Owsley, editors. *The Papers of Andrew Jackson, Volume I*. Knoxville: University of Tennessee Press, 1980.

Smith, William H. *Charles Hammond and His Relations to Henry Clay and John Quincy Adams*. Chicago: Chicago Historical Society, 1885.

Sparks, W. H. *The Memory of Fifty Years*. Macon, Georgia: J. W. Burke, 1870.

Speed, Thomas. *The Political Club of Danville, Kentucky 1786–1788*. Louisville: John P. Morton, 1894.

Stamper, Anita A., and Jill Condra. *Clothing Through American History*. Santa Barbara: ABC-CLIO, 2011.

Stephens, Rachel. *Selling Andrew Jackson: Ralph E.W. Earl and the Politics of Portaiture*. Columbia: University of South Carolina Press, 2018.

Stivers, William B. *A History of Georgia*. New York: D. Appleton and Company, 1859.

Stokes, Nellie T. *Rachel Jackson*. Nashville: Ladies' Heritage Association, 1942.

Swain, Martha H., Elizabeth A. Payne, and Marjorie J. Spruill, editors. *Mississippi Women:*

Their Histories, Their Lives Volume I and Volume II. Athens: University of Georgia Press, 2010.
Wait, Eugene M. *The Second Jackson Administration.* Hauppauge, New York: Nova Publishers, 2002.
Whitwell, William H. *The Life and Times of Judge Caleb Wallace.* Louisville: J. P. Morton, 1858.
Wise, Henry A. *Seven Decades of the Union.* Philadelphia: J. B. Lippincott, 1872.
Young, Alfred F., Gary B. Nash, and Ray Raphael, editors. *Revolutionary Founders: Rebels, Radicals and Reformers.* New York: Knopf, 2012.

Periodicals

American Turf Register and Sporting Magazine, Vol. 8, No. 5. January 1907.
Annual Reports of the War Department for the Fiscal Year Ended June 30, 1900, Report of the Chief of Engineers Part 5, 3060, 1900.
Bulletin of the United States Geological Survey, Department of the Interior, No. 32, 1886.
The Clarion-Ledger, 27 September 2019.
Cubberly, Fred. "John Quincy Adams and Florida." Florida Historical Quarterly, Vol. 5, No. 2 October 1926.
Curry, Bill. "Adventures on the Cumberland." *The Tennessee Magazine,* November 2006.
Durant, John. "Tennessee Turfman." *Sports Illustrated,* 16 July 1956.
Durham, Walter. "Kasper Mansker." *Tennessee Historical Quarterly,* Vol. 30, No. 2, 1971.
Friends of Reform and Corruption's Adversary, published in 1828 by Jackson supporter Moses Dawson by his *Cincinnati Advertiser.*
Gaston, Kay Baker. "Tennessee Distilleries: Their Rise, Fall and Reemergence." *Journal of the Kentucky-Tennessee Studies Association,* No. 12, 1999.
The Gateway, Vol. 11, No. 3, February 1904.
Gillespie, Loretta. "Melton's Bluff." *Moulton Advertiser,* 23 April 2015.
Jackson, Rachel. "Letter Written by Mrs. Andrew Jackson to Benjamin Bakewell." *Western Pennsylvania Historic Magazine,* Vol. 6, No. 1, January 1923.
Journal of the House of Burgesses of Virginia, 1773–1776, Virginia State Library.
Journal of the Kentucky House of the General Assembly, Vol. 7, 1909.
Lepore, Jill. "Bound for Glory." *The New Yorker,* 20 October 2008.
"Marriages." *Register of the Kentucky Historical Society,* Vol. 20, 1922.
Mississippi Department of Fish and Wildlife Services. "Bayou Pierre." Mississippi Sportsman, 24 March 2008.
Mississippi Valley Historical Review, Vol.13, No. 3, December 1926.
Moore, John T. "Andrew Jackson and His Beloved Rachel." *Saturday Evening Post,* 25 July 1925.
_____. *Trotwood Monthly Devoted to Farm, Horse and Home,* Vol. 1, No. 5, February 1906.
Morison, Samuel T. "History and Traditions in American Military Justice." *University of Pennsylvania Law Journal,* Vol. 35, No. 33, 30 October 2011.
Nashville Banner, 24 December 1828.
*The Nashville City and Business Directory,*1859.
The Nashville Whig, 10–12 June 1819.
National Freemason, Vol. 11, No. 1, February 1904.
New Hampshire and Concord Register, 17 January 1829.
New Orleans Times-Picayune, 28 February 2018.
Orlando Sentinel, 20 July 2017.
Pitch, Anthony S. "The Burning of Washington." *White House History IV,* February 1998.
Read, Allen W. "Could Andrew Jackson Spell?" *American Speech,* Vol. 38, No. 3, October 1963.
Report to the Secretary of War to the Two Houses of Congress, Second Session, Fifty-Third Congress, 1881.
Smith, Elbert B. "Now Defend Yourself, You Dammed Rascal." *American Heritage,* Vol. 9, No. 2, February 1958.
Spence, Richard D. "John Donelson and the Opening of the Old Southwest." *Tennessee Historical Quarterly,* Vol. 50, No. 3, Fall 1991.
The Tennessee Magazine, November 2006.

The Thoroughbred Record, Vol. 153, No. 10, March 10, 1951.

Tregle, John G., Jr. "Andrew Jackson and the Continuing Battle of New Orleans." *Journal of the Early Republic*, Vol. 1, No. 4, Winter 1981.

Troyle, Joseph G., Jr., reviewer. "The Life of Andrew Jackson," *Journal of the Louisiana Historical Association*, Vol. 77, No. 3, Summer 1976.

Truth's Advocate and Monthly Anti-Jackson Expositor, published in 1828 by Charles Hammond and his *Cincinnati Gazette.*

"United States v. Walter Jones, Administrator of Benjamin G. Orr." *United States Supreme Court Reports*, Vol. 8, 1918.

Virginia Minerals, Vol. 43, No. 2, 1997. Virginia Department of Mines, Minerals and Environment.

Weisenburger, Francis P. "Charles Hammond: The First Great Journalist of the Old Northwest." *Ohio Archeological and Historic Quarterly*, Vol. 50, No. 3, Fall 1991.

Theses and Dissertations

Burman, Nathan A. "Two Histories, One Future: Louisiana Sugar Plantations, Their Slaves and the Anglo-Creole Schism," PhD dissertation, Louisiana State University, 2013.

Coots, Russell S. "An Angel Has Fallen," thesis, University of Virginia 2010.

Farr, Jason E. "The Glasgow Land Fraud and the Emergence of Andrew Jackson," thesis, University of Virginia, 2016.

Gismondi, Melissa. "Rachel Jackson and the Search for Zion," PhD, University of Virginia, 2017.

Hatfield, Brandi. "Two Become One," thesis, Liberty University, 2010.

Holladay, Robert. "Raging Moderates: Second Party Politics and Coalition of Willing Aristocracy in Williamson County, Tennessee," thesis, Florida State University, 1907.

Hornsby, Sarah Jeanine. "The Protection of An Icon: Nashville and the Ladies' Hermitage Association and the Image of Rachel Jackson," thesis, Vanderbilt University, 1994.

Inman, Natalie. "Networks in Negotiation of Family and Kinship in Intercultural Diplomacy on Trans-Appalachian Frontier," PhD dissertation, Vanderbilt University, 2010.

Koberna, Thomas L. "Moses Dawson: Jacksonian Spokesman of the West," thesis, Xavier University, 1957.

Master, Bettina Drew. "Andrew Jackson: Indian Removal and the Culture of Slavery," PhD dissertation, Yale University, 2001.

Meredith, Rachel. "Somebody Always Dying and Leaving Andrew Jackson as Guardian," thesis, Middle Tennessee State University, 2013.

Ray, Johnathan. "Andrew Jackson and the Indians 1767–1815," PhD dissertation, University of Alabama, 2014.

Stephens, Rachel E. "American Portraitist: Ralph E. W. Earl and Imaging of the Jacksonian Era," PhD dissertation, University of Iowa, 2010.

Thomas, Gregory M. "The Battle of New Orleans," thesis, Louisiana State University, 2005.

Manuscript Collections and Archives

American State Papers, 1789–1838, Library of Congress.

Archives and Special Collections, Xavier University.

Draper Manuscript Collection, Wisconsin Historical Society.

Early Virginia Marriage Records, Research Notes: No, 26, Library of Virginia

Executive Papers of Benjamin Harrison, 1781–1782, Boxes 1–19. Library of Virginia.

Gaines, John Wesley and Edmond Pendleton Gaines Papers, Accession No. 235, Archives and Manuscript Unit, s.

Gay-Butler Family Papers, Mss.4872. Hill Memorial Library, Louisiana and Lower Mississippi Valley Special Collections, Louisiana State University.

Mansell's 1818 Map of Mercer County Kentucky. Science and Engineering Library Map Collection, University of Kentucky.

Marriage Records, Kentucky Historical Society.

Melton Bluff' Receipts, Special Collections, University Libraries, University of Alabama.

Metropolitan Government Archives of Nashville and Davidson County.

Mississippi Department of Archives and History.

North Carolina Department of Archives and History.

Prints and Photographs Division, Library of Congress.

Southern Campaigns Revolutionary War Pensions Statements and Rosters. www.revwarapps.org.

"Springfield," "Three Greek Revival Houses of Mercer County, Kentucky" and "Washington Iron Furnace," National Register of Historic Places, National Park Service, Department of the Interior.

Tennessee State Department of Library and Archives.

Index